WRITING
IN
CONTEXT

WRITING IN CONTEXT

Chris M. Anson Lance E. Wilcox
University of Minnesota

Robert L. Brown
University of Minnesota
Consulting Editor

HOLT, RINEHART, AND WINSTON, INC.

*New York Chicago San Francisco Philadelphia
Montreal Toronto London Sydney Tokyo*

Printed in the United States of America

8 9 0 1 090 9 8 7 6 5 4 3 2 1

ISBN 0-03-007794-X

Library of Congress Cataloging-in-Publication Data

Anson, Christopher M., 1954-
  Writing in context.

  Includes index.
  1. English language—Rhetoric.   I. Wilcox, Lance E.
II. Title.
PE1408.A6185   1988   808'.042   87-12029

Holt, Rinehart and Winston, Inc.
The Dryden Press
Saunders College Publishing

Dedication

The ploughing, planting, and watering of this book
has been the work of literally hundreds
of dedicated teachers of writing
at the University of Minnesota
and Indiana University
over the past 15 years.

We have harvested,
but the crop was theirs.

It is to these teachers,
for their work, their wisdom, and their kindness,
this book is dedicated.

Acknowledgments

It's a humbling experience to write a textbook, to put in several years of diligent labor, and then to look back over the completed work and realize how little of it, finally, is one's own, how little one can actually claim credit for. Some of the ideas and theories and procedural suggestions in this book we did cook up on our own—but not many of them, really. Most of this book seeks only to present—clearly, usefully, and in a lively and entertaining fashion—the wisdom of others. A textbook writer is a kind of merchant sailor, whose only credit lies in delivering the wares of others, complete, intact, and decently packaged. We hope we have done so here.

Our main debt certainly is to those writers and teachers whose works we have learned from and whose wisdom we seek to pass on. Part of the pleasure of teaching writing is the lively exchange and sharing that goes on among those of us dedicated to this odd business. Here then is the real parentage of *Writing in Context* (just in case the offspring is too changed to be recognized).

Peter Elbow's insights and suggestions, as presented in *Writing without Teachers, Writing with Power,* and numerous articles are so woven up in the fabric of this text that it would be impossible to imagine it without them. Linda Flower's work inspires part of what we have to offer on the subject of organization. Young, Becker, and Pike's "tagmemics" and Gabrielle Rico's "clusters" represent two of the more useful suggestions in our chapter on invention. Drafting remains the aspect of the writing process perhaps least understood. In thinking through for ourselves the main issues in drafting, we realized that "stage fright" was the most salient; and in developing techniques for overcoming that archbogey, we found our greatest help in the works of the Russian acting teacher Konstantin Stanislavski and cognitive-behavioral therapist Albert Ellis. We are indebted to many fine theorists and researchers—Rick Beach, Lilly Bridwell-Bowles, Ken Bruffee, Lisa Ede, Sarah Freedman, Barry Kroll, George Hillocks, Andrea Lunsford, Ann Matsuhashi, Lee Odell, Ben Rafoth, Don Rubin, Nancy Sommers, and a score of others—whose studies of writing provided the necessary background and rationale for the book's orientation. Finally we'd like to make a deep bow each to Don Murray and Ben McClelland. Though we have designed our book along somewhat different lines from either of theirs, the generosity and grace of both *Write to Learn* and *Writing Practice* never cease to inspire us, and to set a standard for what a real teacher really ought to be.

Drawing the ring somewhat tighter, we have any number of colleagues who have influenced us in ways too numerous and subtle to describe. Years of conversations with teachers and colleagues have changed our thinking about writing, sometimes by tiny, incremental degrees, sometimes in bright bolts of illumination. Of our colleagues, we owe most to Robin Brown, Don

ACKNOWLEDGMENTS

Ross, Lilly Bridwell-Bowles, Marilyn Sternglass, Barry Kroll, and Michael Flanigan, and to those they trained who carried the good news to other lands, especially (from Minnesota) Mike Klein, Geoff Sirc, and Dene and Gordon Trageser-Thomas. But even these good teachers and friends would be the first to admit that they represent only the tip of the iceberg. The Program in Composition at the University of Minnesota has long been one of the warmest and most entertaining places to teach one could hope to find, and literally hundreds of writing treachers, passing through on their ways to advanced degrees, have made it so. If we thanked all we'd like to, the price of this volume would rise inordinately, but we will mention (at least) Julia Gergits, Anne O'Meara, Laura Brady, Marion Larson, and John Schwiebert. The rest know as well how much they have contributed and how much we appreciate their ideas.

Special thanks must go to Charlyce Jones Owen, senior acquisitions editor at Holt, Rinehart and Winston, for her commitment to this project and her warmth and encouragement; to Kate Morgan, our developmental editor, for her invaluable help every step of the way; and to Andy Paprocki, who mapped the territory for this book almost a decade ago and whose persistence finally convinced us to stake the claim.

We would also like to thank those who have read this book, from the first prospectus through the final draft, whose comments and feedback have clarified and enlightened every page: Victoria Aarons, Trinity University; Nancy Bent, Ithaca College; Paul Beran, North Harris Community College; Joseph Horobetz, Northern Virginia Community College; Walter Minot, Gannon University; Patricia Morgan, Louisiana State University; John O'Connor, George Mason University; William Smith, Virginia Commonwealth University; Judith Stanford, Rivier College; Christopher Thaiss, George Mason University; Dene Kay Thomas, University of Idaho; and John Trimbur, Boston University. For such limitations as the book possesses we cheerfully blame each other, and attribute the rest to our computers (convenient machines!).

The energy and drive we discovered in our writing—for that we thank our students. Their vivacity, diligence, and sheer sportiness keep this writing-teaching business always surprising, always fresh.

Our thanks, finally, to Geanie Anson, to Linda Roberts, and to Nathan and David Wilcox, without whom this book might have been done much sooner . . . but most certainly at the expense of our minds.

The order of authorship is purely alphabetical. Both authors have stared themselves cross-eyed at their respective word processors at either end of the Twin Cities over the past two and a half years, batting out page after page after page, swapping files over modems and phone lines, and rewriting page after page after page of each other's drafts. Where one writer's contribution leave off and the other's begins, even we are no longer sure, especially since Brother Wilcox bought himself a dictionary and quit guessing at the spelling of most common English verbs in their preterit and gerundial forms, and Brother Anson quit hyphenating all his "re" verbs.

C.M.A./L.E.W.

Contents

CONTENTS

Part 2

BUILDING ON THE KNOWLEDGE OF OTHERS   101

Chapter Five

In Search of New Knowledge   109

Chapter Six

From New Knowledge to New Text   140

Part 3

THE WRITING SITUATION   169

Chapter Seven

Why Are You Writing? Analyzing Your Purpose   177

Chapter Eight

Who's Your Reader? Analyzing Your Audience   201

CONTENTS

INTRODUCTION: WRITING IS A VERB

Writing is not words on a page. These sentences and paragraphs you have before you—this isn't writing, it's **prose. Writing** is what got them here. Writing means a college student crawling out of bed on a Saturday morning, sitting down with coffee at her word processor, and making one more attempt to rework a paper for a psychology class. Writing is this decision to overhaul a preceding draft, to see it with new eyes, to tear parts of it out and start them over from scratch, and to salvage other parts while working them over to see what else they can become. Writing is that same college student listening to her coauthor's reactions to parts of the revised draft, and then diving once more into the words to boil and stir them yet again. Writing is this "working and working over"—new ideas, new words, a changed text. (Prose—and lots of it—is what the teacher wants from this student when she's finished with the process of writing.)

This textbook is about **writing**—not so much the noun "prose" but the verbs that create it: composing, drafting, thinking, revising. We're not concerned with the "five-paragraph essay," or the work of professional authors, or the various species of narration versus exposition versus argumentation. We're interested in the **activity** of writing itself, with how you move from the first shadowy thought of something you'd like to discuss (in prose) to the final polishing and editing of the text itself.

For many people this requires a real shift in focus. Most people think of a good writer as someone adept at fixing or cleaning up prose. Learning how to diagnose and treat such ailments as wordiness, awkward constructions, grammatical problems, misspellings, and run-on sentences, is all many people ever think of as "learning to write." These are important skills, but they assume you already have your rough draft in decent shape and that all you have left to do is sandpaper and varnish it. But you know perfectly well how much work and planning and thought went into getting your rough draft down on paper in the first place. That's where you probably felt most at sea, most in need of a lifesaver.

In *Writing in Context,* we'll be leading you through the entire process of writing from first inspiration (or assignment) to presentable text. We'll be helping you to arrive at workable topics for your papers; to develop a rich body of memories, ideas, and information to work from; to select and arrange your material; to get a rough draft down on paper; and to overhaul and refine this into something rich, sharp, and lively. We'll also give you some leads on how to analyze more precisely the writing tasks you face in many different contexts, by raising such questions as "Whom are you writing for, exactly?" and "What do you want this piece of writing to do?" We also want to give you some tips on how to help each other with your writing—even working together on the same piece—and on using word processors.

In recent years, we've begun to understand a lot more about every aspect of writing. We know better now what writers are doing when their writing seems to go smoothly and when it doesn't. We've "looked over the shoulder" of effective writers and discovered what they do that works and how they learned it. We know how writers adapt to different tasks and settings and audiences, how they come up with and revise what they write, and what they pay attention to as they do so.

Perhaps most importantly, we've also learned how much all of these effective strategies depend on "attitude,"on the beliefs about writing you carry into your work. Some very common beliefs about writing, we've discovered, are nothing but trouble. So before going any further, we'd like to clear a little conceptual underbrush.

Some Misbeliefs About Writing

Misbelief #1:   Real writers are born, not made—and they write novels.

Ask anyone on campus to name a good writer, or to name the last really good piece of writing he read, and he'll more than likely answer with a literary author or text: Saul Bellow, Jane Austen, *The Color Purple, Crime and Punishment.* It won't even occur to him that he just received a really sparkling letter from a cousin in Milwaukee, or that the instruction manual for their home computer showed him, with surprisingly little confusion and torment, how to use it. We almost always tend to think of "writing" as "creative," as novels and poems and plays—as a grander thing than the various pieces of prose we happen to produce in our day-to-day activities. Which means we're seriously undervaluing our own work.

For every famous writer—the one who gets on the cover of *Newsweek,* who plugs her latest novel on late-night talk shows, and who signs million-dollar contracts with New York publishers—there are thousands of superb, obscure writers producing sensitive corporate memos; intelligent brochures for family-practice clinics; insurance policies in understandable English; lucid, thorough reports of research on corn hybridization for the federal government; even entertaining and colorful personal letters of their travels about the country. All of these represent very real and respectable writing achievements, yet most of these people never think of themselves as "writers" at all. They think they're "just" engineers or lawyers or supervisors or students or idle vacationers. But that's nonsense. Whatever else they are, they are certainly writers—and so are you, as soon as you put pen to paper.

The "born writer," furthermore, is purely a creature of legend. Some people, certainly, seem gifted with great powers of observation, sharp eyes for detail, excellent memories for places and events. And along with all these gifts they seem to possess a natural ear for prose; their sentences are clear and smooth and rhythmical. But this no more means they're "born writers" than that someone with naturally quick reflexes and great stamina is a "born tennis player." In each case, a tremendous amount of work is needed to turn the innate gifts into productive skills. The same kind of work and study and practice, furthermore, will turn any student, at whatever level, into a substantially more effective and confident writer.

Misbelief #2:   Good writing is good writing, period. It's the same in every situation.

3

Everywhere we go we find writers who believe there is one correct, proper way to write—one style appropriate to all situations. Many writers—students and professionals alike—want us to tell them "the right way to do it," so they can get on with their work.

But both research and common sense show us that writing is not that simple. Writing differs in very important ways from context to context, from audience to audience. (Do you write letters to friends that sound like answers to essay tests in political science?) Good business writing may strike college teachers as blunt and impersonal. An effective liberal arts essay makes a weak legal memo: it's too long, too indirect, covers too many points of view, and doesn't conclude with enough punch. The style, voice, diction, sentence structure, level of formality—all these and more vary as much from situation to situation as the content of the writing itself. This is even true within the college setting. Social scientists don't write like human-ities scholars, who, in turn, don't write like researchers in medicine or phys-ics, who, in turn, don't write like business majors, who, in turn—you get the point.

This may leave you wondering how you'll ever learn to write, if one group is always building their homes with mud and sand, another with trees, and a third group with rocks. If the goal of this book were to show you all the various styles of writing (and thinking) used in the academic and professional worlds, we'd never finish it. What we can do, instead of pro-viding you either the "Secret of the One True Way" or a "Compendium of All Possible Standards," is to provide you with **strategies** to help you dis-cover each group's rules for yourself. We try to show you some ways to discover for yourself if you're in a Mud Group, a Tree Group, or (pardon the pun) a Rock Group, and to adapt your writing style accordingly. If you know the right questions to ask, you can always fit your words to the rhe-torical world you find yourself in.

> **Misbelief #3:**   Writing is a lonely business. As a writer, you've got to go
> it alone.

We tend to see writers as "lone wolves," sickly poets hidden away in musty attics, pouring out their tormented souls. Or, if we're college stu-dents, writing is that business we have to do in the library or our room with nobody around to help or encourage us. It's us, single-handed, locked in combat with our assignment, trying to guess what that vague, misty figure, "The Teacher," really wants. We're wandering in a fog, no one within ear-shot in case we stumble into a mire.

But why should this be the case? If writing is a form of communication, of interpersonal interaction, why do we cloak it in this aura of loneliness? Most of the greatest literary figures knew better. Mark Twain hardly ever sent a book to the printer before letting his good friend (and fellow author), William Dean Howells, go through it page by page, cutting and trimming the weaker material. T. S. Eliot turned over his first draft of *The Wasteland* to Ezra Pound for revision. Hemingway, at Scott Fitzgerald's insistence, cut a long, dull opening section from *The Sun Also Rises*. And on and on. Outside the university setting, it's a matter of course that much writing will be collaborative—with two, three, sometimes dozens of writers working on the same document. A memo might be a solo effort; but a lengthy, elaborate proposal for a new computer system might involve the writing of many people.

In this book we encourage you to break down the dungeon walls, to come out of the hermitage, and do more of your writing "in public." We encourage you to share your ideas, your plans, your problems with one another at every stage of the writing process. In fact, we've dedicated a separate chapter to exploring what writers can do for each other. We're not, obviously, recommending that you crib from each other on essay exams or that you pass someone else's paper off as your own; but short of that, you can gain tremendous insight and encouragement from others at every writing step, from topic selection to final editing. This should not only improve your work, it'll make it infinitely more pleasant as you go.

Misbelief #4: Writing is solely a means of communication. Its only value lies in what it does for the reader.

Although most writing certainly has as its final purpose the exchange of information, we often forget that in the very process of writing, the **writer** is changed as well. We often think that our only goal is to "transmit data" as rapidly and efficiently as possible. We feel we're somehow lazy or stupid if, in fact, we're figuring out what we want to say as we go along. We imagine that a "real writer" or a "real expert" would already know everything and just have to spit it out.

But beyond its usefulness as a means of communication, writing also serves as an excellent way to think and learn in the first place. Especially in college, where much of the writing you do won't actually "inform" anybody, you should learn to view writing as a road to understanding, as well as an expression of that understanding.

This is especially true for really difficult subjects. The more you write about the subject, the better you'll understand it. You might keep a notebook in which you jot down your ideas about what you're learning, or try to get into words exactly what's confusing you, or keep a list of questions that arise as you read or review your lecture notes. We don't mean just taking a few notes, but actually engaging in a sort of personal dialogue with your subject as you reflect on what you've heard or read and try to relate it to your own experiences, thoughts, and observations. Even just trying to restate in your own words the main point of a lecture or book chapter will lead you to grasp it more firmly. Research in education has shown that when students write about the material they're learning, they often score better on tests than students who haven't.

What This Book Offers

So far, we've been trying to expose and debunk some old notions that often get in the way when people are learning to write. Now we'd like to draw together what we've found, turn it all on its head, and see what we can say positively about how we think writing should be understood. If the "truisms" above are in fact false, what is true?

This textbook is based on the following assumptions: By writing we mean all the activities that lead to a tremendously wide range of texts. Any time you're putting words on paper, you're writing; you are being a writer. What qualifies as "good writing" varies widely from task to task and from audience to audience; one size does not fit all. Whatever your present level of ability, you can, by learning and practicing the right strategies, become more effective in a great number of writing situations. Since writing is a form of communication, furthermore, you have much to gain by sharing your work with others at every stage of development; writing is as social an activity as any you can name. And finally, even if no one reads what you write, the act of writing itself will deepen and clarify your understanding of the subject you're writing about.

But why should you believe us? Why take our word for any of this? Actually, we wouldn't ask you to. Nothing in this book, in fact, should be taken on faith. We only ask that you put it to the test. Give our ideas a chance, and see if and how they help.

Think of this book as a series of experiments. Over the next 10 chapters, we will introduce you to a range of techniques and strategies covering every aspect of the writing process. Each technique has been found useful in the past by some writers. On the other hand, it's doubtful if any single writer uses everything we've suggested. What we're offering here is not a complete, tested, air-tight system for handling every writing assignment, but a smorgasbord of possible approaches.

Deciding which approaches work for you is your responsibility. You should try as many of our suggestions as you can. Give each a good run, maybe a few good runs. Then observe for yourself their effectiveness. The question is not which are inherently the best tools, but which tools can **you** work with most effectively. Each time you experiment with one of our techniques or strategies, spend a few minutes reflecting on how it worked for you.

Throughout the book, we've provided places for you to do this. You'll recognize these roadside parks by the words: "Your Turn." Each "Your Turn" asks a few questions to guide you in your observation of your writing process. These aren't meant to be formal writing assignments; they're meant to be freely jotted-down entries in what we like to call your "writer's notebook." You'll find that writing regularly in an informal journal or notebook can help you keep track of your ideas as they come to you and help you to prepare for activities or discussions in class. It can also give you a convenient place to watch your writing grow. Since we already know that writing about something helps you get a handle on it, we'll often ask you in these sections to reflect on and write about your own writing experiences. Our hope is that your experimental log will at some point replace *Writing in Context* as your main source of guidance in this business.

YOUR TURN

To begin, get yourself a looseleaf or spiral notebook that holds at least 100 pages. Then write about the following:

Describe in a few paragraphs your own experience of writing. What kinds of things have you written in the past (e.g., school assignments, letters, a diary, a report at work, a business letter, a college application letter, poetry, stories, etc.)?

Which of these seem to come easiest for you? Which were most successful? Which were most difficult? What might account for the difference?

What is your usual attitude toward writing? How do you feel when you're given a writing assignment? How do you usually feel when you're in the midst of working on it? What part of writing gives you the most trouble?

What would you especially like to learn about writing? What are your hopes for the course you're taking?

Part 1

THE WRITING PROCESS

Overview

Some years ago, in one of his very odd books, B. Kliban presented a four-panel cartoon with the caption "How to Draw a Cat." The first panel showed just a circle. In the second, two triangles stood on the circle, roughly where the ears would be. In the third, the circle had sprouted two tiny circles for eyes and a few lines for whiskers. And the fourth panel showed a perfectly rendered, detailed, professional drawing of the cat itself. It was funny because it was so splendidly unhelpful. It was like saying, "Painting's easy. Just look at the *Mona Lisa* and copy it," or "Writing's a snap. Read an essay by E. B. White and scribble down something similar."

A finished work of art, such as a painting or essay or short story, can be a fine and inspiring thing. But if you're not to some degree a writer already, contact with the work of a master might only intimidate and discourage you. It's so perfect, so polished, so effective. If all you ever see are the final results of the writer's labors, it looks like magic. If, on the other hand, you peek into the writer's workshop, it begins to look a lot more like plain old unmagical, unmysterious work—a lot of work, to be sure, but the work of a mere mortal.

In the next four chapters we will take you on just such an extended tour of the writer's workshop. Rather than examining final products, we'll be laying out for you the various tools of the writer's trade. We'll be telling you how they work, when to use them, what they're good for, and then we'll turn you loose to fill the place full of shavings of your own. Everyone who has ever learned to write has learned the same way—by covering pages upon pages with her own words, seeing how they work (or fail to work), and then covering pages and pages more.

The approach to writing we present in this section parallels that of many kinds of building or creating. In each case, you're trying to create something tangible and structured where there was nothing before: a house, a vase, a piece of furniture, a quilt, a portrait, a ham radio transceiver—or an essay, a movie review, a business letter. The home builder starts with a plot of land, the painter with a canvas, the writer with blank paper. In the end, by a long and complicated series of actions, the worker brings into existence a split-level ranch house, a still life, an analysis of modern farm economics. If we consider what all of these have in common, we find a consistent pattern:

1. *The worker perceives that something should be created.* The maker feels the need or takes the opportunity to use her talents. She has a contract to build a new home, or she has a deadline for a movie review for her school paper.

2. *The worker assembles all the raw material she'll need to carry out the construction.* For the contractor, this means buying bags of concrete, 2 × 4 studs, electrical wiring, insulation, sheetrock, shingles, ceramic tiles, lighting fixtures. The painter will need tubes of paint, charcoal sticks, linseed oil, varnish. The writer develops a rich stock of notes including ideas, memories, and reflections, along with information gathered from outside sources—interviews, statistics, other texts.

3. *The materials have to be sorted, arranged, and assembled.* The painter sketches in the outline of her composition, blocks in the major fields of color, then attends to progressively finer details. The writer works up a set of notes, arranges his material in what seems an economical and sensible order, then tries to get some kind of rough draft down on paper.

4. *Finally, the created object is evaluated and altered as necessary to satisfy the artist's standards.* The builder checks the doors and windows to see that they move easily and keep out drafts. The wiring has to meet "code" or be redone. The painter examines her canvas, and if she didn't achieve the effect she wanted, scrapes the paint off with a palette knife and reworks it. The writer becomes his audience, reading the draft to see what it says, how it sounds, whether it captures his intentions fully, whether it makes sense—then he starts adding, cutting, rearranging paragraphs, opening new lines of argument, developing his examples, polishing his sentences, and double-checking such things as coherence, grammar, punctuation, and spelling.

The four chapters of this section present a number of strategies for approaching each part of the process of "building" a paper (in this case, a narrative paper about a significant personal experience).

Chapter One, "Developing Your Material," focuses on the "collection," or "gathering," phase of writing. We start with a painless way to accomplish what many writers find a terribly difficult task: selecting a topic. We then introduce close to a dozen techniques for developing the topic you've chosen. By the time you've worked through the strategies offered in this chapter, you should have pages of notes to work from. You'll have your lumber and bricks, your charcoal and paints (along with quick sketches and detailed studies for your final work).

Chapter Two, "Putting It All Together," covers roughly the "assembly" phase of the building project. It leads you from an unsorted, undigested pile of notes to a draft of your paper. The chapter offers a useful device for thinking carefully about the organization of your narrative paper—*timelines*. A timeline provides a visual representation of the structure of your paper, letting you plan more effectively the order in which you want to present your material to your reader. The second half of this chapter then concentrates on the process of drafting: the plain hard work of turning your (now carefully organized) notes into continuous prose paragraphs. Since this is the point where many writers freeze up, we've tried to explain something of the psychology of drafting. We try to exorcise some of the demons that haunt us when we're actually committing our thoughts to paper.

Chapter Three, "Seeing It Again," discusses revision. Now you have your draft, what do you do with it? Where do you go with it? How do you turn it from this rough, awkward, misshapen but promising piece of prose into something tight, smooth, and effective? We distinguish in this chapter between "major" and "minor" revisions and offer techniques for both.

Finally, in Chapter Four we present a common sense approach to grammar and mechanics that makes these issues less mystifying and more meaningful by discussing them in the light of how they affect your reader. We end the chapter with a few hints on how to tell, even before checking your handbook, whether your paper is properly "dressed" or not.

Chapter One

DEVELOPING YOUR MATERIAL

GETTING STARTED

Imagine that you're trying to learn some new darkroom techniques in photography, or some ways to make a more powerful serve in tennis, or some good moves for turning quickly while wind-surfing. In each case, you could simply **observe** what highly skilled photographers, tennis players, or windsurfers do, and try to remember their moves. Alternatively, you could go to a series of lectures or read some articles about different lens filters for enlargers, or about the relationship of the ball-toss to the power of the serve in tennis, or about various ways to shift your weight when making turns in wind-surfing.

Certainly, you might learn something valuable in all three cases from watching experienced people or from listening to formal lectures and reading up on new techniques. But without actually **doing** what you're learning about, all the new ideas in the world won't help you to create striking photographs or get that much further toward the finals of your local tennis championship or stay upright in strong winds on your new sailboard. You've got to mess with the paper and chemicals, break strings, get wet. And in the process, you're learning a lot more than the few techniques you're focusing on consciously. Learning, in all these cases, means **doing.**

Just so with writing. Fortunately, right now as a writer you're in the best of all worlds. You'll be learning about a lot of new writing techniques and perspectives from this book and from your teacher. You're also in a supportive classroom with other people whose methods you can observe and who can observe yours. Most importantly, however, you'll be applying all of this to your own work, consciously learning new processes as you improve every aspect of your writing simply by doing lots of it. The film is loaded, the court's been primed, and the wind's just right—now it's time to get to work.

In the next four chapters, we examine the process of constructing a paper from start to finish, breaking the process down into its smaller subtasks, and showing how these are related to each other. We invite you at several points to try out new strategies and to assess how they work for you. The strategies cover everything from how to arrive at a topic, through developing your ideas, explaining yourself on paper, and revising what you've written. For simplicity's sake, we've focused in these chapters on writing to re-create a personal experience, something you can produce from memory without any formal research. The strategies introduced here, however, are equally appropriate to all writing tasks.

Writing to Re-create an Experience

Re-creating an experience should be a familiar enough business for you. It's the goal of practically every personal letter you write and of many of your conversations. When you're having lunch with friends or writing to your family, do you tell them your latest insights into organic chemistry or the causes of the Depression? Probably not. Probably you exchange stories with them, accounts of what you've done and what's happened to you. You went hiking somewhere in North Carolina or bumped into an old friend at a chili-making contest. Or you saw something interesting: the Grand Canyon or a precinct caucus. Or you went to a place that might seem perfectly ordinary but that holds special meaning for you: your grandmother's farm or an outdoor restaurant near campus where you meet with friends. Through your words, you want to make your audience experience these things for themselves as fully and vividly as possible. You want to put them where you've been.

This time, however, you're no longer just winging it over pie and coffee. You've got to get it down on paper—all of it. You won't be at the reader's elbow to explain obscure points or to back up and fill in things you've missed. You may have limitations on the length of your account as well, not to mention a deadline. How does that change the situation?

Getting Started: Some General Advice

If you're like most people, the situation looks most different when you *begin* writing. The Blank Page is terrifying. When you sit down to write, there it is—waiting. Twenty minutes later, there it still is—waiting. The pen fails to move, the keys won't click. You realize that your mind is empty, a permanent void that will never produce another word. Or it's a whirling mass of words, thoughts, phrases, ideas—all of which are embarrassingly stupid. Possibly you force a sentence out, only to scratch it out in disgust; or you retire from the field without having written a word, defeated and harrassed.

Getting started writing means finding the right gear to begin. If you've driven a car with a manual transmission, you've probably discovered what happens if you're not used to the gear mechanism. Sometimes, you'll start the car, slide the gearshift forward, let in the clutch; and the engine either stops dead or, if you really rev it up, barely eases the car forward to cruising speed. At first you're surprised and puzzled, then you notice you've put the car into third gear rather than first. This is what most people are doing when they find it impossible to get started: they're trying to go from a dead stop to highway cruising speed without passing through the intervening gears. Getting moving once you're in first gear is easy enough, as is getting from first to second, second to third, and so on. Going from a standstill to fourth, however—that's when the engine starts chugging, the car bucks and lurches forward and then comes to a dead stop, its gears grinding. You've probably noticed your brain doing the same thing when you try to get something down on that Blank Page.

When you face that first blank page, try to notice what's going on in your mind. Probably you'll find that, all at one time, you're trying to think up a topic, write a catchy first sentence, decide how to organize your thoughts, figure out what evidence is appropriate, and think how much time you have to do the paper. You're trying to work out the solutions to a half-dozen or more separate problems and until you're satisfied with the answers to all of them, you can't possibly write a good first sentence.

The main thing we'll work on in this chapter and the next is developing

15

a feel for the various "gears" you can work in while you write. Whatever your project, there's always something you can do to move it along and to keep it going once you've started. Below are a few general principles to help you with this. If, while you're writing, you find yourself stymied, frustrated, and ready to throw your Smith-Corona down the elevator shaft, then reviewing this section will at least be cheaper (if not so gratifying).

Take a little bite. For the moment, don't think about the project as a whole. If you can't face the whole mountain, pick the next bend in the path; decide you'll get at least that far and stop. Use time limits to set your pace: decide you'll do something on your paper for, say, 15 minutes and then you'll give yourself permission to quit. Or insist on one paragraph, and then promise yourself a movie.

Once you've passed your goal, if you want to keep going, by all means do so. But for this to work, the permission to quit—and quit with a clear conscience—has to be genuine. If you write those three sentences and don't want to go on, take your break and forget about it. Later on perhaps you can do another three sentences or another 15 minutes—but not right then. Don't welsh on your promises to yourself. (This is also an excellent dish-washing and room-straightening technique.)

From the time you get an assignment, work in frequent, short stretches rather than counting on last-minute marathons to meet your deadline. Start early, before the pressure builds up. The more distance between you and the deadline, the less important it is for you to do anything particularly well. You have plenty of time to screw things up and fix them later. And short stretches lessen the odds of your being overwhelmed with either anxiety or disgust—both of which are real dangers in putting words on a page.

If you're really stuck, do something easy. If you can't grind out a single coherent sentence, just jot down the important words. Think of this as verbal doodling. You might do this on scrap paper or on the blank pages of old notebooks—something you know in advance won't "count."

Describe the problem or dilemma itself on paper. Where are you stuck? What's the problem? How are you feeling? You want to rage and snarl at the whole business of composition? Do so in writing. Sometimes all the fuming and fussing going on in the back of your head gets too loud to think over. By writing out your frustrations, you may blow off enough steam to get your head clear and be able to work productively again.

By simply describing your problem, furthermore, you may stumble onto a solution. If you know something's wrong but you can't put your finger on it, there probably won't be much you can do about it. Describing your frustrations often forces them into clarity. This in itself might provide you with the key you need.

Push at what's pushable. If you're really stalled, you probably aren't ready to perform the particular task you're working on. It's time to make a strategic retreat and work on some other part of your project. If, on the other hand, you find your work going well, don't stop, don't question, don't look back—just go with it. Follow the flow, follow the energy. If you push it and it moves, keep pushing it. The vein will probably play out all too soon anyway, and there will time enough then to see what you've produced.

If some of this seems vague or obscure to you, don't worry. We'll be fleshing out these concepts as we go and you may find you understand them better in retrospect than you do now. At some point, you're almost certain to find yourself stuck, balked, brought to a standstill, and you'll know where to find these suggestions when you need them.

YOUR TURN

If you're waiting for us to tell you precisely what constitutes a good personal-experience paper, you can stop. You don't really need us to do that. You've read many descriptions of personal experiences, in one form or another, and already have a good sense of what makes one interesting and another boring.

Think back. What stories can you remember in which someone described something he had done or been through? This could be in the newspaper, in a collection of essays, in a letter you received.

What did you notice about the ones you especially remember or that you got involved in?

What sorts of things bored you or put you off?

In the light of these, how would you like your own personal narrative to come across?

Write your answers to these questions, then compare notes with one or more other students to see what interests them.

Developing a Topic

Do any of these exchanges sound familiar to you?

Parent: What did you learn in school today, Heather?
Heather: (Frowns. Shrugs.) Nothing.

Bacall: (Tossing her head.) Enough about me. Let's talk about you.
Bogie: (Scratching his chin.) I'm afraid there's not much to tell.

Your Friend: Hey, what's happening?
You: Nothing much.

Or have you ever sat down to write a letter—one that was about a month overdue—and couldn't find a thing to write about? Or, you've just been

17

asked to write a narrative paper, to re-create a personal experience, and you discover that in your 18 or 27 or 59 years, nothing has **ever** happened to you? Or is it really that you just can't, at short notice, remember anything that seems dramatic or significant enough to present to an audience? You feel as if one of NASA's astronauts has just described his moon flight and then asked you where **you** went for **your** vacation.

Asked to write a personal narrative (or any other kind of paper, for that matter), you're liable to enter a state of low-level panic until you've "found a topic." Often, just to ease the discomfort, you'll grab at the first idea that occurs to you ("My First Date"). Or you'll remember the assignment your ninth-grade English teacher gave you and start describing your summer vacation—("My Trip to the Corn Palace"). That, or you'll just get out your paper, uncap your pen, and stare at the page until the sweat beads up on your forehead.

This is an excellent place to slow down and think about what you're doing. How many experiences have you actually had in your life—really? (As of your 18th birthday, you have been alive 6,754 days. Surely something has happened.) How many of your experiences interested you, or delighted you, or appalled you, or grieved you, or cheered you? Not your audience—you. (The answer, in case you're still being modest, is in the hundreds, if not thousands.) Now, how many can you remember off the top of your head?

You see the point. You've been through innumerable experiences that affected you intensely. Only a few, though, probably occur to you right away. And the odds of hitting upon the best topic for a paper on the first shot are close to nil. Sometimes it happens—for instance, if you've recently been through something you're eager to discuss. But usually you're holding more cards than you can count, and it would be worth it to look at a number of them before playing.

Instead of writing about the first topic that comes to mind, it is more effective to get down on paper a wide range of possibilities and then to pick the one you want to work on at more leisure. The simplest way to get started is to make a list.

First, list as many experiences or incidents as you can, and do this as quickly as possible. Don't judge yet how interesting they are. Just get as many down as possible.

List even the ideas you suspect may not work. Throwing in the lousy ideas along with the promising ones sometimes lets you see connections you wouldn't notice otherwise or lets you shape a lousy idea into a promising one.

Set yourself some minimum limit for this brainstorming. For instance, decide you won't stop until you have 15 ideas or until you've been at it for 10 minutes. But set only minimum limits. If you've exceeded your standard and your momentum is still strong, keep going. You may be on your way to something more intriguing yet.

YOUR TURN

Every technique we introduce in this book works for some people and falls flat for others. By observing carefully the effectiveness of each strategy we suggest, you will, in time, produce your own "guide to the writing process," tailored to your own particular style and needs.

First try out our suggestions on getting started. When you're done, answer the following questions.

> How many ideas did you come up with? How long did it take?
>
> Do you find anything surprising or unexpected on your list?
>
> How did setting a minimum limit, either of items or time, work for you?

Narrowing the Field

You now have a substantial list of possible things to write about. You have, in fact, already begun to write your paper, though you may not have thought of it that way. Usually, you think of writing as the act of stringing sentences across the page, with the terrifying prospect of somebody actually reading them. It's probably more useful, however, to reserve the word "drafting" for this process. It's obviously a core aspect of producing a presentable paper, but it's far from the whole business (we'll discuss drafting a bit later).

Just as driving entails everything from starting the car to steering, pressing the accelerator, glancing in the rearview mirror, operating the wipers and so on, writing covers everything from the first sketchy listing of ideas to the final proofreading and correcting. So, consider yourself as having begun the writing of your narrative, even if you're miles yet from being ready to draft it.

This also means that, for once at least, you did not have trouble **getting started** on your writing. You are started, after all. You're at least a bit closer to your goal than you were yesterday at this time. And you probably didn't go through the usual agonies, the usual pen-chewing, hair-pulling terrors of staring down the Blank Page. Why not? Because this time, you started in first gear, with something so small and simple and foolproof that you could hardly help but get somewhere with it.

The next order of business is narrowing your list of possibilities. You've been expansive, you've produced a number of ideas; now you need to start being selective. In a small way, this reflects a rhythm you'll notice throughout the writing process: expanding and selecting, drawing and discarding. You will continually be generating material, only to use part of it and toss out the rest. Later on, you'll be drafting and cutting, drafting and cutting. It's the same general process throughout.

In trimming your list, you should indulge yourself and slow down. You may still feel the compulsion to leap to a topic, to pick the first possibility that looks promising and get on with it. But fight it. Relax a little. Study your cards a bit first.

Try the following procedure for easing towards a topic from the list of possibilities you've developed:

If you see any ideas you know right away you won't be developing, go ahead and cut them. Eliminate the deadwood from the start.

Keep cutting the list from the least interesting possibility on up, until you find yourself regretting one. The first time you feel a twinge at scratching one off, stop. And put that one back.

Of the ones remaining, write at least a couple of sentences about each one. What's interesting about it? Why does it appeal to you? What angle might you take with it if you were to develop it at length?

Any time you feel like writing more than a couple of sentences, do so. Get something down on each of them; but if you find yourself involved with one and scribbling away, don't feel obliged to stop.

Now that you've given the "finalists" a little further consideration, see which ones you can now drop or which seem the most interesting or attractive.

Don't feel you have to make a final decision. If, after all this, you're still left with two or more appealing possibilities, that's fine. It's early yet. If of two seedlings in the same pot, one is not definitely bigger and stronger than the other, don't pluck out either of them.

If you're having a hard time making decisions, ask a potential reader which of your possibilities he or she would be interested in reading about. Though the final decision is your responsibility, nothing says you can't solicit some input on it. You are writing not only to express yourself but also to produce the most entertaining reading matter possible. If you can discuss your options with the person or persons who will actually be reading your paper, great. If that's not possible, find someone else you trust and present her with your ideas; describe to her your options, and ask which she finds most interesting. If, of your various experiences, your reader finds one definitely more intriguing than the rest, you might just let that make up your mind.

This is perfectly legitimate. As a writer, you can err in two ways in your relation to your reader. You can write only what you think your reader wants to hear, regardless of whether you think it's true or interesting or not. Or you can vow to write only to please yourself, the reader be damned. Working toward a paper that is gratifying to write and entertaining to read is a more mature and productive attitude than either extreme.

And if after all this, you're still undecided, so be it. Go ahead and start developing your remaining tempting topics as if you intended to write on all of them. The worst that will happen doing this is that you'll lose a little time, but your greater feel for your topics should more than compensate.

YOUR TURN

Take a few minutes now to reflect on what's happened so far in the writing process. In your writer's notebook, jot down some responses to the following questions:

How did this listing and narrowing procedure work for you?

Were you surprised by how much you had to say about any of your items? Did any seem to open up while you were considering them?

All in all, do you think the listing, cutting, and developing procedure produced different results from those you would have gotten by just taking the first idea that occurred to you?

TECHNIQUES FOR DEVELOPING YOUR MATERIAL

Words, Ideas, and Some General Guidelines

Now that you have a topic, you want to collect on paper a wealth of material: ideas, observations, feelings, facts, etc. This is the raw material from which, further down the road, you will be organizing and drafting your paper. Later, when you actually start drafting, the work will go more quickly and easily if you've recorded your ideas on paper where you can see them. The paper itself, furthermore, will prove more engaging and lively as a result of your exploration.

Writing a paper without developing your ideas is impossible. The only question is where you do it. For short works—memos and letters, for instance—you may very well be able to keep everything you want to say in your head. The Blank Page Syndrome, on the other hand, is partly a result of trying to decide how to build a house with your foot already on the shovel.

Exploring your topic on paper relieves you of having to remember everything as you write. The paper serves as an artificially extended memory—a place to store your ideas, so that Brilliant Insight #1 doesn't slip away while you're giving birth to Brilliant Insight #2. Your memory contains remarkable amounts of information, far more than you could ever be aware of at any given time; but this information is organized in a curiously slapdash, haphazard fashion—rather like an immense attic cluttered with photographs in unsorted heaps. When you try to remember the details of an experience, the important facts will not all be lying ready to hand. You'll have to sort through the clutter, throwing out a fair amount of it, before coming across just those "photographs" you need.

This, again, requires that you not limit yourself to only those ideas you can keep in mind. By writing down your memories, you're freer to follow your mind's lead as it "searches the attic." The result may well be that you'll turn up memories of things you hadn't thought of in years: names of friends and teachers from third grade, the hair brush your dog chewed up, the color of the walls in your brother's hospital room, the odd way your aunt had of putting ketchup on her eggs. Once you've written down an idea or memory or description, you're free to forget it and turn your undivided, unburdened attention to something else. You should find this an enormous relief.

Beyond simply jogging your memory, such "brainstorming" allows you to think your paper through at a more profound and subtle level than you could otherwise. Whether you plan to describe a vacation or defend your position on nuclear armaments, exploring your topic allows you to test out hypotheses, pose questions, or review the evidence from a number of perspectives—all at no risk.

The model of writing most people work from doesn't suggest much by way of exploration. It assumes that you come to writing rich in well-formed and well-defined ideas and that all you have to do is find the right words to "clothe" them in. It's a simple, linear model. (See Figure 1-1).

FIGURE 1-1

In most cases, however, when we confront any writing task for the first time, we have only a vague, general notion of what we want to say. We're not primarily looking for "the right words"—at least not yet. We first have to discover what, if anything, we have to say about the subject in the first place.

Writing, however, is a superb way to think, to develop your ideas. If your thoughts on some matter are confused and muddy, forcing yourself to put them on paper is almost certain to clarify and sharpen them. If you don't have thoughts to put into words, start putting down words and see if they lead you into thoughts. Don't think, then write. Write in order to think. Reverse the model, and look at it as it's shown in Figure 1-2. Of course, the

FIGURE 1-2

words you produce may be formless, wandering, perhaps unreadable to anyone but yourself. But then, as those words lead you to further ideas, which in turn lead you to new words, your writing will begin to take shape. The full cycle looks something like Figure 1-3.

The advantage of working from this model is that it relieves you of the pressure to "get it right" too early. It takes questioning and exploration seri-

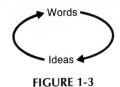

FIGURE 1-3

ously as goals for your early writing. It makes a positive virtue of doubt, uncertainty, and experimentation, of trial and error. To stick doggedly in your writing to what you already know guarantees that you won't learn anything; you'll simply stagnate at your present level of insight. By writing to think and explore, you'll not only produce better material for your audience, you'll find yourself thinking more deeply about your subject.

As you move back and forth between words and ideas, keep reminding yourself that the goal at this point is not to produce "good" writing. No matter how chaotic and sloppy your work, don't worry about it. Great chefs don't keep the cleanest kitchens. The most important goal at this stage is to get down all your ideas—the brilliant and the brainless alike.

For now, focus only on the experience itself, not on your assignment. This is your chance to enjoy your material for its own sake. The more fully you immerse yourself now in your experience, reliving it as intensely as possible, the richer your paper will be in the end.

You may find yourself returning to these activities again and again at many points in the writing of a given paper. At any point during organizing, drafting, or revising, you may find you simply don't have the necessary material available for part of your work. When that happens, you need to return to these activities and produce a rich blend of gold and rubbish until you're ready to pick up where you left off.

Listing

The easiest way to begin developing your paper is simply to start making lists. Make lists of people, places, sights, incidents, clothes, visual impressions, colors, objects, etc. As with all these techniques, work quickly and write down everything—good, bad, or indifferent.

Once you have a few lists, you can start working with them in different ways to explore your experience still further.

Make "chains" of your lists. That is, pick out a few items and use those to start new lists.

Write a paragraph describing each list. What is this a particular list of? What experiences or memories does it bring to mind?

Divide the items in a list into different categories. What smaller lists could you break it into, and how would you name or describe those?

YOUR TURN

Freely and quickly, write a number of lists—at least three or four—related to your topic. Use items from one list to "seed" another as described above. Describe each list in a few sentences. Break each list into related smaller lists and describe these.

How much and what sorts of material did listing produce for you?

Did the descriptions add anything that wasn't already contained in the lists themselves?

How did this technique affect your ability to remember or relive the event?

Clustering

Clustering is like listing but with a difference.[1] You don't so much write a cluster as draw one. In fact, you actually do some of both, writing and drawing. We'll describe the technique here and then explain its usefulness.

Use a large sheet of paper—the larger the better. In the very center of the paper, write some key word ("seed") and draw a circle around it. This might be the proposed title of your paper, or a person's name, or an idea. (See Figure 1-4.)

FIGURE 1-4

That word or thought will make you think of others. When it does, write down a word or two to record your thought, draw another circle around it, and attach a line to it from the central node. This gives you two circled words connected by a line, as in Figure 1-5.

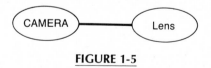

FIGURE 1-5

Let the starting word spark more thoughts and memories and ideas, and write those down—each one circled and connected to the center by lines. You'll start to develop a kind of daisy or pinwheel or spider design as in Figure 1-6.

---

[1]Gabriele L. Rico, *Writing the Natural Way* (Los Angeles: J. P. Tarcher, 1983).

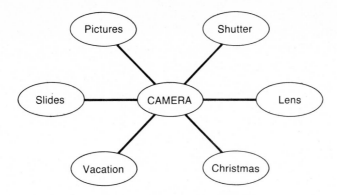

FIGURE 1-6

As soon as you have the slightest trouble thinking of anything associated with the central idea, turn to the circles on the first ring. See what thoughts they provoke. Note those ideas and connect them to the petal or satellite that inspired them.

You'll now have "second-generation" associations growing out of the first round of ideas in a pattern something like Figure 1-7.

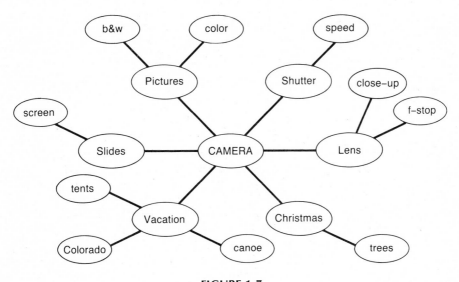

FIGURE 1-7

At this point, start connecting ideas to any of the words already down. A new idea might stem from the original seed, one of the first branches, or even a remote outgrowth. Let your mind range freely over the developing cluster and write in new associations wherever you think of them.

One particular branch may provoke a long series of associations. If so, follow its lead. Whenever it dries up and fails to suggest anything new, skip quickly to another circle. See what fresh ideas or images that one inspires and start extending that part of the cluster.

You may quickly find your page covered, unless you're working on giant sheets of newsprint or a large blackboard. If you run out of room, turn the page, write down the node you were working on in the center of the fresh sheet, and start from there. You might spread these sheets around on a large table where you can see and work on all of them. Otherwise, you can just let them pile up in your notebook and start fresh ones whenever it's necessary.

In Figure 1-8 we've picked up one node of the cluster in Figure 1-7 and worked it out in a little more detail.

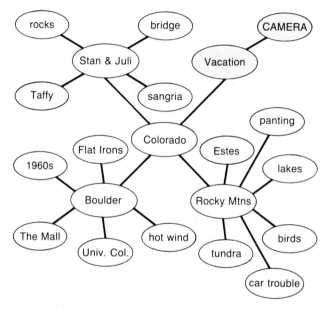

FIGURE 1-8

Many people find clustering the fastest, easiest, and most entertaining way to develop their ideas. Practically everybody gets somewhere with it. Like listing, it's at the furthest possible remove from "writing," and that can be a relief. Also, it's gratifying to see how quickly you can cover a page, or several pages, using clusters.

Psychologically, the technique takes advantage of what the mind does best: making links from one idea to another. Thoughts and memories and images don't surface in our minds in isolation; they always arrive with other images clutching at their heels. In writing out our ideas, we often try to detach them from these other associated ideas, or we simply ignore them. Clustering goes in the opposite direction. Here you want those associations. By following these trains of associations, you can develop a much richer understanding of the original concept. Or you may find yourself going off on a tangent, ending up in a much more interesting place than where you started.

As with all such techniques, you should approach clustering with a spirit of play and exploration. Work quickly. Jump freely from node to node, adding where you can, and moving immediately to another node when the stream runs dry. You can obviously return to old nodes at any time if you think they'll offer new ideas. Plan on several short sessions rather than a single marathon, but if you get carried away with it, great.

YOUR TURN

Do at least two clusters on your paper topic. For one cluster, place your main topic in the center of the sheet and expand from that. For the other, take something from one of your lists and go from there. Then jot down some responses to these questions in your writer's notebook:

How did clustering compare with listing? What do you think would happen if you clustered first and then listed?

What kind of material did you generate using clusters?

When or under what conditions would clustering be especially useful?

Rushwriting

Rushwriting is a brainstorming technique that, unlike lists or clusters, relies on real prose of a sort. It's vital, however, that you don't take it too seriously. You're writing, but not **for** anyone yet. You're still just getting your material down on paper for your own reference. You can ignore spelling, punctuation, grammar, and style; these are not important—yet. In rushwriting, the only mistake you can make in "style" is to give it a moment's thought.

Rushwriting takes advantage of the fact that anything, even writing, can be endured for a limited period. No matter how unpleasant you find writing, if you can stick to it for 10 or 15 minutes, you can make use of this technique. Here's what you do.

Set a time limit. If writing comes hard for you, set a short one, maybe 10 minutes. If you're moderately fluent, try 15 or even 20 minutes. More than 20 minutes and you lose the sprinting quality rushwriting should have. Use a timer or clock and take your time limit seriously.

Start writing, and for the period you've set, keep writing as fast as you can. Speed and quantity are essential. Nothing else matters.

When the time is up, stop. Even if you're following a hot scent, quit for a while. It'll be there when you get back.

Take a break and come back later.
Set yourself another time limit and sprint through it again.

While you're actually rushwriting, keep the following things in mind:

Start from your topic, at least at first. Don't start writing about just anything. There's no good reason to throw away the work you put into selecting a topic.

Don't, however, feel obliged to stick to the topic. If you start to digress, do so. If the writing seems to be leading you somewhere, follow it rather than wrenching it back to the original subject. By following the writing rather than leading it, you may find your way into richer, more profound, and more compelling material than anything to do with your original thoughts. The very worst that can happen is that you will have wasted ten minutes. It's a risk worth taking.

Don't stop writing for any reason, short of fire. Don't stop to debate punctuation, fix spellings, change words, or anything else. Leave all the errors intact. Don't for a moment wonder how your reader will react to what you've written.

Don't hesitate to put down anything. No matter how stupid, obvious, or misguided the thought, write it down and keep going. The road to wisdom is paved with nonsense.

If nothing at all occurs to you, write about that—the problem of having nothing to say. If that doesn't work, write down random phrases or even start repeating yourself. Just keep writing.

Quantity is everything. Don't ask yourself, "Have I done this correctly?" Just count your words. Over time you should become more fluent; you should learn to produce more words in a session. You should also be able to work for longer periods without running out of gas.

What keeps your word count down, after all, is not a lack of things to say or any lack of "creativity" or "inspiration." It's probably inhibition, the lurking fear that nothing you have to say is interesting enough to merit putting into words. Much of it won't be, but some of it will; and if you invite the worthless stuff, the good material may well sneak in, clutching at the other's coattails. In a sense, then, rushwriting teaches you not to make up more but to edit less. Your word count rises by relaxing your critical judgment. You increase your speed not by leaning on the accelerator but by releasing the brake.

Much of the power of rushwriting lies in the time limit. The mild pressure should keep your pen in motion. Forcing yourself to sprint for 10 minutes may produce much more usable material than staring out the window and daydreaming for an hour. Producing words without ideas is, fortunately, almost impossible (except for certain political speech writers). Producing ideas without words is, alas, all too easy. In rushwriting, you concentrate on words—as many as possible, as fast as possible—and expect the ideas to result.

YOUR TURN

Starting with the topic you've chosen, set yourself a 10- or 15-minute time limit, and rushwrite. Answer the following questions in your writer's notebook:

How many words did you produce? Count them, and keep tabs on this over time. You'll probably get faster with practice.

How often and when did you find yourself worrying about spelling, punctuation, grammar, or the quality of what you were writing? Whom did you have in mind while you were writing?

How did this work for you? Describe your material. Any surprises?

Chained Rushwriting (or Loops)

Rushwriting is a vigorous and effective way to create the material you need for your paper, but in a sense it's deliberately inefficient. You have to be willing to produce a lot of low-grade ore, a lot of words, sentences, and paragraphs that will end up in the "circular file," to come up with real gold. Needless to say, 10 minutes of this won't produce much of anything. You don't "rushwrite" once and expect to have all the material for your paper. You do a lot of rushwriting. You squeeze in your short sessions wherever you can: on the bus, between classes, in the library, or after the evening news.

If you think of each new rushwrite as completely unrelated to the others, however, you probably won't use them as effectively as you could. If, for instance, you start each one at random, with the first idea that occurs to you whenever you sit down to write, you might produce a dozen rush-writes and not come anywhere near your subject. On the other hand, if you start each rushwrite with your topic—fresh, as if you had never written on it before—you may cover the same territory each time without making any real headway.

Think of a rushwrite, then, not as a single discrete unit but as a link in a chain. If you know from the beginning that you'll be doing several rush-writes, you can use the whole series to explore your material more systematically and effectively than if you were doing them piecemeal. This more organized, chained rushwriting is often called "looping."

To create such "loops":

First do a rushwrite, using the directions on the previous page.
Take a break.
Now reread your work, circling those words, phrases, or passages that strike you as interesting. Find the intriguing "pointers" in your work: the ideas and images that suggest interesting lines of development.
Pick one of these and write it down, either below the first rushwrite or on another sheet of paper.

29

Use this as the seed or starting point and write for another 10 or 15 minutes on this new topic. Again, write fast, stay loose, and follow any interesting leads that occur to you. When time's up, stop and take a break.

Reread your second rushwrite, marking the interesting parts again as you did with the first.

Select from either rushwrite the most intriguing lead and use that as the starting point for a third round.

Repeat the procedure as many times as you need to.

You could do this, obviously, forever. The procedure geometrically expands material for your paper. With each rushwrite, you produce at least a few leads for later ones; when you write on those, you find more possibilities yet. The longer you do this, the more unexplored and potentially interesting territory you discover. It's startling how, once you start looping, what might have originally seemed a fairly limited topic can grow and develop until it looks almost too rich and complex to handle.

After each rushwrite, you'll find yourself at a fork in the road. It's up to you to decide which of the possible paths you want to follow. Here again you see the pattern we mentioned above of expansion and selection, drawing and discarding. Of the leads you've marked, select the ones that strike you as most interesting and pursue them. Many will simply have to wait for another day.

Other Approaches to Looping

Find the Essence of the Passage. By "essence," we mean the core or central idea that seems to be expressed. Often in working on an expository or critical essay, you'll have some sense of what you want to get across but won't quite be able to find the right words for it. Try writing about it for 15 minutes.

Now, try to restate the main idea of your rushwrite in one clean sentence. (This is sometimes aptly described as "putting it in a nutshell," or "nutshelling" it.) Write this sentence down, however vague or inarticulate, and start your next rushwrite from there. Now reread and try to nutshell the central meaning of that paragraph. Use this sentence to start your third rushwrite—and so on.

Whereas the standard method works largely to expand your ideas, this method can both expand and refine them. You'll find yourself producing arguments, evidence, or further support for (or problems with) your idea at the same time that you're clarifying and focusing it. After a series of such rushwrites, you'll have a clearly developed statement, along with the material to back it up.

Loop Rushwrites Together through Questions. When you review your rushwrites, pretend you're a fresh reader and ask a few questions about the material.

Write down the questions and, selecting one of them as a seed, spend 10 or 15 minutes answering it as well as you can. Then reread your new rush-write and ask further questions. After doing this awhile, you'll have a sort of long dialogue in your notes, almost like the transcript of a thoughtfully done interview. Again, the procedure may simultaneously expand and sharpen the first thoughts you had on the topic.

YOUR TURN

Do a series of rushwrites, at least four or five, linked together by one or more of the methods suggested above. (Do these, if at all possible, for a paper you're working on. Make them count.)

Answer the following questions, recording your answers in your writer's notebook for future reference.

How did this procedure work for you? What did it produce?

Which looping technique—interesting leads, nutshelling, or questions—proved most productive?

Were some rushwrites easier or harder to write than others? If so, how do you account for the differences?

Looping with Partners. Looping can also be done collaboratively, with a friend or a partner, or in a small group working together. Other people can often find possibilities and leads in your notes that you might miss. And sometimes by their very questions and misunderstandings they'll direct you into productive paths that you'd never have found on your own.

Each writer should read one rushwrite to the group at a time.

The group members should then tell the writer (1) what the main idea, the "essence," of her rushwrite seems to be; and (2) what strikes them as most interesting, as worth hearing more about. The writer should write down their answers.

After the session each writer should do a few more rushwrites, based on the most interesting of the group's suggestions. The group can then reconvene and share their progress and perhaps point out further leads for each other. (Chapter Nine, on collaboration in writing, introduces a wide variety of other ways in which writers can be of help to one another.)

YOUR TURN

Work with a partner or small group. Share your rushwrites, either by photocopying them and exchanging them or by taking turns reading them aloud. Respond to the following questions in your writer's notebook:

How did the group's reactions to your work compare with your own?

How would you describe the comments on your own work that you found most useful?

Sketches and Studies

An artist's sketch is usually a simple charcoal or pencil drawing, quickly capturing the main form, shading, and texture of some object. It's not meant to be a formal, public work of art. It's intended rather to capture for the artist some impressions or observations about an object he might use later.

A second use of the sketch is to work out problems in the overall composition of a painting. In this case, the artist may produce a series of sketches, arranging the objects differently in each. The wildlife artist may arrange two eagles, three branches, and a dead squirrel in a variety of poses until finding the arrangement that strikes him as most dramatic or beautiful. He then draws this lightly onto his canvas and begins blocking in the main fields of color.

In writing, you can also produce a variety of "sketches" in preparation for your first full draft. In writing, as in painting, sketching means recording your observations and impressions of something you want to describe more fully later—perhaps getting down a quick description of an interesting character or place or bit of dialogue. Or you can do a series of sketches that are in essence brief "pre-summaries" of your final paper. It might help you to make several attempts to write in one paragraph or page a quick overview of what you want to say. Each sketch would include different elements or episodes arranged in a different order. By trying out a number of these, you might find one that strikes you as especially engaging.

Like a sketch, a study is not meant as a public work of art but as a preparation for one. A study concentrates usually on a smaller subject than a sketch, but attempts to render it in greater detail. In a study, the artist wants to record as much detail as possible about some object he knows will appear in his painting. The wildlife artist might make a very careful drawing, or even small painting, of just the eagle's claws pinning the squirrel to the branch, or of just the eagle's wing, capturing the precise color, texture, and pattern of the various layers of feathers.

For your personal narrative, you might try describing one character's appearance in as much detail as possible, or try re-creating as accurately as you can one incident, perhaps a conversation, you had with the person. If you're writing about a special location, you might go there, notebook in hand, and observe it in detail, writing a description of it for later use. This might even be in the form of a free-verse poem.

YOUR TURN

Do at least two studies and two sketches in preparation for your paper. Answer the following questions in your writer's notebook:

What did you learn new about your topic from writing these?
Which sketch looks as if it would work best as a design for your full draft? Why?

Compare notes with another student on how these techniques worked. What new twists or innovations can you or the other person suggest that might make these techniques more useful?

Dialogues

So far we've discussed ways you can ransack your own mind for ideas, memories, and insights; and we've suggested turning to others to solicit their ideas on how you might develop your material. Another possibility is to create one or more fictional characters and turn the job over to them. By imagining characters with different points of view and letting these "people" discuss your ideas, you can see new angles, new meanings, new lights you might not notice using a more straightforward approach.

Here are the general directions for writing such dialogues:

Think of a character who will have interesting insights or questions about your material: for instance, someone who shares your interest in a subject but disagrees with you on it; or someone from another country; or perhaps a member of a particular profession or group. It might be easiest to start with someone you actually know.

Give your character a label. This could be either a real name or a title to suggest an attitude—something like "Thrill-seeker" or "Farmer" or "Arch-Skeptic."

Once you've named your character, write a sentence or two about him. What is he like? What are his interests?

Carry on a conversation with this person, writing down her ideas, questions, exclamations, opinions, and so forth, along with your replies.

Try to preserve the distinctiveness of the character's personality as clearly as possible. Let "The Artist" stay "artistic," let "The Manager" be consistently "managerial." If you're imagining an actual acquaintance, try to have her say or ask what she really would say or ask in that situation.

The dialogue might look something like this:

Squeamish: You didn't see any bats in there, did you?

Me: Of course there were bats. In one chamber, you could look up into a hole in the roof and the bats poured in almost on top of your head.

Squeamish: Weren't you afraid they'd bite or something?

Me: No. What do you mean "or something?"

Squeamish: You know, get caught in your hair, drink your blood.

Me: No. They're harmless. They swirled around the cave awhile and then headed for the passage outside.

Squeamish: (shiver) How many were there?

Me: Probably a few hundred. Of course, with everyone wearing lamps on their helmets, the shadows on the walls multiplied so that it looked like there were thousands, all squeaking and flapping about.

33

Squeamish: Why on earth would you want to go down there?
Me: [my chance to explain the pleasures of cave exploring]

Once you've got the basic idea, there are a number of wrinkles you can throw in to make this procedure even richer:

Create two or more voices and have them discuss your material with you. You might, for instance, create an "Adversary" who disagrees with you entirely, and a "Peacekeeper" whose goal is to find the common ground between the two of you.

Let the voices discuss your material in your "absence." Rather than writing yourself into the script, leave it solely up to the other voices to develop your material.

Try writing these, like rushwrites, with the clock running.

After a dialogue, mark the most interesting passages and use these to start further dialogues or rushwrites. In effect, "loop" your dialogues.

Try one or more of the following characters: Skeptic, Gullible, Worrier, Confused, Optimist, Pessimist, Your Long-Lost Twin, an Exlover, the Judge, the Movie Producer. Or pretend you're dealing with a four-year-old child whose every line is "Why?"

YOUR TURN

Write at least two dialogues. For one, use a "type" name, such as the ones listed above. For the other, use the name of someone you know. Answer the following questions.

Which dialogue seemed easier to write? Why?

How did this procedure compare with rushwrites or sketches or studies? Which felt most comfortable? most productive?

How might you alter or adapt this procedure to make it more useful?

EXPANDING YOUR MATERIAL FURTHER
Real Life Is in the Details

When you're trying to re-create an experience, the magic is in the concrete, specific details. What brings a personal essay alive are the sights, sounds, smells, and tastes that come through in it. Think in cinematic terms, in scenes. Ask yourself: Do I have enough detail here to enable a movie director, using nothing but my notes, to film this event and get it right? Have I given the set designer, the sound effects people, the actors enough to go on? If not, what's missing? What might the director not include in the picture due to lack of information?

This sounds easy, but it isn't. Every minute of the day, we're taking in an immense amount of information through our senses. Much of it we screen

34

out unconsciously, like parents who sleep through terrible traffic noise but wake up at their infant's first whimper. The rest we translate immediately into general abstract conclusions, depending on our purposes. You'll notice right away, for instance, that Jack is intensely anxious about answering the questions that Karen is asking. If someone were to ask you, "How do you know?", you'd have to stop, observe Jack carefully, and list the details that give it away—his shifting in his chair, the toe of his shoe bobbing up and down, how he's holding his arms folded high up on his chest, the way he's focusing his eyes everywhere but on Karen's face, the tightness or weakness of his voice, the halting way he's selecting his words, the pallor of his skin, the moisture on his forehead.

In re-creating the scene in prose, it's these sensory details that will really make Jack's nervousness apparent to your readers. You could tell your readers, "Jack was nervous"; and in a cool, intellectual way your readers would probably credit your statement. But they wouldn't really experience Jack's plight the way you did when you actually saw what he was going through. You don't want them just to think, or believe, or suspect Jack was nervous; you want them to **know,** to **feel** the brute fact of Jack's anxiety as you knew and felt it. If you present the exact, concrete sensory details—the details that alerted you in the first place—the truth will force itself upon your readers. Note, this doesn't mean fancy or "flowery" writing. It's not a matter of "prose style." It's a matter of evidence, facts, proof.

Hemingway gave some excellent advice for how to practice this skill. He suggested that whenever you walk into a room, you should try to decide first how the room makes you feel generally: cheerful, grave, luxurious, irritable, etc. Try to experience the room's general quality or impression. And then, try to discover the concrete details about the room that cause that impression. The room I'm in right now makes me feel content and comfortable, but a little annoyed. The comfort, when I look for the cause of it, comes from a wooden floor, a blue braid rug (moderately worn), a heavily padded brown recliner, a brass floor lamp giving off a warm yellow light, shelves of books along one wall, and a window looking out on the back yard where a squirrel is rooting around in the Creeping Charlie. The annoyance comes from the clutter: unanswered mail on my desk, papers strewn around another table, stacks of manila folders in one corner (all reminders of work I need to do), and a cracked telephone.

Obviously, you can apply this skill to anything: works of art, people, car interiors, street scenes, restaurants, skies, rocks, movies. It's one of the most useful skills imaginable. Intellectual development means, in part, learning to handle higher and more complex abstractions; but it also means developing a grasp of the particulars, the concrete details of any subject. An architect or artist studies the principles of foreshortening or perspective in order to render more exactly the concrete, specific objects he sees. It's the child, knowing neither the rules of perspective nor attending to what's actually before her eyes, who draws the house showing not only the front but both sides as well.

In this section, we want to suggest some ways of using questions to expand some of the material you've already generated, especially in ways that can bring out vivid and interesting details.

In writing, few things are more useful than good questions. Unfortunately, few things are harder to formulate. To ask a question, you have to be aware of what you know, of what's already given; but you also have to have some intuition of what you **don't** know. This is harder. To imagine the existence of facts, ideas, and concepts not currently in front of you and to form the questions that will lead you to these is difficult. It requires real imagination and energy. The ability to ask useful questions is the distinguishing mark of the great journalist, historian, diagnostician, scientific researcher, criminal investigator, psychotherapist. And writer.

Questions are most useful once you have some possible directions for your paper because they can help you expand your ideas, memories, or information. To help you with this, we're going to introduce a few techniques useful for generating as many questions as possible. Of the questions you produce, there is no guarantee that many will lead you into interesting terrain rather than into a dead end or across barren prairie. But the odds are that the more questions you generate, the more interesting the material you'll discover sooner or later. And the more you'll have for working into your paper.

Story Telling to Evoke Questions

One of the best ways to generate the kinds of questions that will allow you to expand the details of your material is to tap a resource at the heart of all narrative—**other people.** When you tell stories aloud—in the form of jokes, reminiscences, descriptions of recent events, or full-blown ghost stories and folktales—you're keenly aware of the need to create a vivid picture in your listener's mind. And if by chance they want more details, they'll often ask you. As you're expanding your material for your written narrative, a group of "listeners" can help you greatly to know what sorts of details a reader might want to see.

The procedure for this question-asking is quite simple:

Gather an audience. They might be a small group of roommates and friends, family, classmates, or even new acquaintances. (Obviously, they shouldn't be people who already know your story.)

Briefly tell them your story. Explain to your listeners what happened, in as much detail as you feel is necessary for them to get the general "plot" or events as they occurred.

Now get them to ask questions. Chances are your listeners will want to know more information just to resolve their own confusions and misunderstandings—to get the story straight. Then, their own interest in the story will lead them to ask other questions as well—questions about the people involved, and when the events happened, and how you felt—just out of curiosity.

Write down their questions. The most important part of the procedure is recording your audience's questions. You won't remember them all otherwise. If you think you'll be too busy answering the questions to write them down, then have someone in the group keep a record of the questions for you. If at all possible, try using a tape-recorder so you can capture your answers as well. Often your answers will go far beyond someone's simple question, and looking back over the questions later may not remind you of everything you said.

Use the questions as you expand your material. Later, while you're working on your narrative, glance through the list of questions and try answering them in writing, perhaps inserting your responses right into your brainstormed notes. But don't expect that every question you were asked begs for an answer in your narrative. Be judicious. Someone may have asked you a question simply for the sake of asking it, and the answer may not be necessary or useful in your paper.

To give you an idea of how this might work, here's an excerpt from a question-asking session. The writer has described a time when he and his brother and a friend had crawled half a mile up a narrow drainage tunnel when they were about 13 or 14 years old. When they were well into the tunnel, the writer, who was in the lead, spotted what he thought was a huge rat facing him along a smaller, intersecting tunnel, and panicked.

Q: What did the rat look like?

A: It was hard to see; I was using my flashlight, just checking out the little intersecting tunnels. I flashed the light up one tunnel, and suddenly I saw these enormous red eyes and a kind of furry outline, sort of huddling there about ten yards or so in front of me. It was terrifying—kind of an instant shock, you know, like I was paralyzed for a moment.

Q: How come you were so scared? I mean, the rat was probably just as frightened as you guys were, wasn't he?

A: Oh, I forgot to tell you. We'd been sitting around all morning at home wondering what to do. It was the middle of summer. We hit on the idea of exploring the tunnels, and then my mother overheard us planning. She's English, and she started telling us all these stories her mother had told her (I'm sure they were highly exaggerated to scare us) about World War II in London, and how in some bombed out parts of the city the rats were as big as dogs and how they would leap at your throat and tear at your jugular vein and kill you instantly. She's not that graphic, usually, but I think she really didn't want us to go. She probably thought they were sewage tunnels.

Q: Did the rat make any noise?

A: I can't remember. Just before I saw it, I remember how quiet everything was, just an echoey dripping sound. See, every sound we made reverberated for what seemed like minutes. We were all stooped over—the tunnel was like four feet in diameter—and our scuffling along the gritty bottom of the tunnel made a kind of evil sound . . . it's hard to describe.

Q: Evil?

A: Yeah, sort of . . . well, imagine a killer or rapist or something, dragging a body along a back alley, or an evil character with a bad leg, you know, that steady gritty dragging sound. Hunchback of Notre Dame.

Q: Did you scream?

A: Oh, I yelled like hell. But, oh, I forgot, the blank gun! (Laughs.) We were so worried about the rats that we had taken this toy blank gun with us, to scare them off. I remember screaming, "Rat! A rat! Gimme the blank gun!" I was totally out of control. I'd turned around in the tunnel and was frantically trying to shove past my brother and my friend, which was impossible because the tunnel was so narrow. It was pitch-black except for the flashlight, which was waving around crazily because I was so scared. I was imagining that huge rat, it was like a German shepherd in my mind, tearing into my heels with its yellow teeth. And thank God, my brother refused to fire the gun. He was a couple of years older than me and my friend, and he told me afterwards that once we were in the tunnel he'd started wondering what would happen to our ears if we used it. I'm sure we would have all gone deaf instantly; even out in the open the gun was incredibly loud.

You get the point. By having someone ask him questions about the narrative, this writer makes all sorts of new discoveries, not just in the area of details (the sounds, sights, fears, etc.) but also about some important background information he might otherwise not have remembered.

YOUR TURN

Using the procedure outlined above, try generating some good questions for expanding your material. If you feel reluctant setting up a question group, just try telling your narrative to some friends over coffee or on the bus or during a meal. Then explain the procedure and why it will help you, and they'll happily take it from there.

When you've tried this out, answer the following questions in your writer's notebook:

What sorts of questions did your listeners ask?

How useful were their questions? Did they show you where your account created confusion for them? Did they elicit any rich or interesting details from you?

Put an asterisk next to the questions the answers to which you think should be incorporated somewhere in your written narrative. Then take each question and do a five-minute rushwrite on it. Try chains of focused rushwrites if the questions are rich enough.

Assess what you've generated. Do you feel excited about some of your new details? If not, continue working through your question list, rushwriting and looping, until you've expanded some of your ideas to your satisfaction.

Five W's & H

The Five W's & H, otherwise known as the Journalists' Questions, are probably familiar to you, particularly if you've ever done any reporting. You can plug these questions into any writing situation and, in the course of answering them, develop new facts and ideas that might otherwise have escaped you. The questions are, "Who? What? Where? When? Why?" and "How?"

In news reporting, they're often all answered in the first paragraph:

Yesterday [When?], Colonel Mustard [Who?] murdered [What?] Professor Plum [Who?] in the Conservatory [Where?] with a lead pipe [How?], following a dispute over the ownership of a Yorkshire Terrier [Why?].

In organizing your paper, you might find it useful to write such a one-sentence summary of the event you're describing, answering each of the six questions. You can think of this as the most concentrated of thumbnail sketches.

You can also use these questions to generate a richer stock of material for your paper than you started out with. This entails broadening your sense of what each question is asking, moving beyond a mere one-word factual answer to something deeper, more complex, more interesting. Expanded a bit, the questions can be stated as follows:

Who was the main person involved? Who were the minor characters? A full answer will require, of course, much more than a mere name. What kinds of people are your characters? What distinguishes them? How would we pick them out of a crowd? What do they want? What are they like?

What did they do? What is the event you're describing? What were their actions? How did others react? How would you describe a painting of each scene? What directions would you give to a movie director about the events?

Where did it occur? Again, a place name may do for a start. But what else can you tell the reader about the locale? What kind of place was it? What is the ambience or feel of the place? What directions would you give to Universal Studios to help them create one or more sets for the scene? Could the event have happened elsewhere? Why or why not?

When did it happen? As with the question "Where?" the answer to this might require giving an impression of the time of the story generally. Are you writing about childhood? college days? The 1970s? What time of day was it (misty dawn or fiery noon)? What season of the year?

Why did he, she, they do it? Why did it happen? In most cases this will prove the most interesting as well as the most difficult and complex question of all. It's a question of motivation, of goals and purposes.

39

How did he, she, they do it? How did it happen? The answer to this usually entails a sequence of events linked together in a causal chain. "A" happened, then "B" happened, and the two of them caused "C" to happen. Or it will be a question of means, as with the lead pipe in the news story above. Unlike the "Why?" question, though, "How?" doesn't imply a question of motivation. It's more a mechanical question than a psychological one.

YOUR TURN

Apply the Five Ws & H to your own material. Write both a one-sentence capsule summary and a fuller development based on the questions. Answer the following questions in your writer's notebook:

How did this technique work for you? What new material did it generate?

Which question proved the most fruitful or interesting?

Now write a dialogue (see pages 33–34) with a Journalist and yourself as the characters. The Journalist should be a complete newcomer to your situation, with no previous knowledge whatsoever. Let the Journalist probe you repeatedly with these questions until he's satisfied with your account. (This may give you an excellent idea of what kind of information your reader will need to understand your experience.)

Particle/Wave/Field

The particle/wave/field technique is the richest and most complex technique for generating questions we have to offer. Once you have any kind of rough topic, even just for a starting point, the P/W/F approach spawns all kinds of useful and interesting questions almost automatically.

First developed by composition experts Richard Young, Alton Becker, and Kenneth Pike in their book, *Rhetoric: Discovery and Change,*[1] the P/W/F technique asks you questions about your topic from three different approaches: as a static entity, as an entity in flux, and as an entity that is part of a larger system. Put simply, "particle" questions ask for discrete details and facts related to the object of your focus. "Wave" questions examine the changes and developments of that object. And "field" questions probe the relationships between the object and other entities with which it interacts. Below, we'll explain each of these rather abstract concepts more fully and show you how you can use them to expand your material.

---

[1]New York: Harcourt Brace Jovanovich, 1970.

Particles. Seeing your topic in particle form involves describing simple, dis-crete facts, ideas, images, memories, statistics—the small grains of truth that make up your topic. In short, it calls for lists. If you've already drawn up lists, you can use those here. If you've used clustering, turn your clusters into lists and use those. You can also, of course, draw up further lists starting from any "seed" you like.

Once you have your lists, write above them the word "particles" and the symbol **X.** Think of each entry on the list as an **X,** a variable almost in the algebraic sense. You'll be plugging these **X**s into simple question-asking for-mulas in the following sections.

To illustrate the approach, we'll start with a simple list and work it into a set of wave and field questions:

PARTICLES : **X**s

Caves	helmets
rope	bats
stalactites	stalagmites
boots	carbide lamps
mud	bad air

Waves. Wave questions look at the developments, the changes in your topic and in the particles of it. From these questions you can start working toward process descriptions, how-to's, cause-and-effect analyses, historical studies—any number of subjects that involve development.

The formula for producing such questions is this: "How does **X** change over time?" You might even write that at the top of a page before you start. Once you've done so, plug in your general topic for **X** and then each sub-sequent item on your list. Another way to phrase wave questions is: "How is **X** different before and after some event?" or "What is the history (or future) of **X**?" Note that the length of time involved in such changes is arbi-trary. Some things, such as unstable atoms and the emotional states of tod-dlers, change in fractions of seconds; others, such as the creation and ero-sion of mountains, are best calculated in millions of years. In asking wave questions, you can set the time limits yourself. You might even ask several wave questions using one particle, simply by varying the length of the time you consider.

By plugging the short list of particles above into the general wave for-mula, we can produce the following questions.

"How Does **X** Change Over Time?"

Cave exploring: How has it changed? Who did it first? Prehistoric tribes? Mod-ern times? When did it become a sport? Who were the earliest cavers for pleasure? Where did it begin? France? America? How has the sport developed? Societies? Magazines? Specialty Shops? Safety regulations, habits?

Caves: How do caves change? How are caves formed? A geological question. Which caves? Say, central Texas. Long-term changes: When did these form? How did they form? Limestone laid down when? Water level dropped when? Longhorn versus Natural Bridge—one older or younger? Short-term changes: history of exploration, opening to public—damage from public? Changes in ownership? Policies?

Ropes: How have ropes changed? What materials have they been made out of? Hemp? Nylon? How has their construction changed? One strand to several strands? Originally woven by hand, but how done now? Development of machines for this? Have ropes evolved specifically for cave exploring? Has their use changed? History of knots?

Stalactites: How do stalactites change over time? How do they develop? Water dripping and mineral deposits—but what minerals? How long does it take to form one? Then what happens?—columns? fall and shatter? Changes in their formation over time? Soda straws turn to solid bodies. How does that happen? Something plugs them. What? Movement of air in caves? More recent changes? Damage from cave explorers? Souvenirs? Oil from hands? Smoke from lamps? (a new topic?!?)

As you can see, any item from a list can produce half a dozen questions. If your lists are at all extensive, you may have to simply pick and choose the most interesting items to plug in. You can stop after simply asking "How does **X** change?" for each particle. Or, as we have done here, you can write down all the related questions you can think of as well. The best guide to follow is your own interests. If you find yourself led down a fascinating side road (or tunnel or chamber), you should follow it.

Field. Field questions are the most abstract. In fact, the sequence, particle-wave-field, represents a steady movement from the most concrete to the most conceptual. In practice, this makes field questions the most difficult to frame and to answer, but also the most interesting. The richest topics for most academic papers usually tend to be field questions.

Field questions concern relationships: part to whole, claim to evidence, similarities to differences, etc. All organized fields of knowledge—everything from physics to economics to literature—are attempts to answer more or less sweeping field questions. How is energy related to mass? How do supply and demand affect prices? What role do changes in language play in the history of poetry? In working through the P/W/F technique, a rich body of particles and waves will help you formulate field questions. But if you find yourself slowing down with field questions, don't worry. Field questions simply require more thought than waves or particles.

There are a number of field questions into which you can simply plug your existing material. Use these to get started, and return to them if you run out of ideas, but don't feel obliged to restrict yourself to them. As with the wave question formulas, you might jot one or another of these on a sheet of paper and write the resulting questions under it.

"How do any two **X**s go together? How do they relate to each other?"
"How are these two **X**s similar? How are they different?"
"What parts can this **X** be broken into?"
"What different things is this **X** a part of?"
"What is this **X** the effect of?"
"What does this **X** cause?"
"What does this **X** point to or remind me of beyond itself? What other things is it like?"
"What use can be made of this **X**?"

You can also apply field thinking to entire lists. You might take one of your lists and ask the following questions.

"What parts does this list naturally fall into? How might I arrange the items into sublists? How would I label them? How would they be related to each other?"

The short list we've been using might be broken down as follows:

A	B	C
Caves	ropes	mud
stalactites	boots	bats
stalagmites	helmets	bad air
	carbide lamps	

Once you've sorted your list, you then name or describe the subcategories and start considering the relationships between them. With the list here, you might produce the following ideas in rushwrite fashion:

What subgroups have I got? (A) geological formations, (B) equipment, and—(C) what?—hazards? But then, the equipment itself was all designed to meet hazards, wasn't it? So the items of lists B and C should be related. Boots, I suppose, qualify as a way of dealing with the "hazard" of mud. What other hazards are suggested by the equipment list items? Ropes: steep places, cliffs and vertical drops, narrow ledges, crawlways? Boots: sharp stones, snakes? Helmets: low ceilings, stalactites, falling rocks, falls? Carbide lamps: Darkness, also indicates bad air by dimness of flame. (Working backwards:) How do you handle bats? You don't. (Bat spray?) How about bad air? Surplus oxygen? Does anyone actually carry this?

This is the kind of creative pondering that field questions can provoke. Notice that nothing is settled. But you have a wealth of questions to consider, and an interesting paper idea might grow out of this at any point. Note also how useful this sort of questioning becomes for types of writing other than the narrative.

As another example of something the P/W/F technique might do, let's take two possible wave questions and ask the field question, how are they related?

Wave #1: How has the sport of caving grown in popularity and extent over the last century? (Social changes)

Wave #2: What physical changes are apparent in caves over the last century? (Geological changes)

Either of these could be answered separately. But considering them together, we can ask the further question: "How has the increased popularity of cave exploring affected the physical conditions of the caves themselves? Have cavers, like backpackers, become aware of the environmental damage of their own sport? Are they developing a code of honor about protecting natural formations? What could be the future consequences of all this?" Here, all of a sudden, you might have an excellent paper topic. By superimposing one wave question onto another, you've developed a sophisticated question of cause-and-effect.

Another possibility is to take a relationship (a field question) and plug it into the formula for a developmental (wave) question: e.g., "How has the relationship between_____and_____changed over (time period)?"

Here are a few examples of what this formula produces:

How has the relationship between Cuba and the United States changed over the past 30 years?

How has the relationship between coal burning and ground water purity changed during this century?

How does the relationship between Huck Finn and Jim change over the course of their raft trip south?

How does the mother/child relationship in Somaliland typically change between early adolescence and early adulthood?

The possibilities for intellectual play with this model are endless. Each of your separate particles provides the material for several possible wave and field questions. The latter in turn will sometimes drive you back to listing more particles just as the "equipment" list above provoked a string of fresh "hazards." You can work wave questions and field questions back and forth into each other in an infinite variety of ways to produce more questions than you could ever reasonably answer in a lifetime. On the other hand, you shouldn't let the potential complexity of the technique throw you. You should use it for all it's worth, but if you get little farther than writing lists of particles and a few simple wave questions, you've still made real progress in the development of your ideas.

The first few times you use the particle/wave/field technique, it may feel strange and stiff to you, but stick with it. Here are a few things to keep in mind.

The P/W/F technique is extremely untidy and haphazard. You'll cover a lot of paper, leaving questions and lists strewn everywhere. So be it. Later on, you can sort it all out, throw away most of it, and tidy up the rest; but don't give it a thought while you're actually cooking up your questions.

As with all such techniques, work quickly, follow the instinctively interesting leads, and don't even think about your reader. If you're stuck, push somewhere else. If you're on a roll, keep moving.

Don't be shy of using the technique in as clumsy and mechanical a way as you want, particularly in the beginning. The technique's strength is producing questions almost automatically. List your particles and start plugging them into the question formulas provided. Many of the questions will prove trivial or unanswerable. Others will lead to immensely interesting and provocative material. The technique can't distinguish one from the other. That's where your own imagination and judgment come into play.

If you've thought of a question, **don't** stop to ask yourself: "Is this a particle, a wave, or a field question?" Just write it down and keep going. You use this procedure to invent questions, not to categorize them. If the question makes you think, if it opens up issues and ideas you hadn't considered before, then it's done its duty. It makes no difference what kind of question it is.

When do you stop? Whenever you have to, or whenever you're sure you have more than enough material. The technique works to expand rather than to focus your ideas. It continues to mushroom into further questions and angles and ramifications as long as you work with it. It won't, however, lead you to a conclusion. At some point, dictated probably by the scope of the assignment and your time constraints, you'll have to call it quits and begin sorting out what you've got.

YOUR TURN

Sit down for at least two sessions with this technique and churn out as many questions as you can. Then answer the following questions in your writer's notebook:

What new material did you develop? What new leads did this open up for you?

Where did you have problems with it? How did you get past these?

IN SUMMARY

The techniques we've suggested for generating and developing your ideas all assume that you'll be sitting alone for at least a short time for this specific purpose. But remember along the way how valuable other people can be as you generate and expand material before beginning to draft a piece of writing. Make mental notes of how you present your ideas, what background you find yourself explaining to your listener, what details you intuitively reach for to make the story interesting. And notice how your listener responds. What is she excited by? When does her attention flag? What questions does she ask? All of this will help you determine what to present and how to present it when you start drafting your story with readers in mind.

Remember also the value of keeping a notebook handy. Once you've started thinking about a topic, you'll notice that the idea acts as a magnet, drawing to itself a world of related ideas, images, and memories, even when you're not deliberately working on it. These often flash into your consciousness at the oddest times: while you're in the shower or behind the wheel or in the middle of jogging or when you're not quite attending to a lecture or meeting. Often, furthermore, their half-life is painfully brief. If you don't get them down right away, they'll fade from your mind, and no effort of memory will recall them. This is especially true of those splendid insights we all have just before dropping off at night. So keep a notepad with you everywhere.

The point of all these techniques, again, is simply to amass material for possible use in your paper. You want to have more than enough, more than you can ever use before you shift into third gear and start organizing and drafting. It may seem a sloppy, inefficient way to work, but it's really not. It's a case of the long way around being the shortest way home. It's much better (both for your work and for your general mood) to be able to select and arrange from an abundance of material than to find, after carefully writing and polishing three pages of a six-page paper, that you've run out of things to say.

Chapter Two

PUTTING IT ALL TOGETHER

If you've put time into any or all of the techniques discussed so far, you should have more than enough material. This could be in any form, from notes to dialogues, from lists and clusters to long passages of straight prose paragraphs. The one thing it's not likely to be is neat. For some time now you've been barrelling along in what we've called Second Gear—moving swiftly and easily, with few backward glances at your reader—and you've covered a good many miles. Now it's time to start taking more seriously the prospect of producing an essay someone else would enjoy reading. It's time to move into Third Gear: organizing your material and working up a draft.

There are two main points to remember about Third Gear. One is that it's not Fourth Gear. Which is to say, though you're taking your reader more seriously than you did before, you're still not working on your presentation draft. You're still not producing a document that anyone besides yourself (or perhaps one or more sympathetic helpers) is likely to see. You don't have to worry about how it looks. You can misspell words. You can make grammatical and punctuation errors. You can phrase ideas with any amount of clumsiness and lose nothing by it. You'll have a chance to get back to all of those things before you're done. If you worry about them now—if you try to jump from Second straight into Fourth—you'll probably only slow yourself down.

The other point to remember is that, though you don't want to slide into Fourth Gear just yet, you can always downshift if the going gets tough. At some point, in trying to describe a particular camping spot or recall an argument you had with your sister, you may find yourself bogged down. You may not have all the details you need, and trying to come up with the details and draft at the same time may cramp your style. If this happens, you might take time off from the drafting, and return to one of the techniques detailed in Chapter One. Set your draft aside, get out your notebook or a scrap of paper, and do some rushwrites or particle/wave/fields or whatever it takes until you're satisfied that you have the material you need. Then pick up the draft where you left off.

You may find you need to do this repeatedly. In fact, the longer the paper you're writing, the more certain it is that you **won't** have all the material you need when you start to draft. Jumping to a higher gear before you're ready can cause real trouble; dropping from a higher to a lower gear and then moving forward again is often the quickest way to proceed.

Before we tackle the process of drafting, we want to describe a useful technique for organizing your material. This technique helps you get your ideas and reflections and information arranged in an attractive order before you commit any part of a draft to paper. Like other organizing techniques, it makes use of graphic aids—visual representations that let you see the shape or structure of your paper. Such graphic aids, as we'll show in more detail in Part 2, can help you make decisions about the organization of your work more flexibly and effectively than if you tried to work out all the problems in your head. They also have the advantages of easy access and speed. Because you're working with diagrams rather than with words, you can experiment with different ways of arranging your material with little time or effort.

The technique we'll explore in this section is useful mainly for organizing narrative material—events sequenced in time. In Part 2, we'll show you another organizing technique for use with a range of academic papers: essays, explanations, arguments, and research reports—as well as for writing outside the academic setting.

ORGANIZING YOUR NARRATIVE

Think back on the detective stories you've either read or seen. What's the first thing that happens as you read or watch the story? Usually, it's the crime either being committed or discovered. "Two shots rang out. A body hit the floor." Or, "Lady Grimsley opened the door. A blood-curdling shriek escaped her lips. There was Lord Grimsley, hanging by his suspenders from the blades of the slowly revolving ceiling fan . . . dead!"

But though the murder or discovery may be the first scene the author presents to us, it's usually not the first event that happened **chronologically**. A long series of events led to that murder, most of which will be revealed as the story unfolds. In fact, the uncovering of the events before and during the crime is usually what provides the drama of the events after the crime. Every clue Hercule Poirot uncovers moves the story forward while revealing previous events. It's only in the police report that the events will ever be presented in a straight line from start to finish, and the police report won't be half as interesting to read as Dame Agatha's novel.

We have, then, two distinct series of events. One is the **historical** sequence, the chronological Monday-Tuesday-Wednesday string of occurrences. The other is the **rhetorical** sequence, the order in which the author presents these events: first the crime, then the investigation, then (by way of the investigation) a return to the events leading to the crime, then forward again to the arrest. For some kinds of writing (accident reports, biographies) the historical and rhetorical sequences may be the same. In history, they almost always are. But in works meant largely for entertainment, some rearrangement of the historical events is usually more interesting than the straight A-to-Z-format.

Your own material may lend itself very well to some sort of rhetorical rearrangement. Rather than assuming the first thing that happened is the place to start writing, you should consider which incident will best catch the reader's attention, which you might save for flashbacks, which to skim over lightly, which to render in detail, and so on. We'd like to lay out for you here a technique for thinking about these possibilities. The technique relies on the use of timelines—much like those you may have encountered in history courses and textbooks.

How to Draw a Timeline

Working with timelines gives you a much clearer picture of the story-telling possibilities within your material than you can get any other way. Instead of being overwhelmed by the material you've developed, you have a graphic representation of the main points of your experience, their chronological relationships, and their potential for exciting your reader. This means you can now start making some considered rhetorical decisions about how to **present** your story to your reader. By giving you a better handle on your material, timelines allow you to shape and structure it in a way that will capture and hold your reader's interest.

A timeline is a sort of blueprint you can draw and revise (repeatedly if necessary) that gives you a sturdy foundation when you start drafting. They're useful because they're quick, easy, and cheap. Revising a timeline takes a matter of minutes, sometimes only seconds. Making major structural changes after you've drafted a piece may take hours.

The first time you work with a timeline, expect it to feel awkward and a little confusing. But follow the directions carefully and you'll find that, like clustering, it's an easy and entertaining way to get a particular job done.

Draw a horizontal line representing the passage of time.

Mark the major events you want to write about with vertical lines running up from the first line. (Note: the horizontal line should extend beyond the first and last events.)

Label the events with A, B, C, etc., beneath the horizontal line.

Make a list of what event each letter stands for.

So far, you should have something that looks like Figure 2-1.

A   B   C   D   E   F   G   H   I

FIGURE 2-1

   A: Lord Grimsley serves tea to Aunt Dragonia
   B: Grimsley accidently exposes Idaho terrorist gang
   C: Pick-up trucks seen surrounding Grimsley Manor
   D: Lord Grimsley discovered dead on ceiling fan
   E: Police investigate; are, not suprisingly, stumped
   F: Poirot called in; discovers belt buckle with secret code
   G: Poirot cracks code; identifies terrorists
   H. Chase through streets of Milwaukee leading to capture
   I: Poirot recounts story to nephew, Felix

The next step is to *extend the vertical lines upward to varying heights;* the more exciting the event, the higher the line should be drawn.

With the present example, this produces something like Figure 2-2.

50

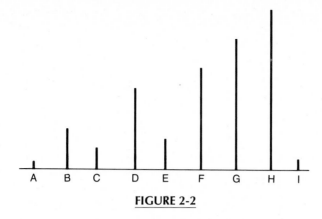

FIGURE 2-2

You now want to *redraw the line to space the events horizontally* to chronological "scale." That is, events that occurred close in time should be close together on the line. Events separated more widely in time should be separated more widely on the line.

Events which extend over a long period can be drawn as flat boxes rather than as peaks. In Figure 2-3 the police investigation (E), taking place over several weeks, represents one of these extended periods.

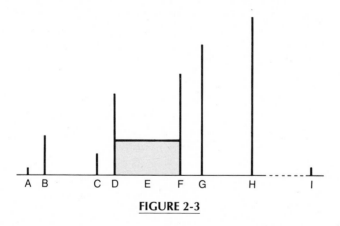

FIGURE 2-3

Now that you've drawn your timeline, what decisions can it help you make? Let's look once more at Figure 2-3. What decisions might this time-line lead the writer to make, simply on the basis of how it looks?

One thing he might notice immediately is how short the vertical lines are that represent events "A" and "I." In drawing them like this, the writer has discovered that, compared with the more powerful incidents of the story, events "A" and "I" don't greatly interest him. Lord Grimsley serving tea to Aunt Dragonia, and Poirot recounting the incidents of his adventure to his nephew Felix, both fail to excite him as a writer. And chances are that the events won't excite the reader either. The writer would probably decide to jettison event "A" entirely. Event "I" might make a clever, low-key punch-line for the story, but he certainly won't spend much time on it.

Next, the writer notices the flat box at Event "E." There's no real question of cutting this section: the events are somewhat interesting, and the results of the investigation are certainly necessary to the story. On the other hand, if he renders "E" in detail, it could take far too long, thus bogging down the story and losing the reader. He realizes that his technique for writing about "E" will differ substantially from the technique he uses for "H." Because "H" is highly exciting, he will want to present it in the fullest, richest detail possible: careful descriptions, actual dialogue—the most nearly cinematic presentation he can manage. "E," by contrast, will call for some quicker, sketchier procedure: less detail, less dialogue, perhaps only a summary of the investigation and its results.

This suggests a general principle for the writing of any narrative, whether essay or fiction: the more exciting the incident, the more detail you want to use in presenting it. The less interesting it is, the more general and abstract you can afford to be. Richness of detail makes an event more real and vivid to your reader, but it also takes more time. A more general treatment is less engaging, but quicker. If you render an exciting event too sketchily, your reader won't really feel or experience the interest the events hold for you. If, on the other hand, you render an intrinsically uninteresting event in too much detail, you'll probably bore your reader cross-eyed. With timelines, you indicate by the height of your vertical lines which events are most intrinsically exciting, and in most cases those will be the ones which deserve the fullest treatment.

YOUR TURN

Draw a timeline covering the events you plan to write about. As described above, space the events more or less to chronological scale and draw the vertical lines to represent the innate excitement or interest of each event. Then answer the following questions in your writer's notebook:

How would you describe the general shape of your timeline? Is it fairly flat, rolling, or mountainous? Does it build toward a single peak, or are there several high points spread throughout?

Do you find any flat or low spots? What kind of events are they? How might you handle these in your writing?

Arranging Your Events for the Greatest Dramatic Impact

Once the timeline is drawn, the writer already has a better idea of which events to include, which to cut, which to develop in detail, and which to summarize more briefly. There is still one very important decision to make, however, and it's the one we began this section by discussing: namely, in what order should the events be presented? Should the **rhetorical** sequence be the same as the **historical** sequence, or should it differ? By arranging and rearranging the letters denoting the different events, the writer can construct a number of possible alternative "plots" in a matter of minutes.

Suppose, for instance, the present writer goes with the straight, chronological sequence, the story opening with Event "B": Lord Grimsley accidently exposing the band of Idaho terrorists. (The writer, again, has already cut Event "A" completely from the story.) The rest of the story would simply reel off in the order:

B   C   D   E   F   G   H   I

This might work. Event "B," after all, is pretty interesting in its own right. And the plot as a whole certainly has the virtue of simplicity. If the story hooks the reader in the first place, it at least won't confuse her. But since the writer has long since learned not to stop with his first idea about anything, he continues searching for alternative ways of presenting the same events.

Suppose now that the writer draws a plot beginning with Event "D," Lord Grimsley revolving slowly from the broken ceiling fan. This certainly has shock value. (Have you ever priced a good ceiling fan?) If the writer does this, however, he'll still need to reveal events "B" and "C" at some point for the story to make sense. This will require one or more "flashbacks," which would probably come up as Monsieur Poirot pieces together each event from the clues he finds. The order for this would come out something like:

D   E   F   (C)   G   (B)   H   I

Events "C" and "B"are the flashbacks embedded in the story running from "D" through "I."

The writer could even begin with Event "F," showing Poirot at work from the first page. An order for this might be:

F   (C D E)   G   (B)   H   I

Thus Poirot, during the early part of his investigation (F), pieces the story together, working from the arrival of the pick-up trucks (C) through the police investigation (E). Later, he decodes the belt buckle (G), and realizes the fatal secret Grimsley had stumbled upon (B). And then we have the chase and capture (H) and the aftermath (I). Arranging the letters like this and thinking carefully about how the story would have to be told, the writer would probably already foresee a couple of possible difficulties in such a plot. The opening scene, for one thing, wouldn't have the attention-grabbing power of event "D." The story might also be hard to follow: so much material comes between "F" and "G," the reader might lose the main thread of it.

Yet another option might be to present the entire story as told by Poirot himself to his nephew Felix. In that case, event "I" (Poirot's talk with Felix) would act as a frame for the story as a whole; and Poirot might well begin with his own arrival on the scene. As Poirot experienced the events, after all, they did begin with the phone call from Commissioner Jowls requesting his services. This kind of "narrative frame" plot runs something like this:

I - [F (C D E) G (B) H] - I.

Event "I" is, in a sense, the only event we directly see: Poirot talking to Felix before a roaring fire, a snifter of brandy in his hand. The rest of the story we get "second hand" from Poirot; in a sense, it's all flashback. From within that framework, Poirot describes simultaneously his investigation and the series of events it revealed, the latter occurring as flashbacks within his own story. Poirot might be sitting with Felix in November, discussing an investigation he did in August that revealed events of the previous May. Trying to keep all this straight without a timeline would be mind-boggling. With a timeline, you can do it rather easily.

The last point—how Poirot himself would have experienced the events of the story—brings up one final consideration: point of view. The order you present the events in depends on who's telling the story. If Poirot tells it, it begins with "F." What if the police inspector tells it? Or Lady Grimsley? Or the Idaho terrorists? Or Lord Grimsley? (Perhaps more to the point, where does it end if Lord Grimsley tells it?) In your own work, this probably won't be an issue, but it may be worth thinking about.

Some Cautions

The success of a timeline in helping you to arrange your material for a narrative essay comes largely from its way of laying out the actual (chronological) sequence of events in your experience and letting you consider alternative arrangements for those events. Like all other techniques for writing, however, it doesn't work "automatically." You still need to judge the results and use some caution in making any major decisions for writing your paper:

Not every story lends itself to rhetorical rearrangement. Events that happen in one spot over a short continuous period of time often work best in simple A, B, C, D order. An afternoon at the zoo hardly calls for any fancy plotting.

If you use flashbacks, be very careful not to confuse your reader. Mark the moves back and forth in time as clearly as possible. You might read a few of the short stories of Flannery O'Connor to see this handled by a master.

Flashbacks usually work best built into the quieter rather than the more active parts of your story. Usually a character will be thinking back on an event or telling it to someone. The character will need a little peace and quiet to do this. You don't want to break off a chase scene or a sword fight to introduce an episode from your hero's tormented childhood.

YOUR TURN

Using the timeline you developed for the last "Your Turn," do the following:

Think of at least three different ways you could arrange the events involved in your story.

For each arrangement, write a sketch (see page 32) giving a brief summary of the plot as your audience would read it.

Briefly note the advantages and disadvantages each arrangement would have in terms of its effect on the reader.

DRAFTING: HOW TO BEGIN

You've found an excellent topic, developed lots of material, and worked it into a splendid structure. The moment finally arrives when you have to start putting words on paper with the eventual goal of having them read by someone besides yourself. If you haven't stalled before, there's every chance you will now.

Drafting is probably the hardest part of the writing process, for novices and veterans alike. This is the point when you'll first notice what a mess your room is, how badly the dishes need doing, how long it's been since you called Cousin Fritzler in St. Paul—anything to get out of writing. Interviews with professional writers are remarkably consistent on this point: when it's time to start drafting, everything else in the world suddenly overwhelms them with its pressing urgency. We all do this: magazine reporters, technical writers, us, you. And we all know what nonsense it is. If the dirty laundry has been accumulating this long, the pile can wait a bit longer. But at the moment of sitting down to draft, other demands seem terribly pressing. One writer, in fact, described the secret of writing as simply being able to keep your tail in your chair for an hour or more at a time. You can wriggle—just don't get up.

Avoiding Pitfalls in Drafting

Completely overcoming the problem of procrastination is too much to hope for. The fact is, every phase of writing takes work, and all work requires a certain amount of discipline, of simply getting to the task and staying with it. But though no one has ever discovered a way to make drafting easy, we're often remarkably adept at making it more difficult, nerve-racking, and unpleasant than it needs to be. As if it weren't enough that we have to walk uphill, we find ways to tie our own boots together and put rocks in our backpacks as we go. For the next few pages we'll try to pinpoint some of these self-defeating habits and suggest ways to prevent falling prey to them.

The Need for More Material.   One of the difficulties in drafting is unavoidable. That is, when you sit down to draft, no matter how well prepared you think you are, no matter how much material you've developed, there's always a lot more clarification and development left to do before your ideas will make sense to anyone else. You may have worked up more than enough to write about. You may even have thrown away pages of brainstormed material as excess. Nonetheless, when you start drafting, you'll find that it's more than just a matter of finding words for the ideas you already have.

In drafting, you're necessarily looking at your material more closely than you have before; and in doing so, you'll discover more gaps and sketchy spots than you were previously aware of. Your brief note about the bank of lights behind third base tells **you** everything you need to know, but unless this is explained in a healthy sentence or two, **your reader** won't have the slightest idea what you're talking about. The note "Alice—jittery" may require a paragraph to develop fully. And, of course, you may find as you draft that your paper takes on a strange vagabond life of its own, wandering hither and yon, only really finding its focus after several pages, or not even until the concluding paragraph. To some degree then, you're always creating new material as you draft, and this will always slow you down.

Anxiety.   The other main difficulty in drafting is simple anxiety. This takes a number of forms. You may really feel nervous as you write. Or you may develop a temporary nausea for the whole writing business. Then again, you may just be bored and distractible, even though you're usually interested in your topic. You might, on the other hand, work diligently but find yourself making scores of small, stupid mistakes and wasting a lot of time correcting them. Or you may have a sudden fit of literary perfectionism and find yourself spending hours obsessively honing and polishing what you've already written.

Don't be fooled. Every one of these is simply a more or less sophisticated form of stage fright. At a low level, stage fright won't interfere with your work at all. It may even keep you alert and provide you a certain useful "nervous" energy. On the other hand, such nervousness can make drafting a terrible burden, keep you from your desk, or bog you down in the silliest, time-wasting details. This isn't helpful—or necessary.

In dealing with with these two problems—the need to invent new material, and the varieties of stage fright—keep in mind the place of drafting in your overall writing strategy. You're only producing **a** draft; you're not producing **the** draft. It's not your presentation copy. You're playing, but you're not playing "for keeps."

Commit Yourself to Revision.   The kindest favor you can do yourself is to take a solemn oath that under no circumstances will you turn in the draft you're working on. Commit yourself to a careful and thorough revision before even starting. Don't get up on that rope before you've got your safety net spread securely beneath you. (One easy way to guarantee you'll keep your vow is to draft on unpresentable paper, such as the backs of old exams or canary yellow "second sheets.")

If you commit yourself to a thorough revision, and your first draft suddenly veers off course and heads down another road, you can afford to follow its lead. You have a shot at discovering whole new landscapes, whole new approaches to your topic, perhaps even a new topic, even as you write. You may find that as you draft, your topic seems to shift and change under your hand, perhaps altering its focus or tone, until at the end you've arrived somewhere totally different from your original destination.

This is the time **not to take your original blueprint too seriously.** Your brainstorming and timelining are guides, maps, aids; they should not be straightjackets. If you've worked carefully on your blueprint, experimented with a variety of structures, found one that seems comprehensive yet simple, and sketched it in with the necessary information and details, it should speed up your drafting considerably. But it's not carved in stone.

Sometimes as you draft, you'll feel the logic of the events or ideas pulling you away from your original direction. You thought your account of the "haunted house" on Cedar Creek led naturally to the anecdote about your falling through the stairs and being injured. In writing it, however, the story itself seems to want to pull toward Robbie Berkhoff's first encounter with the "ghost" who lived there. Follow the ghost. Your notes and blueprint will still be there long after the vividness of the memory of Robbie and the ghost has faded.

In Short, Plan Carefully, and Then Take Your Plans Lightly.   Follow your map when it works, but if the bridge is out or another route beckons, go the other way. Don't cling to your outline with such a deathgrip that you choke off fresh creativity. If you do, you may in fact be able to plough ahead, following your blueprint, but the odds are high that you won't feel any enthusiasm for the work, and your writing will lose something of its sparkle and freshness.

Committing yourself to a revision in effect blurs the line between developing your material and drafting it. If, after all your work, your draft turns out a complete shambles, you can always toss it off as an extended brainstorm and start another draft from scratch. It will not in any case have been a total loss. Even if the draft as a whole doesn't work, you can usually salvage a number of facts and insights from it; and the mere fact that you recognize the draft's problems shows that you have a better grasp of your topic than you did when you started. The second draft should come easier for knowing what to avoid.

Knowing that you will be revising your draft leads to another useful guideline for producing it. On the draft itself, **whenever you're in doubt about including something, throw it in.** You're not sure whether you need to explain a particular concept? Explain it. You suspect (though you're not sure) that the anecdote about pulling the calf out with a winch quite fits? Write it. Sometimes you'll know exactly what needs saying and what doesn't, in which case you should trust yourself: you're probably right. But in case of doubt, when you're drafting, include it.

The reasons for this are twofold. Anything that keeps you going, keeps you getting words on paper, is all to the good. Keeping up a steady rhythm of work is of the essence in drafting. Any long brooding pause may slow you to a standstill. If you consciously write more than you can use, you'll produce some waste, but at least you'll maintain your progress. That's one reason.

The main reason, however, is that when you're revising, it's much easier to cut material than to add it. If you have indeed overexplained the economics of ethanol production or gone on too long about Max's prize heifer, you'll see this on the draft fairly clearly, and fixing the problem will entail but a few slashes of the pen. If, on the other hand, there are gaps in your account, (1) you'll have a harder time finding and diagnosing them, and (2) treatment will mean more actual drafting. Carving away the excess from a draft is swifter, easier, and surer work than plugging holes with fresh material. You do well to produce more than enough the first time, by including everything that may be appropriate. We call these "Kitchen Sink Drafts" (as in, "She threw in everything but. . . . "). When it's time to revise your work, you'll thank yourself if you've written one.

Your major obstacle in all this will almost certainly be your own excessively high standards for the draft. Instinctively, we all hate to see words come from our pens or typewriters that we feel aren't worthy of us, writing that we'd hate to have "pinned" on us. But on a rough draft, you'd best just learn to accept it. As some wise scribbler put it, "You have to be willing to write badly in order to write well." Or as the late E. B. White, a prodigiously wise scribbler, reminded himself on a sign over his desk: **Don't Get It Right, Get It Written.**

The more you insist on writing splendid prose the first time, the more slowly and less efficiently you'll work, and the more awful the whole experience will become. When this gets too bad, when you set your standards so high that you can't get anything down, you've given yourself what is known as "writer's block"—an ailment writers are always quick to attribute to everything but its real cause, their own inflexible (and unhumble) notions of what they ought to be able to produce the first time they set pen to paper. Writer William Stafford suggests that if you can't hit the ball over the net, you should lower the net. If you still can't get the ball high enough, you should lay the net on the ground and roll the ball over.

Keep Up the Momentum. Drafting is the real bricks-and-mortar part of writing, the workaday grind. The earlier phases, the brainstorming and elaborating and arranging, are the playful parts of writing, the courtship and honeymoon with a topic. The later phases, revision and editing, are the most gratifying and intriguing; the work is interesting and the results are heartening. The middle phase, getting the original stuff down on paper, feels the most like Monday morning.

So let it. Since the really crippling danger in drafting is anxiety, a steady, matter-of-fact, workaday approach may be the safest and most useful. **Try to draft steadily and try to draft rapidly.** Keep paddling, or peddling, or climbing, or however you see it. This is no time for long window-gazing. And it's no time to be obsessively revising what you already have (which, again, is simply a sophisticated way of avoiding the real work, that of creating fresh prose.) Try to get a version of your (carefully developed and blueprinted) paper **down on paper** where you can work with it—where, in a **later draft,** you can make it into something really significant and sharp and colorful.

Banish the Critic. If you find as you write that you keep getting flustered and scratching things out, you may be letting your imaginary audience intimidate you. You may be imagining your actual intended reader going over your work, shaking his head with disgust at every third sentence. Or you may be suffering a visitation by the Critic.

The Critic is a loathsome, nasty, ill-natured, sour-faced pedantic wretch who crawls sooner or later into the back of every writer's head and starts carping. "What a stupid idea! You can't say that! Can't you be original? How dull you are! You call that grammar? You write like a hick! Scratch that out; that's not at all interesting or original. You can't write. That's the worst kind of TV slang! You're really going to get found out this time. Your teacher will probably read this aloud to the class and everyone's going to giggle and point." And on and on and on.

If The Critic were physical, we could lock him away somewhere out of earshot. As it is, all we can do is refuse to listen, or at least buy him off with a promissory note. If he starts in after you, tell him he can attack the draft all he wants—**after** you're done with it. But until that time, he has to crawl back in his box. Insist on it.

And don't argue with him; it only encourages him. Defiantly and pointedly ignore him and go on. He may continue to fuss and grumble and snigger for a while, but he does find being ignored discouraging. If you do this, you may suddenly realize at some point that you've written two quick, easy pages without hearing a word from him. When you revise those pages later, you'll probably notice that they sound smoother, livelier, and more natural than most of what you've written. If, however, you let The Critic control the drafting, he has a habit of maiming and crippling people's prose into dry, bloodless, awkward, hesitant stuff that even a tax lawyer would find dull reading. It may be "correct," but no one will enjoy it.

Unfortunately, your readers may sometimes look suspiciously like The Critic; they may even have acted like him in the past. In this case, our advice to ignore The Critic may at first strike you as a contradiction; after all, we've been suggesting that in drafting you should begin thinking more carefully about your readers. How can you attend to your readers' needs and at the same time banish them to the soundproof Critic's Cell so you can get on with your work?

If you find yourself not knowing whether the reader staring over your shoulder will turn out to be The Critic in disguise—then think up a sympathetic audience while you're drafting. Imagine that you're writing a letter to share your material with a supremely indulgent and interested friend, or perhaps your mother. Later on, in reworking your draft, you can let your real readers—critics or just plain folk—back in. Knowing that you've already drafted the paper will give you the confidence to deal with their reactions maturely, without being intimidated.

YOUR TURN

Healthy realism means seeing your situation as no better, **but also no worse,** than it really is. If you're stiff, anxious, or "blocked" while drafting, work through the following steps. They might help bring you back to a more valid appraisal of your case and set you on a more even keel.

Write your worst fantasies about what's going to happen when you turn in your paper. Indulge yourself in the wildest kinds of imaginable terrors. What will people say about you? What will they think about you? Stretch this into the bizarre and beyond—into the absurd, the ludicrous, the comic. (Most of these are probably "giggle and point" nightmares of one sort or another.)

Now write what probably will happen if, in fact, you produce fairly poor work. Don't exaggerate this time. Be as exact and matter-of-fact as possible.

Now describe the best you can realistically hope for if you perform at the top of your skill. Again, don't exaggerate. You'll probably get an "A" and a few flattering comments in the margin. You won't get the Pulitzer Prize. You won't get your essay published in *The New Yorker*.

Now describe (as accurately as possible) what will probably happen if you do your typical work.

Finally, imagine yourself one year or five years or fifteen years down the road. How much will you even remember about this paper? How much difference will the quality of your performance actually have made for better or worse?

Now that you're back on the planet Earth, go back to your drafting. You'll still want to write a rich and interesting paper—and you should. But at least you won't spend the whole time tottering on the edge of certain humiliation, or anguished at the thought of losing your Pulitzer.

The Drafting Environment

Because the most destructive opponents to steady, creative drafting are Intimidation, The Critic, Procrastination, Self-Doubt, and other members of their terrorist gang, we've spent considerable time in the last section on some **attitudinal** defenses that will protect you from their hand grenades. If you can sit in your chair, promise yourself a revision, and keep The Critic off your back long enough, you're bound sooner or later to produce a draft you can start turning into something presentable.

Beyond these and other psychological techniques for Authorial Liberation, a great deal of what happens inside your mind as you produce a draft will depend on what's happening on the **outside**—in your writing environment.

What Physical Arrangements Encourage You to Write? Where do you work best? In your own room? At the library? At a small restaurant? Beside the pool? Do you write best always in the same setting? Or does a change of location help from time to time? For some writers, the low-level commotion of a public area drives them in upon themselves and helps them concentrate more effectively, whereas others work best in the most perfect stillness and solitude they can find. One of our students says that she finds it "hard to get ideas down unless there are some minor distractions. And I burn out if I don't take little breaks to sit and think about something else." Another student says that he has to draft all at once, "on Saturday afternoon to early evening when it is very quiet, no people, at a table or desk." But don't guess which kind of writer you are. Try both and find out for sure.

What Writing Schedule Proves Most Productive for You? Do you draft best in long stretches, a couple of hours or more at a time, or do you work in short snatches? For brainstorming, and particularly for rushwriting, we suggested grabbing every open 15-minute slot you could find. This might also work for drafting; but then again, it might not. You may need to keep your sessions short in order to face them at all. On the other hand, you may find yourself getting frustrated at the slowness of your progress unless you can sit down and push your text along for hours at a stretch.

As a general rule, you draft best when you draft regularly. Writing a five or ten-page paper may seem overwhelming. Drafting for a set regular time—say 8:00–10:00 every Monday, Wednesday, and Friday morning—is simply another two-hour job. The more businesslike your approach, the easier it'll be. If the writing goes well, that's great. If it doesn't, at least you put in your time. No guilt attaches to your lack of productivity. It makes life a lot more enjoyable between sessions.

Adjust Your Schedule to Your Most Productive Time of Day.   Most people are at their most intellectually efficient early in the morning and at their worst shortly after meals and after sunset. Your own biological clock, however, may run on a different cycle. Try writing at several different times and take note of your mental state—your concentration or distractibility, your alertness or drowsiness. And note the amount and quality of the writing you produce. This may help you decide when to schedule your regular hours, if you decide to go that route.

You might also find that your "writing clock" ticks haphazardly. Sometimes at 11 P.M. you'll feel utterly drained, exhausted, and intellectually comatose. Go to bed. At other times you might slide into bed at midnight with a thousand thoughts and great ideas swimming in your mind, converting themselves almost magically into perfectly formed sentences. If you can afford to, get up. At least jot down some of the more interesting of your ideas for later use. If you can sleep in the next day, you might even take an hour to try drafting something. Go with it. When your energy's sapped you'll know it.

What Tools Work Best for You?   What physical materials make the act of writing itself most attractive? Special pens? Pencils? Colors of ink? Size, shape, and color of paper?

Can you draft at a typewriter or computer keyboard? If you can, you'll probably make drafting a more pleasant and efficient business than if you still grind out your text longhand. For most people, their first experiences drafting at the keyboard feel stiff and detached; but once they get past their initial discomfort, the sailing is generally smoother. (For more on word processors, see Chapter Ten.)

YOUR TURN

Before beginning this "Your Turn," completely alter your environment, typical writing time, and writing materials. Then proceed with the exercise.

Where do you usually write and under what conditions?
What materials do you typically use?
Have you ever in the past made any deliberate changes in your environment, schedule for writing, or materials? If so, did you notice any changes in how your writing went as a result?
Now analyze the alterations you made to complete this exercise. Ignoring the fact that this type of writing differs significantly from writing

longer, formal papers, what are you noticing about your writing behaviors that differ from your usual behaviors? Would you attribute any differences to the changes in your location, writing materials, or writing time?

Techniques for Getting Words on Paper

The actual process of drafting—of trying to produce coherent prose that begins to resemble a connected, extended paper—varies greatly from person to person. One writer in our class told us that she finds it impossible to draft anything after she's been studying her textbooks. Another's magic for drafting is to work only at night, when it's "subtle, subdued, and dark, with a can of coke and a typewriter." And even after lots of self-analysis and experiments with different environments, schedules, and methods, a few writers can't predict exactly what helps them draft well or why.

Nevertheless, if after considering all we've discussed, you still "choke up" when you draft, a few common-sense techniques may help ease the tension and help you to put something on the page that you can work with.

Try Pushing Your Blueprint Closer to a Prose Text before Starting. Imagine that you've hired a ghost-writer to do the actual draft for you. But here's the hitch: you're not allowed to see or talk to her. Instead, you have to leave your notes in a form she can figure out for herself. This will probably mean a fairly thorough outline—probably with complete sentences at each major and minor heading—along with all the back-up material needed to fill it in. Once you've gotten this far, it should be possible to fill in the gaps with a little English prose glue and create a draft you can work with.

Make the Difficult Easy. Analyze your own behavior: what's the hardest part about drafting? What makes you feel most like quitting or procrastinating? If you can locate the source of the pain, you'll be that much further toward easing it.

For many writers, what hurts most is the strain of moving ideas from their minds to the draft only to find that the words don't belong or are misplaced. In this case, it helps to lighten the load. Don't feel compelled to create full sentences if you're worrying about other matters like structure. Use shorthand for getting your main ideas down quickly and don't flesh everything out until later. One of us, for example, writes a first draft filled with "et ceteras": "In this case, it helps to lighten the load. Don't feel compelled to create full sentences, etc." Then, in working through the draft later, it's relatively simple to expand the "et ceteras" into full ideas and complete sentences.

It's also helpful to write a few sentences of one paragraph or section and then jot down key words or ideas for later expansion:

63

Finally, we could see the summit rising up out of the fog. Biff, exhausted from the climb, etc. (Biff's anger at Mary for accidentally burning the trail map in the previous night's camp fire; was the altitude getting to him? His spirits lifting as we neared the top.)

You might also try writing directions to yourself for when you return to work on the section in more detail. This relieves you of the burden of producing finished sections of your paper but still reminds you of the ideas you had in mind as you were drafting:

Three days into the trek and 50 miles from the nearest shelter, we were suddenly paralyzed by an accident. It happened quite innocently, when Mary was, etc. (Develop the scene here; Mary's foray into the forest for firewood; our warnings; include John's offer to accompany her, and Suzanne's look of jealousy. Maybe work that in as a theme or idea somehow—how our pettier emotions on the trip always seemed to lead to accidents or danger because they broke down cooperation. Keep that in mind for other sections.)

When she emerged from the woods, we knew at once that danger had struck. Her breathing was already becoming shallow and rapid, and her face had taken on a pallid hue. John quickly twisted his bandana into a tourniquet and Judy hunted through her knapsack for the snake-bite kit. (etc.—describe our argument over the tourniquet, and include details—venom, suction cup, how close the bite was to her artery, John's careful incision, etc.).

Listen to the Writer's Voice in Your Head and Trust the Sentences It Offers You.   Often you'll find, somewhere between your ears, a quiet voice suggesting sentences as you go along. If you're nervous about your audience or if The Critic has got you, you may keep rejecting these suggestions again and again, frantically trying for something better, something more striking and original. Don't do it. Trust that inner voice. Accept those sentences and write them down. You can always go back to them if need be; but when you do, they'll probably prove the plainest, most natural, most usable words you've written.

Finally, Don't Count on Anything to Replace Sheer Hard Work and Courage.   These are the essentials. Drafting is intrinsically effortful, and putting words on paper always exposes you to some degree. The only way through the forest is step by bold, deliberate step. Don't "wait for inspiration." And don't expect the techniques we've introduced here to work magic. A change of tools, a change of place, a change of time, an appealing imaginary audience—any of these might make drafting easier, even fun (some work is fun, after all). But words only appear on the page when you put them there—and leave them there. Reliance on inspiration or on technique, like obsessive revision in the early stages, are symptoms of anxiety, if not laziness. **Drafting is work.** It's a job. You do it, then you keep doing it, then you do it some more after that. And after a while it gets done.

Chapter Three

SEEING IT ALL AGAIN : REVISION

To Jackson Pollock

~~Some say that~~ the process
~~of~~ (writing) is ~~simply~~ (a matter)
(of) ~~getting things you can write~~
not simply ~~taking composing~~
thoughts on paper. ~~It is~~
~~difficult Composing~~ Writing
is ~~tough~~ hard ~~to do to~~
~~accomplish easily~~ work.

MICHAEL C. FLANIGAN
University of Oklahoma
Norman

WHAT DOES IT MEAN TO REVISE?

From afar, it may seem that experienced writers rarely need to change their writing once it's on the page. When you see the final efforts of good skiers or famous chefs or concert pianists, it's difficult to imagine them struggling with their work: wiping out on the slopes, bungling the recipe, destroying a simple melody. But if you observe anyone who's good at what he does, writers included, you'll find that he is constantly revising, rethinking, and refining what he's doing. Good writers produce draft after draft after draft, making each new version more powerful or enjoyable to read.

Becoming a more skillful writer doesn't mean reaching the point where the words flow right onto the page in their final, polished form. Instead, becoming a skillful writer means spending more and more time on **revision.** We know from research that poor writers don't revise much. They crank out a draft and decide they're done—the job is over, they've managed to fill three pages, and they can relax. No wonder their writing isn't working! They're not even giving themselves the chance to create better writing; they're stopping when they've just begun.

If you've been working on your draft through Chapters One and Two, you will have seen that writing is at first necessarily messy, tentative, and imperfect. Revision allows you to "resee" what you've produced, sometimes changing it, sometimes thinking up whole new parts for it, sometimes cutting pieces you realize you don't want or need. The process of revision, of course, begins the moment you start writing and making changes as the words appear on the page. You might even have "revised" your brainstorming notes, changing your plans for the paper without having drafted a single word yet. In this chapter, however, we're referring to revision as a systematic, careful rethinking of a mostly complete rough draft.

By revision, we also mean **taking your audience seriously**. Now is the time to borrow someone else's eyes, to read through their minds, to experience your text freshly, from another reader's point of view. To bring this notion of "reseeing" more sharply into focus, let's think through the writing process again, this time in terms of what you're looking at and whose eyes you're looking through at each stage.

Developing Your Material. While you're developing the material for your paper, it's a good idea to focus your attention wholly on the **experience** itself. Forget about your reader, forget the details of the assignment, even ignore the fact that you're planning to write a paper at all. Just stay focused on the subject or experience you'll be writing about later. Let that alone fill your thoughts, and get down, in whatever form you can, all that you remember, think, or wonder about. It's just you. Your audience is nowhere in sight. You're looking only through your own eyes and forgetting everything but the details of the experience itself. **Relive** now, **report** later.

Drafting. Here your focus shifts a bit. You're still gazing mainly toward the experience itself, but now you're sharing it with someone. You've got your imaginary reader standing there next to you, interested and eager, as you point out the details of your experience. Imagine you've returned to your hometown, after having been away for twenty years, and you're showing it off to your spouse or grown-up child or coworker. Your mind would be filled with the objects you were sharing; but, in a sense, you'd be seeing only partly through your own eyes. You'd also be seeing your old stomping grounds through the eyes of the other person. You'd want your friend to see every significant detail—the city block where you played streetball, the corner store where you used to hang out, or the remnants of your old tree-house. And not only would you want to show each detail, but you'd want your friend to understand why it was significant, why it amuses or horrifies or excites you even now. That's the spirit that makes for energetic and fluid drafting—that desire to share the experience with a sympathetic audience.

Revision. In revision, you turn around, shift your gaze entirely, and even in some sense abandon your own "eyes." Now you turn your sight away from your experience and focus it **on the writing itself.** It's as if you had the chance to go back and give your friend a new tour of your hometown, this time thinking carefully about **her** experience—and then turning up more exciting streets, going to more interesting spots, capturing funnier memories—in effect, improving your **performance** as a tour guide. Revision—in writing, at least—allows you to discover and change those parts of your account so that they will have more desirable effects on your reader. It lets you cut the rather stiff graveyard scene or write in a section on the mysterious old mill. It gives you these opportunities **before** there's a chance for your companion to get bored, hungry, frustrated, or foot-weary.

In focusing on your paper itself, that collection of paragraphs that has somehow developed under your hand, you're looking at it as an object, as a document meant to accomplish certain goals. And you look with the eyes of someone who has never seen your paper before, who has no idea what you think, or what you've been through, or what you intended to say, other than from what's on these pages. The business of revision entails reading your paper in this detached, naive sort of way and then working out the answers to these questions:

What do I actually read here? What do I see and hear and think and wonder about while I read this paper?

What else does this lead me to think or ask? Where could I go with this?

What do I want my real reader to experience?

How do I change this draft so later readers will experience it the way I want them to?

In other words: What's here? What else might be here? What do I want here? How do I **get** it here?

If you think about revising in these terms, you'll probably notice that, to some degree, you're revising the whole time you're writing. While drafting your paper, you stop over and over again to ask yourself, "How does this sound?" or "Is that really how she looked?" And often enough you change a phrase or reslant a paragraph right then and there, before moving on. In fact, we know from studies of people writing that rescanning what's on the page before moving on is an essential part of the writing process and often leads to revision in the middle of drafting.

But if you revise too much too early, if you keep your attention focused too narrowly on the paper itself, you'll slow your work down painfully. As a result your paper may wind up stiff and cautious, with none of the verve and enthusiasm it might have had if you'd shared your ideas more freely and carelessly in the beginning

Your main goal in revising, then, is to see your draft with new eyes, specifically with the eyes of your intended readers. But this is difficult. If, throughout your planning and drafting, your mind has been filled with the experience itself, it's very hard to clear that away and see your paper without it. The original ideas and images act like a backdrop for the writing, filling in your experience as you reread it. **You** know exactly what the corner store or the schoolyard or the treehouse looked like; all you need to conjure it up again is the word "PS-159" or "our treehouse" or "Sam's Grocery." But for your reader, these words don't mean anything.

The sad truth is that just because you're thinking while you're writing doesn't guarantee that you're writing what you're thinking. The words that come off the end of your pen or move haltingly across your word processor screen may or may not capture and communicate to another reader the memories and ideas moving through your mind. It's all too easy while drafting to leave significant gaps in your text without realizing it. Your familiarity with your material makes it difficult to experience your text the way someone else would.

Before going on to sketch the process of making major and minor revisions, we'd like to suggest two trade secrets for overcoming this problem.

1. *Get someone else's feedback on your draft.* No matter how good a writer you are or become, you'll always benefit from the responses of a sensitive, helpful reader before you revise. Find someone you can trust: someone who won't either baby you or tear you to shreds. You want someone whose judgment you trust, and who will respectfully and straightforwardly let you know how your draft comes across. Then it's up to you (after you've recovered from the shock) to decide what to do with your draft in light of this feedback. (More on this in Chapter 9.)

2. *Put the draft away, out of sight, as long as you can afford to.* The worst time in the world to revise is immediately after finishing a draft. If you can stash it somewhere and forget about it, the more time that elapses before you read it, the "newer" your eyes will be. At the very least, you should put it away overnight; a few days would be better.

    The key phrase here is "as long as you can **afford** to." Don't use this strategy as an excuse for procrastination. For classroom work, one night might be all the time you have. Newspaper reporters usually have less—just a coffee break—or no time at all. As with any task, the best advice is to study the assignment, look at your calendar or "to do" list, and work out the most sensible schedule you can.

When you do begin revising, try not to be intimidated by the problems you discover. As with planning or drafting, you want to maintain some sort of steady progress. If you hit a section that disturbs you, but can't decide why, put a question mark in the margin and come back to it later. Push at what's pushable. Try to keep moving. We keep harping on this because whenever you're working on a paper, it's so easy to grind to a halt and find yourself stuck and discouraged, staring into space in despair.

YOUR TURN

Think back over all the writing you've done, both in and out of school. Make a list of your most significant writing memories. Then answer the following questions in your writer's notebook:

Can you remember revising these significant pieces of writing at all? If so, describe what you did. Did you produce one or more rough drafts? How changed was your final version compared with earlier ones?

Did you revise the same way, in the same amounts, for all the different kinds of writing you did? If not, how did your revising process vary? Why?

In your experiences, was there a relationship between the amount of revising you did on a paper and the effect it had (e.g., a grade in a course) on your readers? If not, what circumstances might explain why there wasn't a relationship?

MAJOR AND MINOR REVISIONS

To revise effectively requires time and care. It calls for more than correcting misspellings and bad punctuation and replacing vague words with more exact ones. It usually requires drafting fresh material, slicing away large clumps of deadwood, and rearranging broad sections of the text. This sort of revision we'll call **major revision** because it's so important to the purpose and meaning of your writing. **Minor revision**—working with smaller language units—may change your meaning somewhat, but it mainly helps to **refine** and **polish** your writing, making it easier or more enjoyable to read.

Let's take a look at each type of revision. One of our students, Jeremy, is writing a letter to the mayor of his hometown about the problem of road conditions. He hopes his letter will influence the mayor to take note of the problem and do something about it. His first draft of the letter begins like this:

Dear Mayor:
I have noticed that over the years the south side of the city has had fewer road problems than the north side. Every pothole is located in the north sections of town. Also the repair crew does a poor job repairing such holes.

After rethinking his letter for a while and experimenting with some revisions, Jeremy finally settles on an entirely different opening paragraph:

> Dear Mayor:
> I must congratulate you on what a good job you've done as mayor. I really think you try to meet the needs and wants of the citizens of this city. However, this letter is to make you aware of yet another problem that has arisen over the years thanks to careless asphalt companies or whoever is in charge of fixing the roads in the north section of town.

In discussing his revisions during a taped interview, Jeremy explained that once he had begun to think about the mayor's **experience** reading the letter, he realized that it would be better not to sound as if he were angry at the mayor; and that meant not launching right into the problem:

> Well, it's just that after I read through this paragraph [in the first draft], it was a little, uh, not so much short as it was . . . , really it was an angry letter, it's more angry than this one [revised version]; this one has more balance to it, sort of praising the mayor. . . . It's a good way to get his attention, by using positive compliments rather than starting out with a problem.

As you can see, this is a substantial, or major, revision; not only has the language changed, but so has the entire purpose and meaning of the opening paragraph. And its effect on the mayor will change correspondingly.

Now let's examine **minor revision,** which focuses on smaller units of language and meaning. Dan, another student, is writing a letter to his senator on the issue of handguns. He thinks the federal government should restrict the sale and ownership of handguns, and he wants his senator to know how he feels. He hopes, perhaps, to influence the senator's vote on the relevant legislation. In the second paragraph of his letter, Dan writes the following sentence:

> Whether there was intent to kill or personal accident, the gun decides its seriousness—not the gun user.

In this case, Dan is fairly satisfied with the whole paragraph, but he's not happy with that one sentence. The language is a little rough, and he wants to refine the structure to help smooth out the final draft. He changes the sentence to read:

> The issue is not whether there is intent to kill, but that the gun decides the seriousness of the accident—not the gun user.

Here, the meaning has become **clearer,** but it's not fundamentally different from what Dan intended in his draft. In other words, Dan thought about the major aspects of his letter first. Satisfied with **what** he was saying in the paragraph, he could then turn to **how** he was saying it. There he found some problems, so he revised at a minor level.

The important point to remember here is that it would have been silly for Dan to spend a lot of time making minor revisions if what his letter needed was major revisions. Why? Working that way is like folding all your clothes before they've been ironed, or ironing them before they've been washed. Jeremy, for example, might have tinkered around with his first draft for hours, pressing out the rough sentences, pleating the uneven paragraphs, picking off the lint here and there, only to realize later that the whole thing needed to go right back in the hamper.

Of course, often the two sorts of revision overlap considerably in your thinking. A garbled sentence might show you a major problem with the meaning of a whole paragraph—and vice versa. But clearly, at the start of your revising process, it helps to consider large questions before small ones—as a builder would be sure the foundation, framing, and roof were all sound, for example, before putting up the mailbox or attaching the doorknocker.

Both kinds of revision—major and minor—can take every bit as long as brainstorming and drafting, which means that you have to leave yourself ample time to do them. You should keep this in mind when planning your work on a paper—and try to begin by asking yourself questions that can lead to major, not minor, revisions. You'll need to set yourself a deadline for the rough draft well in advance of the due date. Obviously, if you finish your draft with just a few hours to spare, your revision won't amount to more than the most superficial tinkering. And if the foundation and the framing and roof are weak? Well, there'll be a nice new mailbox and shiny doorknocker lying by the rubble.

YOUR TURN

In Appendix B, we've included drafts of essays written by students. Locate and read the drafts titled "Bear Problems" and "Bearly a Problem." Then answer the following questions about the drafts in your writer's notebook:

What are the key differences, for you as a reader, between the rough and final drafts of the essay?

Describe the major and minor revisions the writer made. How are you distinguishing between the two? What effect do they have?

Are there any revisions (either major or minor) that you think don't improve the essay? Describe them and discuss your reasons.

Having read the rough draft, do you think there are any other directions for revision that you'd have suggested to the writer?

HOW TO MAKE MAJOR REVISIONS

As we've suggested in our distinction between major and minor revision, effective revision means working over your paper in "layers," rather than simply starting on page one and moving through, sentence by sentence, to the end, as if you were feeding a piece of beef into a meat grinder. Your draft will demonstrate strengths and weaknesses at several levels: overall organization, coherence of ideas, richness of detail, structure of paragraphs, grace and clarity of expression, precision of word choice, etc. You can no more look at all of those at once than you could develop, arrange, and draft your paper at one time. Instead, you'll probably need to go over your paper several times, focusing on different aspects at each pass.

In this section, we want to begin with a likely "first pass" through your paper—one that will lead you to make major revisions by considering the overall content and structure of your essay before worrying about sentence structure or word choice.

Revising the Essence

When you stop drafting and begin revising, you should read your whole draft once through quickly, without bothering to mark or change anything as your go, just to give yourself a sense of the overall effect of the piece. Keep your pen behind your ear until you reach the end. Then analyze how it affected you. As a reader with "new eyes," how did you feel reading it? What was its tone? How did the writer come across to you? What feeling did the paper leave you with?

Write your answers down, either on the draft itself or on another sheet of paper. You might also try to "nutshell" your paper—to state in one pithy sentence what it really says. Then write down anything else you noticed or can remember about the experience of reading it, either as a whole or at certain memorable points. Then read it again, and perhaps a third time, until you're sure you know your way around it.

Then the big question: **Where can I go with this draft?** Notice we didn't say, "What's wrong with it?" but "Where can I go with it?" The difference is crucial. Most people think of revision as merely getting the bugs out of their first draft. But such an approach seriously limits your range of options. It assumes that your rough draft is in good shape already and needs only a little fine tuning and adjusting. But it's more often the case that although your draft isn't bad, you might be able to rework it into a substantially richer, fuller, more interesting paper still. It's an opportunity you'd hate to pass up, but it will require a revision that's more than sandpaper and furniture wax.

Consider how you might refocus your draft. Ask yourself, where is the real **life** of the draft—its **essence?** Where is it quickest, liveliest, most energetic and engaging? How can you get a grip on that part of it and pull it into the spotlight? Not all of the paper will interest you to the same degree. Effective revision is to some extent spotlighting the essence of the paper, then sloughing off the dull stuff and rearranging everything else accordingly.

You might also ask yourself whether someone, after reading your draft, might say "So what?" **Is** there, in fact, some essence to your paper above and beyond the simple details of the experience itself? What does the experience "say?" Why are you telling about it? If you're writing about the first time you had a car accident, will your readers care? What is it about your accident—and car accidents in general—that your readers might be interested in?

To give you some idea of how thinking about the essence of your writing can help you to resee and reshape your draft, let's look briefly at part of a narrative paper written by Sharon, one of our students. Sharon's paper is about a time when, as a young high school student, she was almost raped by a stranger in the woods. In her first draft, Sharon told the story as simply as possible, as if she were giving the facts to a reporter. The part of her paper we want to focus on is close to the beginning, when she is setting the scene for the attempted rape:

> The woods had lots of interesting places: the pond, the creeks, trees, animals, and quarries; but the quarries were dangerous and off limits to us children. When I got to be a little older, my father would escort my brothers and me swimming in the nonproducing quarries that had become filled with rainwater. Then I grew old enough to venture into the quarries by myself.

As Sharon began working on her draft, she realized that all she had done was simply **recount** her experience. In response to the "so what" question, she wrote in the margin: "So what—right. Just tells about the rape. What's the point—just the experience?" Then, in working through the structure of her paper, Sharon wrote next to the paragraph we've quoted, "tells about the quarries—setting. Off-limits, scary. Makes them not attractive. Do I want that?"

Sharon told us that as soon as she wrote down these questions about the setting of her paper, she realized something very important about her whole paper, about its **essence:** it gave the impression that the attempted rape hadn't changed her at all. In reality, much had changed; she had come to view the world more realistically, not as a Garden of Eden but as a place filled with dangers, with problems to be solved, with new attitudes and beliefs to form about society and men and women. This realization led her to rethink the place of the attempted rape—the quarries—as a setting for her discovery. If she wanted to show how **she** had changed, she could do this through her description of the **quarry.**

Here's the revised version:

> The woods were filled with wonderous things: the ponds, teeming with curious wildlife; the creeks, winding their way below the steep cliffs and jutting rocks; the dense trees, alive with the activity of squirrels and birds; and the quarries, for years abandoned and now filled with water and fed by streams that had broken their way through the earth in search of lower ground.
>
> When I got to be a little older, my father would escort my brothers and me swimming in the larger of the quarries. There, we would jump from the limestone rocks into the cool, clear water, laughing and splashing each other, and then lie on the embankment in the hot summer sun, and talk about our family and our dreams. These were times when even the big clouds seemed to smile down on me, and I imagined them embracing me with their goodness.
>
> Then I reached the age when I could venture in the quarries by myself. . . .

Clearly, Sharon worked quite a bit on the detail of her paragraphs. But notice that now she has eliminated all her references to the danger of the quarries, details that might give the impression that it was a place where evil lurked, in one form or another. Instead, she has painted the quarries as a beautiful place, a place untainted by evil. Now she can lead into the attempted rape scene against the backdrop of this Eden-like setting, where for so many years everything had been good and blissful.

As a result of this one revision, Sharon's paper gains a lot of interest, and loses its "so-whatness": it's about a terrible and ironic coming of age—how a young woman began to understand the world for what it is, a place filled with both beauty and ugliness, both sadness and joy. That's a pretty substantial revision—a revision that began with the paper's essence and rippled all the way through it, right down to Sharon's choice of words and details.

YOUR TURN

As far as possible, follow the directions above while rereading and describing the draft you've written. Then answer the following questions:

How long were you able to put your draft out of sight? How was it different from the way you remembered it when you reread it?

What strikes you as the essence of the draft? Where is it most vital, most engaging? How did you answer the question, "So what"?

Where can you go with it? What other papers could you make out of this material? What's the most interesting direction you could take with it?

Revising the Structure

Part of your paper's essence may be reflected in its larger rhetorical units—its structure, the arrangement of its major pieces. At a high level, your paper contains several large chunks of material—just as this chapter contains sections on different kinds of revision. If Sharon were asked to justify including the section on the quarries in her paper, she'd offer reasons like these: the section sets the scene for the attempted rape, provides necessary background information, and creates a kind of visual metaphor to show how Sharon's own attitudes changed as a result of the incident.

Do the same for your paper. Ask yourself if every main part of its structure deserves to be included. Are there large chunks that could be dropped without the reader missing them? Are there gaps that need filling or things just hinted at that need fuller explanation? Are there sections that are too long or complex—overgrown chunks that could be split up into two smaller pieces? Should you grab that exciting passage about finding yourself face-to-face with 10 members of the Fallen Angels Gang at 1 A.M. on a back street and expand it, perhaps into a whole history of the gang and its eventual demise? Should you take those three paragraphs about Frank falling into the pen with the sow and merge them into a single, less tedious paragraph? Should the present concluding paragraph be moved to the introduction and the paper reshaped from there?

As you ask yourself these questions, you'll find yourself working on the structure of your paper from two perspectives: its inner "flow" and its outer "shape." Think of the inner flow as the subjective experience readers will have following the chain of your ideas, and the outer shape as the arrangement of the objective parts of it—the pieces you can put labels on in the text itself.

Inner Flow.   In assessing the inner flow of your paper, simply start by reading through it from beginning to end (again, as if you'd never seen it before) and note your subjective reactions to it point by point. Write your reactions in the margins as you read. Note only your reactions themselves; don't adjust anything yet. You'll do that later. Ask yourself:

> Am I interested in this part of the paper? Am I reading quickly and eagerly? Or am I bored? Am I having to force myself through this?
>
> Is this part clear to me? Or am I confused by this? Do I feel as if I've missed something?
>
> Do I know where the writer's going? Or have I lost track of the argument or the story? Do I know what the point of this section is?

Count on these reactions to guide you in what to keep, what to discard, what to expand. You can revise your paper, in fact, according to a "survival of the fittest" theory. Keep the healthy, the swift, the vigorous; sacrifice the lame, the impotent, the dreary—unless you're willing to work long and hard to bring those sections back to health (and by then it may be you who's dull and lifeless!).

Outer Shape.   The other approach to assessing the structure of your paper is to focus on the organizational "shape" of it. If the paper feels somehow out of control, unfocused, meandering, you may be losing sight of the forest for the trees. In drafting, your attention is so wholly taken up by the trees that this seems almost inevitable. But now you need to strip your paper down to the framework, so you can see its structure at a glance.

Here's one way to get a grasp on its outer shape:

1. Number each paragraph of your paper in the left margin.
2. Go back and read each paragraph in turn, and write down in a word or phrase its main point. What does the paragraph really **say,** in a few words? As you do this, you may find that a particular paragraph has several main points and can't be readily nutshelled, in which case you've already identified one organizational problem.
3. Now try scanning through the paragraphs again, this time stating what each one **does** for the whole paper. What is its function? Why is it

there? If you find yourself writing what it **says** instead of what it **does,** try filling in the sentence, "This paragraph is here at this point because it serves to _____." In the first draft of his letter to the mayor, for example, Jeremy answered this question by saying that his first paragraph served "to tell the mayor what I'm angry about." By thinking about the function of that paragraph, placed where it was at the start of the letter, Jeremy was led to make a revision. He then said that his new opening paragraph served "to praise the mayor for the good job he's doing, and encourage him to keep reading about further problems he could maintain his reputation by solving."

Once you've analyzed the content and function of each paragraph, the organizational strengths and weaknesses of your paper should be more apparent. To reveal them even more clearly, however, you might try turning the list into a formal outline. If it doesn't hang together the way it is, try rearranging the large pieces in a few other ways. What are the two or three or four main points? How should lesser points be arranged under these? Can you see, just by looking at the list, which paragraphs might be extraneous or which points might need fuller development?

For a narrative, of course, a formal outline may not be as useful as a more subjective sense of its structure—how it flows, what sort of narrative voyage it takes you on. Just because your descriptions of someone's character are spread throughout the paper doesn't mean they should all be grouped together into one section; perhaps there's a good reason for adding details cumulatively. On the other hand, you might find that many of your later details are afterthoughts that you remembered to put in while you were drafting. In that case, your subjective sense of these randomly tossed in details might lead you to pluck them all out and put them together in a character sketch early on.

Part of revising the structure of your work also means trying to cut repetition. If you find that the labels you've used to describe paragraphs #3, #5, and #9 sound suspiciously similar, you might go back to your draft to see if two or three can be dropped, or consolidated into one. You probably sensed in rereading your draft that you were repeating yourself, but the skeletal outline of it can show you exactly where and to what extent you were actually doing so.

YOUR TURN

Assess the organization of your draft, using the strategies we've suggested. Answer the following questions:

What did you notice about the flow of it? Where was it rapid and engaging? Where did you have to drag yourself through it? What seems to be going on in these passages?

From your outline of the draft, how would you describe the shape of it?

Does the outline reflect what you noticed in the flow? Or do the two ways of assessing your paper seem at odds? Where do they overlap or provide different information?

What ideas for revising the paper do these questions generate? Are you seeing anything new in the essence of the paper by looking at its structure?

Making a Mess

After all this, it's time to return to your draft again, this time with a flame in your eye and vengeance in your heart. With your new outline beside you and your comments in the margins, it's time for surgery. Find the lifeless sections and draw boxes around them with broad slash marks from edge to edge. Write out new sections, label them, and indicate where they belong. Draw circles around other paragraphs or parts of paragraphs and indicate with arrows where in the draft they **really** belong. If you need to, grab scissors and paste, cut your draft into pieces, and reassemble it in several different ways on the dining room table or the floor of your room. Be bold. Add. Cut. Rearrange. And watch how the draft seems to gain clarity and shape, how it toughens up and gains color and life and vigor even as you work on it. The egg is in pieces, but the eaglet is alive and noisy.

And, whatever you do, don't be afraid to be **messy.** How messy? That will depend on how much you **think.** The blueprints might be perfect; the materials could be the strongest available; and you could have great faith in the construction. But until you've gone over it with a shipbuilder's eye, don't assume the boat will float. We've found, over many years of helping people to revise, that there's a pretty reliable relationship between the quality of a final piece of writing and the **quantity** and **depth** of revision. Revision requires thought—and thought is what leads to improvement.

If it's hard to imagine just how messy a good revision can be, take a look at the page by novelist Jon Hassler (Figure 3-1).

MAKING MINOR REVISIONS
Revising Language and Style

Once the big pieces are all there and all in the right place, then you can start on the minor revisions—the honing and polishing—concentrating on the style and grace and clarity of the language.

In doing this, it helps to read your draft **out loud.** Go off by yourself and read the draft slowly, sentence by sentence, aloud, and listen to how it sounds. Or find someone who can be a temporary audience, and read it to

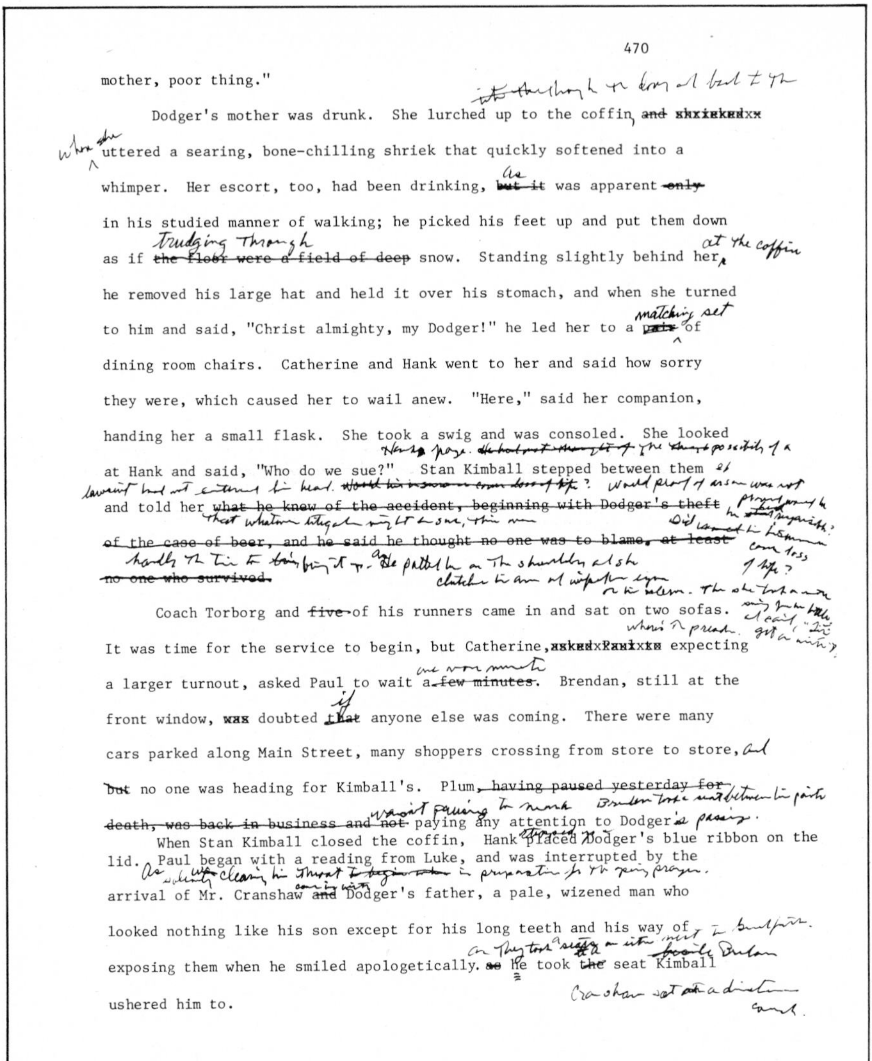

470

mother, poor thing."

Dodger's mother was drunk. She lurched up to the coffin ~~and shrieked~~ uttered a searing, bone-chilling shriek that quickly softened into a whimper. Her escort, too, had been drinking, ~~but it~~ was apparent ~~only~~ in his studied manner of walking; he picked his feet up and put them down as if ~~the floor were a field of deep~~ trudging through snow. Standing slightly behind her, at the coffin he removed his large hat and held it over his stomach, and when she turned to him and said, "Christ almighty, my Dodger!" he led her to a ~~pair~~ matching set of dining room chairs. Catherine and Hank went to her and said how sorry they were, which caused her to wail anew. "Here," said her companion, handing her a small flask. She took a swig and was consoled. She looked at Hank and said, "Who do we sue?" Stan Kimball stepped between them and told her ~~what he knew of the accident, beginning with Dodger's theft of the case of beer, and he said he thought no one was to blame, at least no one who survived.~~

Coach Torborg and ~~five~~ of his runners came in and sat on two sofas. It was time for the service to begin, but Catherine, ~~asked Paul to~~ expecting a larger turnout, asked Paul to wait a ~~few minutes~~ one more minute. Brendan, still at the front window, ~~was~~ doubted ~~that~~ if anyone else was coming. There were many cars parked along Main Street, many shoppers crossing from store to store, and ~~but~~ no one was heading for Kimball's. Plum~~, having paused yesterday for death, was back in business and not~~ wasn't pausing to mark paying any attention to Dodger's passing.

When Stan Kimball closed the coffin, Hank ~~placed~~ Dodger's blue ribbon on the lid. Paul began with a reading from Luke, and was interrupted by the arrival of Mr. Cranshaw ~~and~~ Dodger's father, a pale, wizened man who looked nothing like his son except for his long teeth and his way of exposing them when he smiled apologetically. ~~so~~ He took ~~the~~ seat Kimball ushered him to.

FIGURE 3-1

When we read the work of professional authors, we're sometimes led to despair by the seeming effortlessness of their prose. Jon Hassler, author of several highly acclaimed novels, writes as clear and graceful a style as anyone now working. As this page from the "fifth but far from final draft" of his novel *Grand Opening* demonstrates, such apparent "effortlessness" costs even the best writers great effort indeed. (Feel free to make a similar or even worse mess of your own rough drafts.)

him. All the jolts, bumps, awkward phrasings, long-winded sentences, rough spots, unfocused meanderings, stiff language, unnatural word choices, and strange constructions will jump out at you when you actually **hear** the paper. With your worst sentences, in fact, you'll probably get tongue-tied and out of breath. Those passages, on the other hand, that sound smooth and natural when you read them aloud should be left alone. Not everything will need to be changed. Certain parts of your text—maybe even quite a bit of it—may be just fine as they stand, and you don't want to cut away any healthy tissue. Learn to trust your own ear. If it fails, then someone else's will pick up on the problems and you can revise accordingly.

Finally, after all this time, after all the slashing and the redrafting and the rearranging, after all the reading aloud and rewriting paragraphs and rephrasing sentences—after all this comes the final inspection: that search for any visible flaws, any tiny defects in the finish, any little dents and scratches, in preparation for going public with what you've created. **Now** you can check punctuation, making sure that sentences end in periods or question marks. Now you can get **there, their,** and **they're** straightened out and make sure you haven't used **it's** where you mean **its.** This is where all the grammatical, syntactical, and mechanical training you've received over the years comes into play.

Groan. We know: it's also the part of the process that often gets the short end of the stick. You're rushed. It's well after midnight. The paper's due at 9:00 A.M. in Professor Throckmorton's class. The last page is rolling off the typewriter. Your eyes are turning into paperweights and your body aches for bed. Why check it over again? It's done, it's done, it's done. Staple it, slide it into your notebook, cross your fingers and hit the sack.

But not before setting your alarm to wake you an hour earlier tomorrow. Because if you're smart, if you value the effect your writing will have on your reader—Prof. Throckmorton or anyone else—you'll do one more careful reading of your paper: checking for errors.

We don't, of course, urge you to wait until the last minute to proofread your work. Why not? Because the writing process is not that simple. When writers spot errors, the **act** of discovering a problem often causes them to reformulate a whole sentence, and that might cause them to resee a whole paragraph, and then . . . well, back to square one. As we've made clear in this chapter, you can't resee your draft and make major constructive changes in the hour you've got before class.

But whenever you do it and whatever process you use, making your text error-free is **very** important. So before you turn anything in, read on. . . .

YOUR TURN

Below are the rough and final versions of one paragraph from a student's narrative. It describes how his team won the state high school swimming championship largely because of his personal victory in one of the last races of the meet. The paragraph begins at the moment when the starting gun was fired. Read these two excerpts through quickly, noting their similarities and differences.

Excerpt from Rough Draft:

Suddenly, "Bill-ie, Bill-ie, Bill-ie. . . . " [writer's name] resounded through the pool area. I knew this was the moment. The first 50 yards were easy; no change in places. During the third length, however, I felt myself pulling away, going after the West High freshman who was their anchorman. As I came into my final turn, I saw his feet and knew I could take him. The final 25 yards I swam in slow motion and experienced every inch I gained on him.

Same Excerpt, Revised Version:

I exploded from the block and was instantly immersed in the strange underwater silence. As I broke the surface, I heard the pandemonium of the crowd distorted through my water-filled ears. I hit my first turn perfectly and felt myself pulling away from Jefferson and St. John's and gaining on West. At the 50, I was one body length ahead and three behind. During the third length, the crowd was going wild and I felt them calling to something inside me to rise up and conquer. I felt myself swimming with uncontrollable strength, surging through the water . . . I had one length to go.

Now, in your writer's notebook, spend a few minutes jotting down your observations about the revisions: which are major, which minor? In your opinion, how much of an improvement is the final version? Why? What further revisions of the paragraph would you suggest to the writer?

Chapter Four

COMMON SENSE ABOUT GRAMMAR AND MECHANICS

Sofa!? R then we? VeCo. Veredt, he major! Stages soft—he ''writing pro''—ces from . . . (first con). 'Cept ion top resent. At ion-draft.

Let's try that again—

So far, then, we've covered the major stages of the writing process from first conception to presentation draft.

Better, no? Notice how, just by moving around a few dots and dashes and spaces, the gibberish suddenly snaps into focus as a readable sentence.

At the end of the last section, we just touched on the issue of grammar and mechanics. Here we want to pursue the subject a little further by considering why grammar and mechanics are important and what you can do about them if they give you trouble. We'll take a common sense approach to grammar and mechanics, one that relies a good deal on what you already know as a reader and what you can discover by reading your own and others' writing, especially when it's in draft form.

Before we get to the "hows" of the approach, though, it's a good idea to place grammar and mechanics into some sort of perspective: where they come from, what they are, and when and why they're important.

SOME SENSIBLE WAYS TO THINK ABOUT CORRECTNESS

Where Do Grammar and Mechanics Come From?

At the simplest level, the rules of grammar, mechanics, and spelling are **conventional.** By conventional, we don't mean stodgy and unoriginal; we simply mean that they carry authority only because everyone agrees upon them, like the rules of a game.

As an example of purely conventional signs, consider traffic lights. There's obviously nothing special about the colors red, yellow, and green that leads us to stop, slow down, or proceed. When we face these colors on the road, what we do is controlled neither by divine revelation nor by primitive instincts. We've simply agreed that red "means" stop, yellow "means" proceed with caution, and green "means" go. And we know what we risk if we don't play along.

The rules of any language get their authority in much the same way. Right now, you're reading this text by moving your eyes from left to right across the page. This seems natural, but there's nothing inherently better about reading from left to right than from right to left, as would be the case if you were reading Hebrew, or in columns from top to bottom if this were Chinese. Or take the formation of plurals. There's nothing magically better about adding an -s to designate two or more of the same thing. Any number of changes would work just as well if everyone agreed on them. In other languages, for example, the plural can be formed by adding -en (German), or -eaux (French), or -im (Hebrew), or -ata (Greek), or -a, -ae, and -i (Latin).

When English borrows words from other languages, it often borrows the plural forms as well: we say "alumni" or "alumnae" instead of "alumnuses." Sometimes, however, we change the plurals to the standard English -es: who would ever say he saw ball games at three stadia in two days? In still other cases, both plural forms may be used: both "syllabi" and "syllabuses" are acceptable according to the *Oxford American Dictionary*. Here we have a case where we don't agree on a single form. If you have trouble with "who" and "whom," to take another example, it's partly because some older "agreements" are giving way to new ones. The same process explains why a very large number of educated people now use split infinitives (note the line from the old "Star Trek" series, *"To boldly go* where no man has gone before").

Correctness, then, is defined by common usage—and common usage changes over time. In the nineteenth century, using the phrase "clear out" or the word "ice-cream" (for "iced-cream") or the noun "cab" (for "cabriolet") or "mob" (for "mobilus") was considered incorrect—even barbaric. Today, these usages are perfectly acceptable, having, in fact, replaced the earlier forms.

We learn most of the rules and conventions of our language **effortlessly** and **unconsciously;** they're part of the system—how things "should" sound—and we hear it immediately when they're violated. Take the rules of word order. All of us have an unconscious system in our minds of how English sentence structure works—what it will allow and what it won't allow. Often we can't explain what the rules are or describe our judgments, yet they still exist as part of our internal knowledge of the language. Let's look at an interesting example. Consider these two sentences:

(a) Jody called her mother up.
(b) Jody called up her mother.

In both (a) and (b), "up" may occur either before or after "her mother." We know the sentences are both acceptable without having to explain why we can place the "up" in either position. If we had to write a "rule" for these sentences, we could say:

Rule 1: "Up" can occur either before or after "her mother" (the object of the sentence).

But what about the next pair?

(a) The cat climbed up the tree.
(b) The cat climbed the tree up.

Here, we know immediately that (b) is unacceptable or strange; it sounds weird, and it destroys the meaning of the sentence. In this case, the "up" can occur only **before** "the tree." If we were to write a rule for these sentences, we'd have to say:

Rule 2: "Up" can occur only before the object of the sentence.

See the problem? Rule 1 contradicts Rule 2, yet the two pairs of sentences seem identical in structure.

You probably can't explain this phenomenon (which has to do with the difference between prepositions and "verbal particles"). But you don't need to. When it comes to forming such sentences, you follow the rules automatically. You'd never say that the cat "climbed the tree up" to mean "climbed up the tree."

If you were to analyze your speech, you'd find that you make errors like "climbed the tree up" very rarely (if ever). You might incorrectly use "I" instead of "me," as in "John came along with Billy and I," or use incorrect verb forms, as in "I should have went with them," but your listeners will get the point nonetheless. When you make these kinds of errors, you don't risk **not** communicating; what you do risk (if your listener is educated and knows the difference) is being stigmatized because you're using language "incorrectly." Most of the time in speaking, we ignore each other's little slips of grammar because we're concentrating on meaning, not running a check on the propriety of each other's expression.

But in writing, the game changes. Writing is a code for speech (which itself is a code for meaning), and this written code carries many additional rules and conventions. In writing, it's quite possible to make the kinds of mistakes you don't usually make in speaking—mistakes that put obstacles between your reader and your meaning. Remember that your reader has to "re-create" your meaning—and that takes effort. The more roadblocks you put in the way, the more frustrating the effort becomes.

One reason why it's easier to blunder in writing than in speech is because writing lets you elaborate your sentences, lets you make them more sophisticated and longer than normal spoken sentences, especially through the addition of clauses and structures that might otherwise over-burden not only your own short-term memory but the short-term memory of someone who happens to be listening to you (as in this sentence, for example, with its several clauses and its final parenthetical phrase—an apt example of a structure that might not be found in such complexity, unless it was carefully planned out, in a normal conversation). There are many more eggs to juggle in sentences like that one, and your movements need to be precise. You have to pay more conscious attention to your sentence structure because there's a greater chance that you'll drop an egg on your foot.

But sentence structure is not the only extra egg to juggle in writing. There are also conventions that help the reader restore some of the details of speech that are otherwise lost in writing. Speech is littered with little remarks and phrases that help you to communicate. You give your questions a rising tone toward the end. You lower your voice and speak faster when you're adding a parenthetical remark in the middle of a sentence. You often pause between major parts of sentences. And you use your body and face in various ways—hand gestures, frowns, winks, and the like—to emphasize what you're saying. But how can you wink, or frown, or give a rising tone to a question, or make an audible pause in writing?

The "sound" of writing can only be "heard" by your readers if you've replaced these signals with the marks that represent them. Commas, semi-colons, colons, exclamation marks, indentations, question marks, apos-trophes, dashes, parentheses, periods—these are the visual signs that replace the devices you use in speaking—the pauses, the question tone, the winks and nods.

To get a feel for their importance, look at what happens when they're taken away from a short paragraph. This is an excerpt from Studs Terkel's book *Working,* a collection of interviews with people about their jobs. Try reading the paragraph aloud:

> Im a dying breed a laborer strictly muscle work pick it up put it down pick it up put it down we handle between forty and fifty thousand pounds of steel a day laughs I know this is hard to believe from four hundred pounds to three and four pound pieces its dying

As you can see, this paragraph is written using only the actual spoken words as Mike Lefevre, a steelworker, spoke them during the interview. When Terkel wrote down the words, however, he had to resupply as many of the little pauses and rhythms and natural sentence boundaries as he could. Read the passage aloud again, this time with Terkel's punctuation:

> I'm a dying breed. A laborer. Strictly muscle work . . . pick it up, put it down, pick it up, put it down. We handle between forty and fifty thousand pounds of steel a day. (Laughs) I know this is hard to believe—from four hundred pounds to three- and four-pound pieces. It's dying.[1]

You probably noticed that in the first passage, your sentences ran together, your speech rhythms were erratic and odd, and you had to back-track whenever you realized you'd been reading incorrectly. In the second passage, you probably found that your reading was more fluent; you knew where to pause and where to put your stress and intonation.

As this example shows, the conventions of writing are partly natural—in the sense that they're based on the normal (unconscious) cues that help people speak to each other. In writing, though, you have to pay conscious attention to all these special conventions—both for correctness and style. And, like it or not, that takes effort.

YOUR TURN

Below are two speeches from different plays, stripped of their original punctuation. Read through each passage until you have a sense for how it should be spoken, then resupply the necessary conventional signals. In your writer's notebook, jot down a few remarks about how you see mechanics: if there isn't one right way to punctuate these passages, what does that tell you about the difference between "correctness" and "style"? Which of your changes or additions to the passages were obligatory and which were questionable or optional?

---

[1]Studs Terkel, *Working,* New York: Pantheon Books, 1974, p. 1.

From Arthur Miller's *Death of a Salesman*
[*Willy is speaking to Happy and Biff:*]

I been wondering why you polish the car so careful dont leave the hubcaps boys get the chamois to the hubcaps happy use newspaper on the windows its the easiest thing show him how to do it biff you see happy pad it up use it like a pad thats it thats it good work youre doin it all right hap biff first thing we gotta do when we get the time is clip that big branch over the house afraid its gonna fall in a storm and hit the roof tell you what we get a rope and sling her around and then we climb up there with a couple of saws and take her down soon as you finish the car boys I wanna see ya I got a surprise for you boys[2]

From Shakespeare's *Hamlet*

To be or not to be that is the question whether tis nobler in the mind to suffer the slings and arrows of outrageous fortune or to take arms against a sea of troubles and by opposing end them to die to sleep no more and by a sleep to say we end the heart ache and the thousand natural shocks that flesh is heir to tis a consummation devoutly to be wished to die to sleep to sleep perchance to dream ay theres the rub for in that sleep of death what dreams may come when we have shuffled off this mortal coil must give us pause theres the respect that makes calamity of so long life for who would bear the whips and scorns of time the oppressors wrong the proud mans contumely and the pangs of despised love the laws delay the insolence of office and the spurns that patient merit of the unworthy takes when he himself might his quietus make with a bare bodkin who would fardels bear to grunt and sweat under a weary life but that the dread of something after death the undiscovered country from whose bourn no traveller returns puzzles the will and makes us rather bear those ills we have than fly to others that we know not of[3]

Why Care? The Solution Is Attitude

Recently, one of us was in a bookstore and noticed a guide for writing résumés. It was called *Do You Want Your Résumé to Wear Blue Jeans?*

We like that metaphor. The conventions of language are, indeed, a kind of "clothing" your writing wears—a reflection of your self. All language carries more than a single message. In one sense, it expresses ideas or facts through words. In another sense, it expresses something in the same way that clothing styles do—that is, something about the speaker (or wearer).

Consider, for example, two different versions of the same letter of request:

---

[2]From *The Heath Introduction to Drama,* 2nd ed., Lexington, MA: D. C. Heath & Co., 1983, p. 811.

[3]A. L. Rowse, ed., *The Annotated Shakespeare,* Vol. 3, New York: Clarkson N. Potter, Inc., 1978, p. 225.

Deer sir
My name is Andrew Johnson I'm a senier at Spaulding college Im conducting a experiment relating to partical wave theories were studing here. I wander if I could set up a intreview, with you to diskuss your'e companies work in this area which I'd be much ablidged if I coud meat with you as soon as posible.

Dear Sir:
My name is Andrew Johnson. I'm a senior at Spaulding College and am conducting an experiment relating to the particle-wave theories we're studying here. I wonder if I could set up an interview with you to discuss your company's work in this area. I'd be much obliged if I could meet with you as soon as possible.

Clearly, these letters are almost identical in language and content. They differ only in a seemingly trivial way: one is dressed like a slob—cluttered with spelling mistakes, run-on sentences, and other mechanical problems. The second is flawlessly neat.

In reading the two versions, you might be struck by how much more sophisticated or mature the second version seems compared with the first. If the contents are so identical, how can this be?

By showing blunders in grammar, spelling, and punctuation, the first version is telling the reader that the writer either 1) doesn't know the mechanics of the written language, or 2) hasn't taken the time to revise and edit the letter. In either case, the impression is not a good one: the writer appears at best incompetent, at worst downright lazy. In contrast, the writer of the second letter is expressing precision, care, and professionalism.

If you extend this example to think of important reports, letters of application for jobs, term papers in courses, feasibility studies, stories sent to creative writing journals—any and every sort of writing you do—you can begin to see how important that second layer of meaning is. In every case, you're giving a message about yourself in terms of how diligent, professional, and precise you are in your writing.

The second (and no less important) reason for caring about correctness in your writing says something about how **considerate** you are toward your reader. Writers and readers enter into an unstated contract: readers expect writers to do the most they can to make life easier for them, by giving them a smooth ride with a nice view—not one filled with bumps and jolts and frequent breakdowns. Readers want to be entertained, educated, enlightened. In return, they're willing to put plenty of their own effort into understanding what the writer is saying. But they're also easily frustrated when a writer doesn't live up to her part of the bargain. When the writer breaks the contract runs sentences together leaves punctuation out. Makes sentence fragments but, also puts commas, in the wrong places. Misspels alot and used tenses wrong or inconsistantly. Fails to finish the sentence see what we mean the contract is broke you feel like putting the page in the trash. Along with the writer.

Of course, there's more to being considerate of your reader than avoiding simple errors. Readers also expect you to use a **style**—sentence structures, word choices, and organizing techniques—appropriate to the kind of writing you're doing and to your purpose. (We'll touch on this idea of a flexible writing "wardrobe" a bit later in this chapter.)

Why, then, care about correctness? Because if you want to be heard, you should care about your reader. This is especially true of your teachers. Teachers, whether of writing or of any other subject, are like all other readers; they're bothered by the same problems and errors and confusions that annoy everyone else. Often they're more sympathetic than general readers. Instead of throwing out a document riddled with errors, teachers painstakingly point out where those errors are and what you can do about them. But they too have their limits. They'd much rather spend their time explaining errors with which students honestly need help than circling mistakes made from laziness or sloppy proofreading. The more you can do to improve your writing in this area, the better your chance of getting constructive, helpful criticism on the **substance** of what you're writing.

IN THE SHORT RUN: HOW TO DO AWAY WITH ERROR

Where Does Correctness Belong in the Writing Process?

There's no question about it: correctness is very important. It can sometimes mean the difference between an "A" and an "F" on a term paper; the acceptance or refusal of a bid; a commitment to publish your story . . . or another rejection slip. At the same time, however, we believe that worrying about correctness has a time and a place.

As you've seen throughout Part 1 of this book, different activities are easier at different times. Some things, such as clustering, you can dive into from the earliest moment with little struggle and great effectiveness. Others, such as revising the structure of a paper, you do better to wait on. But what about grammar, mechanics, usage, and other "surface" matters? When and how should you attend to these?

The answer depends largely on how comfortably you now handle the conventions of written English. For some writers, standard grammar, punctuation, and spelling are almost second nature. Even their most seemingly chaotic brainstorming still falls naturally into correct and properly punctuated sentences. If you're one of these, the question of when to consider these matters really doesn't arise; you're taking care of them all the time, often as you work on voice and style.

If you haven't developed this control, though, you need to decide more consciously when to refine this part of your work. As a general rule, we would suggest the following: During most of the writing process, **maintain the grammar and mechanics of your writing as correctly as possible, with-**

out letting them interfere with larger writing concerns. The last thing you want is to allow your thoughts about the most important things in writing—ideas, organization, audience, and purpose—to be constantly interrupted by little nagging questions of correctness. If correctness is second nature for you, if it doesn't require any real thought on your part, keep it up as you go along. If it's difficult for you—for instance, if you constantly have to refer to your dictionary to check your spelling—you'd probably do better to forget about the spelling until the end. You might sound the words out as best you can, draw large circles around them when you're uncertain, and keep going. Just be sure to get back to them before your presentation draft. You can do the same thing with respect to grammar and punctuation.

If your control of these matters is so-so, how careful you are might depend on where you are in the writing process. In any sort of brainstorming, you can pretty much ignore grammar and mechanics entirely. No one will see it, and getting your ideas down quickly and freely is of the essence. (When did anyone care about correctness while taking notes during a fast-paced lecture?) In drafting, you might be more careful (as much as you can be without disrupting the flow of your writing). Then, in revision, you'll want to spend considerable time thinking about grammatical questions, punctuation, and spelling. As long as you do the clean-up before the paper goes to its final audience, that's soon enough.

Looking for Error—and Learning from It

Many techniques have been tried to help writers overcome problems in grammar, usage, and other surface details of composition. Unfortunately, there's no magical, easy way to learn the surface conventions for writing. Again, a great deal of your success will depend on your own attitude toward the problem. If you resist learning, you'll remain frustrated. If you rely entirely on someone else to tell you when you make mistakes, you'll learn slowly and unhappily, by trial and error. But if you concentrate on the mistakes that are pointed out to you and practice recognizing them in other texts you write, you'll learn quickly and effortlessly. In addition, you can search your writing for error **naturally,** without needing any special knowledge or fancy rules. Here are some strategies:

Read Your Writing Out Loud. We've said this before in our discussion of revision, but it bears repeating. Probably the most effective way to uncover your grammatical and mechanical problems is to read each of your sentences **out loud, one at a time,** and **listen closely.** Your ear is often much better at picking up syntactic train wrecks than your eye. If you've written a sentence fragment, you'll hear it. You'll feel yourself. Left hanging. If you've written a run-on sentence, and you force yourself to keep reading until you reach a period, you'll feel a strong tug to stop right where the missing period should go putting the period back in is then a simple matter. If you've slipped up on noun-verb agreement and you've written "he run" or "they runs," the error will go off like a bell when you actually hears it, though your eyes might not pick them up on its own.

If you read your sentences out loud, you'll not only discover the technical grammatical flaws, but you'll also find the awkward, meandering, wordy, or muddy sentences as well. That's because many grammatical errors are caused by problems in the expression of your meaning. And, too, a sentence that is unpleasant to read aloud is probably unpleasant for your audience to read silently. All of which leads to another useful guideline: if a sentence is clear, it's probably at least close to correct. If it's unclear, it doesn't matter how technically correct it is; it still needs to be revised.

Use a Reader Approach.   Whether you read your work aloud or scan it silently, one of the best ways to spot errors is to use what we like to call a "reader-based" approach to reviewing your work. In a reader-based approach, you try to put your own involvement in what you've written completely out of your mind. Pick up your paper and act as if you've never seen a single line of it before. Then start reading, always keeping in the back of your mind that this is a **new** experience. This way, you may well discover problems that your writing will create as it's **read,** and often these result from making certain kinds of errors.

To illustrate this reader-based approach, think for a moment about the spoken language. Speech can create ambiguity because so many individual words can carry more than one meaning. Consider, for example these sentences:

> The dogs race past the barn.
> The dog's race passed the barn.
> The dogs' race passed the barn.

Spoken aloud, these three sentences sound exactly the same. But in this case, the writing system allows us to avoid the ambiguity. On a close examination of the written form of these sentences, you notice that the meaning of sentence #1 is distinguished from the meaning of sentences #2 and #3 by the different spellings of two words that sound identical: "past/passed." Just as important is the use of the apostrophe—something many people forget to include when they're writing. In sentence #2, the apostrophe clearly signals to the reader that the meaning is to be taken differently than the meaning in sentences #1 or #3.

Let's take a more relevant example, this one from a student's essay:

> Early in the 20th century, the field of psychology was not very fully developed. During the previous two centuries scientific thought the belief that one could understand the human psyche was not considered.

If you're like most readers, you probably stumbled when you reached the second sentence and had to go back and figure out what went wrong. You

were, in other words, "led down the garden path" as you read. Let's reconstruct how you may have read the two sentences.

You probably had little difficulty understanding the first sentence: it says
simply that the field of psychology was in its infancy early in the 1900s. No
problems so far. But then you began reading the second sentence: "During
the previous two centuries . . ." At this point, you probably understood the
phrase to mean, "during the two centuries preceding the 20th century,"
and then you were **anticipating** a statement with a noun: "During the previous two centuries, something happened," or "During the previous two
centuries, psychology was in such-and-such a state." But then you reached
"scientific," not a noun but an adjective—not "scientists," not "psychology," not "science," but "scientific." So you figured that "scientific" pre-
ceded the main noun, "thought": "During the previous two centuries scientific thought was in such-and-such a state."

In a split second, then, you tentatively resolved this first problem. But
reading on only made things worse. Expecting a verb, you were puzzled to
find "the belief," another noun phrase. Perhaps you figured that you'd misread "scientific"—that it really said "scientists": "scientists thought the
belief that. . . ." In any case, you were frustrated and had to go back again
and try to figure out where you went wrong. And your problem arose
because something was stopping you from figuring out the **meaning** of the
sentence.

In this case, however, it wasn't **your** problem (often the reader blames
himself before blaming the writer!). Instead, the problem was in the writing;
the writer had left out a seemingly trivial little symbol, one of the conventions for helping readers to create meaning without being frustrated by
ambiguity. Read the sentence once again, this time with the symbol
included:

> During the previous two centuries' scientific thought the belief that one could
> understand the human psyche was not considered.

Suddenly the pieces fall into place: "previous two centuries' scientific
thought" is to be understood as a whole clause—"the scientific thought **of**
the previous two centuries"—and then the rest of the sentence makes
sense.

But even in this second version, the sentence isn't very sensitive to the
actual reading experience—the way readers process and unravel the meaning of a text. This is where **revising** and **proofreading** begin to merge
together. How? Because by spotting an error, you may be compelled to
rethink larger aspects of your writing.

In recognizing the absence of the apostrophe in our sample sentence,
for example, you might find yourself reconsidering its whole structure. First,
you might consider putting in a comma to separate the first part of the sentence from the second and give it the kind of sentence pause that helps
readers to sort out the pieces:

During the previous two centuries' scientific thought [,] the belief that. . . ."

Still, the sentence seems clumsy and abstract. In thinking about the separation of the first part ("During . . . thought"), you might find yourself reconsidering the second part ("the belief that . . . was not. . . ."). And so you might revise the whole sentence to make it more direct:

> During the previous two centuries, scientists did not take the belief that one could study the human psyche very seriously.

This version is much clearer. A further revision could then bring the parts of "take . . . very seriously" closer together:

> During the previous two centuries, scientists did not take very seriously the belief that one could study the human psyche.

Perhaps then you might see some wordiness in "take very seriously the belief that," so you revise once again:

> During the previous two centuries, scientists did not seriously believe that one could study the human psyche.

You could further revise the sentence, of course, to make it more stylistically appealing, and each revision could open up new problems that, in turn, could lead to further revision, especially if you find that your intended meaning is changing because of the revisions. ("Did not seriously believe that," for example, sounds a shade less contemptuous than "did not take very seriously the belief that.") But at the very least, you've created a sentence that your reader won't stumble over or misinterpret.

As this example shows, by paying attention to how the conventions of grammar and mechanics can help your reader, you'll find more incentive to make your final drafts error-free. As we've tried to show in the last three chapters, there are more important (and difficult) concerns in writing than the simple placement of a comma or the spelling of a single word. On the other hand, you can have the most creative ideas, the most convincing arguments, and the most carefully researched information, but if your writing is cluttered with errors, if it consistently slows your reader down because of the "garden-path" phenomenon, you'll leave a very poor impression. Why compromise your excellence in the important areas because of a few silly oversights in the simple ones?

Use Other People. In Part 4 of this book, we've devoted a whole chapter to writing collaboratively. But we can't overstress the importance and usefulness of asking other people to go over your writing for you. They may discover all sorts of errors or problems with the surface details of your writing, and you can do the same for them. Once these problems have been brought to your attention, they'll become part of a growing storehouse of problems you can recognize on your own.

If you get help from others, though, be a sport about it. Make sure you've gone over the draft yourself and gotten it as error-free as possible before asking the other person's help. And don't have your helper **fix** your lapses; let her merely bring them to your attention, perhaps by putting question marks next to them (she may be uncertain herself whether something is really an error). It is still your task to come to an understanding of the problem so you can recognize it in the future.

This process—having someone point out an error and then learning to recognize it once and for all—is quite simple, with a little concentration. For example, many people mistakenly use "your" (possessive pronoun) when they mean "you're" (contraction—you are). In fact, this kind of error is pervasive in writing, even though it's one of the easiest to correct. Just think: it's taken you about fifteen seconds to read about this error and concentrate on it. If you've been writing "your" when you mean "you're," these 15 seconds may be enough to bring the error to your attention so that you're never going to make it again. It's that simple. In a few minutes, then, you could learn:

> when to use "can not" instead of "cannot";
> never to confuse **their** (as in "their house") with **they're** (as in "they're drunk") or with **there** (as in "look over there");
> and never to use **to** (as in "she went to the store") for **too** (as in "there isn't too much sugar left").

Just think what 10 minutes or half an hour of such concentration, one error at a time, once a week or so, could do for those common errors you make!

YOUR TURN

Using the procedures we've suggested above, give your narrative paper a complete "error workout." First, read through your paper as if you had never seen it before. If you discover points where your reading process is slowed down or made difficult, see if you can identify any errors. If you can't, just try revising your writing to make it read more clearly and smoothly. Check also for any obvious omissions or incorrect uses of punctuation, any words whose spellings you're unsure of, and so on. Take a few minutes to look up those questionable words in the dictionary—you'll be surprised at how many you'll remember the next time you use them in your writing.

When you've done all you can to spot errors, then exchange papers with someone else. Each of you should circle any additional errors you spot or place question marks next to sentences or phrases or words you're uncertain about.

When you're done, exchange papers again and go through your own writing, trying to analyze the errors your partner has noted or questioned. If you recognize the problem, fix it. If you're still unsure why (or whether) something is an error, ask your partner to explain it to you. If neither of you is sure, consult your teacher, other members of your class, or a reference book.

BEYOND ERROR: MECHANICS AND STYLE

Writing and Clothing Revisited: Dressing the Part

Earlier, we drew a comparison between correctness and clothing: the more correct your writing, the more distinguished or professional or mature your appearance as a writer. In short, we implied that your writing wears clothes, and they should look nice.

But in reality, "error" is not as simple as that. It's not a matter of being right and wrong, as if we could never wear torn, dirty jeans. As with clothing, what counts as an error in one setting (wearing formal dinner wear to do gardening and lawn work) may be perfectly acceptable in another. Part of understanding error, then, requires you to be sensitive to the variety of forms writing can take in different contexts—something we'll spend more time on later in Parts 2 and 3.

Throughout this textbook, for example, we've made a decision to use contractions in our writing (as in this very sentence). We've tried not to sound overly complex and abstract. And we've made important decisions about the "voice" of our writing (you'll find occasional sentence fragments used for stylistic reasons. To be curt. To be emphatic. Or to list items in series).

We've made these choices consciously, based on educated guesses about our audience (you) and what will be most useful to you. If we were writing a grant proposal to the federal government, or a lesson for third-graders, we'd make different decisions.

Having a flexible wardrobe means giving yourself power as a writer. Imagine that a writer has no idea if he or she is making grammatical or punctuation errors in writing. In a sense, that writer has no choice—as if she had only a single kind of clothing to wear. And because she has no choice, she has no way to adapt herself to different situations; she's stuck wearing the same outfit to a beach party, a lecture at college, a house-painting job, and a wedding reception.

To take a more radical example, consider the following passage:

> Yeh've gone t' d' devil, Mag Johnson, yehs knows yehs have gone t' d' devil. Yer a disgrace t' yer people. An' now, git out an' go ahn wid dat doe-faced jude of yours. Go wid him, curse yeh, an' a good riddance. Go, an' see how yeh likes it.[4]

This passage is from "Maggie: A Girl of the Streets," a novella by Stephen Crane. Clearly, Crane has played havoc with the standard rules of spelling

---

[4]William M. Gibson, ed.,*The Red Badge of Courage and Selected Prose and Poetry,* 3rd ed., New York: Holt, Rinehart and Winston, 1968, p. 167.

and grammar. But if we see the passage for what it is—Crane's attempt to capture the sounds of a particular dialect—his violations make perfect sense. In fact, Crane is actually using the conventions of writing to show us his deviations: the apostrophes in "gone t' d' devil," for example, signal that something has been omitted. This control of the conventions shows that the violations are systematic and intentional. There's a world of difference between deliberately making "errors" and just plain blundering. In this case, Crane's violations are desirable—the passage loses a lot of its power and interest if all the errors are removed:

> You have gone to the devil, Mag Johnson; you know you have gone to the devil. You are a disgrace to your people. And now, get out of here and go away with that doe-faced Jude of yours. Go with him, curse you, and good riddance. Go, and see how you like it.

Of course, this creative control of the language—having a closet full of outfits and disguises so that you can use "error" when you want to or know when something is an error in one context and acceptable in another—may take years to acquire. But gaining a more basic kind of control—enough simply to recognize errors in your own writing, especially the academic kind you're doing in college—isn't as overwhelming a task as most people think.

Refining Your Skills over a Lifetime

All writers, no matter how experienced, continue to learn about grammar and mechanics as they write. As we worked on this textbook together, both of us learned from each other several problems in our own writing mechanics. At one point, for example, we began questioning our use of the word "awhile": was it one word or two? After looking in the dictionary, we learned that both "awhile" and "a while" are acceptable, but under different circumstances. "Awhile" is fine if it's used as an adverb ("I think I'll stay **awhile**"). But if it follows a preposition, then the "while" is a noun and must be separate from the "a" ("I think I'll stay for **a while**"). It's that easy.

But if grammar and mechanics really **are** that easy, then why all the brouhaha (yes, we had to look that up, too)? Why all the difficulty? Why so many red pens and so much frustration? Perhaps the two biggest blocks to gaining control of grammar and mechanics are discouragement over the apparent size of the task, and anxiety about looking foolish when you make mistakes. But these worries shouldn't stop you from wanting to master the conventions. From time to time, try reminding yourself of the following principles.

1. Correctness can be learned relatively easily.
2. It doesn't need special instruction or whole courses or hours of memorization and study; it can be learned as part of the writing process.
3. Once you see how simple being correct is, it will reduce your anxiety for writing in general.
4. The rules of correctness make sense; they're simple and logical.

5. Other people reading your work can help you catch the problems, and you can help them catch theirs.

Finally, correctness is achieved in the "long run"—not right at this moment, while you revise and check over your narrative paper, but as you do so for other writing years into your future. Here then is one final principle—the Grand Truth about error: **Most errors disappear *"by themselves"* if you read and write often.**

Acquiring the rules of grammar and mechanics is normally something that happens naturally, over time. You may not even be aware of it, but each day you're learning something new about the language—new words, new constructions, new expressions. Acquiring language is like watching a clock: you can't see the hands move, but after a while, time passes. In fact, you've probably learned 99 percent of what you know about spoken language unconsciously, without any formal instruction at all.

The same principle works for writing—find some papers you wrote in grade school or high school, and you'll see what we mean. You may not have seen the hands moving, but a lot has changed since then, and probably only a little as a result of direct, consciously learned rules.

But although you might learn correctness in writing **naturally,** you can't learn it by sitting there idly. You have to use the written language as much as possible and in many circumstances. That means that you should write and read **a lot**—just as you've talked and listened a lot to learn what you have about the spoken language. You can't become a successful gymnast, one who impresses judges not only with your style and individuality but also with the flawlessness of your performances, by studying rule books about good gymnastic form: you have to **do** it, again, again, and again.

Postscript

AM I FINISHED YET?

So, you've chosen your topic; you've developed a wealth of material; you've selected and arranged it carefully; you've drafted freely and openly, sharing your experience with your imaginary, interested audience; and now you've reread your draft, added to it, cut from it, rearranged it in a new and even more striking form; you've read it aloud over and over, each time unsnarling tangles, clarifying meanings, enlivening the imagery; and finally, you've carefully corrected spelling, grammar, and punctuation.

You probably think you're done.

Well, you might be. Or you might not. This is a purely practical question. Are you satisfied with the version you've got? Are you ready to wash your hands of it and have it read by its intended audience? Are you willing to be judged by it? Have you reached the point where you just can't bear the thought of fiddling with it further? Or have you simply run out of time? If any of these is true, then **for all practical purposes** you're done. Turn the paper over to its final reader—whether this is an instructor, a business associate, or an editor—and wash your hands of it.

But if you're still not satisfied, or if you've had a sudden brilliant insight or idea for a new direction in your work, and if you've got the time, you might consider revising it again. So long as you're really developing your paper, and not just worrying it or tinkering around with punctuation or a word here or there, it might be well worth your while to write a third draft, a fourth, or even more.

There's no absolute law for how much or how often you need to revise. Some famous authors claim to have produced 30, 40, even 50 drafts of a single story or novel. Furthermore, it's hard to quantify revision: some people make so many changes **as** they write that they only produce one or two actual **copies** of their writing. Others make all their changes **on** their rough drafts, and these changes make the drafts so messy that they have to recopy them many times.

But there is a point of diminishing returns. How significant are the improvements you think you can make in the draft? How much time and energy would it require to make them? Is it worth it? You don't want to turn in third-rate work if, by revising your draft one more time, you can genuinely produce first-rate work. On the other hand, you don't want to fall into mad, obsessive perfectionism either, turning in the perfect drama review three weeks after the play has closed.

How thoroughly or often you need to revise a piece varies widely, both because of the kind of piece you're writing and how you write it. If a business situation is especially complicated, with many audiences and sensitive information, then you may need to revise copiously. If, on the other hand, you're keeping a journal of impressions about all the movies you see, then you won't revise at all—unless you expect that your descendants will one day discover your journal in the attic, and you want them to know you were a skillful writer!

How carefully you planned your writing, furthermore, also has an effect on how much you'll revise it. The more carefully you designed the draft, the fewer revisions it's likely to need—unless, of course, you decide to head off in a radically new direction with it after it's done. Certain kinds of writing with very rigid formats—some kinds of lab reports, for example—are, in a sense, planned for you in advance—and require less revision as a result.

But in another sense your paper is never really done. The paper is the fruit of a long process of development, and the process could continue indefinitely. A famous poet once said: a poem is never finished, it's just abandoned. The same is true of all writing. Throughout Part 1, we've avoided talking about a "final draft." Instead, we've called the version you present to your reader the "presentation draft." We've done this because "final drafts" are mythical creatures. They don't really exist. With any draft, with any piece of writing whatsoever, you can always pose the question, "Where can I go with this? What else can I make of it?"

And then you're off and running again. . . .

YOUR TURN

1. Describe your "presentation draft." How is it different from your first draft?
2. If you were to do another draft, what would you do? Where would you go with it this time? What else would you change? What would be involved in such a revision in terms of developing, organizing, and drafting fresh material, changing tone, etc.?
3. Where else might it go? What other papers could you turn this draft or material into?

A Final Encouraging Word

The point we can't stress enough, finally, is that all of these processes—planning, organizing, drafting, revising—run together and blend in with each other. All the "gears" are available to you at all times, though at any given moment, one gear may move you along more readily than any of the others. The most efficient writing process continually shifts between them, depending on where you are at the moment in the development of your work.

The terms themselves, in fact, even become a little slippery if you try to grab them too tightly. When you redraw a tree or a timeline, for instance, is that developing or revising your paper? When you've found a gap in the logic of your draft and you brainstorm some notes on it, is that drafting or developing your material? If you complete a draft, then decide to go off in a whole new direction, what happens to that draft? Does it stay "a draft," or have you reclassified it as a long "free write"?

For the sake of presentation, we've organized the various composing activities in Part 1 rather rigidly—into separate chapters—as if they always occurred in the same sequence and were not connected to each other. In reality, the writing process is like juggling. Think of all the mental and physical writing activities we've discussed—and many more to come—as a bunch of different fruits you're trying to juggle at the same time. Getting better as a writer means that you can keep more **types** of fruit in the air at one time—even greater numbers of each type—and then begin juggling faster! Until then, it can't hurt to juggle one kind of fruit at a time, getting used to focusing your attention on each shape. Before you know it, you can even handle the unwieldy bananas pretty well. Then you'll soon find yourself mixing the fruits together, increasing the speed, adding more. And dropping none.

Of course, there's probably no "best" order to these various processes. Some writers move through the steps in a fairly straightforward, one-two-three manner—just as we've organized Part 1. Peter Elbow, on the other hand, author of an excellent book called *Writing with Power,* merely starts scribbling away on his topic, doing something like chained rushwrites, until he's "rushwritten" himself all the way to a final version. He goes over his ground many, many times; but it would be impossible to say when he's "developing his material" and when he's "drafting" or "revising." Only through long experimentation and careful self-observation will you discover what approach to writing suits you best.

Finally, whether you call something rushwriting or revising or drafting or whatever, perhaps the most important thing is, it's **all** development—both of the paper and, more importantly, of you as the writer. The paper itself can't be any richer or clearer or more original or acute than your own thinking. Muddy, wispy thoughts don't produce a strong, clear paper. But no matter how muddy or wispy your original ideas, you can, just in writing the paper, develop clarity and strength and energy in your thinking. Writing the paper is, in that sense, a sort of dialogue; and both you and the paper become wiser, more intense, more acute and distinctive even as you work. When you write, then, you're not just creating your **writing:** you're creating your very mind!

99

Part 2

BUILDING ON THE KNOWLEDGE OF OTHERS

Overview

In Part 1, we showed you some strategies for developing, organizing, and presenting your material. Essentially, you were making important decisions about what to tell your reader—decisions about what events to relate, what to include in describing each event, what people to give background information about, and so on.

In writing your narrative, however, you were selecting from a certain pool of already existing material, a pool that exists in your own mind in the form of memories. In developing your material, you may have elaborated on these memories to some extent, trying to visualize events and surroundings that had become dulled over the years. Or you may have embellished a few details that would otherwise have seemed too ordinary or uninteresting. Maybe you even called up your parents or a sibling to ask for some extra details, a second set of memories about your experience. Still, for the bulk of your material, or content, you didn't have to go anywhere but inside your own mind.

In much of the writing you have to do, however, including the great bulk of college writing, the ideas and knowledge and memories you have ready to hand won't be enough. You'll need to discuss issues you're not already familiar with. You'll be asked to analyze and report on matters you haven't in the past given much time and attention. You'll need to go beyond your own present stores of knowledge and, one way or another, start tapping the minds of others. Whether through personal interviews, letters of inquiry, or library research, you'll need to draw on the experiences, ideas, and speculations of other people to flesh out your own understanding of a subject. Then you'll need to digest and assess this information to present for a third party your new understanding of the subject in light of what you've learned.

Colleges and universities are trading posts stocked with great stores of knowledge—facts, data, analyses, written records of people's ideas and beliefs, research tools, histories, fiction and speculation. The library is often the intellectual core of the university campus, where thousands of texts contain everything you've ever wanted to know about . . . everything, from the most obscure to the most mundane. Computer technology is making much of that information accessible to us at a faster rate than ever; books not available at one library can usually be had from another in a matter of days through computer lending networks and interlibrary loans. Fancy photostat machines can make paper copies for us of two-hundred-year-old newspapers stored on hundreds of little reels of microfilm. Data retrieval systems can get us just about any information we need, and modern electronic printers can supply the most extensive bibliographies anyone would ever want on a topic with just a few commands on a computer keyboard.

In the classroom, the story is the same: information abounds. Dozens of books to read, formulas and terms to understand, lectures to be digested and integrated into your thinking, discussions that challenge everything you thought you knew about a subject. It's almost dizzying to think for a moment about all the information you're exposed to during your college career. With all the extensive subject matter you're expected to be learning in a particular discipline, you probably wonder why you're asked to **write** about it, as if you were the expert and your nationally famous scholar-professor were a rank beginner.

Learning to Write.   Part of the reason for doing papers on various subjects in college is to give you practice in the process of writing itself. Above and beyond your specific knowledge of any given field, you also need to develop the capability to communicate this knowledge to others. Writing is in itself a skill every college and university should impart, as part of its general educational mission. Every opportunity to write furthers the goals of college instruction as a whole.

Writing also makes you think. Organization, discrimination, logical analysis, weighing of evidence, informed judgment—all of these are at the center of your intellect. You learn to think by thinking, and writing makes you think. If you step back and observe what you're doing when you're thinking through a problem, you'll notice that you're making attempt after attempt to put something into words. You're trying to phrase or formulate some idea in clearer and less ambiguous language in your own mind. You start with the frustrating feeling that you "know what you want to say but just can't say it," and after several muddied attempts, finally do get it into some sort of language. Much of thinking is this labor to work your hunches into definite words, whether you ever then speak the words to another person or not. Being asked to write about something forces you through this very process.

To use an analogy from sports, you can't exercise your heart directly. You can't just decide to do so many heart beats in five minutes. You exercise your heart indirectly by running, swimming, walking, or doing something with your large voluntary muscles that forces your circulatory system to work harder. In the same way, you increase the breadth, precision, and flexibility of your thinking by making yourself write. Writing often seems hard because it puts some stress on your thinking. But do it often, and the prospect of writing a 30-page paper won't give you nearly as much concern.

Writing to Learn.   There's another reason for writing papers that focus on intellectual content: just plain learning—of the ideas, facts, concepts, and knowledge shaping any given field, and of the interconnections among these.

As we suggested in the Introduction, writing changes the writer. You probably have a new perspective on the personal experience you wrote about in Part 1; certainly you discovered some feelings or memories you weren't aware of, and if you've told your experience to other people or allowed them to read about it, their responses may have told you something else you didn't know about yourself or the memories you related.

Gathering external content—material based on the words or ideas of others—and then writing about that seems to many people like picking raspberries and boxing them for sale. The information goes from the source (picker) to the destination (buyer) via the text (box) that you produce. But if life were that simple, we'd let computers do this sort of writing by choosing the right target information and then splicing it together, perhaps in the form of abstracts or short lists of data, for readers to use.

What's missing in this model is merely the most important part: what **happens to you** as a writer. Everything you gather and analyze and think about is filtered through your mind, before, during, and after you write. Your understanding of the material must be transformed in some way before you commit it to paper and, ultimately, to the reader waiting at the other end. At the beginning of a paper you see the material one way; as you write and revise, you change your thinking, so that by the time you've finished, you understand the material in a wholly different way— more thoroughly and profoundly—than you did before you started. In short, you only really learn the material through the process of writing your way through it in order to give it to someone else.

Instead of the intellectual content somehow getting into a box and moving to the reader by itself, you stand in the middle of the entire process. But unlike a kind of automaton that does the same job the same way over and over again, you change in the process of writing. And later, when the reader reads and thinks about your work, she is changed too. Everything—information, writer, text, and reader—is in a state of flux: growing, evolving, and changing in the very processes that allow knowledge or information to move from mind to mind.

Writing and Working. Finally, there's a very pragmatic reason behind all this writing in college: namely, writing at work. If you're among the great majority, you'll be doing a good deal of writing in your career—writing whose main goal is taking raw factual or conceptual material and presenting it, for one reason or another, to a body of readers. Very few jobs don't demand at least some formal writing for other audiences. Lawyers, for instance, may be paid richly to produce a single contract. Engineers specializing in materials research and testing earn their living by the reports they write.

Unless you've actually experienced working in an office or business, you may assume that work-related writing can be reduced to a few types of reports and documents, as well as memos or letters that can be handled by competent secretaries who translate your dictation or hurriedly scribbled notes into neatly typed pages. But recent studies of the professional workplace have shown that writing is one of the most important job-related skills for most college graduates, and that writing consumes a substantial portion of the working day for almost **all** college-educated workers—at least one day of writing in each five-day week. Two reasons for writing were identified as "vitally important" across a variety of job categories:

1. To objectify a situation so that its essential elements and interrelationships can be analyzed; and
2. to present the findings in a document to be transmitted to the relevant, authorized personnel.[1]

In plain English, you write on the job to find out what on earth is going on, and to tell somebody about it.

---

[1]Paul V. Anderson, "What Survey Research Tells Us about Writing at Work," in L. Odell and D. Goswami, eds., *Writing in Nonacademic Settings,* New York: Guilford, 1985, pp. 3-83.

Writing to write, writing to learn, writing to prepare for the world of work—three good reasons why you face formal writing tasks in a variety of college classes.

In Chapters Five and Six, we'll be focusing on **academic** writing—on the process of using the knowledge and experience of others in your own writing. We assume you're already familiar with the writing process as presented in Part 1—such things as different brainstorming techniques, drafting strategies, and ways of assessing and revising your material. Here we'll be taking those for granted and building on them. Chapters Five and Six, in fact, explore a sort of "alternate route" through the writing process for whenever you're writing about issues that require you to go beyond what you already know.

Chapter Five looks mostly at the process of research. We discuss how to develop a sensible and interesting question and plan your research around it. We then present three ways of gathering the kinds of information you might need on any question: direct observation, interviews, and the use of printed texts.

In Chapter Six, we look at how to present your information to your reader. Here we briefly raise an issue we discuss in greater detail in a later chapter, how to take into consideration the special needs and characteristics of your audience—in this case, your college classroom instructor. We then present a graphic aid for structuring your paper, called "trees." These do the same job as the timelines discussed in Chapter Two, though for nonnarrative material. Finally, we provide some guidelines for how to incorporate the material you've gathered into your text. How do you best draw into your paper the words, ideas, and data of others, and give credit where credit is due? These are tasks you'll be asked to perform throughout your college career and probably afterwards as well.

YOUR TURN

It's worth giving some thought to just what kind of writing you might be asked to do in your career. Note down a few of the jobs you might someday be interested in pursuing. Then for each, brainstorm a list of all the ways those jobs might involve some writing.

What kinds of letters, reports, or other documents might you be asked to produce? What kind of writing do you think you'll be asked to do most often? How much of your time would you guess will be spent writing?

Now check your guesses by finding one or more people in your field, people with the sort of job you'd like, and ask them how much and what kind of writing they find themselves doing.

Chapter Five

IN SEARCH OF NEW KNOWLEDGE

WRITING BEFORE RESEARCHING

Whenever you've been assigned to write a paper using outside sources, the great temptation is simply to run to the library and either grab and use the first three remotely relevant sources you can find or read everything you can lay your hands on. The second approach, of course, leaves you drowning in a sea of information. Just managing to stay afloat takes tremendous energy, much less trying to navigate your way toward some piece of land you can't even see yet. The first approach, on the other hand, leaves you with less information to manage but with the difficult task of pulling together several barely related sources into some kind of unified theme. Suppose your topic was teenage pregnancy, and the first three articles you discovered were, "Decline of Sex Education Programs in the Schools," "What You Should Eat When You're Pregnant," and "Maternity Clothes for the Young at Heart." No matter what you title your paper, it's in effect going to be, "Crazy Random Facts about Pregnant Teenagers," and everyone will know it.

From the very beginning, you want to have as clear an idea as possible of what you're actually writing about. You can't possibly cover a really broad topic in enough depth to be interesting, so you need to find a smaller slice of it you can handle. Furthermore, you can't stop at a mere "topic." You need to push on to a real **question,** a real **problem.** "Teenage Pregnancy" would require volumes to discuss adequately. "Teenage Pregnancy and Nutrition in Seattle" is perhaps narrow enough, but the topic still sits there like a sort of inert lump. Topics, you'll discover, never motivate research. Questions do. "Topics," in fact, are only useful insofar as they lead to questions. Try something such as, "To what degree are the nutritional resources available in Seattle for unwed, unemployed, pregnant teenagers adequate to the demand?" Now you've got something to find out.

How do you develop a **question** (or questions) from a sufficiently narrowed **topic?** In working through Chapter One, you developed a wide variety of approaches to developing material out of your own thoughts and memories. All of those are useful again here. You move from a topic to a question by thinking about it, by wondering about it. And the best way to do that is by **writing,** by doing rushwrites or clusters or dialogues or a particle/wave/field or whatever else seems useful to you.

Notice how different this advice is from the way you may have gone about doing a research paper or formal report in the past. The standard model is: 1) think of a topic, 2) collect "quotable stuff," and 3) write it up. Here we're suggesting that you **start writing from the very beginning.** The paragraphs you produce at this point, of course, will probably never find their way directly into your final paper. But by writing from the start, and by continuing to write the whole time you're carrying out your research, you'll stay in better control of your material. You won't just produce an undigested list or collection of facts. You'll present a carefully thought-out analysis and interpretation of some important question, using the ideas and expertise of others. You write to think, and the time to start thinking is now, before you start doing interviews or paging through the *Reader's Guide* or scanning library shelves.

So, go back to Chapter One and list a range of topics you might be interested in researching. At this point they can be as broad as you like. Follow the instructions under selecting a topic and weed the list out, developing ideas on several topics as you go, until you find yourself drawn to one.

Then start using the various brainstorming techniques to sort out what you know, what you don't know, what your feelings and opinions are, and what you'd like to know more about. The odds are, you won't choose to write about any problem you've never even heard of before. Your familiarity with a topic so far may be only from snippets you've read in magazines, gossip from your friends, an interview or two on a talk-show. But whatever the topic, you probably know (or think you know) something about it already. Take some time to get down even that little bit.

Now go on to write about your feelings on the topic. What parts of it interest you or disturb you? What parts of it leave you cold and indifferent? What about it puzzles you? How does it affect you? If you've stumbled onto something that hardly affects you at all—say, real estate tax law in Greenland—maybe you really should consider a new topic. On the other hand, in mulling over your topic you may realize that what at first appeared rather dull—like the federal deficit problem—may strongly affect your own well-being for decades to come.

Think (on paper) how the issue affects someone else. It's unlikely, for instance, that as a male college student in your early twenties, living in Portland, Maine, you'd have much direct use for food banks in Seattle. But you can probably imagine young women whose health and well-being, and that of their children, depend on the food banks. Given a chance to talk to a food bank coordinator and to some of the teenage mothers themselves, you might become very concerned indeed. That concern might be enough to drive you to question city and state political leaders and spend time rummaging around the library, checking into the factors that make for the successful operation of food banks.

Nothing is significant in the abstract, in a vacuum. Whatever is significant or interesting or worth researching is so because it affects **someone's** well-being. Try to discover who that someone is and how he or she will be affected. And don't worry about being wrong at this point. You're not gathering information yet, after all; you're just trying to decide what information is worth gathering. Once you have a reasonable guess who might be affected by some issue, you've already moved toward turning a dry, lifeless "topic" into a living, breathing "problem."

By thinking and writing about the problem in advance, you'll also be able to narrow the range of your research. The more specific your sense of what you're trying to discover, the quicker and more efficiently you'll uncover precisely the information you need. If you go into a library to "do some research on acid rain," you'll be only too well rewarded. If it's sources you want, if your goal is basically a long bibliography, we promise you success. On the other hand, you'll never be able to use a fraction of the sources you discover, and what you do use may have little rhyme or reason.

If, on the other hand, you've put time and thought (on paper) into your topic, you may start your research, not looking for "stuff on acid rain," but seeking an answer to the question: "What are the probable results of recent state legislation concerning acid rain on small mammal populations in Lake County, Minnesota?" Trust us, you'll still find plenty of information. But it won't even compare to the vast number of articles and book titles you'll be able to **exclude** from consideration immediately. In a world drowning in information, a sound guide to what you can safely eliminate can be a life-saver. For this reason alone we'd advise you to write first and do research later. Any 10 minutes you put into narrowing your topic now will save you a solid hour or more in the library.

Finally, by writing before researching, you'll develop a rich set of questions in which you'll have some genuine interest. This is important. A paper written by an author who's really not concerned with her topic rarely goes beyond the dully competent and businesslike. The engrossing papers come from students whose genuine, deep-felt concern with the topic drives them to be careful and meticulous in their research and shrewd and thoughtful in their interpretation of what they discover. It's when you've developed a question or set of questions that you really need to answer, that the research itself becomes much more engaging and your paper promises to have some life and energy.

YOUR TURN

Follow the steps just outlined to arrive at and develop a question for research. Then answer the following questions:

How much did you discover you already knew about the topic? How does that compare with what you **thought** you knew?

At what point did you really begin to feel you were "on to something"? When did the topic seem to start generating questions almost on its own?

How did your feeling about the topic and the paper itself change as a result of writing about these issues in advance?

PLANNING YOUR RESEARCH

The difference between planning your research and simply marching grimly into the library and shuffling through the card catalogue is like the difference between studying a map before driving somewhere new and jumping in the car and heading off (you hope) in the right direction. Either way might get you where you're going, but one's going to be a lot quicker and more rewarding than the other. So if you feel some impatience about all this writing before starting your research, remember: all we're really suggesting is that you look at the map for a bit first.

After you've defined a research question for yourself, or at least acquired some idea of what you want to know and why—you should consider whether your present general background in the area is enough. If you've chosen to write, for instance, about the role of John Dean in the Watergate scandal, you need to decide if you know enough about Watergate itself already, or if you need to get more background on it first. Or suppose you're looking into the significance of certain traditional patterns of quilts. Do you know where quilts originally came from? Who brought the custom of quilting to America? What's the rough historical background of those people? Don't know? Maybe you should do some leisurely browsing in the stacks or spend a little time poring over volume PQ of the encyclopedia before settling down to serious business.

Needless to say, your preliminary explorations may radically change the nature of the question you actually research. Which brings us to a paradox: on the one hand, the better you've defined your question, the more efficient your research will be. On the other hand, you should never be completely committed to any one question you develop. Both are true, if seemingly contradictory, statements. You want to have a route mapped out in advance, but you must be flexible enough to take an interesting new turn as you're exploring the landscape. You'll also find yourself having to change your route under circumstances you can't predict from just looking at the map, such as:

1. *Roadblocks or dead-ends:* Something about the way you've framed the question makes it impossible to answer;
2. *Untravelable terrain:* You discover that your question could be explored or answered, but it's so complicated and sophisticated that you wouldn't survive the journey, given your present provisions (time, resources, knowledge);
3. *The hazardous unknown:* You've posed a question to which **no one** yet has a satisfactory answer (think of the "world" maps of the Middle Ages that showed the Earth simply stopping amongst a sea of dragons about the middle of the Atlantic); or
4. *The path you missed:* You've spent some energy climbing to a summit only to see that a left turn at the crossroad below would have taken you toward the beautiful tarn you couldn't see at that low an altitude.

The most likely (and most fortunate) of these would be #4. This is the best reason in the world not to be too rigid about sticking to your first question, no matter how carefully framed. Once you start researching anything, you never know what's going to come flying up out of the bushes. If you did, most of the usefulness and all of the intrigue would be gone. If any of these turn out to be the case, then you want to be able to cut loose of your present question and go after a new one. But keep your notes. The bird in the hand might turn out to be the best one, after all.

Once you have a question, you should work up as rich a collection of collateral questions as possible. To understand fully the core issue you're researching, what other questions can you think of that need to be answered? How many related questions to the main one can you devise? If your question concerned quilt patterns, you might also brainstorm a list of side questions like the following:

> Who made the quilts? How were quilting bees developed? What was the procedure for a quilting bee? What did people do there? Were men ever involved or was this purely a women's ritual? Was it only married women? Unmarried women? Where were the children? How long did the bee last? Was there food or drink provided? If so, by whom? How often were these held? Any special time of year? What were quilts made of? What served as dyes? How were they assembled? What kinds of materials did they use? What kinds of patterns were there? Did they have national or clan or family significance? Were they all traditional or was there room for innovation?

Any of the techniques introduced in Chapter One will work to develop such a list. The best perhaps would be dialogues, rushwrites linked together by questions, and the particle/wave/field method. The richer your list of side questions, the richer the material you'll ultimately be able to bring to bear on your main question.

If you plan to search through card catalogues, the *Reader's Guide to Periodical Literature,* or other alphabetically arranged guides for locating information, you should make a list of all the topic headings under which your subject might be found. To look up material on quilting, you might look under Quilting, Folk Art, Blanket Making, Appalachia, Crafts, Pioneers, Bedding, American Folk Art, and Community Customs, among other headings. In hunting up the information you need, some of these listings will probably prove dead ends, but it's good to have a range of options. You never know where the really interesting information on something will be hidden.

You should also consider the form the information you're looking for is liable to take. Are you looking for complete books, chapters in books, articles, news stories? Will your information take the form of maps, charts, graphs, photographs, statistical tables, historical documents, personal accounts by arctic explorers, statements by politicians, interviews with people on the street, television news, or statements from the *Congressional Record?* Will you learn what you need through direct observation, experimentation of some sort, interviewing certain persons, taking a poll, or doing traditional library research? Some questions can be approached a number of ways; others virtually dictate one specific form for the relevant data. The better the idea you have of what you're looking for, the more quickly you'll zero in on it.

Finally, you probably always do well to work from some sort of timetable. Work backwards from the date your presentation draft is due. When is PD-

Day? Now, if you're to do a good, thorough, careful revision of your rough draft before presenting it, when will you have to have the first draft done? How long will it take you to write your draft once you've gathered the information you need? How much time does that leave for the research process?

Once you've blocked out your time constraints, you should, at least tentatively, arrange the order of your tasks within those constraints. Should you get the interview with Professor Wilkerson done before prowling the stacks or after? Do you need time to do some background reading on Tazmania before researching your specific question about the devils? When should your working bibliography be ready so you can read all the journal and magazine articles you think you'll need? Are you comfortable burying yourself in the library for a full day at a stretch, or can you only work in two-hour blocks? How much total time do you expect to need? (Now add 50% to that number.)

If you work through all the steps we've suggested here, think what you'll have accomplished:

1. You'll have a research question sufficiently narrow that you can say something about it beyond textbook generalities.
2. You'll have some sense for the human significance of your question, of its importance and seriousness.
3. You'll have a good idea of what you already know, feel, and suspect, and of what you need to acquire by way of background knowledge before proceeding.
4. You'll have a wealth of side questions, the answers to which will flesh out the findings on your main question.
5. You'll have a range of headings and subheadings you can use to guide your use of the card catalogue and other indexes.
6. You'll know roughly what form the information you're seeking will take and what you'll have to do to find it.
7. You'll know in what order and by what date you need to finish your various research tasks.

Now when you begin your research, you won't have that sick, sinking feeling of being faced with tens of thousands of volumes and countless journals, holding a slip of paper with the word "Russia" written on it.

For the remainder of this chapter, we'd like to discuss three major ways of finding information on any given subject: direct observation, interviews, and printed sources.

GATHERING DATA FROM OBSERVATIONS

Sometimes you'll need to know more about a subject, but the information you need doesn't require that you go to any other person as a source. The information may be lying right out in the open, available for any interested party. Are the hamburgers at Slaphappy's any good? Order one and find out. Is the intersection of Franklin and Lyndale really more dangerous than that of Randolph and Cleveland? Spend a few hours at each one some Saturday night and count fender benders. Is the liquid in this bottle an acid or a base? There's the litmus paper; have a go at it.

Many courses in college will require you to make careful objective observations on your own to develop an understanding for how the firsthand data in a given field looks. Chemistry labs aren't intended to reveal new truths; they're to let you experience for yourself how the current knowledge was discovered. The interesting phenomenon in an animal learning lab isn't the rat; it's the Skinner box. And part of such courses is almost always writing up the results of the observations you've made. Each field has not only its own research methodology, but its own structure and language and style for reporting its results. For any of these courses, you'll need to learn how to observe the noteworthy events and how to put down on paper what you've seen in a form useful for other researchers in the field.

Other writing situations require you to combine one form of external information with another. One of our students, for example, was writing a research paper on companies that were allegedly dumping toxic wastes into the Mississippi River. During an interview with an executive at one such company, our student was asked if he'd like to have an instructive tour of the area where the plant's fluid wastes were passing into the river. That tour gave him considerable additional material, which he then used to guide his further reading on the subject.

Some writing will necessarily involve these sorts of observations: lab reports, police reports, time studies in factories, experiments on physical phenomena, legal and social counseling involving visits to specific sites where injustices are occurring, and all sorts of news reporting. These and many more kinds of writing are based on visual data-gathering. It helps, then, to think for a moment about the most productive ways to gather this kind of information.

Before the Observation

At first, it might seem that there's nothing to do until you actually observe or experience the phenomenon you're writing about. But it helps to have some ideas about what to look for before you go into the situation. That way you won't find yourself, a day or a week later, thinking, "Why didn't I think of looking at the layout of the plant more carefully?" or trying to remember just what color was the stone of the Plattsburgh National Bank facade, and not quite being able to do it.

To get an idea of how you might prepare for experiencing or observing something, let's take a common example—the review of a restaurant. All over the world, writers are eating at restaurants with the deliberate intention of assessing their experience, especially of the food, and writing about it in the form of an evaluative review. If you were to write a restaurant review, you'd want to ask yourself questions like these:

1. What do I want to know about this restaurant before I eat there?

You might want to know, for example, how long the restaurant's been in business; who the manager is; who the owner is, if different from the manager; what background the head chef has; what the exact location is; and whether it has operated under any other name in the past. This information could be useful not only in your final draft, but also as a background against which to evaluate your experience. If the restaurant claims to serve the finest haute cuisine in the city, you'll probably think about your experience somewhat differently than if it promises to serve you your pizza in five minutes or give you one free.

2. What do I want to look for when I eat at this restaurant?

This is your most important question, because it acts as a kind of mental organizer for your visit. Of course, you could take the view that the most outrageous or finest or awful qualities of the restaurant will stand out the most, so you need do no preparation. But it's wiser to think carefully about information that your reader might want in addition to what strikes you as important. For example, the prices at the Cottontail Inn might be absolutely average—a finding that doesn't seem remotely as interesting as the fact that all the waiters and waitresses are dressed as rabbits. But that doesn't mean that average prices aren't important to prospective diners.

So what do you want to look for? That's where planning can help. Brainstorm a list of specific items to evaluate; these may soon lead you to some general categories. These general categories in turn might lead you to think of further specific items. For example, "How good are the hamburgers?" might lead you to list "Quality of Food," and that in turn might remind you that you'll want to evaluate appetizers, main courses, desserts, and salads. After all, some places cook the best steak in the world, but the cheesecake is like sawdust.

Once you've created one or two categories, the rest will come to you quickly. "Quality of Food" leads to "Quality of Service." That gets you thinking about the "look" of the place, the "Ambience." Then "Value" (see if you can take home a menu after you've finished, or write down some prices right there, as you eat). Then "Location." And then maybe even back to the material you've generated in Item #1: How does the restaurant measure up to its claims or reputation?

As you can see, planning for an experience helps you know what to focus on, and that helps you to be more observant, more aware of the data you're collecting. A teacher we once knew was constantly bemoaning the human tendency not to use our senses as much as we should. To make his point, he used to walk into his class on the first day dressed as a motorcycle gang member (he was an actor as well as a teacher and had a splendid collection of disguises). He'd walk to the back of the class with a beer and sit down, putting his feet up on the desk in front of him, and start making a fuss because the teacher was late. Soon he'd start ranting and raving about how rotten the academic scene was. Eventually he'd leave the room, change his clothes, and come in as the teacher he really was. Then he'd tell the class that he was detained because of a faculty meeting about a half-crazed guy in a motorcycle jacket who was causing disturbances around campus. The class, of course, would frantically tell him that the biker had been sitting right there a few moments before. The teacher would say, "Well, since I didn't have anything planned for today, that'll make a good first assignment. Why don't you take out a sheet of paper and in the next half hour describe what happened as clearly as you can." Eventually, the students got the point—they really hadn't "seen" as much as they could have if they'd been prepared.

During the last week of class, our teacher friend would tell his students that a crazed woman in a tattered dress, carrying a plastic submachine gun water pistol and wearing an AM radio around her neck was roaming around the campus, and to be on the lookout for her. On the last day, lo and behold, there she was in their classroom, trying to give a speech on the increasing passivity of today's students. Again the teacher, in full disguise, would leave the room and return as himself. But this time, the students were ready—and it showed in their final description of what happened.

3. Is there anything I should know about what I'm experiencing or observing to help me to understand what I'm seeing? If so, where can I get that information?

So far, in planning for your restaurant review, you've generated some categories of information to be examined more closely. But now it's time to think about the specific characteristics of each item or category you've listed.

Let's take the most important category, "Food." Imagine that you're reviewing a French restaurant that claims to serve the best *endives à la reine* in the entire area. If you don't know French food, you might go to the restaurant and trust your own instincts. If the *endives à la reine* taste slightly sweet, and generally good, so be it: the place gets your top rating. But say you notice a sort of semibitter taste, a kind of bite to the palate, as you're eating, which gets offset by the sauce covering the endives. Unknowingly, you might write that the restaurant's *endives à la reine* aren't what they're cracked up to be, when, in fact, that taste is very important to the dish when it's really well-prepared.

If you're in this situation, you might want to consult with someone, or perhaps read some additional material, to prepare for your observation. No one is a "complete" expert; and when you base your writing on data gathered from outside yourself, very often you must rely on other people or authorities to help you make the best inferences and judgments about your observations.

Making Your Observation

Suppose you're now at the restaurant. Your planning has given you a list of things to pay attention to. Now you need to make your observations and get the data back to your writing desk. Don't trust your memory for this. You need somehow or other to record what you're seeing or learning.

Take along a pad of paper. On the top sheet, have some reminder of your planning: a list of categories or items, or perhaps some questions to ask yourself. Or write each category at the top of a separate piece of paper so you can be sure you cover all the important features of what you're observing.

Then try to distinguish carefully between the actual, concrete, exact experiences you're having, and what you make of them—between what you see, taste, and smell and what you think about those experiences. We discussed this briefly in Chapter One: the difference between observing someone tapping his foot, breathing shallowly, fiddling with his glasses, swallowing often, evading questions—and inferring, "Joe is nervous." (Even one of these "observations" is an inference. Which one?) Keeping facts and inferences separate is much harder than it sounds, especially if you're new at it.

Because all the evidence in an observation has to travel through your consciousness before you record it in your notes, it's easy to draw conclusions about the facts as they're passing through. Later, what look like facts in your notes are actually generalizations based on your interpretations. If you're conducting a study of rat conditioning, for example, you might write, "Tuesday, 9 A.M. Charlie the rat very tired today." That may seem like a fact; but imagine that Charlie was just not very responsive in pressing the bar for a pellet of food. The fact that Charlie pressed the bar only three times in the first hour, compared with the usual 12 times, might be explained by many other factors than his feeling tired. Maybe he was getting a cold. Maybe some other psychology students fed him by accident. Maybe he was losing his appetite for the cheap pellets supplied to the laboratory. Maybe he was developing a brain tumor. Any of these would do as well as "tired."

Some recent methods for analyzing data, on the other hand, allow for more deliberately subjective interpretation than has been common in the past. Inferences, even the most instinctive responses, can often give you opportunities to develop new angles for further investigation. So don't be afraid to make speculations or write down your interpretations. But keep in mind that the actual observations should be recorded as precisely as possible, and your interpretations of the information should be kept separate from them.

Be careful also not to leap to generalizations during the observation. If you're taking a walk and you see a jogger holding a gun on an older man in a suit, don't leap immediately to the conclusion that the runner has gone mad from the heat and is ruthlessly murdering innocent people. You may find that the older man had tried to shoot the runner, who managed to wrest the gun away and was holding the man at bay until the police arrived. Or imagine that you're reviewing an elegant restaurant, and you notice that your waiter keeps letting drops of wine fall from the lip of the bottle onto the white tablecloth as he fills your glass. If you were keeping notes on your observations, you might write, "the restaurant has sloppy service." But without further facts, your generalization might be misleading—for instance, if the rest of the service is impeccable (that particular waiter might be a trainee or may have just been fired).

The best way to avoid this situation is to use a simple procedure for your observation: put brackets around everything you write that is an inference or generalization or conclusion based on the facts: "Waiter has dripped some wine on tablecloth. [Sloppy service?] Steak entrees start at $16.95. [Overpriced for this area. Not worth the money.]" When you're using the information later, you'll find this especially useful for helping you to remember what you actually experienced, and what you thought about the experience. You might also find that too much of what you're writing has brackets around it, and you'll focus more of your attention on getting good, hard facts for later analysis.

YOUR TURN

Assume that you're doing a movie review for a local paper. Whether or not you actually write your review for class, try following the procedures we've outlined in this section. First, choose the movie you'll see. Then ask yourself if there's anything you'd want to know about the movie before seeing it. Next, brainstorm a plan for seeing the movie: try generating categories of data or information you'll want to get.

Now see the movie and take notes (as well as you can in a dark theater) using your categories. When you've finished, compare your movie-going information with that of other members of your class. What differences in the styles, contents, and depth do you notice in the notes? What differences in the categories? How do you differ in the percentages of facts versus inferences or generalizations?

Work out similar plans for observing one or more of the following:

A routine dental appointment.
A match between two teams in a sport you don't know well.
One hour at a daycare center.
The work of a construction crew.

INTERVIEWS: WHY, WHO, AND HOW?
Why Interview Someone

One very direct, interesting, and efficient way to learn what you need to know is to find an expert and **ask** him or her about the problem you're researching. By presenting your expert with specific, relevant questions, you let him do the screening and sorting for you. You don't have to scan dozens of pages looking for the specific fact you need. You pose your question and let the expert scan **her** memory for the relevant data. The material she presents is liable to be more focused and useful than what you would discover any other way.

The expert can also throw some intriguing and useful surprises into your research. A live human being is a much less predictable thing than a published book or article. The startling opinion, the snappy one-liner or moving anecdote, the behind-the-scenes gossip is more likely to turn up in conversation than in cold print. The human angle on any problem, in fact, surfaces more quickly in a live interview. In her published work, for instance, a marine biologist may be forced to write at a level of objectivity and scientific precision that would leave anyone but another researcher quite uninvolved. In an interview, on the other hand, she's free to talk about how she got into the field, to describe her childhood in the Florida Keys, the skin-diving expeditions she used to go on as a teenager, or the octopus she kept as a pet and how her mother once found it in the washing machine.

The expert, furthermore, no matter how much he writes, always knows much more than he can ever make public through the available media. Think about your own main interests for the moment. Pick one area: rock climbing, poetry, baseball, child psychology, music, anything. Reflect on how much you actually know about it. Now, how many pages would it take you to describe all that in perfect detail? How long would that take you? Your expert is in the same position. The fund of information anyone has at his fingertips greatly exceeds what he could ever get into print, even if he did nothing but write every day for the rest of his life.

Experts also tend to know where to find more information of the sort you need. A chemist from the Environmental Protection Agency could steer you toward the important books, articles, and other sources more easily and efficiently than you ever could by wandering aimlessly through the stacks. Someone in social services could tell you where the statistics on food banks are kept, where to find copies of city and state legislation, and who else you might want to talk to about the problem. Finding a likely interview candidate and talking to him early in your research may save you a lot of wild goose chasing later.

So who are these experts anyway? Where do you find them? For the purpose of research, we suggest a very broad definition of the term. An "expert" can be anyone who has specific experience of the problem you're writing about, whether that experience is academic, professional, or personal. A 75-year-old sport fisherman in upper New York state may be an "expert" on acid rain if he can tell you from his own experience what it's done to the fishing. An unwed teenage girl with a 10th-grade education may be an "expert" on how well the food bank keeps one going between welfare checks. Your goal is to add the experiences of others to your own stock of ideas and impressions, thereby coming to a fuller understanding of some problem. Anyone who has "been there," experienced the something you're investigating, is to that degree an "expert."

In deciding whom to interview, you should try to get a range of viewpoints. Just as you'd hardly judge a legal case by listening to only one side's attorney, so you shouldn't base your own conclusions on just one interviewee's statements. Find people you suspect will be on different sides of some issue and interview them all. For the acid rain issue, you might talk to a Sierra Club activist, a senior engineer for a Northeast power company, and the old fisherman mentioned above. By the time you sort through all they have to tell you, you'll have a reasonable idea of the ecological and economic arguments in the issue and some feeling for how the problem affects the general public.

This sounds like a lot, we realize. You were probably wondering where you were going to find anyone at all to interview, and here we are suggesting you interview a number of people. The fact is, you have an embarrassment of riches. For a problem of any scope, there are dozens, maybe hundreds of people you could talk to. Your task—and here you'll see the expansion/selection process at work once again—is to brainstorm a list of all the people who might make useful interview candidates, then select those few who would give you the widest, deepest, most interesting range of experiences. We've sketched out here a procedure you might follow for doing this.

Rather than start by trying to think up specific names of interview candidates, start with types or categories. What **sort** of people are likely to be concerned with your topic? To answer that, you need to think through the range of issues your topic might involve. The technique of choice for this is clustering (see pp. 24–27). Place your topic in the center of a page or blackboard and start working out a cluster of all the things it might influence or be related to. We've worked one out for food banks in Figure 5.1.

Once you've done that, use the cluster to help you brainstorm a list of the types of people who might have some interest in the subject. These can be groups based on profession, on age, on religion, on physical health, and so forth. Such a list for the cluster in Figure 5.1 might read as follows:

unwed mothers	"unwed fathers"
social workers	directors of food banks
legislators	police
teachers—inner city high schools	families—parents and children
	ministers
shelter volunteers	medical people
pediatricians	ob/gyn doctors
public health nurses	daycare teachers

From this brainstormed list, make your tentative selection of who might make interesting interviews. Again, try to select an interesting **set** of people,

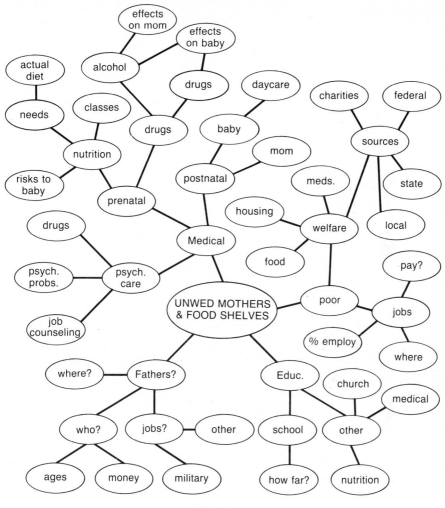

FIGURE 5.1

a group that will give the widest possible range of experiences, knowledge, or opinions.

Finally, check phone books, newspapers, and libraries to find specific individuals who fit each category. Pick at least two for each slot, in case the first is unavailable. Some, of course, you may not be able to find this early— the phone book doesn't usually list unwed mothers in the yellow pages— and others may only appear on the horizon after you've already done some portion of your research. The food bank coordinator or public health nurse, for instance, might put you in contact with a spirited young single mother who could give you a great interview.

YOUR TURN

For each of the possible research questions given below, do the following things:

1. Draw up a cluster to explore the range of things each problem topic might influence.
2. From the cluster, brainstorm a list of the sorts of people who might be concerned with the problem.
3. Select a few of these that would make an interesting set of interviews and write down in a few sentences what makes this particular grouping attractive. What different angles would you hope to cover by interviewing this set of persons?
4. Use the phone book, newspaper, library, or other sources to supply actual names of persons you could talk to, either in person or, if need be, over the telephone.

(Note: you can do this exercise by yourself, of course, but it will probably be most helpful if you work at it in groups of two to four.)

Questions:

1. A chemical company is applying for permission to build a new plant in your town. What would be the environmental effects of building the plant?
2. It's been revealed that the members of your varsity football team have been using steroids. What should be done about this?
3. An unmanned spacecraft has passed through the orbits of Jupiter and Saturn, revealing interesting and unexpected findings. How are these changing our understanding of planetary formation?
4. How effective is the use of hypnosis as a substitute for Novocaine in dental work?

Preparing for the Interview

For any given interview, you'll have a limited time, usually no more than half an hour. You need to make the most efficient use of this time possible. Just as in doing firsthand observations, the secret is planning. By the time you arrive at your interviewee's office or doorstep, you should have a clear idea of the kind of information you're seeking, as well as questions or topics for questions designed to elicit this.

If you've followed the steps above, you're already well on your way. You've thought about your topic at some length; you have notes covering what you know and what you want to find out; you've considered a number of possible subjects for interviews, and you've selected those that seem most interesting. Somewhere in your notes, you should also have the reasons that led to your decision. With this and your other notes, you should have a good sense for what it is you want to ask.

Before the interview, you should discover all you can about the person you'll be talking to. If she's written articles or books or has been interviewed anywhere, familiarize yourself with these. If she works for a business or government office, try to find out in what capacity, or with what duties and powers. It's a waste of your interviewee's time to ask for information readily available through other sources. If the person, for instance, has just been interviewed in the city paper, read that article first. Use the subject's answers there as springboards to new questions and answers, rather than just combing over the same old ground. If you can refer to other writings or statements, your subject will know you've put some time or thought into the interview and will be that much more willing to help you.

When you arrive at the interview, you'll want to have a list of questions ready to ask. The nature of the information you need will suggest how to phrase your questions. If it's specific, concrete data you're after, you should formulate specific, concrete questions—as many as necessary. If, on the other hand, you're interested in the broader experience or outlook of the subject (as is usually the case), you want to develop open-ended questions that encourage the interviewee to answer at greater length, to think out loud, to explain relationships, analyze causes, or assess results, rather than making simple statements of fact. Questions that can be answered with yes or no, for example, should be avoided.

Consider the following questions. All concern the introduction of "flextime" scheduling at a local company. (In flextime, the number of hours per week is specified, but the scheduling of those hours is open.) The interviewee in this case might be a personnel manager or supervisor.

One set of questions might call for specific **facts** about the company's use of flextime:

> When did your company first introduce the use of flextime?
> How has absenteeism for the various branch offices been affected since the introduction of these new scheduling options?
> What changes in employee productivity levels have you noticed?

All of these call for factual or statistical data. The first calls for a specific date. The last two can be answered with percentages, plus or minus. This may be precisely the information you're looking for; and if so, these are the sorts of questions you need. If, on the other hand, you want more wide-ranging, **interpretive** statements, you'll need to use questions like the following:

> What led your company to adopt flextime? What was behind that decision?
> How has flextime been received by your employees? What's been your impression of their response to it?
> What advice would you have for a company contemplating the adoption of flextime?

The questions you want to avoid, closed questions, are those that invite one-word answers. They too often produce this sort of exchange:

You: Would you say flextime has proved popular with your employees?
Interviewee: Yes.
You: Would you say it has raised or lowered productivity?
Interviewee: Lowered.

Try to cull an interesting quotation from material like that!

If you do ask a question like that, you can always follow it up with a second question designed to probe further:

What makes you say that?
What have you seen that leads you to that conclusion?
What's your response to that?
Why might that be the case?

These are all old workhorses in interviewing, but they're still effective in helping to get at a rich vein of ore that might otherwise play out too early. (You'd be surprised, in fact, at the kind of mileage you can get out of "Really?" or "That's interesting," or "How so?")

Moving from short, concrete questions to more interpretive ones can work wonderfully for the interview as a whole. You'd do well, in fact, to use the specific closed questions to get the interview started and the richer, more open-ended ones to broaden it.

YOUR TURN

A good way to pilot your questions is to let a partner pretend to be your prospective interviewee and role-play the interview with her. The "subject" should try to give plausible answers to the questions. That is, she shouldn't be unusually taciturn, nor should she be too forthcoming. She should give each question the answer it calls for. On the other hand, every time you ask a closed question, she should give you a one-word answer and make you work for a better one with an appropriate follow-up.

After the mock interview, ask the "subject" what she thought of the various questions. Let her tell you which seemed interesting, which were most challenging, or which ones she found unpleasant or offensive. These, of course, should be reconsidered and at least rephrased before the real interview.

Arranging the Interview

This is both the easiest and hardest part of the interview process. The mechanics are simple. Once you've selected your potential interviewee, call her, introduce yourself, tell her exactly what you're working on and something about the information you need, and ask for an appointment. Be courteous, calm, and matter-of-fact. Don't ramble, don't plead, don't bully. Simple.

Or so it would seem. Nonetheless, for most people, including some of the most experienced journalists in the country, making this first phone call is the most anxiety-provoking part of their work. Nobody enjoys doing this. You should just get it over with as soon as possible; procrastinating only makes it worse. And keep in mind, people really do want to share their ideas and opinions. Most people rather enjoy being interviewed, having a chance to play the expert. Sometimes you'll be turned down—the person will either be out of town or is legitimately too busy—but only very rarely will the person be rude or hostile and refuse out of sheer orneriness. If it's your peculiar fortune to run into one of these, congratulate yourself on a narrow escape. You didn't **really** want to spend 30 minutes in the same room with that person anyway.

If you plan to tape the interview—generally a good idea—ask now if your interviewee would have any objection. Most won't. If someone does refuse, however, or seems unusually cautious, either drilling you with questions or insisting on staying anonymous, do the person and yourself a big favor. Bow out gracefully and go on to the next person on your list. The person will feel relieved and grateful, and you'll get to interview someone ready to give you richer, fuller, more interesting material for your paper.

Conducting the Interview

The first order of business in an interview is introductions. Repeat what you said over the phone: your name, what you're working on, and how the interview will be used. Let your subject know who will be reading your paper. Some people who would avoid the press will gladly talk to a student.

If you plan to tape the interview, ask permission again, and set up the machine. Bring a long-playing tape so you won't need to change it once the interview is in progress. Also, don't trust the machine entirely. Take thorough notes on the session as you go. This will help you focus on what you're doing, what topics you've covered, and what leads look interesting, and provides a back-up in case there's a problem with your machine.

Once the preliminaries are over, dive right in. Don't try chatting the nervous stiffness away. This never works. Start in on the business at hand, and the nervousness will go away after a little while by itself.

The time that you spend with your interviewee is **yours,** not hers. You've asked for it as a favor, and she's granted it to you, made you a present of it. It's both your right and responsibility to make the best possible use of it. This means that you should take the initiative for directing the conversation from the beginning and should maintain it throughout. You know (or should know) what topics you want to cover, what information you need, and the nature of the answers (whether statistical, anecdotal, or interpretive). It's not the interviewee's job to intuit your needs or guess at the material she thinks you want. It's yours to ask the right questions and make sure they get answered.

Sometimes this will mean keeping the subject from flying off on a tangent. In this case, you need to politely but firmly interrupt him and return to terse, more specifically factual questions until you've covered the necessary ground. Then, if you like, you can let him take off again. More often your subject will rely on you to get the conversation started and to keep it going. In this case, you might start the interview with specific, concrete "particle" questions and build over time toward the more open-ended "wave" or "field" questions, falling back when necessary on the old workhorses "That's interesting," or "Oh?"

Once you've asked a question, keep silent until you either 1) get an answer, or 2) the interviewee asks you for a clarification. Silence can be nerve-racking, but it's usually a good sign. It means the interviewee is thinking carefully about what you've asked and trying to formulate the best answer. Avoid repeatedly rephrasing your question just to break the silence. By presenting your subject a string of not quite identical versions of the question, you're forcing him to shoot at a moving target. That really can be frustrating. Ask your question and wait it out.

Above all, **listen to your interviewee.** Ask about the things that puzzle or surprise or interest you. Keep your ear open for the story behind the story, the buried treasure hidden in the cave. Don't stick rigidly and mechanically to your prepared questions if you think you've stumbled onto a vein of more interesting material. The real problem here is time. It's limited and you'll have to make choices. You can't go chasing every rabbit that darts out onto the path; but if one runs by, nervously consulting a pocket watch and muttering something about being late for the Queen's Ball, you might want to follow that one.

When your time is nearly up, break in gracefully and tie up any loose ends. Double-check important details—dates, statistics, spellings of names—then ask if the interviewee has anything in particular she'd like to add. Before you leave, thank her and ask if you could contact her again, even just over the phone if you find any gaps in your notes or have any further questions. You can also—though this is entirely optional—volunteer to send the person a copy of your final paper.

After the Interview

As soon as you can, sit down and fill out your notes. Try especially to reconstruct as accurately as possible those quotations for which you only got the core words and phrases. Do this while it's still fresh—and be warned, it gets cloudy and vague with astonishing speed. An hour after the interview you'll remember more than you will that night. The next day, a fair amount of it will have slipped away. A week later, you'll be doing well to remember anything at all.

Once you've gotten your notes into shape, start working up the material the same way you worked up the topic. Think about what the interviewee said and didn't say. What do you make of it? How does it confirm or fail to confirm what you expected? Does it agree with or contradict other interview or textual material you've gathered? What do you make of the contradictions? How does it change your own understanding of the problem? What new questions does it raise?

You should do a series of rushwrites answering these questions. After all, you don't want just a collection of facts; you want a broad, well-grounded understanding of a complex problem. You turn **facts** into **understanding** by thinking about them, and a good way to think about them is. . . .

YOUR TURN

Plan, conduct, and evaluate an interview according to the previous directions. Answer the following questions.

What kinds of questions proved most useful in the interview?

If you had this particular interview to do over, what would you do differently?

Which brainstorming techniques are either leading to the most fruitful directions for inquiry or are helping you most fully to analyze and interpret the material you're uncovering?

USING PRINTED SOURCES

In most of the academic writing you ever do, your main source of information will be printed material of some sort: books, magazines, newspapers, reports, brochures, etc. The process for using printed sources in your own writing can be divided into five general activities:

1. Deciding what kind of sources you want.
2. Finding the sources.
3. Assessing the sources you've found.
4. Carrying away the information you need.
5. Incorporating the source material into your text.

In this section we'll be focusing on Steps 1, 3 and 4: the main planning, reading, evaluating, and note-taking parts of the research process. Step 5, on how to use your written sources, will be discussed in the next chapter. Step 2, where to find what you need, we won't cover at all. This is an important and necessary ability, but your teachers, peers, and (above all) a competent reference librarian can give you more helpful information than we can.

Selecting Your Sources

In selecting your sources, you might follow the strategy outlined above for choosing people to interview. That is, don't just wander to the card catalogue or the *Reader's Guide* or the shelves and start browsing with the intention of snapping up the first three articles that look good. Instead, start with a range of publications that might be useful, and from those select a tentative set to pursue.

How many publications do you imagine you have to choose from? How many pieces of writing come into print every year in this country alone? Think about it. How many books and periodicals do you see in a day—in the library, in the bookstore, on magazine racks in drugstores, or by grocery store check-out counters, in the hands of bus riders, under the arms of students? Which one of those do you think will carry the information you're seeking?

If you dwell on this even briefly, you'll realize your first task in selecting your sources is screening—ruling out as many unuseful sources as you can, so that you can attend more carefully to the likelier candidates. Fortunately your topic helps you do this to some degree. You know perfectly well not to thumb through back issues of *Cat Fancy* for an article on supernovas, or through *National Geographic* for an in-depth analysis of the writings of Kurt Vonnegut.

But suppose you were interested in something to do with hypnosis. Then where would you look? What books or magazines might carry something on that topic? Below are just some of the possibilities:

Periodicals:

> *Psychology Today*
> *National Enquirer*
> *American Psychologist*
> *Time*
> *Newsweek*
> *Self*
> *Journal of Consulting and Clinical Psychology*
> *Journal of Abnormal Psychology*
> *Christian Science Monitor*
> *Science News Weekly*
> *Woman's World*
> *Omni*

International Journal of Clinical Hypnosis
Ladies' Home Journal
The Atlantic
Scientific American
[Your school paper]
Journal of the American Medical Association
Journal of the British Society for Parapsychological Research

Books:

Hypnosis and the Control of Pain by Professor Ernest Hilgard
Any standard "Intro Psych" textbook
Your Magical Mind: How to Control Your Friends and Enemies through Witchcraft, Hypnosis, and Voodoo by Doctor Whirley De Fraudo (Magic Pentangle Paperbacks)

If every subject was covered by one and only one journal, finding the information you needed would be much easier. But for every subject you can name, you can probably find at least one specialty periodical—one dedicated just to hypnosis, or windsurfing, or needlepoint, or Colonial American history—and articles on the subject in numerous others. How then do you decide which of these sources will be most useful to you? How, if you're doing a paper on hypnosis as a dental anaesthetic, for instance, do you judge which of the sources above would give you the most trustworthy and reliable data?

You probably already have some sense how you'd rank different sources based on their reliability. Consider for a moment the following six periodicals and two books:

National Enquirer
Journal of the American Medical Association
Newsweek
International Journal of Clinical Hypnosis
Woman's World
Science News Weekly
Hypnosis and the Control of Pain by Professor Ernest Hilgard
Your Magical Mind: How to Control Your Friends and Enemies through Witchcraft, Hypnosis, and Voodoo by Doctor Whirley de Fraudo (Magic Pentangle Paperbacks)

Rate these as high, medium, or low on how reliable and accurate you would expect them to be as sources.

Most people, confronted with this question, would give high ratings to the two professional journals, middle ratings to Newsweek and Science News Weekly, and put National Enquirer and Woman's World at the bottom. Professor Hilgard's book would receive high marks; Dr. De Fraudo's would rank dead last. The following "Your Turn" should reveal something about the relationship between such ratings and the usual readership of various printed sources.

YOUR TURN

For each magazine and book in the list immediately above describe the **audience** to which it seems to be directed. Who might typically buy and read each of these publications? What are their ages, educational levels, familiarity with the specific subject matter, reasons for reading, professions, interests, life styles, genders, and so on? You might do this with one or more partners, working together to build up your theoretical composite picture of the readership for each of these periodicals and books.

Now compare that with your rating of each source's trustworthiness. What pattern do you see?

If you worked through the steps of the previous "Your Turn" section, the point we're making should be pretty clear. Though many publications discuss the same subject, an important difference between them is the nature of their respective readerships. The most trustworthy and sophisticated sources will be written to an audience of well-educated, highly trained experts in the field. Publications aimed at an educated but nonspecialist audience (as in *Science News Weekly,* for example) will respect their readers' intelligence and desire for accurate reporting, but won't go into the same level of detail as a professional journal. Publications like the *National Enquirer* know their audience is more interested in amusement than intellectual sustenance or scientific truth, and they tend to conjure up their "facts" accordingly.

Does this mean you must always consult only the most specialized, technically sophisticated journals in a field? Of course not. For one thing, you'll probably be unable to read what in some fields can amount to a foreign language. Most professional journals require several years of advanced training in the subject area to be read with any real critical judgment. Carefully controlled, statistically analyzed research of the sort that appears in the *Journal of Consulting and Clinical Psychology* remains, for the most part, beyond the abilities of all but specialists to fully understand. You might, therefore, need to lower your sights until you hit upon the best and most accessible sources for your purpose. For your paper on hypnosis and dental anaesthesia, *Science News Weekly* or even *Psychology Today* might be an appropriate choice.

Your selection of sources should also follow from your purposes in using the source. You can do other things with articles and books besides simply citing them as expert witnesses to make particular points. You might, for instance, be less interested in the legitimate medical uses of hypnosis than in the popular myths and misconceptions surrounding it. In this case, the *National Enquirer* or Dr. Mephisto's *Guide to Mind Messing* might provide documentary evidence of some of the more engagingly lunatic notions surrounding the field. *Science News Weekly* would be of less use in this case, and the professional journals less useful still.

On Judging a Source by Its Cover (and a Bit More of Its Anatomy)

Once you realize what a publication's intended audience tells you about how you might use it, you can strategically violate the old (and largely wrong) adage about not judging a book by its cover. Of course, the only way finally to judge a book or article is by reading it carefully, underlining and taking notes as you go, summarizing and analyzing its major arguments and evidence. But you're not to that stage yet.

Before beginning to read and take notes on anything, examine it to determine whom it's written for. Knowing who the author is addressing will tell you a lot about the author's outlook, his possible biases, the credibility of his information, the kinds of things he'll emphasize or play down, and whom he's liable to praise or damn. You'll be able to make an educated guess on all of these even before you read the article's opening paragraph.

Clues to a magazine's readership can be culled from virtually every page of it. You might examine and consider all of the following:

The title (and subtitle, if any);
The nature of the cover art;
The masthead (Table of Contents, list of contributors, organization responsible for publication, etc.);
Titles of all articles and departments;
Illustrations throughout the magazine;
Advertisements;
Classified ads (if any).

The work of inferring the readership from these clues, besides being eminently useful, is also fun. There's a Sherlock Holmes quality about it that you may rather enjoy. As an example, we'll go through an issue of one particular magazine, note what we find, and infer what we can about the intended reader.

Title and Subtitle: **Sierra: The Natural Resource.**   The title, *Sierra,* is the name of a mountain range in California. As a one-word title, it's probably more likely to be a popular magazine than an academic journal. With a mountain range for a name, it's likely to concern outdoor activities: mountaineering, hiking, camping, etc. The subtitle, *The Natural Resource,* confirms this. The word "natural" is a "buzz-word," or signal, for ecological, outdoorsy, whole-wheat-and-yoghurt sorts of interests.

Cover Art.   A splendid photograph of a spare, strangely bent pine tree jutting out of a flat grassy swamp. In one corner is the title of the article the picture apparently illustrates: "Restoring the Everglades." The cover is beautiful but not strange or showy; the audience is presumed to be more interested in landscapes than in photographic technique. The article's title not only concerns a famous wilderness area, it concerns the "restoration" of it—an issue the audience is presumably interested in.

Masthead.   The table of contents (page 5) gives the names and topics of the articles and small pictures to accompany them. The pictures—again all straightforward, precise, and unexperimental—show an otter, a bee, a plant, a desert landscape, and a young man with glasses, a moustache, and a cowboy hat. The man looks more like a college teacher "gone country" than an authentic Wyoming cowhand. This again suggests the intended audience.

A glance at the page numbers shows the articles running between 5 and 8 pages each—standard magazine length: longer than newspaper articles, shorter than academic research reports. The masthead, on page 6, gives not only the editorial staff, but officers of an organization. Unlike *Time* or *Redbook*, this isn't a commercial magazine; it's the official publication of an organized special-interest group, The Sierra Club. The readership then will consist in large part of dues-paying members of the club, people already committed to its goals of environmental protection.

Titles of Articles.

"Restoring the Everglades"
"Toxics on the Home Front"
"Whatever Happened to Energy Conservation?"
"Grassroots Profile"

There are also short articles on "billboard blight," toads, the Arctic Wildlife Refuge, nuclear radiation hazards, sea otters, the Surface Mining Act, various wildlife areas, and a collection of pictures from a photo contest.

The articles cover biological and ecological questions, outdoor activities, and political controversies over environmental policy. The "typical" reader would probably have a four-year college education, enjoy outdoor activities, and be politically active.

Advertisements.

Inside front cover: Big opening spread advertising a complete set of the Roger Tory Peterson field guides.

Page 4: Grape-Nuts (a health food). An attractive young woman on the front porch of her lakeside cottage enjoying the morning sunlight, the fresh breeze in her hair, and her bowl of cereal. Slogan: "For you, Grape-Nuts is as natural as the morning."

Page 7: Another pretty young woman—open sky behind her, wind in her hair—in bluejeans and a sport shirt. The sport shirt is being advertised, presumably to other pretty, young, outdoorsy women.

Page 8: A camera ad. Pictures of the camera in several severe outdoor settings.

Page 9: A mutual fund that only invests in ecologically clean industries; above that, foreign language instruction tapes.

Pages 11–12: Himalayan tours; raised relief maps; Book-of-the-Month Club introductory offer.

The consistent themes through all of this are: 1) travel and the outdoors, usually with a camera in hand; 2) "natural" materials, processes, etc.; 3) ecological awareness, including an understanding of the economics and politics of conservation; and 4) education and self-improvement (reading, recognizing critters and bugs, speaking French).

Most of the models in the advertisements are youngish (late 20s to early 30s), but not teenagers. They are without exception white, in good physical condition, and in no financial distress. They are outside enjoying themselves and have an attractive rough-and-ready appearance about them. They are dressed for sport, not fancy dining.

Advertising in the next 90 pages or so represents variations on the same themes. The classified ads parallel the major advertising.

From this characterization of the readership of *Sierra* you can make some logical inferences about the nature of the articles you'll find here, and from that, the uses to which you might put them. The articles will describe wilderness areas to visit; provide information about biology, zoology, and botany; discuss ecological problems and conflicts; give accounts of famous or important environmentalists in the past (e.g., John Muir) and present (Stewart and Morris Udall); and so forth. Given the status of the organization the magazine represents, the articles will be trustworthy and accurate but will fully and adequately represent only one perspective: that of the conservationist. For an article on acid rain, you'd find plenty of usable material, but you might want to supplement it with another, more pro-industry, source.

The articles, furthermore, assume and play to a general undergraduate background in the sciences but aren't written at the level of detail and thoroughness that a research zoologist would require to enrich her own knowledge. For a course in social issues, the coverage of acid rain in *Sierra* would be very helpful. For a research paper in advanced organic chemistry, you'd have to go elsewhere.

YOUR TURN

Get the most recent copy of some magazine—preferably one you've never read. Go through it as we did above, describing in detail what you find under each category (title, advertising, etc.), and what it tells you about its readership.

Then imagine a paper you might write for which the magazine could serve as a source. How would you use the magazine? What kind of help could it give you? For what sorts of assignments would it not be useful even though it covers the relevant subject matter?

Suggestion: this is another excercise that goes best with two or three people working collaboratively.

"Interviewing" Your Written Sources

The kind of analysis just described gives you a good idea of the kind of material you can expect from an article, the trustworthiness of the information it contains, and the angle it will probably take. These are important as background and will help guide you in your use of the source. But such a general review of the magazine is no substitute for reading the specific article. The article says what it says, and there's only one way to find out what that is: by reading it—actively, purposefully, and with pen in hand.

We've called this section "**Interviewing** Your Written Sources" to stress the active, probing, analytical way in which you need to read when doing research. Too much of the time, we indulge in passive reading: half attending, half somewhere else, letting the words wash over us without leaving much trace; or slogging through an article from start to finish, not really quite following it, certainly not interested, but wearily, doggedly marching down the paragraphs, and finally carrying away only a vague impression of its content.

The way you read should follow from your goals in reading. Passive reading isn't necessarily wrong—on the beach in July with a florid romance or convoluted spy novel, why not relax? But for research, it's slow, inefficient, and terribly energy-sapping. When you're doing research, you have an important question you need to answer. To answer the question, you need certain kinds of information. Your goal should be to find the most useful and telling information available as swiftly and efficiently as possible and to spend the bulk of your time thinking about what it means.

Just as in interviewing, to make the best use of your time with your sources, you need to have developed some questions in advance. You need to "pose" these to the article, and you need to record the relevant answers in your notes. At the same time you need to be thinking—keeping your eyes open for intriguing or fruitful new avenues of exploration; asking yourself what a writer's statement really **means**, both to you and to her, beyond what it says on the surface; trying to see around her statements to what she **isn't** saying, to the questions she **isn't** answering. And, of course, all of this will prompt you to "ask" more questions yet, either of this source or of others. Needless to say, this means you won't just be reading; you'll be reading and writing simultaneously.

Getting Acquainted: Reading First Units. Faced with any written document, your first task should be to develop an overall sense of its purpose, what main points it hopes to make, and how it's put together. You want to do this before reading through it. You want to map the size and contours of the forest before wandering in amongst the trees.

The simplest way to do this is to read according to the "Principle of First Units." No article or book is made of one long, unsorted, unbroken string of words. Books and articles are built in hierarchical patterns of smaller units combining to form larger ones. This book, for instance, breaks first into an Introduction and Body. The Body comprises four major sections, each usually with a short overview. Each section contains two to four chapters. Each chapter breaks into smaller units yet, indicated by first-, second-, and third-level subheads. Each smaller unit is divided into paragraphs, and each paragraph into sentences.

To discern the general shape and scope of a work, first examine how the book is structured. Study the table of contents, if any, and look at the major chapter headings and subtitles. Then read the first unit in each of the various series of units: the first chapter of the book, the first section of each chapter, the first paragraph in each section, and so on.

To get a good feel for the contents of this textbook, for instance, you'd probably read first the Introduction and then the overviews to the large sections. After that you might read the opening page or two of each chapter and look over the headings and subheadings it contains. Then you'd go back and read the first paragraph of each chapter subdivision and the first sentence of each remaining paragraph. Once you'd done all this, although you might still not know the book's message in full detail, you'd be able to reconstruct the greater percentage of it; and you'd know with practical certainty whether or not any given question was covered.

By following the "Principle of First Units," you can read between 5 and 10 percent of a book or article and pick up about 80 percent of its conceptual content. And you'll know where within the source to look for the specific information you need. This can save you reading a lot of material that's only tangentially or loosely relevant to the question you're trying to answer.

Reading in this way, you'll discover, requires more energy and concentration than stolidly slogging through uncharted swamps of prose. It may leave you more mentally tired afterwards, but it's much quicker, it returns you much more information for the time and energy you put in, and it's much less likely to bore you.

"Interviewing" the Text.   Ready to begin? Right now, while you're thinking about it and before you write down a single note, record all the relevant information for your footnotes and bibliography. Write down, **this instant**, the author's name, the title of the article, the name of the magazine, its date, volume and issue number, and the page numbers of the article. All of this has to be recorded with complete accuracy for your final paper; and if you don't get it down now, you could well forget it and have to make an extra trip later to look it up.

Next, note what kind of publication you're dealing with. Go over the clues discussed previously and describe in your notes the kind of reader this publication is intended for, and what that leads you to expect from the source.

Then start your serious reading, questioning, analyzing, and note taking. You should read with your major questions and interests always in mind. You should constantly be asking, what does this writer have to say about my question? How does this information concern my research? If it doesn't actually address the issues you're researching, skip it and go on to the next source on your list. If it does, note what it says and its relevance or use. Don't just read with a blank, lazy, empty mind—nothing will register. You're just wasting your time. On the other hand, if you find yourself fascinated with the article, follow it, even if it leads you astray for a while. You never know when you'll be led into a better research issue altogether.

Somewhere in your notes, try to nutshell your source: to state in one sentence the main point of it. What's its major claim or conclusion?

From there you should note the major arguments and evidence the writer uses to support or elaborate his claim. What kind of evidence does he rely on: statistical? observational? anecdotal? What is the logic of the major arguments? You should try to write these in your own words and see if they make sense. Compare your version with the original. How accurate a paraphrase did you write? If you find it extremely difficult to restate the major points or arguments of the article, it may well be that the author himself is vague or illogical.

As you record the material you need, keep asking yourself what use you might make of it in your final paper. This will suggest to you how nearly word-for-word you have to be in writing down what you need. If you find a passage you think you might want to quote directly into your paper, make sure to copy it exactly as it stands. Don't move so much as a comma. If you have access to a photocopier, you would do well to make a copy of at least the passages you intend to quote.

And most important, **keep up a running dialogue with your source right in your notes**. Respond to what you read. React to it. Believe it. Doubt it. Wonder about it. Let it provoke new questions and ideas. Compare it with other things you've read or people you've talked to. Mull it over. And do all of this in writing, right in amongst your notes as you go. If you want to keep your own reflections separate from the material you're copying down, you can put them in brackets [ ]. But don't postpone thinking about what your sources are saying until you're done "doing your research." Do your thinking and researching together, as one unified activity, and let all of it— the observations you're using from others and the thoughts and reflections and questions you have to bring to it—appear in your notes throughout the research process.

Finally, when you've finished with the source, spend a few minutes more continuing this probing, questioning, and reflecting. What new questions or issues does the article raise? How does it change your knowledge or understanding of the original problem? What do you know or comprehend now that you didn't before? And where, in the light of this new understanding, do you think you should go from here? How does this article alter your future research plans?

The rough pattern for your notes on any source, then, should look something like the following:

1. Precise bibliographical reference.
2. Apparent audience for the source.
3. Nutshell and Overview (from reading First Units).
4. A blend of information from the article and your reflections on it.
5. Summary reflection. Plans for further research.

How much you write on any of these depends on the scope of your research and on the source you're using. Each item from 1 through 3 and 5 might be no more than a sentence or two. The longest section will usually be for item 4. On the other hand, an article may not actually add much to your knowledge, limiting the amount of information you draw from it, but it might open up entire new areas for research and consideration. In this case, only item 5 might be extensive.

You might also decide to save this full a treatment for only your most important sources. You might, for instance, have a much longer list of sources than you'll ultimately be able to use. In this case, you might simply glance over and nutshell each of them on the basis of a quick first units reading; and then, when you've got some idea of which ones contain the most relevant and valuable material, go back to those for a more careful probing.

Controlling Your Sources.   The point of all this, finally, is **to keep you in charge of your paper**. Make sure every source **serves your purposes**. Formulate your own questions and problems and use the sources to help you answer them. The great danger in writing a paper based on outside research is that the sources can overwhelm you and wind up dominating your paper. Instead of a careful examination of the relevant evidence on a given issue, your final product is little more than a loose string of summaries of randomly selected articles,**very** loosely tied together in a "concluding paragraph."

The pattern "Intro, Source 1, Source 2, Source 3, Conc" is a dead giveaway that the writer hasn't really digested, thought about, and worked with her source material. She's merely written thumbnail summaries of them and strung them along like beads on a string. The more impressive papers are organized by concepts and arguments, with each section representing a rich blend of evidence and analysis from a range of sources. Unless you actually think about (and that means write about) your sources as you're using them, you'll carry away only the notes from which to reconstruct summaries (with perhaps "a quote" or two), and you'll be in great danger of writing a mere "string-of-sources" paper.

The time to gain and keep control of your topic is early on, before even starting your research, and every minute as you go along. Waiting for later to mull over what you've gathered may be too late.

Chapter Six

FROM NEW KNOWLEDGE TO NEW TEXT

Everything we suggested in the last chapter was aimed at one goal: helping you to increase your knowledge and understanding of a given question. Whether you looked into environmental problems, the development of education in the American West, recent discoveries in astrophysics, or when and how your high school chose its team name, you followed the same general process. You started with a question, turned up relevant information through observations, interviews, or reading, and turned the material over and over in your mind (and in your notes) until some sort of pattern or solution emerged. If you worked through the suggestions in Chapter Five, you now comprehend a lot more about your chosen topic than you did at the start.

Now comes the other side of your task: presenting what you've learned to your reader. Somehow you have to get your new, deeper, more thorough knowledge of your subject onto paper, where someone else can enjoy it and benefit from it. You need to develop a finished paper in which you present your best considered judgment of the question in the light of the information you've uncovered. This, again, doesn't mean reeling off a list of summaries; it means offering your own best assessment of what the truth is on this issue, using your sources to clarify and document your claims.

In this chapter we present a number of strategies to help you mold the inchoate mass of notes, statistics, quoted passages, and firsthand observations you've developed into a coherent paper. We assume you've been through Chapters Two and Three and already have a handle on the processes of drafting and revision discussed there. What we offer in this chapter are techniques specifically related to shaping researched material into a presentable text. In particular, we'll be discussing the following:

Audience: How to write for a college instructor who may or may not be pretending to be someone else.

Organization: How to use "trees," a graphic aid somewhat like timelines, to help you organize an explanation of something rather than to tell a story.

Incorporating Source Material: How fairly and accurately to draw into your paper the ideas, facts, speculations, and quotations from the people and texts you've consulted.

WHOM ARE YOU WRITING FOR, ANYWAY?

Between your understanding of the issue, whether recorded in your notebook or on index cards, and your final paper, there is one problem you have to consider immediately—that of audience. Who are you writing for? In every batch of papers college teachers receive, there's always at least one where the student has obviously done a thorough job formulating, researching, and answering some interesting question, but the paper still doesn't quite "come off." It feels oddly inconsistent—stiff and pedantic in some places and downright chatty in others. Or the writer assumes the reader to have different amounts of knowledge on different pages. In some paragraphs, the writer is clearly addressing an expert in the field; in others, she's talking to an eighth-grader. Or, if the writer completely forgets what she's about, she starts talking to the instructor personally: "As you said in class last Tuesday, and I think it made a lot of sense, if Huck is innocent, the entire society is guilty."

All of these suggest a failure to think through carefully and consistently the problem of audience. The writer hasn't decided once and for all who she's writing for and what's appropriate in addressing this particular reader. The problem of how to analyze and adapt to any given audience is a broad one—so broad, in fact, we've dedicated an entire chapter to it later in this book. For now, however, we'd like to mention the issue as it relates specifically to the academic paper.

In writing for the classroom, you're addressing an inherently strange sort of audience. When you write about the position of women in Victorian England, do you really expect to tell your instructor much that she doesn't already know? Sometimes you might, especially if this is an in-depth term paper. But in most cases, you won't be adding much to your reader's actual knowledge. Instead, you'll be writing to demonstrate your own comprehension and judgment concerning a subject your reader knows better than you do.

Then why is your instructor reading your work if he doesn't stand to gain from it what a less informed reader might? The half-true/half-cynical answer is, to assess it. But your instructor probably assigned you the paper in the first place to accomplish a number of laudable goals: to compel you to read and think through the course materials, to push you to investigate some aspect of the course in more depth, to challenge you to engage the material more actively and consider its meaning and ramifications for yourself, and to give you practice in expressing your thoughts and findings in writing. Your instructor will want to see that you've accomplished these, and you shouldn't be shy about showing her.

Different instructors put the emphasis in different places. Some primarily seek evidence of deep and thorough research; others are eager for signs of independent thought and evaluation; still others look for clarity and precision of expression. Most students, by the time they've reached college, are past masters in the art of "psyching out" the teacher—detecting, as if by a sixth sense, what the instructor will be looking for. This is exactly as it should be. By learning to write about a variety of subjects and for a variety of instructors, you develop a broader and more flexible repertoire of writing skills than would be possible if instructors were unanimous in what they wanted.

Still, though the emphasis will be different from class to class, a few guidelines will hold true in most academic situations. There are a few things that you can safely assume almost all instructors will value.

1. *Depth.* It's usually better to be a specialist than a generalist. It's usually more impressive to demonstrate a thorough and detailed knowledge

of a small slice of some subject than a superficial and elementary knowledge of the whole.

2. *Unity.* Discuss one problem per paper. Keep everything in the paper focused on that problem. If you "tree" your draft (see pp. 145–159), every part of it should hang logically from one top node. If you've written about two things that you vaguely feel belong together, you'd better get down on paper the exact nature of that relationship—or drop one of them.

3. *Originality.* Suppose you were teaching a class of 50 students about your favorite subject—skiing, thoroughbred horses, Jane Austen's novels, "Dallas," fine wines. Now suppose that you're reading 50 papers on that subject. A good many of them cover the same ground and come to about the same conclusions. Here's one, however, that, although not "off the wall," nonetheless follows a fresh and untried approach to the subject, looks at the information in a new way, comes to original and unique conclusions—even, in fact, shows you things about the subject that, after 30 years of teaching it, you hadn't noticed before. Can you imagine how refreshed and awake you'd feel after that? And how grateful?

We're not recommending that you cook up some off-beat or absurd thesis just to be different (though some teachers might even welcome that). We're suggesting you look long and hard at your material and that you look for **yourself,** through your own eyes, trusting your own judgment. And don't be in a hurry to come to a conclusion. The first things you find to say about any topic will be the obvious, cliché-ridden truisms the instructor has read all too often before. Instead, be patient, watch carefully, watch long, and in time you'll see patterns that others have overlooked. Not crazy things, but deeper and subtler things. Get those down and offer those to your instructor, and you'll be surprised at the results.

Writing **for** an instructor is not, however, the same thing as writing **to** an instructor. The latter has its place—for example, when writing a note asking for an appointment or apologizing for a late paper or some such—but not in an academic paper. In an academic paper it isn't generally a good idea to address the instructor personally and directly. Your task is not, finally, to learn how to write for a specific teacher but to learn how to take part in a broader, more extensive **academic conversation**—one involving a variety of persons, none of whom you will necessarily ever meet. You want to write so that a range of people, all interested in the same general subject, will benefit from reading your piece.

You might think for a moment about letters to the editor in a newspaper. Those letters aren't to the **actual** editor; in most cases, the writers couldn't tell you the actual editor's name. The letters are to the readership of the newspaper at large. It would be more accurate to describe the letters as **through** the editor than **to** him. The same sort of thing holds true for college classroom writing. You're writing **for** the instructor, not actually **to** her. In a sense, she's acting like an editor—deciding whether your letter is appropriate for the newspaper's larger readership, whether it's ready for "circulation" among the academic community.

You need, then, to have some other reader than your teacher in mind when you write. You need someone besides your instructor to direct your comments to: an expanded collection of people potentially interested in what you have to say. If your actual reader (the instructor) won't do as a target audience, you need to create for yourself a consistent and logical "make-believe" audience and address them. You invent a purely fictional readership and write for their benefit, knowing all the while that your instructor is sitting in the wings, evaluating how well you're reaching "them."

If some cases, the nature of this audience will be given as part of the assignment. In teaching technical writing, for example, we'll sometimes ask our engineering students to describe some instrument or process so that a technically untrained business executive can understand it. Similarly, a political science instructor might ask you to analyze some social dilemma in your city and to write your results in the form of recommendations to the mayor and council.

In most cases, however, you won't be given such explicit directions; instead, it will be up to you to concoct a useful mock audience on your own. You'll need to decide who your "audience" is, what they know about your subject, and why they would be reading your paper. For most classroom assignments, the most useful "readership" is the one nearest to hand; that is, the exact sort of readers you and your classmates were before you started doing any work at all on your topic. In using your "preresearch self" as a model audience, you'll want to answer the following sorts of questions:

> What, precisely, did you know about the general topic of your paper before you started working on it?
> What false preconceptions did you have?
> What did you need to have explained? What could the writer have safely counted on you to understand in advance?
> What would have sparked your interest in this subject if someone had tried to talk to you about it?

You should work out the answers to these questions in as much detail as possible.

Finally, it helps to think about your "readers'" knowledge in broad levels. If you assume they know calculus, you should also assume they know algebra. If they've read the poetry of Matthew Prior, a minor English poet of the early 1700s, you can be fairly sure that they've read the work of Alexander Pope, a much more important poet of the same period. On the other hand, a knowledge of algebra doesn't guarantee calculus nor does a familiarity with Pope suggest any reading of Prior. In a similar vein, you don't want to assume on pages 1–3 that your reader has a firm grasp of plate tectonics and then on page 4 give a careful explanation of continental drift.

In short, create a plausible audience, using your own educational background as a guide (unless instructed otherwise), and address that same audience in every page, every paragraph, every sentence of your paper. Be consistent.

Now, what was it you wanted to say again?

ORGANIZATIONAL TREES

Timelines, as you'll recall, provide a graphic aid in the organization of narrative materials. They allow you to see, and thereby control, the structure of your story before you actually set about drafting it. Also, because they require so little time to draw and redraw, they permit you to experiment rapidly and freely with various possible organizational structures before committing yourself to one in prose. Organizational "trees" perform exactly the same service, though for conceptually rather than chronologically structured materials. Timelines help you tell a story: first this happened, then this, then this, and so on. Trees help you explain concepts, make arguments, analyze a situation, present a case—anything where the content of your writing breaks down into hierarchically structured units rather than sequential events (e.g., "Three Reasons Why the Americans Won the Revolutionary War," "Aspects of Clothing Design," "Arguments for the Equal Rights Amendment").

This covers most of the writing you'll ever do, unless you become a newspaper reporter or fiction writer. The great bulk of nonfiction writing lends itself more readily to arrangement according to a tree structure than by timelines. Even for your personal experience essay, you may decide that, rather than a chronological story, you want to write a reflective, impressionistic piece on some person or place that's been of special significance to you. In this case, trees may be the tool you need.

How to Construct a Tree

Organizational trees work somewhat like clusters (see pp. 24–27) in that they use circled codewords to represent concepts, arguments, facts, or other units of thought. But whereas in clustering, nodes were attached to each other only according to how you happened to think of them, the nodes in trees are carefully arranged to show the relationships between ideas. The kinds of relationships that trees can show include parts of a whole, causes of an effect, examples of a category—anything, in fact, in which one idea can be broken down into or gives rise to several supporting ideas. A few examples might make this clearer.

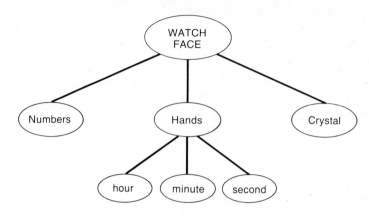

FIGURE 6.1

PARTS OF A WHOLE

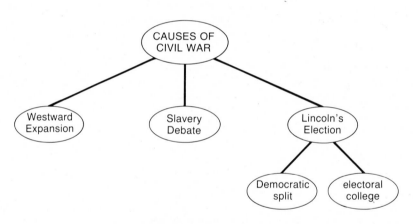

FIGURE 6.2

CAUSES OF AN EFFECT

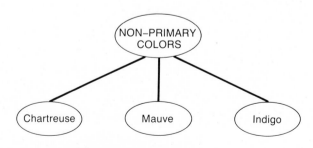

FIGURE 6.3

EXAMPLES OF A CATEGORY

In the first example (Figure 6.1), the tree graphically represents numbers, hands, and crystals as parts of a watch face. The node representing "hands," furthermore, subdivides into kinds of hands: hour, minute, and second. The second tree (Figure 6.2) suggests that westward expansion, the slavery debate, and Lincoln's election all qualify as causes of the Civil War. Lincoln's election, in turn, appears from this tree to result from two other causes: the split in the Democratic party and the counting of votes in the electoral college. The final tree (Figure 6.3) represents chartreuse, mauve, and indigo as examples of the category "nonprimary colors."

YOUR TURN

Draw trees to represent the relationships between the items in each of the following lists.

1. red, primary colors, yellow, blue.
2. monitor, keyboard, disk drive, microcomputer, printer.
3. The Boston Tea Party, The Boston Massacre, The Battle of Lexington, Events Leading to the Declaration of Independence. (For convenience, you might label your nodes: Tea, Mass, Lex, D.I.)
4. Springsteen, musicians, Bach, Madonna, classical musicians, Beethoven, popular musicians. (Label your nodes, if you like, just using whatever initials or code letters are convenient.)

What's the really obvious difference between the tree you drew for list 4 and the trees you drew for 1–3?

If you got the tree for item 4 of the previous "Your Turn" to look fairly sensible and symmetrical, you probably understand most of what you need to know about the technique. You've got the main idea and the principal mechanics. But so far, this has been at a very simple level. A more fully worked out tree for a report might look like Figure 6.4.

You can see the general logic of this tree for yourself, without even needing to know what the paper is actually about. The subject of the paper stands at the top. Below it and branching out from it are the most important, most general, and most sweeping two arguments. These each branch into their supporting arguments and evidence. These minor arguments subdivide, as indicated by the connecting lines, into supplementary details, and so on. The very lowest nodes, "a," "b," and "c," might be examples of "2," which is a cause of "A," which illustrates the major argument "II," which is half of the problem the paper discusses.

As the "Your Turn" exercises and Figure 6.4 demonstrate, there are two fundamental and vitally important principles for drawing trees.

1. On all organizational trees, the **higher** the position of **the node, the more abstract** and general it is. The **lower nodes** represent comparatively **more concrete and specific** material.

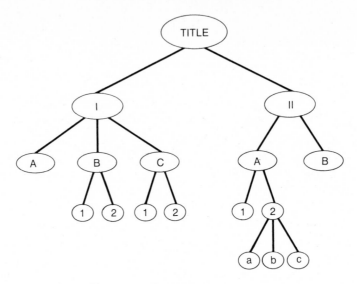

FIGURE 6.4

2. All of the nodes along any one horizontal band should represent about the **same level** of generality or detail.

Though both principles are essential to using trees in organizing your paper, the latter is the trickier problem for most people. Judging the level of abstractness or concreteness of different ideas can often be subtle. Furthermore, you'll need to sort your material out into different middle-range categories before it will make any sense. You may understand your topic in a general way and have a hatful of specific facts; but to make anything useful of your facts, you will have to gather them into subcategories that will make them easier to interpret and present.

You've probably often found yourself in this situation between researching and drafting a term paper. You were writing about the novels of Mark Twain, and you had stacks of notes about different characters, images, dialects, symbols, etc., but shaping the material into a coherent design seemed almost impossible. Nonetheless, some kind of sorting was absolutely required if you were to present anything but a jumble of findings.

Consider, as an illustration of these principles, the tree in Figure 6.5 intended for an introductory guide to auto mechanics.

Notice the confusion of levels. The writer starts sensibly enough, dividing the parts of cars into the broad categories of electrical systems and mechanical systems. He then breaks mechanical systems, again quite sensibly, into propulsion, transmission, and control systems, and subdivides the last category still further into brakes and steering. Under "Electrical Systems," though, instead of developing comparable midrange categories, he simply starts listing off all the electrical parts themselves.

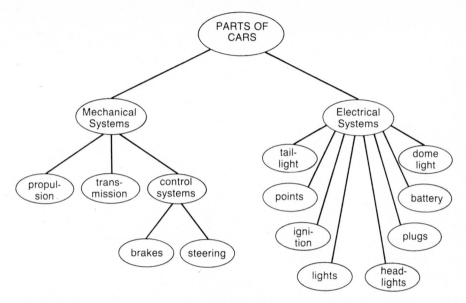

FIGURE 6.5

If he organizes his manual according to this tree, he's going to lead his reader into a maze. He's liable to end up with a 15-page chapter on the engine, 10 pages on transmission, perhaps 12 pages on control systems (divided between brakes and steering), and then a long series of 1-page chapters on each tiny part concerned with electronics. The reader may follow the early part of the book fairly well but will probably feel completely at sea throughout the rest of it. His task, then, is to sort the separate items under "Electrical Systems" into coherent, labeled sets, and then redraw his tree using these as a middle level of categories, as he did intuitively under "Mechanical Systems."

YOUR TURN

1. Bail out the technical writer whose manual is sketched out in Figure 6.5. Decide what subtopics you might use to sort out the parts of the electrical system and redraw that half of the writer's tree to make more sense.

2. Now try building another tree from a collection of individual items. Following is a list of parts of the human body. Each item has been given a code letter or initial for the sake of convenience in treeing. Pretend you were writing a textbook, and you wanted to assemble your discussion of human anatomy into the most sensible and understandable pattern. Draw a tree structure, using these items, that will result in the most useful structure for your book. Create whatever

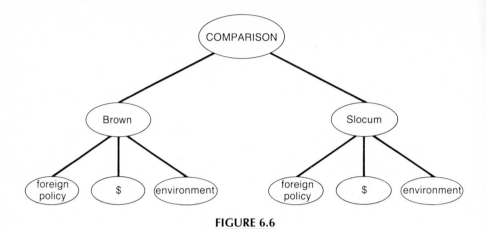

FIGURE 6.6

middle range categories—between "human body" at the top and "nerve endings" at the bottom—that you think will be necessary to make sense out of these items.

ITEMS

large intestine [LI]	spinal cord [SC]
skull [Sk]	heart [H]
brain [B]	small intestine [SI]
arteries [A]	ligaments [L]
cerebrum [CM]	veins [V]
esophagus [E]	cerebellum [Clm]
appendix [Ax]	capillaries [Cpl]
brainstem [Bst]	aorta [Ao]
cartilage [C]	nerve endings [NE]
stomach [S]	bones [Bn]

So far, the examples we've offered have lent themselves fairly readily to one particular tree structure. There might be minor variations in the ways different students arrange the nodes of these trees horizontally, but that's all. There won't be any radical structural differences between them. In real life, however, it's rarely this simple. In most cases, your material can lend itself to a range of different tree structures, none of which may be clearly better than the others.

To take a simple example, suppose you wanted to write a paper comparing two presidential candidates on their stands on foreign policy, economics, and environmental protection. On the face of it, you have two obvious ways to arrange your material—either by candidate or by issue. If you arrange your material by candidate, you get a tree that looks like Figure 6.6.

Your paper, after suggesting your topic, will enter into an examination of Senator Brown's positions on foreign policy, the economy, and the envi-

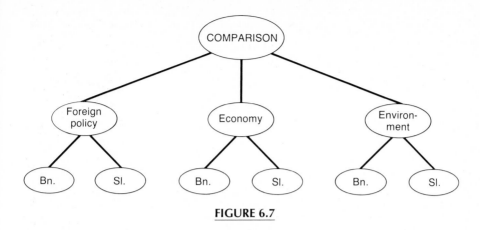

FIGURE 6.7

ronment. Once that's done, you'll turn to a discussion of Vice President Slocum's views on the same three issues and then come to some conclusion.

If you decide, on the other hand, to arrange your paper by issue, you produce the kind of tree in Figure 6.7. In drafting this paper, after writing your introduction, you'd contrast the candidates' views back-to-back first on foreign policy, then on economics, and lastly on the environment. Then you could draw whatever conclusions were warranted.

These are both reasonable options, though they result in quite different papers. Since neither approach is clearly more logical than the other, you'd choose between them on rhetorical grounds. Your choice might depend on several factors: length of your paper, complexity of the issues, degree of real difference between the candidates' views, as well as your goals in writing the paper. Is this a cool, objective, judicial analysis of the two candidates, or are you deliberately campaigning for one over the other? How does that change matters?

YOUR TURN

Project 1

Give some thought—either in your notebook or in class discussion or both—to the factors that might lead you to adopt one of these tree structures over the other for writing a paper on these two candidates.

Which tree would work better in a one-page letter-to-the-editor? Which would work best for a careful 20-page report?

Draw the tree that would be most effective if you were deliberately backing Brown over Slocum. Explain why you drew the tree as you did.

How would you draw your tree if, for example, you wanted to discuss Brown's views on the Middle East, the farm problem, and wildlife preser-

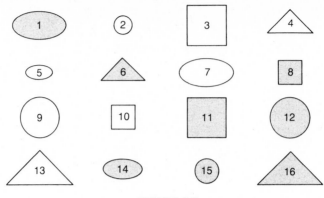

FIGURE 6.8

vation, while discussing Slocum's positions on Central America, urban decay, and nuclear disarmament?

Which structure would work best if you were comparing the candidates on only two issues? What about if you were comparing their positions on six issues? What else might you do in that case?

Project 2

The following exercise requires you to face two of the problems we've discussed in forming coherent trees. The task is to arrange the geometric shapes in Figure 6.8 into a sensible tree formation. To do this, you'll need first to decide how to sort out the shapes, i.e., what kinds of sets you'll gather them into. Group them according to type and then say what each type is; that is, label the categories you're using. (You'll notice immediately that each item fits into several. Most things do.)

Once you've developed your categories, arrange them into the most coherent, sensible, useful tree structure you can. Since it should be readily apparent that a number of trees will work, you might draw at least three, arranged according to different hierarchies.

Compare your own trees with those of others. (For extra credit, calculate how many logically coherent trees could be constructed to handle these items.)

Using Trees to Develop Your Material

Organizational trees can be useful in every phase of the writing process. Early in the development of your material, you can use trees as you would clusters. Once you have any topic, try breaking it down in different ways to get a sense for what you already know about it, where your strengths and

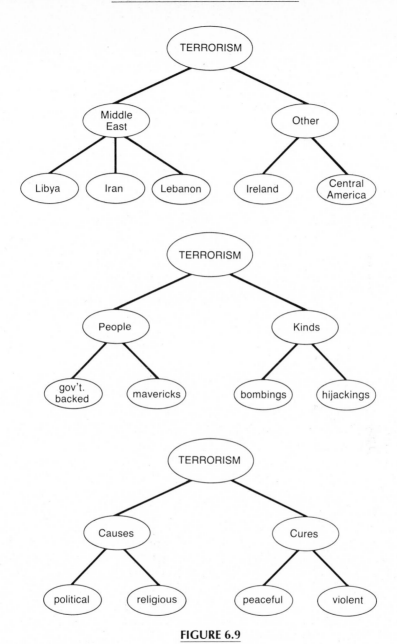

FIGURE 6.9

blindspots lie, and what directions you might take in your research and analysis. You might start by sketching as many trees as you can, branching each one only one or two layers down. In dealing with a topic such as terrorism, you might sketch something like Figure 6.9, just to see how the subject might be approached.

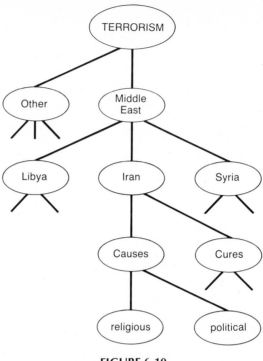

FIGURE 6.10

After sketching a number of small trees, you might try combining these to drive your tree as deep as possible. Combining the first two trees above, you can see how each branch might be elaborated. (For convenience, we've drawn only one branch full length; the others we've drawn out to the margin. You could obviously develop all of the branches to the length of the one we've focused on.)

Once you've developed a tree in this fashion, it becomes a very easy matter to control the breadth and depth of your topic. Almost always when you begin a paper, you define your topic much too broadly; this excessive breadth forces you to write a paper with no particular detail—you produce a "once-over-lightly." Later drafts almost always entail narrowing your topic and developing it in more depth. With a tree such as Figure 6.10, you can do this easily. To narrow your topic, you simply slide down any branch one or more nodes. If the topic of "terrorism" is too broad, slide down to Middle East terrorism. If that's too broad, slide down to Iranian terrorism. Still too broad? Try "Causes of Terrorism in Iran." Narrower still? Try "Religious Factors in Iranian Terrorism." Still too broad? Then you'll want to tree one of your lower nodes out further and see what even more refined question you can formulate.

If it happens that you overshoot the mark and come up with a topic so narrow that you can't find much material on it, the tree again helps. Simply

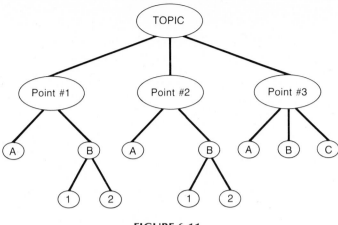

FIGURE 6.11

slide back up a level or grab the next node to either side of the one you're on. "Religious Causes of Iranian Terrorism" too narrow? You have two directions you could go. You could discuss political causes along with religious; or, referring to one of your earlier trees, you could either add another country or focus on religious issues in the entire Middle East.

As you conduct your research, it's worth it every so often to sort out your material according to the trees you've developed. If you do, you'll discover right away which of your subtopics you're ready to develop in detail and which still require more concentrated research.

Drafting from Trees

The primary use of trees is to help you organize your material for drafting. The visual representations trees provide allow you to think more clearly and flexibly about the relationships between different parts of your material. By either breaking down your topic from main ideas, to minor arguments, to details (drawing your trees from the top down) or by combining related items into sets and building those into progressively larger categories (building your tree from the ground up), you prepare a pattern or blueprint for your paper that you can then use to guide your actual drafting.

When you draw a tree, the shape of it can tell you fairly clearly whether it's likely to work or not as a structure for a paper. Consider Figures 6.11 and 6.12. Think for a minute what kind of paper each tree is bound to produce.

The tree in Figure 6.11 seems symmetrical, balanced. If you could turn it into a mobile with thin metal wires and Christmas tree bulbs, it would hang nicely just as it is. A paper written from it would reflect this symmetry. It would fall into three major arguments, all developed in about the same

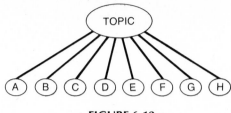

FIGURE 6.12

detail with no rambling or abruptness. Symmetry in the tree makes for clarity in the paper.

Now consider Figure 6.12.

How would you describe this one? Octopoid? The writer has come up with a string of arguments or points or ideas for his topic, but he hasn't worked out any of them in detail. If he were to write his paper in this shape, every paragraph would open a new topic, dropping it after only a sentence or two. If you were reading the paper, you'd be left feeling frustrated, cheated, unsatisfied by all the undeveloped hints and ideas. The lack of any grouping of the units promises a loose, chain-like structure—point 1, point 2, point 3, point 4—with nothing holding them together.

As it happens, there is a valid use for such a structure, and you've heard it a thousand times. "In the news tonight these stories: Congress passes aid package for widows of Swiss submarine captains; President visits Hockey Hall of Fame in Eveleth, Minnesota; Rain and gloom moving into the Seattle area tonight, continuing through 1993; and the Port Aransas Fighting Sandcrabs kicked sand in the face of the Clear Creek Wildcats, 47 to 14, after being beached at halftime. All the details right after this word from. . . ." You'll also find in most newspapers a column of news briefs: a headline and a paragraph or two for each of several minor stories. In both of these cases the "octopoid" structure is appropriate.

By examining the shape of an organizational tree, then, you can predict with some accuracy how the final paper will look. You can see problems in your structure quite clearly before committing them to prose and thereby making them much harder to fix. By cutting, expanding, rearranging, or otherwise revising your tree, you may save yourself a major organizational overhaul once your paper is in draft form.

What you look for in a tree for most nonfiction writing, again, is at least a rough symmetry. It doesn't have to be perfect. You don't always need three major arguments, each with two minor arguments, and each of those supported by three details. Real life is rarely that neat. A paper based on so tidy a pattern might appear pedantic and artificial—and dull as a result. But a moderate symmetry, such as that in Figure 6.11, allows your paper to move along at an even pace and helps your reader comprehend and remember what you've told her.

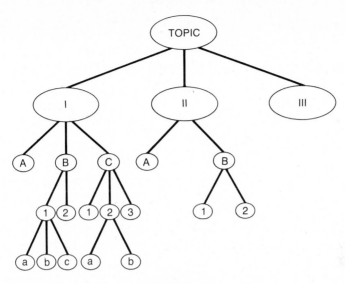

FIGURE 6.13

Using Trees in Revision

Even after the draft is done, trees continue to be of use. By working backward from a written draft to the organization that seems to underlie it, you
can use trees in the structural revision of your paper. Trees allow you to
diagnose problems in organization you might not otherwise be able to see.
It often happens that you'll write a paper (or read one) that just doesn't feel
right. It feels like it's wandering, or dragging, or missing the point, or you
keep feeling as if you're losing the train of the argument. Yet you can't say
for certain where the problem is. Something is out of control, but you can't
form a clear enough perception of the paper as a whole to say what it is.

An organizational structure gone astray shows up vividly if you try to
draw a tree based on the conceptual units of the paper. In the margin of
each paragraph write a word or two noting its topic. If the paragraph is long
or detailed, you might label every sentence or every few sentences. Then
using these labels as your nodes, try to draw the shape of the paper as it
stands. The results will often be revealing (even amusing).

Consider the reconstruction of a student's paper in Figure 6.13. What
sort of paper do you imagine this was, and what might have happened to
the writer to cause it?

When you read the paper, the organization feels lopsided, unbalanced,
out of whack in a particular way. Of the three points being made, the first
one takes up several pages and is rich in supporting detail. The second feels
thinner, though not too bad. The third, however, is entirely too abrupt and
sketchy. You're rolling along on the momentum of the paper's arguments,

157

and suddenly you come to a screeching halt, as if a tire had blown or your boat had run up on a sandbar.

Everyone who's taken essay exams has written this kind of paper. You actually have a lot to say about all three topics, but by the time you reach #3 you have two minutes left to write—and this is what results. On larger papers you might be seduced into this if, after firing off two of your three conceptual cannons, you find you've satisfied the minimum length requirement of the paper, and you don't want to write any further. (There's no real excuse for this, but exhaustion is exhaustion.)

If, when you retree your draft, you discover something like this, you'll definitely want to correct the problem when you revise. Your simplest option in the present case might be to drop branch III entirely, develop branch II a bit more fully (through more brainstorming, interviews, or whatever), and let branches I and II carry the paper by themselves. Or you could even be more radical, cutting away everything except B and C under branch I. That looks like your richest material, after all.

Another option might be to reverse the order of your arguments: start with the short, sketchy branch III; move to II; and finish with the very well-developed and supported branch I. Trotting out your arguments in the order of increasing complexity and power might give your paper a very effective rising momentum. What you finally decide to do will depend, of course, on your purpose, the nature of the assignment, your time limits, the material you have that you didn't include in your first draft, and a host of other factors. In any case, your decision will be better informed and more effective for seeing so clearly the shape of your paper as it stands.

YOUR TURN

Project 1

By now you should be able to glance at a tree and tell several things about it. Look at Figure 6.14 and answer the following questions:

1. What would the draft be like that resulted from this tree? What would the experience of reading the draft be like?
2. How might the writer have written a paper with this particular structure?
3. If you found your own draft had fallen into this pattern, how might you reorganize it during revision?

Project 2

Try reconstructing the organization of some piece of writing. You might tree a draft of your own, an essay in a magazine, the work of a fellow student, or one of the drafts in the back of this book.

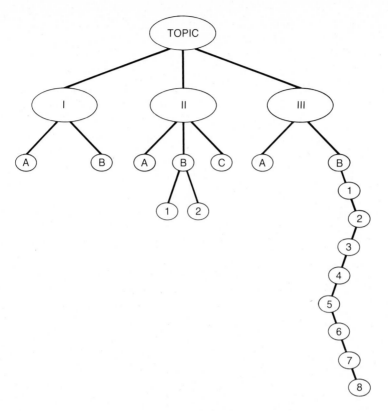

FIGURE 6.14

Then describe your tree. How balanced is it? If it's lopsided, where is it too heavy or too light? How might it be improved?

HOW TO USE WHAT YOU'VE GOT

As you brainstorm for possible directions for your paper, ask yourself why someone would want to read about your research. If you think about your imagined audience's purpose, you may find yourself eliminating some bits and pieces and focusing more sharply on others. Let's say you started out by gathering information on hot-air balloons, perhaps because you've always found them interesting and exciting. Along the way, though, you read some material about the famous Hindenburg disaster. Before you knew it, you were shifting the focus of your research to the early dirigibles and zeppelins created during World War I. Then suddenly you discovered that the Japanese had sent bombs on powered unmanned dirigibles over the United States during World War II, and that one of these had actually exploded in the Northwest. You'd always thought, along with most everyone else, that the United States had never been physically under attack

159

(except during Pearl Harbor) since the time of the Revolution and the Mexican-American war. And soon you were off digging up everything you could about the Japanese balloon bombings.

As you think about your audience, consider the range of information you've collected. Would your readers be more interested in learning everything you've found about hot-air balloons and related devices—a kind of all-purpose history—or would they prefer a focused examination of one topic? Let's say you decide to focus on wartime uses of hot-air balloons. Does that mean that everything you found about weather balloons has to be scrapped—two days in the library? Maybe not. You could, after all, always begin the paper with a kind of overview of hot-air balloons. What if you set the wartime focus against a backdrop of hot-air balloons as wonderfully peaceful devices? But they're not just peaceful because they're used for peaceful purposes, such as gathering weather information, but also because they're peaceful to ride: in between the blasts of propane, you hear nothing but the wind, and you view the beautiful world below from a little hanging basket in the air. Then . . . presto! The article in *Sports Illustrated* comes to mind, the one in which the three balloonists who flew across the Atlantic talk about their personal feelings while floating above the sea.

The kind of thinking illustrated in this "organizational" brainstorming came from thinking about the who and why of your writing—questions you may have considerable latitude with in some open-ended writing assignments. Just as easily, however, the process can work in reverse. In reviewing your research material, you might discover a different reason for writing and even a different imagined audience.

Using Sources while Drafting

While writing, many people focus on the new material they've gathered, instead of on what they want to say in the paper and how they plan to document or illustrate it with their research. Again, writing papers in which you incorporate outside sources is not a matter of collecting information and then arranging it in the paper, like setting the table for dinner. It's more like cooking the dinner: you have to decide what you want to do with the ingredients you've collected. In this case, though, there's no recipe to tell you how much of what to put in. Instead, you're creating the recipe as you go along, sampling the stew every once in a while to see if it tastes the way you want it to. You may have some goals—giving it a full-bodied, herby flavor by using oregano and sweet basil—but you must be open to new surprises, new discoveries as you go along. And, above all, the creation is yours—not a random collection of ingredients, but a carefully planned and tested dish.

How much of your source material should you eventually use? The most frustrating source papers to read are those in which the writer has merely strung together a collection of quotations like a line of Christmas tree bulbs. Because there's often no point, no direction for these quotations, the paper reads like it was spat out by an unsophisticated computer with a "quote and print" program. Here's an example of what this "program" does:

A Study of Pearls

According to a recent survey, six out of ten people find pearls attractive on women.[1] Johnson notes that pearls have been around for centuries.[2] In comparing the difference between natural and man-made pearls, Smith found that natural pearls have a certain sheen that cannot be reproduced synthetically.[3] According to Robertson, the pearl industry has seen a recent growth by as much as 15 percent over the past six years.[4] The earliest mention of pearls in the *Oxford English Dictionary* is 1450.[5] Cummings, in his book on the natural formation of pearl, says that some oysters. . . . (And on and on and on, ad nauseam).

To avoid falling into this pattern, constantly keep in mind that the goal of including the source material is to document or illustrate your own conclusions.

The decision how and when to use your source material depends, again, on you and your audience—on why you're writing your paper, and why "they" are reading it. If, for example, your main purpose is to show your reader why it's profitable to invest in pearls at the present time, ask yourself what specific information will help document that. In the few lines on pearls above, for example, much of the research that's cited won't help inform people about investing in pearls—so scrap it. Sometimes you can make the research fit the purpose, and that can lead you along some interesting paths. The information about people's attitudes toward pearls, for example, could be used to show that the value of pearls is mainly in the eye of the consumer, and if consumers are big on pearls at the moment, it will mean a higher demand and a greater return on your reader's investment.

But don't try to make irrelevant information fit just because you've gathered it. You may be tempted to cite everything you've collected—just because you put in the time to get it and because you think that lots of citations look impressive. Resist that temptation: use a critical eye when evaluating whether any of your sources fit your developing purposes. Start from purpose and work your way back through the sources, rather than the reverse.

Quoting, Paraphrasing, and Summarizing

When you've decided to use a source in your paper, you have to make an important decision: how you'll incorporate it into your own writing. If just drafting sentences of your own is hard enough, now you must lead your way into someone else's ideas or someone else's language. But first let's define these three options.

Quoting.   When you quote someone, you use his or her exact words. And we do mean exact. Let's say you're writing about an interview with Shardun, a woman who wrestles with huge lions as part of a circus act, and one of her statements on your tape recorder is, "Well, only, um, only one time did I get hurt, see, and that was when Robby—he's our biggest lion, the one you see there thrashing around in his cage—when Robby swiped at me while I was bowing to the crowd, and caught me right on the fanny, ha ha ha, and over I went and the crowd they thought it was hilarious, see, but meanwhile I'd got a pretty bad gash back there and had to have some stitches." If you quote Shardun, you should use her exact words, although you can, if you wish, edit out the "ums" and the laughs and coughs and other bits and pieces not directly related to her words.

You should quote as exactly as possible to protect your interviewee (or the writer of your source) by not misrepresenting them. This is especially important for written sources, since the writing won't include the "ums" and coughs that speech will. With this principle in mind, you can see now why we stressed the importance of working carefully with your source materials before you begin drafting: if you transcribed the words of Susan Smith from an article she wrote on firefighting in the Northwest as, "Forest fires decreased by 26 percent over the five years before Oregon set up the Firefighters Cooperative," and she had actually written "increased," you're in trouble, particularly if you've built a whole point or paragraph around that information.

There's another point to be made about the Shardun quotation above. The main reason why you'll want to quote someone directly (whether it's their speech or their written words) is because the language of the quote is revealing, or beautiful, or well phrased. You might find, however, that Shardun's language isn't any of these. In this case, you'll want to use some other method for presenting her memories or ideas. (We'll mention two other methods in a moment.)

If you do quote one of your sources directly, you'll want to prepare your reader for the quotation rather than just dumping it into your paper and expecting your reader to figure out why it's there. Remember: the quotation is evidence, illustration, proof. Handle it as such.

Think how a lawyer handles evidence to prove her case in a courtroom. She would hardly just toss a revolver onto a table and cry: "Proof that the accused is guilty!" No one would know what she was talking about. Instead, she'd preface her introduction of the evidence with something like:

> As we have maintained, the accused entered the victim's store at
> approximately midnight, fired the fatal shots, and fled. At 12:15, Captain
> Hanson reached the scene, found the body, and also discovered this. (Here she
> lays the gun on the table.) The ballistics report concludes that the bullets in the
> victim's body were shot from this revolver. The lab then took fingerprints from
> the gun and matched them to those of the suspect's on file. (Here she sets
> blowups of both sets of prints on an easel.) As you can see, and as the
> fingerprint expert, Dr. Helms, has testified, the prints on the gun exactly match

those of the accused, proving that it was this man (pointing to accused) who fired the shots that ended the life of Sycamore Q. Farnsworth.

You see the pattern. You tell your jury (the reader) what point you're making; then you place your evidence (the quotation) on the table (your text); and then, as a rule, you follow it up with some comment demonstrating its relevance or tying it into the concerns of your paper. This final comment isn't always necessary—sometimes your quoted material supports your point so plainly that nothing further need be said—but in case of doubt, make the relevance explicit. Here's an example of how this might be done by someone writing a paper on the novel *Pride and Prejudice*:

> Jane Austen's novel *Pride and Prejudice* tells the story of a family in the early 1800s with five single daughters, all in search of husbands. Though Austen sympathizes with the plight of the family, her novel is comic rather than serious. She finds the man-hunting funny. Austen sets the subject and tone of her novel in her first sentence: "It is a truth universally acknowledged that a single man in possession of a good fortune must be in want of a wife." The tone of the sentence is deliberately formal, pedantic, "school-teacherly," although what it says is obviously wrong; single, rich men aren't all looking for wives. In fact, as the first chapter shows, it is the young women in the novel (and especially their scheming mothers) who are "in want of" a husband. Austen thus lets the reader know what to expect of her work—a comedy about courtship and marriage, all of which looks rather silly to the detached, ironic storyteller.

Again, the same pattern:

You state your claim ["Austen sets the subject. . . . "];
you present the evidence "'It is a truth. . . . '"];
and you show how the evidence supports or illustrates your claim ["Austen thus lets. . . ."].

Showing What's Borrowed. When you use quotations, your reader will want to know exactly which words are yours and which you've quoted from someone else. This isn't just polite or convenient, either; it's legally mandatory. The failure to distinguish your source's words from your own is plagiarism—a serious offense, and one you certainly don't want to stumble into through carelessness. (In other words, listen up!)

In Chapter Four, we discussed matters of grammar and punctuation as "conventions," as agreed-upon ways to communicate in prose. For quoting the words of others, there are also two main conventions. For short quotations, three lines or less, you place quotation marks around the borrowed words but leave them within the body of your paragraph. This is the way the writer of the Jane Austen paper handled her material.

For a longer quotation, you separate it into a paragraph of its own; but unlike the rest of your text, you indent every line, moving the whole left margin in a bit. If you're typing and double-spacing your paper, the quoted material should be indented and single-spaced. The whole paragraph, with the longer quotation included, should look something like page 164.

Dr. Soniksen has long been an advocate of the legal recognition of so-called Living Wills. Such documents express the desire of a patient to have further life-support systems turned off or removed at the point his or her medical condition becomes hopeless. The will says, in effect, if my condition is terminal and if I'm no longer aware of things around me, I want the heart-lung machine (or other support machinery) removed. Dr. Soniksen defends his patients' right to refuse treatment on these grounds:

> Life cannot be adequately defined purely in biological terms. In the absence of consciousness and any future hope thereof, a body with an operating heart and lungs is rather an "animate corpse" than a live human being in any meaningful sense.[1]

Though, as a medical researcher, life may for Dr. Soniksen be a matter of biochemical processes, as a physician, it's the patient's personality, the patient's very consciousness that's important. A patient who is comatose and will never regain consciousness is, in these terms, already deceased, and keeping the "animate corpse" going on a heart-lung machine becomes pointless.

Pointing out to your reader by one of these conventions which words are borrowed is a necessary part of your job, but not all of it. You're also obliged to let your reader know exactly where your material came from (often called "documenting your sources"). Somewhere you need to give an exact reference—author, title, publication, date, issue, and page for periodicals; author, title, publisher, city, state, date, and page for books—of anything you quote. Since it would clutter up your paper intolerably if you gave all this information with the quotation itself, a number of neater, more sensible systems have been developed.

The whole purpose of the various footnoting schemes is to inform your reader of what secondary source each quoted passage comes from. The raised number at the end of the quoted passage tells the reader: "These words, facts, or ideas are not really my own. I borrowed them. If you want to find the original source, match this number with the one at the bottom of the page or at the end of my paper, and I'll tell you all you'll need to know." Again, making this information available to your reader isn't just politeness or fairness; it's the law.

Many are the systems of documentation. The Modern Language Association has an "old MLA format" and a "new MLA format"; the American Psychological Association has its own "APA format"; medical personnel have another; lawyers yet another; and so on. The fine points of each, furthermore, take usually dozens of pages to describe. Your best option may be to decide on the basis of either your paper topic or your major field of study which system to follow. Otherwise, ask your instructor to choose one. Then get a printed guide to the system and follow it exactly.

Paraphrasing. A useful way of incorporating someone's words into your text without actually quoting them directly is called paraphrasing. A good paraphrase translates the author's ideas into your own words. The best strategy for doing this is to read the author's statement once, trying to understand its main point. Then, without looking at the original text, draft in your own words what the author said. Finally, double-check to make sure you captured the author's **meaning** while avoiding her **language.** Try as much as you can to keep your paraphrase consistent with your own style; don't be influenced by the style of the text you're paraphrasing.

To give you a sense for how this works, consider the following direct quotation from a technical article:

With the advent of computer technology, many secondary school teachers began to undergo ideological shifts concerning their assumptions about cognitive development. Instead of adhering to the teacher-centered model of learning, which vests the teachers with the power and authority relative to their knowledge, many educators began to develop curricular materials based on a student-centered theory of development.

If you're writing a paper to a general audience on the effect of computers on education, you might want to use this idea; but because the language of your paper is likely to be less academic, you'll want to avoid sticking too closely to the original language in your paraphrase. Using the method we've suggested, you might write this paraphrase of the author's main idea: "After computers came into the schools, many teachers began to rethink their ideas about how children best learn. Instead of assuming that they were always responsible for their students' learning, they saw ways to encourage students to learn on their own."

This paraphrase makes good use of the original text: it's true to the author's meaning, it's clearly and tersely written, it captures most of the ideas in the original, and it uses a language more appropriate to the paper.

Occasionally you may find that you want to let some of your source's language creep into your paragraph. Let's say you decide to paraphrase Shardun instead of quoting her directly. You like her anecdote about being hurt by the lion, so you weave that into your draft:

> Although Shardun feels secure that the lions she wrestles won't turn on her during a performance, she hasn't escaped completely unscathed from her many bouts with the huge creatures. Once, when she was taking a bow for the crowd, the largest of the circus lions swiped at her, gashing her fanny and sending her to the hospital for stitches.

Now, if you've drafted this paraphrase, you might find that the word "fanny" seems stylistically awkward, even a bit silly. How do you get around the problem? Use "buttocks" or "derriere"? Since those options are hardly any better, you might in this case lift part of Shardun's actual statement and splice it into your paraphrase:

> Although Shardun feels secure that the lions she wrestles won't turn on her during a performance, she hasn't escaped completely unscathed from her many bouts with the huge creatures. Once, when she was taking a bow for the crowd, the largest of the circus lions swiped at her, gashing her "right on the fanny," and sending her to the hospital for stitches.

Get to know your sources well. Then, as you're drafting, you don't even need to look at them; you know that Smith said such-and-such, so you can write his ideas down in your own words. Then, in working your way back through your draft, you might check each of the references against your source material and decide if you want to quote it directly, or if your paraphrase is accurate, or if there's anything else you might want to include from the source.

Summary. A third way of incorporating your sources into your text is through summary. When you summarize something, you boil it down so that you're arriving at its essence or main ideas. Including summaries of source material is easy if you've already written summaries as you did your research.

Summaries can also be used across sources. Let's say you've done three interviews with circus performers, all of whom report getting injuries at some point because of their work. In that case, you could summarize all three of your interviews as follows:

> Although most circus performers love their work, they are aware that it entails certain risks. During interviews with three members of the Bam-Bam Traveling Circus, for example, I learned that they had all been injured severely enough while performing to send them to the hospital.

Usually, your writing will contain a combination of summary, paraphrase, and direct quotation. These three methods should always be seen as ways to incorporate your sources within the larger context of the points you are trying to make in your paper. Above all, don't let your research take over your ideas. Think hard about the overall significance and meaning of your paper, and the data will fall into place naturally.

YOUR TURN

As an exercise in gathering and incorporating source material into your writing, go to the library or some other place where you can get written information, and obtain a single source. Then think up a purpose and an audience for a piece of writing no longer than two pages. As you draft your minipaper, try to incorporate something from your source material into the paper using 1) direct quotation, 2) paraphrase, 3) summary, and 4) a combination of these methods.

When you've finished, think of a way that your minipaper could become part of a larger research project, assuming you'd have more source material on the topic. What you've now demonstrated is a useful strategy for building a paper: creating subsections, one at a time, and then working them together using appropriate transitions.

Part 3

THE WRITING SITUATION

In Part 1, we devoted most of our attention to the **process** of writing. We used the narrative to illustrate this process because writing a narrative is relatively familiar to you and because it could be written for people in your immediate context: your teacher and classmates. In Part 2 we widened this "immediate context" to consider the kind of writing most often found in academic settings. Although there's a great deal of variety in what we might call "academic writing," from book reviews to legal briefs to news writing to lab reports to analyses of art objects, many introductory and intermediate college courses require papers in which you synthesize a body of research and present it for an educated audience.

In Part 3 we want to widen the circle a bit more by considering two concepts fundamental to all writing, within college and beyond; these are the concepts of **purpose** and **audience.** But because we don't want to privilege a single "type" of writing or context (such as corporate or business writing), we'll be discussing purpose and audience somewhat generally, without as much "hands-on" practice as you've found in Parts 1 and 2. Much of that practice will be up to you to supply, using some of our strategies and suggestions and perspectives, as you work through writing tasks you're already engaged in or as you complete the deep cases in the Appendix.

As you'll see in the next two chapters, purpose and audience are complex and multifaceted issues, partly because they're never the same in any two pieces of writing. But fundamentally, they boil down to these two essential questions: **why** are you writing, and **whom** are you writing to.

Before launching into the first of these concepts, though, we want to explain why we've chosen to focus on them, so that the goals of Part 3 will be clear to you from the start.

The Writing Situation: Purpose, Audience, and Text

Everything you write—from this week's grocery list to your last will and testament—exists in some sort of situation, some **context** that gives it meaning. Take your narrative paper, for example. The situation for that paper was an academic one: you were writing in response to an assignment, for teachers and other students, as a way to practice the writing process. If you were writing a narrative for the *New Yorker,* on the other hand, your situation would be quite different. You'd be writing not for an assignment (unless the *New Yorker* commissioned you to do something for them) but for your own purposes (to become famous, to make money, to have your fiction read by thousands, etc.). Your content might be influenced by your knowledge of what the readers (and editors) of the *New Yorker* like in narratives. You probably wouldn't, for example, send them a crazy, pulp-magazine-type science fiction story, just as in your class you probably wouldn't turn in a graphic account of your first sexual experience as your narrative paper.

Furthermore, with your *New Yorker* piece, you wouldn't have the same sense of your audience's immediate presence as you had with your narrative paper. With your narrative paper, you knew exactly who would be reading it: Carlos, that biology wizard from Amarillo in your group, or Stephanie, who got that medal in gymnastics. You could even predict where it would be read: in your classroom or the library or the local hamburger shop. When you're writing for the *New Yorker,* on the other hand, your sense of audience is necessarily more vague and ill-defined. Where do your readers live? Well, sort of all over. Who are they? Mostly white, mostly middle class, mostly college-educated—but still, that hardly gives you any concrete, personal sense of them. Your "reader" is little more than a statistic—a shadowy "average" or "typical" reader, not someone you're liable to bump into up in the stacks.

By the "writing situation," then, we're referring to a combination of features in your writing environment—an environment which is not always "surrounding" you physically, but which nevertheless influences your writing mentally. Two features of this writing situation are its "why-ness" and its "who-ness," or its purpose and its audience. When you see how many of the important decisions you have to make as you write and revise come from these two concerns, you will begin to understand how important they are to becoming a really successful writer.

But so far, we've been talking pretty abstractly. To illustrate, let's see how purpose and audience influence the **texts** of two pieces of writing (two memos) produced in two different situations. The first is a short note written from one business executive to another in a large corporation:

Bill—
Just spoke with the people at Collins about the recall on the diffs w/the design flaw. Nothing to report as yet. Some media hype, of

course. Watson to give me a run-down when he returns from Pitt tomorrow. Meantime, hold tight. See you at the BD meeting.

—Cliff

As you glance through this memo, notice some of its textual characteristics. It's economical—so economical, in fact, that some of the sentences aren't even complete, making it read like a telegram (perhaps "w/the" means "with the"?). It seems very casual, like a phone conversation. It uses undefined terms that assume some prior knowledge (what's Collins? who's Watson? what's the BD meeting? what's a diff? what's Pitt?). And so it's hard (at least for us) to understand. We can only guess at its purpose. It seems to be saying, "Everything is status quo; I'm just letting you know that I'm still working on the problem."

By getting some information about the memo's situation, though, we can begin to explain some of these textual characteristics. First, Cliff and Bill work together and know each other, which explains the relaxed, familiar tone of the memo. Because they work together, they have lots of shared knowledge, which is why Cliff didn't have to explain things like "BD meeting" (they both know that this is an abbreviation for "Board of Directors"), or "diff" (differential), or "Pitt" (Pittsburgh). Cliff is a little worried, though, that Bill is making important decisions without his consent or knowledge, and the two men are also a little competitive. In this case, Cliff doesn't want Bill to do anything yet concerning a problem with a machine part that another company manufactures for them. His purpose for the memo, then, is partly to let Bill know that he's got things under control. That way, Bill might be influenced not to make decisions about the matter without Cliff's knowledge—or get any credit for resolving the problem, either! And so the text of the memo is different from what it might be if the two men weren't competing, or if Cliff weren't worried about Bill's one-upmanship. In that case, Cliff might not have said anything about Watson's reporting to **him** the next day. Complicated, no?

With just these tidbits of information about the context of the memo, you can see why Cliff made certain important decisions in his text. He based these decisions on his purpose (keep Bill from doing anything at this point) and his audience (Bill, a close but dangerously competitive colleague).

Now look at a second memo:

Dear Cardholder:
It has come to the Credit Office's attention that payment of your last statement is now overdue. If payment has already been made, please ignore this reminder and accept our apologies. If payment has not been made, please do so immediately to avoid collections procedures. Thank you.

Shamrock Department Store

Once again, look closely at the text itself. The language is more formal than the first memo. There's not much ambiguity; everything makes good sense to us as readers. It sounds a bit more "mechanical" than the first memo, as if it were written by a machine rather than a live, breathing human. And it avoids personal pronouns ("the Credit Office" instead of "our"; "if payment has been made" instead of "if you have paid your bill").

Like the first memo, the specific characteristics of this text can be explained by thinking carefully about its situation. First, consider its audience. Unlike the first memo, this one has many potential readers—people who hold credit cards at Shamrock Department Store and haven't paid their bills on time. The obvious purpose is to get these readers to pay their bills. Why not just say, then, "Pay your bill, or else"? Well, partly because although the readers are "delinquent," they're also clients. If you're a store owner, you want to be firm but diplomatic, so that you don't alienate sensitive customers and lose their business. And you want your language to sound professional, even a little clinical, so that the reader is reminded that this could become a legal matter.

All of this is true at Shamrock—and more, too. The manager has told the Credit Office to be less dictatorial about reminding customers to pay their bills, because last year the Credit Office mistakenly sent over a hundred reminders out to people who had always paid their bills on time. The reminders were very blunt, and many customers complained. So the Credit Department, in revising its reminder notice, became more abstract to avoid sounding accusatory. Furthermore, the old memo had used "we" instead of "The Credit Office," which had the unhappy result that lots of card holders with questions about the reminders called the wrong department. By saying "The Credit Office," there was no more question about whom to call. The purpose and audience of the memo, then, explain why the writer made these specific textual decisions.

Another way to understand the importance of purpose and audience is to consider a writing situation first, and then to look at a text that is clearly inappropriate for that situation. Imagine, for example, that Susanne, an account executive, has flown to Atlanta recently on a major airline. During the flight, Susanne noticed that the flight attendants seemed short-tempered and tired, rarely smiling, going through the flight preparation routines in a brusque manner, becoming impatient when passengers asked for assistance, and seeming almost rude in their actions as they served the drinks and snacks. Susanne had paid a lot for the airline ticket and so decides to write a letter to the airline. Here's her letter:

> Dear Pilot of Flight 308:
> I'm telling everyone I know what a lousy time I had on Flight 308. It's without conscience to run an airline in this manner.
>
> > Disgruntled Passenger

It doesn't take any special expertise as a writer or reader to see that the text of this letter has serious problems! And chances are that if you explain why, you'll find yourself referring to its purpose and audience. We'll let you explain why Susanne has missed the mark here, but to help you out, here are some questions:

1. What might be Susanne's purpose for writing the letter? Is that purpose realized in the memo? Why not?
2. Who should be Susanne's audience? Why? What would happen if the pilot read her memo? Would that help the purpose of Susanne's memo? Why not?
3. How can Susanne improve her text by thinking more carefully about her purpose and audience? What specific textual decisions would she make if she thought more carefully about these?

After answering these questions, you could probably do a better job of writing this memo without even having been on Flight 308! Go ahead and try in your writer's notebook. As you do so, try jotting down some notes about the important textual decisions you make and how your analysis of your purpose and audience affected these.

One final word about purpose, audience, and text. Clearly, all three aspects of writing are intertwined, as our examples have shown. You can't really talk about how to create a piece of writing without talking about why you're doing it and whom you're doing it for (or whom you're trying to affect in some way). But just as we analyzed separate parts of a simultaneous process in Part 1, we think it's a good idea to look closely, one at a time, at the concepts of purpose and audience that make up your writing situation. As you work through the chapters in Part 3, try to integrate your new thoughts about purpose and audience into the writing you're doing. And remember that these thoughts can enter into any part of the writing process, from early planning to final revising and editing.

Chapter Seven

WHY ARE YOU WRITING? ANALYZING YOUR PURPOSE

SOME THOUGHTS ABOUT PURPOSE

As we pointed out in the Introduction, when many people imagine a "writer," what usually comes to mind is the professional literary person, someone whose picture might appear in the *New York Times Book Review,* someone who has that special "gift" or "knack" of producing page after page of beautiful or interesting or entertaining prose. That impression exists because we often associate good writing with the purpose of creating something very large or artistic—a monumental novel or a volume of great poetry. These artistic purposes for writing, of course, have led to some of the highest expressions of written language—in the same way that the purpose of much great architecture has been to create the most beautiful or esthetically interesting buildings out of available materials.

But let's face it. A lot of the world's writing isn't very monumental or lasting. Like useful, functional dwellings, it serves its purpose in carrying on the world's affairs at a particular moment in time. It tells people about things. It requests action. It documents agreements and sets down resolutions. Future generations might study what remains of this writing, perhaps as a way to understand history. And, of course, much writing never intended to be historically important has, in fact, become so: the loose, unstructured journal entries of Charles Darwin, Anne Frank's diary, Martin Luther King's "Letter From the Birmingham Jail," or the newspaper stories of Woodward and Bernstein that played a major role in the Watergate scandal of the 1970s. All these seemingly "temporary" writings have become important historical documents, fueling further thinking, reading, writing, and new knowledge.

But you shouldn't be deceived into thinking that good writing must always have the lofty purpose of making artistic or cultural history. The truth is that a staggering amount of ordinary routine writing in a great variety of forms is created every day by the government, industry, the news media, public services, and academic institutions—in fact anywhere people are carrying on scholarly, business, and scientific activities and sharing them with others. And each separate piece of writing, from the three-line memo by an executive in a busy corporation to the 200-page government document reporting the results of a research study on bicycle safety, has its own general and specific purposes. So varied are the purposes for writing, in·fact, that they could be compared with the purposes for any human behavior. Name a human activity, and it's probably embodied in one form or another in writing. Ordering. Confessing. Marrying. Damning. Expressing love. Attacking. Denying. Greeting. Deceiving. Learning and discovering. Protesting. Singing. And teaching.

But "purpose" is a tricky concept—tricky because it's often discussed abstractly, in a way that may not be very useful when it comes to actually writing something. Being told to "have a clearly defined purpose for your essay," for example, probably doesn't give you much direction in discovering what your purpose is. Or saying "my purpose is to convince my reader" probably doesn't help you to think very fully about what it means to "convince" someone of something or of how you'll go about doing it.

In this chapter, we want to explore the concept of purpose in writing. But we won't be giving you hard and fast rules about purpose. That's because, as we've shown you in Part 1, the writing process involves asking

ing yourself lots of questions and coming up with tentative answers. The last thing we'd want to do is to try to give you an exact prescription for achieving all the specific purposes you have for your writing. To begin with, it's a process that can't be done separately from the writing task. In addition, no set of formal rules can cover every situation. What we can do is to show you some strategies for thinking about your purposes—and how best to accomplish them through your writing.

Because each purpose for writing is different, the writing that accomplishes each purpose will have to be different as well. When we use the term "purpose," then, we're referring not to a set of easily remembered rules or a formula for what your writing should do, but to some ways of thinking about, even **discovering,** your general and specific goals for writing. We'll provide you lots of maps, but the exploration is up to you.

YOUR TURN

In your writer's notebook, spend a few minutes thinking about the various purposes you've had for writing in the past. Why were you writing? What were you trying to accomplish?

Now think more fully about each purpose you've identified. If you wrote "doing an assignment" or "getting a good grade in a course," try to think of some more specific purposes. Were you trying to "sell yourself" or your intelligence to a teacher? If you wrote "writing on the staff of the high school yearbook," what were some purposes you remember thinking about: trying to be "neutral" so that no group of students would feel left out? Trying to entertain your readers? Trying to give as full or representative a picture as possible of the school, its teachers, and the class?

If necessary, dig up some old writing you've done and use that for your analysis.

Modes, Patterns, and Purpose

Writing is sometimes divided into certain kinds or forms that are thought to be related to writers' purposes. You're probably familiar with the terms "description," "narration," "exposition," and "argumentation." Descriptive writing tries to portray something seen or heard or otherwise experienced as accurately as possible. Narration, the form you practiced in Part 1, tries to tell a story; it's one purpose of novels and personal anecdotes. Exposition is mainly informative; it tries to present facts and details objectively or discuss ideas in a reasoned, balanced way. An argument tries to sway the reader's opinion, make a point, or support a position.

You may also be familiar with, or even have practiced, the "patterns" often used in writing: comparison/contrast, cause/effect, process analysis, definition, and so on. These patterns are often treated as if they're essentially the same as your purpose: to compare and contrast two things (or people or approaches or ideas); to define a concept; to show how something works.

Although it can be useful to practice these patterns and modes as purposes in and of themselves, in reality writing doesn't work so simply or mechanically. It would be very strange for you to sit down and think, "Now I'm going to write a description of my car," or "I think I'll compare and contrast my cat and my dog." Instead, you might draft a description of your car because you're selling it and you want to make a poster to hang up somewhere; or you might have just gotten your first cat and you're writing a letter to a friend, comparing the cat's behavior with your dog's.

Similarly, your purpose in writing a narrative in Part 1 was partly to analyze your own writing process, partly to practice some new strategies we introduced to you, partly to explore one of your personal memories or experiences more fully, and partly to inform or entertain members of your class. Your purpose wasn't **just** to write a narrative anymore than walking is **just** walking, and not to try to get somewhere or lose weight or enjoy a sunny afternoon. Essentially, the patterns and modes are the *whats* of writing—its various forms and characteristics. But purpose is a term that relates to the *whys* of writing—the goals you want your writing to accomplish.

Patterns and modes also overlap in most writing. Imagine, for example, that you've had a little fender-bender and your insurance company has asked that you send them a brief account of the accident. You'd certainly want to use some description. You might narrate the whole event from start to finish from your own point of view. You could also find yourself comparing your account with the account the other driver insisted on at the scene. You'd probably want to argue your own position, while trying to seem objective. And you might inform your readers about certain key points relevant to the accident: the road conditions, the fact that the traffic light was broken or that a dog ran in front of your car.

In working on your response to the insurance company, you'd probably find some of these strategies more important or relevant than others, but they'd all be equally possible as you drafted and revised your writing. Modes and patterns like description, cause and effect, and argument are, then, not ends in themselves; they're forms of writing used **in the service of** some larger purpose. Writers are generally unaware of the modes and patterns as they write; they use the patterns naturally to accomplish the purposes that do stand out consciously as goals to be met through writing.

Because the modes and patterns aren't actual purposes for writing and because they're most often used unconsciously during the writing process, we're not going to spend any time discussing them in this chapter. Instead, we want to explore the concept of purpose from a more realistic, goal-directed point of view. We also want to help you to use the concept of purpose to make decisions and choices as you plan, draft, and revise your writing.

YOUR TURN

Briefly examine the following excerpt from the monthly newsletter of a national club's local chapter.

> When I reached the old Frazer farm, I was greeted by Polly Frazer, a pleasant woman, the daughter of the late Sam Frazer himself. She soon showed me what I had come to see: the Model T Ford in the dilapidated barn behind the farmhouse.
>
> Wading our way through the cobwebs at the barn door, we soon reached the car. According to Polly, it had sat there, untouched, for nearly 50 years, the last will and testament of old Sam, forgotten now in the wake of his death some years ago. Polly herself had had no interest in the car; she had never learned to drive, and, in an odd twist of heredity, she had shunned all things mechanical.
>
> With a piece of rag I found by the door of the barn, I began wiping the dust from the fender of the Model T. Slowly, like a photograph emerging from developing fluid, the gleaming black splendor of the car appeared, and soon, as if bringing back something from the dead, I had revived the front of the car: the fenders, curling over the wooden-spoked wheels; the eye-like headlamps; the front hood, receding back to the glimmering windshield.
>
> To make a long story short, I had discovered there a car which, by any standards, is as perfect as that day so many years ago when it rolled off the Ford assembly line and made its way, by train, no doubt, to Simsville and to the garage of Sam Frazer.
>
> Under the circumstances, I think that we should buy the car immediately. Polly's asking price is high—but there's absolutely nothing that we need to do by way of restoration. And, because everything is intact, it is truly authentic, and should take many medals for our chapter in the annual antique car show.
>
> We would like to urge members of the Simsville Chapter of the Whelks Club to pledge as much as they can to purchase this marvelous automobile, which will then become the property of the Chapter and its members, for use in parades, shows, and a host of other Whelks Club activities.
>
> If you would like to see a picture of the car, I have placed a Polaroid on the bulletin board outside the club dining room at the West entrance.
>
> Thank you, fellow members, for your support.
>
> Ronald Thurston
Member, Whelks Club

Now consider the range of purposes Mr. Thurston may have been trying to accomplish in writing this piece. Why would he have spent so much time describing the car in such high-sounding language? Can you imagine alternative ways he could have tried to achieve his purpose? Try drafting a few lines of such alternative material or sketch out a plan for it.

Deciding What to Say

At the end of the last section, we said we'd be presenting some alternative ways to think about—and use—the concept of "purpose" in your writing.

To begin, let's consider the spoken language. Think of the last time you tried to summarize the plot of a movie. "Summary" is often used as a label for a particular kind of writing or speaking, as if it were a purpose in and of itself. Now, on the surface, just summarizing a movie for someone may seem like an easy task: all you do is open your mouth and tell him what happens in the film. But speaking to someone is not as simple as doing something by formula, which is often what comes to mind when we think of a summary. No one "summarizes" in a vacuum.

Let's assume you're about to summarize a movie during a casual conversation with a friend. Consider some of the questions you'll need to answer quickly and unconsciously as you decide what to say: 1) Should you make judgments about how good the movie was, or how you felt after seeing it? 2) What should you select to tell—should you describe the characters, the plot, the scenes, the camerawork? 3) Which specific details will you focus on? 4) Should you provide information beyond the film itself—who directed it, who acted in it, where it's playing, how much it costs, how long it is, what the radio or newspaper or TV reviewers are saying about it? 5) How much will you tell—was there a surprise ending you wouldn't want to ruin for your listener? And who **is** your listener? (You'd probably make different choices in your selection of details if you were summarizing a bloody, gory movie for a retired minister than if you were summarizing it for a friend who's crazy about high-tech special effects!)

Seems hard, doesn't it? Yet we make these and many other very sophisticated decisions almost effortlessly whenever we tell someone about a movie or a performance we've seen. If we didn't need to, then saying anything at all would be fine: "Then I got some popcorn. Then Robert Redford drove away in his Maserati. Then the person behind me kicked my seat. Then someone whispered. The camerawork was really outstanding. The film was shot on location in Sicily. The film was badly scratched."

What allows us to make these sophisticated decisions? First, of course, we follow certain obvious rules of communication—no one wants to know that we went to get popcorn, unless it explains a gap in our knowledge of the film or is related in some way to the movie experience. Beyond these rules, however, we make more fine-tuned decisions for our "summary" because underlying the simple purpose of summarizing something are more specific purposes, both our own and our listeners': convincing them to see the movie, giving them information about it, keeping a conversation going, showing that we're "up" on the movie scene, revealing aspects of our personality.

Thinking of summarizing very generally, without thinking of specific reasons for summarizing, is what leads many people to assume there's such a thing as **a** summary paper. But any piece of writing whose purpose is to summarize also has more specific underlying purposes influenced by its context. These underlying purposes allow us to make many of our important decisions about what to tell and how to tell it.

To illustrate, let's take the movie example a little further. Let's say you're talking to a friend who's been having some family problems; her parents have been making her feel depressed, always criticizing her career choice, making her feel guilty because she doesn't visit them enough, bugging her about one thing or another. The movie you've seen is about a character who faces a similar problem, and you think it could help your friend to gain some new perspectives on her own life. In summarizing the movie for her, you might be trying to convince her to go see it, in the hope that she'd be consoled or enlightened about her own situation. You are, in other words, using what looks like a "summarizing" purpose to accomplish a "convincing" or "advising" purpose:

> You know, Sharon, I saw this really interesting movie the other day, called *It's My Life*. It's all about this guy whose parents kick him out because he sits around and plays the guitar all the time and doesn't help out enough in the bakery that they own. Then he joins a band and his father almost goes insane over it; they have this huge fight, and the father takes a golf club and smashes the headlights and fender of the guy's Camaro, and he starts living in the woods in this shack, playing his guitar in the high school gym at night, breaking in after the janitors leave. But then after a year or so the band starts to get really famous, and from then on it's all uphill. He gets super rich and the last scene is great—he goes into the bakery in disguise and buys everything in the place, like five hundred donuts and a hundred loaves of bread and all these cakes and everything, with a thousand dollar bill. And then he takes his shades off and all, and he and his parents hug and his father's just about crying, and it's like all he wanted was his own dreams and then they realize this and everything works out great.

Now imagine you've been asked to be in a friend's wedding and you're at the rehearsal dinner. You've never been very close to your friend's parents, though, and they've always suspected that you're a "bad influence." So you're a little apprehensive, in spite of your elegant appearance, dressed as you are in your finest clothes. Everyone is behaving very formally, and the discussion at the table is rather intellectual. Someone's raised the issue of obscenity and violence in the media, and several people have come down in favor of governmental controls over what can be shown at the movie theater or on TV.

Let's imagine that you don't agree, and you want to make the point that a lot of what might be considered "obscene" or "violent" has the purpose of helping us to be less obscene or less violent by exposing these things in a bad light. You're reminded of the movie, so you begin to summarize it as an illustration of your point. In turn, the summary serves the purpose of expressing a point of view, which in turn you might be using to show the wedding party something about yourself, your intellectual status, and your beliefs. At a very personal level, you might also have the purpose of demonstrating to your friend's parents that you've got some intelligence—that you're not the degenerate they think you are. At the same time, you're careful not to sound too radical, which would only confirm their view of you:

> Well, I'm not so sure, Albert. I mean, so much is in the mind's eye, isn't it? And many decisions about what we should or shouldn't see would have to be made

by someone whose opinions about violence or obscenity we might not agree with. Look at those TV evangelists—a lot of them would probably want to cover over every piece of art in the Louvre that had the slightest hint of nudity. You know, I saw this really interesting movie the other night; it was about a young guitar player whose parents kicked him out of the house because they thought he wasn't using all his God-given potential to become a baker like them and help run the bakery. The scenes of him with his friends in the band are pretty violent, and there's some quite explicit sex and a lot of bad language. But underneath it all, the movie has a really good message; it's all about understanding and reconciliation, and the main character comes to see how his decadent, violent lifestyle has almost destroyed his family, and how he'd really learned those behaviors from his own parents. So the sex and violence and bad language aren't really corrupting anyone. If someone else had already made the decision that I couldn't see the movie, then I'd have missed the chance to think about the whole issue a little more deeply. I'm not all that crazy about violent films, you know, but I think that one touched me in a special way.

Clearly, these two scenarios show how the same sort of information, presented in the same form—summary—can be used for different purposes in different settings. And because each summary serves a different purpose in a different context, its content, language, etc., will differ. Thinking about purpose at such a high level of generality as "summarizing," then, may not be as useful as thinking about the more **specific** purposes you're trying to accomplish—and these specific purposes depend upon who your readers (or listeners) are, the context you're in, and the knowledge you have of the situation.

YOUR TURN

Below is the first page of a rather elaborate menu that one of us discovered in a restaurant called "Hannegan's," on LaClede's Landing in St. Louis, Missouri.

> The time is 1932. The arrogance and flamboyance of the '20s had suddenly, by the events in 1929, turned to depression and despair . . . a great nation built by diversity and strength is drowning in a common sea of poverty . . . its faith in itself nearly gone. Even the weather, with drought and freezing cold, has turned against a frightened, humble people.
>
> The new majority, the nation's poor, elects a new president and suddenly hope and purpose burst across the land and people—together—begin to fight the unknown forces that have defeated them.
>
> Our restaurant seeks to celebrate this rebirth of hope, this spirit that saved America. Hannegan's is of no party, right or left, Whig or Tory. But Hannegan's does have a cause—to remind us of a time when people came together with common purpose and gave honor to the political process.

The actual menu—the bill of fare—is sandwiched in the middle of all sorts of interesting information about a local politician, Hannegan, who was prominent in St. Louis during and after the Depression.

184

In your writer's notebook, spend some time analyzing this section of the menu for its possible purpose(s); why would the restaurant want to tell people about the depression? What general purpose might the information serve, and what specific purposes could some of the actual sentences in the excerpt have within the context of the menu or restaurant?

WORKING WITH PURPOSE DURING THE WRITING PROCESS

In the last section, we tried to show how some of the general terms used to describe "purpose" in writing were not very useful for actual writing situations. We suggested that it's more productive to think about specific purposes defined by the situation you're writing in. These purposes, in turn, can help you to make appropriate decisions as you write and revise.

In this section, we want to shift our attention to writing and provide you with some useful ways to think about and work with purpose during all stages of the writing process.

Making Purposes Your Own

To most people, the word "purpose" immediately suggests free will—you do something with a purpose because **you** want to do it. The motivation comes from within you and drives all your actions toward a goal. In writing, this suggests that every time you sit down to compose something, you're developing and trying to accomplish your own, exciting, self-motivated purposes.

We know many writers, however, who wouldn't write nearly as much as they do unless they had someone (or something) pressing them onward at all times, urging them—sometimes even forcing them—to sit down at a desk and make meaning with a lot of funny little marks. You might ask yourself this question: what percentage of the writing you've done in the last week was purely self-motivated, produced because you had your own intrinsic interests and your own goals to accomplish? If you're like most people, the percentage is likely to be low.

Let's be honest: much of your writing—probably most of your college writing—you do because someone makes you do it. In one important respect, then, your purposes for writing are defined "by default"—you write because you're given a task to accomplish. Not completing the task has consequences beyond the writing itself: you fail the assignment, perhaps you fail the course, your grade point average declines, you become less competitive on the job market, it takes you longer to reach your goal of having your own law practice or poultry-processing plant or whatever.

Millions of people face essentially this same situation daily on the job. They sit down at a desk and they create meaning with little marks because someone is making them do it. Often the tasks they face are handed to them, just as is an assignment for a class of students. At other times, the task is part of the normal expectations for the successful performance of the job: they receive a letter from someone at another corporation, and they're expected to answer it. Again, an employee's failure to complete these tasks can lead to unpleasant consequences: a client gets angry because the employee isn't answering her requests; the employee's superior takes him off an important account; he loses a small fortune for the company because of his negligence; perhaps he's fired; he can't find another job; the bank forecloses on his mortgage; and he loses the chance to start his own law practice or poultry-processing plant.

At other times, however, your purposes for writing are yours and yours alone. You have your own goal for writing and accomplishing it has certain rewards for you independent of what anyone else is requiring of you. One of us, for example, recently wrote a letter to the manager of a restaurant because it advertises its German cuisine as "authentic." The food was so bad, and so inauthentic, that something had to be done. The purpose beyond the letter, then, was to right a wrong, to call attention to an injustice—even to let off steam at being misled. But clearly, failing to write the letter wouldn't have had any bad consequences for the writer, except perhaps that he would have had to keep some emotions pent up instead of releasing them.

The problem with "assigned" purposes is that all too often, completing them begins to seem like a chore more boring and more frustrating than scraping the peeling paint from a hundred clapboard houses. But that feeling comes from focusing all your attention on the **source** of the purpose—the reason you're being asked to write ("gotta do it; have no choice; it's right here on the syllabus")—and not enough on the more specific purposes that **you** can develop within the task.

Consider the following academic assignment: "Write a five-page paper, based on an interview, which describes someone's job." Your obvious purpose in doing the assignment is to complete a requirement of the course, perhaps to satisfy an "area" requirement and move that much closer to graduation and "real life." Result? Immediate tension, or boredom, or frustration, or dread.

You could relieve a lot of tension, come up with more ideas, and enjoy your writing more, however, if you tried to develop **your own** purposes for writing—to **make the writing assignment yours,** even though you haven't actually set the task from the start. Cheryl, one of our students, found this out recently as she began planning a paper in response to the interview assignment we've described.

Cheryl's best friend's father was a mortician. He spent a good portion of each working day with dead people, embalming them and preparing them for funerals. Cheryl had heard a few things from her friend about the activities of morticians, but as she thought about it she became more and more curious about the personal aspects of their lives: what attracted them to the job, what were the rewards, and so on. She decided that she'd like to interview a mortician—not her friend's father, who was miles away in Cheryl's hometown, but someone near her university.

As Cheryl began working on her interview questions, she became even more interested and excited. How do morticians feel about their jobs? How can they take a lunch break in the middle of their work and eat something? Do they ever have dreams about corpses? What are the most outrageous experiences they've had? What do they tell people who ask them what they do? Are there differences between public stereotypes of their work and what actually happens behind the scenes?

In a sense, Cheryl's curiosity became **her own** purpose for doing the paper. She also realized that her topic would probably be of interest to the whole class. Another of her own purposes, then, was to try to inform and entertain the class as well as complete the assignment for her teacher. In short, writing the paper became an interesting challenge for Cheryl. She'd found her own motivations for doing it, and these helped her to make wise decisions as she wrote and revised her paper.

Purposes Within and Beyond Your Writing

Before we turn to specific questions about purpose that you can ask yourself at various stages in the writing process, one more useful distinction needs to be made, and it concerns the two kinds of purpose that surround the writing act: purposes **beyond** your text and purposes **within** it.

Purposes.   Purposes beyond the text are your very general reasons for writing. Usually, they're what you hope to accomplish **outside** of your writing, as a result of it. Most college writing, again, is completed for the course requirements. If you probe a bit further, however, you'll usually find some other, more useful beyond-text purposes that help to define "doing what's required." But that means thinking more specifically about each assignment you're given.

Imagine, for example, that you're writing a term paper for a psychology class. At a high level, your purpose beyond the text might be "doing what the teacher requires" or "passing the course." At an even higher level, your purpose for doing the paper might be defined by your purpose for pursuing higher education: finishing your degree, getting a job, realizing your life's ambitions. At a lower level, your purpose for doing the paper might be to show the teacher that you've acquired the basic concepts of psychology, or to investigate a phenomenon not explored in class, or to show which group of scholars has the better evidence for one or another claim about human emotion. Your purpose for writing, in other words, is really several purposes, some close, immediate and pressing, and others farther off, more abstract.

Purposes Within the Text. Imagine you want to win a long-distance race in the varsity track meet. To accomplish this purpose, you'd probably develop a lot of strategies, or more **specific** purposes, that would govern your actions before and during the race. You might load up on carbohydrates a day or so before the meet. You might work out hard for three days and then, the day before the meet, ease off considerably. You might check out the course beforehand and work out a plan for running it. You might even try to find out something about the other women or men who will be your major competitors. In short, you'd develop a lot of specific purposes for behaving in certain ways. If someone asked you, "Why are you eating so much spaghetti this week," you'd explain this specific purpose in terms of your more general purpose—to win the race.

In writing, each of your purposes beyond the text—like "winning the race"—must be realized somehow **within** the writing you're doing—like eating spaghetti, studying the competitors, etc. The specific ways you carry out your purposes beyond the text are your purposes within the text—and these can be as small as a single word in what you're writing. If you ask yourself the question, "Why did I choose this word (or structure, or style, or information)," then you're asking a question about your purposes within the text. The beyond-text purpose of "passing the course" might involve making very careful decisions about your writing so that it receives good grades. And that might mean spending considerable time revising certain sentences, choosing certain words, organizing ideas, and so on, in keeping with the specific expectations of your audience (perhaps your teacher) and the situation you're working in (lab section of Bio. 101).

Most of us can identify within-text purposes if we've had a reader who clearly likes or hates a certain style, or even certain words or conventions ("Avoid, at all costs, using the personal pronoun!"). To achieve our purposes beyond the text, we usually make specific writing decisions based on this knowledge: "I want to do well on this paper [beyond text] to ace this course [beyond text] and get my degree [beyond text], and I know that Dr. Brady hates scientific papers that use the personal pronoun, so I've avoided that in my description of the experiment on page 3 [within text]." The same thing holds true for what information you include in your writing: "I'm trying to convince Acme Department Stores to begin selling our line of toy dolls [beyond text] and I know that they're concerned about safety, so I'll mention that our lab tests show that our dolls' eyes cannot be detached from the doll [within text]."

To take a more specific example, let's consider the purpose beyond the text of writing an article for a popular science magazine on the mathematician John von Neumann. To realize this purpose, you'll have to ask yourself many questions and make numerous decisions within your writing. Let's say you've written part of a draft, and your title and first sentence read something like this:

Science as a Game: The Life and Work of John von Neumann

John von Neumann was born in 1903, in Hungary, the son of a Jewish family.

After writing this first line, you might find yourself rethinking it, wondering whether you really want to start that way. Where does the incentive for this rethinking come from?

Many of the decisions writers make as they compose and revise their writing come from thinking about whether the words on the page are realizing their purposes, given their readers and context. When you begin thinking about specific decisions in your writing, you're often pondering whether your **within-text** purposes are realizing your **beyond-text** purposes; this leads you to test alternatives, to reread earlier parts of the text, to wonder about the reactions of your readers, and so on. Often these "sticking points" seem like conflicts to be avoided; in reality, you should think of them as necessary and desirable. They're an essential, productive part of the writing process.

Let's assume that you think the first line of your article on von Neumann is too plain, not catchy enough. Here, then, you may be thinking about one of your purposes beyond the text—to entertain the readers of a popular science magazine with an enjoyable and informative article about this mathematician and his theories. Your purpose within the text—to begin by giving some background information on the subject of your paper, John von Neumann—is not working as a way of realizing your purposes beyond the text. And so you try again:

Science as a Game: The Life and Work of John von Neumann

Morra is a "finger game" played between two players. Both players move at the same time, showing each other either one or two fingers and, simultaneously, calling out the number of fingers they think the other player is displaying.

Here, your purposes within the text have shifted a little. Instead of beginning with some background on the life of John von Neumann, you've decided to start by describing a game that Neumann discusses in his important book, *Theory of Games and Economic Behavior*. Because von Neumann's theories of mathematics are so tied to gaming, you figure it's an appropriate way to begin. After all, how many people associate great scientists or mathematicians with fun and games? Your new beginning should help you to realize your purposes beyond the text more effectively: the title suggests the essay's topic, and the description of the game is an intriguing and unusual way to begin a paper on someone's life and work. That might spark your readers' interest, get them involved in what could otherwise be seen as a boring article.

Very often, problems in writing occur because we think too much at the general level beyond the text and not enough at the specific level within it—or we fail to recognize how important the connections are between the two levels. This is one of the chief causes for lack of revision: we believe that once the text is complete, it's accomplished all our purposes beyond the text. But when we ask whether the specific parts of a piece of writing really are the most appropriate to accomplish our purposes, we're often compelled to rethink (and revise) the writing, thereby improving it considerably.

YOUR TURN

In this assignment, we're giving you a topic: hamburgers. Imagine you're writing a letter to someone—for example, the chief executive officer of a hamburger chain, the owner of a meat-processing plant, or the editor of a daily newspaper. Before you can choose your audience or begin writing anything, you'll need to define your purpose(s) beyond the text. Take a few moments to brainstorm in your writer's notebook for a purpose beyond the text and an audience for your letter.

Begin drafting your letter. As you write, keep track of your thoughts every now and then on a separate page. During these reflective pauses, look back over the specific decisions you're making in your draft: structure, choice of words, style and tone, etc. Focus also on things you change while writing. Then jot down some hypotheses about these choices and changes (your purposes within the letter). To what extent are they influenced by your purposes beyond the letter?

Analyzing Your Purpose: Open and Closed Tasks

Before you can begin writing a response to a task someone has set for you—whether it's in a corporation, a public service agency, a factory, a laboratory, or a college course—you should spend some time thinking carefully about the purposes that are evident in the way the task is put to you. Some tasks are relatively "open," able to be defined in many ways. Others are narrowly focused well in advance of your own thinking. For example, "Write a five-page essay on a topic of your choice" gives you a whole supermarket to wander through, whereas "Summarize in two pages the attached article by B. F. Skinner" pretty well blocks you off in the gerbil food section of the pet supplies aisle.

The advantage of school is that you have at least some opportunities to write in response to open-ended tasks. You have the luxury of leaning back and discovering your purposes both beyond and within open-ended writing assignments, assignments such as "Write about utopian societies. You may choose your own audience, style, format, and length, but integrate some of the ideas we've explored this term in utopian literature." In these cases, you have lots of freedom to decide for yourself what sort of writing you want to do and why you're doing it. You might write a mock planning document for your town based on new social or utopian visions; produce a pamphlet for social service agencies describing ways for families to realize some of their own "internal" utopian ideals; invent a utopian society of your own and write it up as a travelogue; write a history of utopias in American film.

In many other writing situations, your task is not defined for you in a "specs" sheet, but may nevertheless severely restrict your options. In the world of work, for example, your options are limited by goals that are set up in advance by your business or corporation. Even if you run your own business, the workings of the business will dictate what and why you write: to place an ad for your products in six magazines; to order fifteen cases of blue dye #6 from a company in Houston, Texas; to reply to an inquiry from a hiking store in Anaheim, California, about what happened to its 600 orders of freeze-dried yams; and so on. In cases like these, when your purposes beyond the text are clearly defined for you before you write, you'll benefit most from spending your time working on your purposes within the writing—in other words, how best to achieve through your writing the purposes that are already defined for you.

Imagine, for example, that you work with stained glass, and a church in town is looking for someone to repair extensive damage done to their windows during a severe thunderstorm. The church will sign a contract with the stained-glass expert whose bid appears the most thorough for the cost. In other words, they'll choose the person who gives them the best work for the least money. In writing up your bid, your purpose beyond the text is simple: get the contract. How you go about doing that, however, leaves you with many questions to answer: How much detail should you provide about the work you'll do? How persuasive should you sound (should you, for example, include a paragraph on all the previous work you've done in the past few years)? Should you provide a description of the damage so it's clear what you'll be doing, or should you assume that the church knows exactly what's broken and what needs to be repaired? How much should you promise and at what cost? These questions will relate directly to how badly you want the contract.

Planning for Purpose

As you begin to plan for any writing task, you'll find that a few minutes of focused brainstorming—thinking mainly about your purpose—can guide the direction you take in your writing. Instead of feeling as if you're in a maze of choices, you can reason your way through some options and find yourself making progress even before you've started the serious work.

The best early step in deciding your purpose, once you've analyzed your writing task, is to try to find some interest in the writing yourself—to make it **your** purpose, instead of someone else's, as Cheryl did in the mortician paper discussed above. That will, of course, depend on how restricted your assignment is. If you're not enjoying studying the psychology of human learning one bit, then being forced to write on the difference between operant and cognitive behaviorism may not be much fun.

If you're stuck in this situation and nothing immediately exciting comes to mind, try to relate the topic to other interests you may have, even if this means building a scenario that gives you new purposes. Say you're writing a paper in psychology about the difference between these two learning methods and you can already describe each and say something about the people who had a part in shaping them. If you think hard enough, there may still be some room for your own ideas and input. Perhaps you might argue that cognitive behaviorism seems truer to the way people really learn. Imagine that you've been called in to act as an expert witness at a kind of intellectual trial between cognitive and operant behaviorists. Imagine that whichever method "wins" at the trial will become the dominant method for psychologists and psychiatrists. Keeping that imaginary purpose in mind—as long as it's in sync with the purpose reflected in the task—may give you some added incentive and interest as you write and revise your paper.

YOUR TURN

Below are three open-ended writing assignments of the sort you might be given in college courses. Within the general framework of each, define for yourself a more specific writing purpose you would find interesting to pursue.

> Attend the university theater's performance of *A Midsummer Night's Dream* and write about it.
>
> Write an argumentative essay on the subject of teaching creationism in the public schools.
>
> Do a paper (4-7 pages) on any question concerning the development of new medical technologies on public policy.

Assume the assignment can be cast in virtually any form and addressed to any audience. For each assignment, make a few notes on how your choice of audience and purpose would affect the way you would actually write the piece.

Define Your Purposes Beyond the Text.   What will the writing accomplish beyond itself? What do you hope will happen as a result of writing? Are these purposes defined in the task or situation? Write down as many possible options as you can. Remember that the process of brainstorming can lead you to discover your purposes beyond the text if they're not defined in advance. You may not be aware of them or even know what they are, until you begin thinking about them.

Try some focused prewriting before you really begin to explore your chosen topic. Return to Part 1 and try using some of the techniques we've suggested there—freewriting, various kinds of brainstorming like listing and particle/wave/field, etc.—to think carefully about what purposes your writing might serve. Try drawing a cluster of purposes with your task at the center.

Define Some Purposes Within the Text.   You can't predict many of the specific decisions you'll make as you write until you begin drafting and revising. But sometimes you can give yourself a head start by deciding some of your within-text purposes in advance. What might be the best way to accomplish your purposes beyond the text? If you're complaining about the bad food at a restaurant, is it best to launch right into your feelings, or begin by explaining when and what you ate? What reasons would you give for doing this, in terms of your purposes beyond the text? If you're writing a letter to the editor responding to a newspaper article that made you angry, should you begin emotionally or coolly? Should you summarize what the article said, or should you assume your readers already know? Once you've made some planning decisions, ask yourself what effect each decision may have in terms of your beyond-text purposes.

YOUR TURN

In the piece of writing you are now working on, spend a few minutes planning for your purpose by following our suggestions above. Then answer the following questions in your writer's notebook:

Did you notice any changes in your purposes, either beyond or within the text, as you went through the planning activities? If so, what were they?

How was your planning affected by the specificity of the task you're responding to?

To what extent were you able to make the purpose for the task "your own," as opposed to someone else's?

Drafting with Purpose

Once you've analyzed a writing task, you've discovered the task giver's purpose for your writing and planned out one or more directions for it based on your own purposes beyond the text. Now it's time to take your directions and purposes and plans all less seriously. They gave you a map to start off with, but once you've started drafting you reach new territory, cross some borders. It may be time to redraw your maps.

The most important thing that happens as you actually begin drafting is the **discovery** and **refinement** of your purposes. You might have had a good direction in mind when you began, but you'll soon notice that the very process of writing begins to change your intentions. As you're writing that first section on the life of John von Neumann, you realize that what you really want to do is an article on the mathematics of games—and von Neumann becomes a little patch in a larger quilt.

Whatever you do, don't be afraid to **redefine** your purposes as you write. You might find, for example, that the purposes you had originally set for yourself are too difficult or large to accomplish. So redirect them. Take a small helping, one you know you'll finish. Narrow your purposes and leave some of the others for later.

On the other hand, don't let your preoccupation with purpose overwhelm you as you write. Don't ask yourself at every step of the way, "Am I realizing my purpose? What is my purpose? Is this working?" You'll freeze with indecision. Instead, when you reach a natural pause in your drafting (when you get up for a Coke or take a break for lunch), reexamine your purpose in light of the text you've written so far. The following questions will help you to focus on your developing purposes:

Discover Your Purposes Beyond the Text. Have any further general purposes developed from discoveries you've made as a result of writing and rereading what you've written? If you began by assuming you'd change someone's mind about an important issue, does this still hold true? Has your own mind changed? If you'd planned to complain to the manager of a restaurant about the food, do you still want just to complain or are you now asking for your money back? Are you threatening something? What response are you now looking for—an apology, a refund, something else again?

Discover Your Purposes Within the Text. Are you thinking any differently after doing some drafting about the structure, language, or content of your writing? If you're writing an article for a journalism class and you notice that a local magazine is looking for new material along the lines of what you're working on, will this change your purposes within your writing? If you've decided that the restaurant is probably unaware that its food is so bad, are you reconsidering the harshness of your criticisms? Would a less brittle, legalistic style suit your redefined purpose more effectively?

YOUR TURN

Below are the beginnings of two pieces of writing on the same topic, both written by Gerri, one of our students.

The first excerpt is from the final draft of an interview paper Gerri wrote for her composition class. The second excerpt is from an article she wrote at the same time for the university newspaper.

Words Can't Express Who She Is

Linda Levine waltzed into the room with an embracing smile radiating from her innocent face. She was dressed in a pair of denim overalls with a bandana tied around a loop of the overalls and wore a pair of blue tennis shoes. Was this the same face that was covered with white make-up and the same girl who transfixed the audience with her repertoire of mime skits?

I began my interview with Linda by asking her how she got started in mime. At around age fourteen, Linda grabbed any opportunity to watch mime. Whenever stores would have grand openings, mimes would be hired to gather outside and try to draw customers into the store. Linda would stare breathlessly at the mimes for hours. She began taking mime lessons but at first did not realize the essential key for effective miming. Finally, after two years of hard work, she realized that if she wanted to be a good mime, she would have to feel what she was doing. "You could be taught to climb a mime ladder—one that doesn't exist," she explains, "but until you're prepared to see it and feel that once you go up a little bit you'll have to be afraid of falling down, you'll never be a good mime. . . ."

Words Are Superfluous to Student

In the dark Collins/LLC coffee house, a girl calling herself "Rainbow" stood with her face covered in white makeup at the edge of the small room. With no props or words, she brought the audience to tears and laughter.

A week later, Linda Levine, a freshman who will be performing at Kiva at 9:30 tonight, waltzed into a McNutt dorm room with an embracing smile radiating from her face. She was dressed in a pair of denim overalls with a bandana tied to them and wore a pair of blue tennis shoes.

Was this the same face often covered with white makeup and the same girl who transfixed audiences with her repertoire of mime skits?

At 14, Linda grabbed any opportunity to watch mime. . . .

After reading these excerpts carefully, spend some time in your writer's notebook speculating about Gerri's purposes in each. How might her beyond-text purposes have differed for the two pieces? What evidence in her specific decisions within the two texts suggests those differences?

Revising: Testing the Results

Once you've completed a full draft of your writing—whether it's a corporate memo or a term paper for Principles of Macroeconomics—you'll be fairly well set in your purposes for writing. You'll know what you've been trying to accomplish, and how this has helped to guide your planning and drafting.

In revising your writing, you'll want to focus most of your attention on the relationship between your purposes beyond the text and the specific decisions you made within it. Now is the time to weigh each word, look at each paragraph, think carefully about the tone and style of each sentence. If you reread your writing through the lens of your ultimate purpose, you can make expert judgments on these matters with greater ease.

Furthermore, you don't have to do this alone. Throughout this book, we've urged you to use other people in your writing and revising processes. Because you can't be sure whether you've accomplished your purposes beyond the text until someone reads your work, now is an excellent time to give your writing a "dry run."

Before you get feedback on your draft, however, you might want to jot down some questions for your readers so that they can provide you with the sort of information you need.

1. What do you suppose is the main purpose of this piece of writing?
2. To what degree do you think it accomplishes that purpose?
3. What specific features of the writing do you think help it accomplish its purpose(s)?
4. What specific features do you think get in the way?
5. What suggestions would you make for revision so that the purpose of the writing can be more effectively accomplished?

Using this feedback, you can then match your own stated purposes against those your reader discovered in your draft.

You can also make up a list of your purposes beyond and within your writing to give your readers before getting feedback. This way, they can tell you whether you've accomplished those purposes—and, if not, where the problems lie.

One excellent method for getting this kind of feedback is to ask a reader to write a "purpose summary" of your paper. First, number each of your paragraphs in the left margin. Then, on a separate piece of paper, try stating what each paragraph does to realize your purpose beyond the text. In our stained-glass example, you might write next to the first paragraph of your bid, "gives the background for my work to show that I'm competent and experienced." Next, ask a reader to do exactly the same thing without showing him your own purpose statements. Be sure, however, to tell him who your prospective audience is and what purpose you hope to accomplish beyond the text. When he's finished, compare your lists of purpose statements. Did he interpret your reasons the same way you did?

YOUR TURN

Read the text below and answer the following questions about it:

To whom does it appear to be written?
What purpose does the writer want it to achieve?

196

What seems to be the relationship of the writer to the people who will be reading it?

Once you've done that, go through paragraph by paragraph and try to define what each of the five *does* to further the writer's purpose. Does it inform, explain, give evidence, pull rank, wheedle, or what? Try to avoid summarizing the paragraphs; don't simply paraphrase what each one *says*, say what each *does*. Use the correct *verb* to label the main action or purpose of each.

FUNDING REQUEST

1. The Peace Covenant Workshop would like to have Lawrence James conduct a one-day workshop on the theme of *Personal Peacemaking*. The workshop would be on Saturday, April 25, and would run from roughly 9:00 a.m. until 3:30 p.m. with a break for lunch.
2. The workshop would examine the place peacemaking has throughout our lives—from inner personal peace, peace among family, friends, and coworkers, to issues of peace in the world at large. Although the activities of the Peace Covenant Workshop focus largely on the issues of nuclear war and weaponry as discussed by the United Methodist Bishops' recent statement, the workshop conducted by Mr. James would not be so narrowly conceived. It is both Mr. James' intention, and the desire of the PCW, that the workshop treat peace in the life of the Christian in the broadest, most spiritually grounded terms.
3. The pages attached describe the sorts of peacemaking workshops Mr. James typically conducts, and give a good indication of the direction and emphasis he would take in his workshop for us. We hope and trust that the workshop will appeal to a segment of the Lake Hamilton congregation well beyond the PCW itself. We think that for such a workshop we can reasonably shoot for about 30 to 40 participants—about the number that joins the Adult Retreat each January.
4. Mr. James' background and qualifications are laid out fully in the pages attached. He has degrees in history and in theology, and has been involved in religious and peace education for over 20 years. He now conducts workshops on such topics as a full-time profession, and is author of a forthcoming book on peacemaking entitled *The Elusive Olive Branch*.
5. Mr. James met with Reverend Ellis and myself some weeks ago and discussed how such a workshop might look. Both Reverend Ellis and I were impressed with Mr. James' background and ideas. On behalf of the Peace Covenant Workshop, we request the Foundation to grant us Mr. James' fee, so that we can further the Christian mission of peacemaking in the lives of the people of Lake Hamilton United Methodist Church.

After developing or getting from someone else such a paragraph-by-paragraph purpose analysis of your own draft, you can now revise your paper by thinking about how well your own stated purposes match those identified by your reader.

In addition, try using the following more general questions during the revising process:

Rethinking Your Purposes Beyond the Text. Are you quite clear about what the writing is supposed to accomplish? (Here is a good time to think about alternative purposes that parts of your writing could accomplish in the future. If you've written a report of an experiment, for example, could you use this report to create a different kind of text which gives advice to parents?) If you were reading this piece of writing for the first time, and without any background information, what would you **infer** were the author's purposes?

Rethinking Your Purposes Within the Text. Now reread your draft a few times, thinking carefully about whether the specific within-text decisions you've made can be justified given what you're trying to accomplish. Is the language the most appropriate to meet your goals? What about the structure? Have you said enough? Too much? Think of alternatives, and try them out or jot them down for later use. Use the comments from your "dry-run" here to make new decisions and discoveries.

YOUR TURN

Read the cover story of a news magazine such as *Time* or *Newsweek*. Get comfortable with the subject; reach the point where you can say something confidently about it. (This will also work for textbooks from one of your courses or some subject about which you have a lot of knowledge.)

Now choose two very different reasons for providing the same information in a short (one-half- to one-page) piece. (Choose different audiences if this helps.)

Plan and write the two short pieces, but as you do so, keep jotting down in your writer's notebook some observations about how your purposes began, how they changed as you wrote, and how they influenced specific textual decisions you made along the way or after you'd finished and began making changes. Share your two pieces with your classmates and ask them to discuss them, pointing out the differences beween them. Then compare what they observed with what you wrote in your notebook.

WHAT'S READING GOT TO DO WITH PURPOSE?

When you read, you unconsciously bring purposes to the act that help you understand what you're reading. Let's say you pick up a newspaper. Your purpose for reading the newspaper may be to locate a new recipe, to find out the score of a game, to look for a job, to see the outcome of some important political event, or to check someone's story of a national or local happening against "the facts" as reported in the paper. Or you may just be getting the paper so you can have something to pass the time with on the bus.

With all these purposes, you also have certain **expectations** about what the paper will yield. You know that many daily newspapers often carry recipes. You know that there's usually a sports section. You know that facts about current events are going to be as accurate as possible. In short, you know a lot about the contents and language of newspapers—even about their audience (people like yourself).

If you extend this concept to think of other sorts of texts you commonly read, you'll find that you know a good deal about them too. When you're in a supermarket and you see a little metal stand with paperback books whose covers show pictures of attractive young women standing alone in the moonlight by the seashore, their hair and negligees blown by the wind, you have certain expectations based on your knowledge of popular romance fiction. Or when you walk into a college or university library, you know that you're unlikely to find *Superman* comics or pornographic magazines, because libraries tend to house materials considered to be of intellectual or scholarly interest.

Readers, then, bring all sorts of expectations to the things they read, and they base these expectations on their own purposes for reading. But when these expectations are violated, readers become confused or frustrated; the reasons **why** they began to read have been foiled. And that's generally something to avoid, unless you're writing avant-garde fiction. As a writer, you should try to be fully aware of your readers' expectations and purposes.

Of course, sometimes pieces of writing are read for completely different purposes than those the writer had originally intended—personal diaries for their historical significance, for example. But this shouldn't concern you. The best advice is to keep firmly in mind the purposes your specific readers will bring to your work and the contexts they are likely to read it in. The following checklist should help:

Why will your reader be reading this? What general and specific purposes might your reader have for wanting to read what you've written?

In what context will the piece be read? This concerns both the form of the writing (its physical appearance) and the physical surroundings in which it will be read. Would your piece most likely appear in a magazine sold on local newsstands, a course paper distributed to students in class, a booklet of instructions for assembling a lawn spreader, to be inserted into the carton? How does this context influence the purposes the reader will bring to the text, and how, in turn, does this influence your writing?

What are some of the expectations of style, format, etc., your audience will have, based on their purpose and context for reading? How does this influence your within-text purposes as you write?

Again, it's a good idea to test your writing on real readers who can help you answer these questions more fully. If your test reader is very different from your intended final reader, have your test reader role-play, seeing your text through the eyes of the audience it will eventually reach.

A FINAL WORD ABOUT PURPOSE AND LEARNING

We've suggested earlier how a "requirement" can turn into something exciting by helping you to acquire new knowledge. Although much academic writing may seem to be judging or testing you in some way, there's a very high-level purpose beyond all the texts you write in college: to make you wiser, more thoughtful, and more knowledgeable. Why else would so much time and energy be devoted to school writing, most of which seems to serve no purpose beyond the class for which you write it?

We can't overstress the point that once you believe in this purpose for academic writing, you'll begin to see **yourself** in the writing—your own goals and interests, rather than those of your teachers or the curriculum. The writing's not there by accident; it's there for you. Use it, enjoy it, give it the sort of purpose you'd give anything that's your own. You'll find that as a result your writing will be livelier, better, more interesting to read, more fun to write . . . in short, more **purposeful,** both for you and your audience.

Chapter Eight

WHO'S YOUR READER?
ANALYZING YOUR
AUDIENCE

Several times in the previous chapters, we've mentioned the importance of **audience** in the writing process. Thinking fully about a real or imagined reader is one of the most valuable things a writer can do.

As we pointed out in Chapter Six, audience plays an important role in academic writing. You may, for example, find yourself thinking about how your different teachers will read your writing: what style does each prefer? Will they be especially hard on you if you make grammatical mistakes? Are you supposed to give information back to them, or should you state your own opinions? Clearly, the answers to such questions will vary considerably from teacher to teacher. But even though they're all different people, in some ways teachers represent a limited audience; writing only academically, only for academic readers, doesn't give you much practice considering the needs of different audiences.

In the past, you may have been asked to write for a "general audience" or "the average reader." Defining your audience in that way, unfortunately, isn't very helpful. The "general audience" is shrouded in vagueness, and it's hard to tell how they'll respond to your writing unless you know more about their specific characteristics, beliefs, and so on. Also, your school writing may not ever have reached any audience but the teacher; instead, it's often used to assess your writing ability, help you learn complex material, or practice the sorts of writing people do in the "real world" beyond the classroom. The classroom, then, seems rather artificial compared with the many writing situations outside of school.

At the same time, though, the classroom can be an excellent place to experiment with and learn how language can be adapted to various audiences. First, there's less risk involved: you can write an advertisement in a classroom and, if it misses its mark or if it's unintentionally misleading and false, you haven't lost a three-million-dollar account or gotten into trouble with the Federal Trade Commission.

There are also many opportunities in a classroom to get the same kind of feedback you might get if your writing really were to reach its intended audience. We've suggested how writing for a conference group or for other class members can provide you with a sense of purpose and a feel for your readers. Just as easily, you can ask them to play the **role** of any other kind of reader, and they'll give you useful comments and ideas.

Finally, the classroom as a writing workshop is an ideal place to discuss and explore what we mean by "audience." You'll find that talking about and role-playing audiences in the classroom helps you not only to invent ideas but also to work with language as you draft and revise your writing.

In this chapter, we'd like to expand the concept of audience by considering some ways of thinking about audience and by trying out some writing for different sorts of audiences. The aim of this chapter, then, is to provide you with some new perspectives and some "audience strategies" that can help you to draft and revise all your writing, both in school and beyond.

YOUR TURN

Think about all the different writing you've done in school settings. For what sorts of audiences did you write? Can you think of two or three teachers who seem to you radically different as audiences? How did they differ? What effects did those differences have, if any, on the way you thought about and produced your writing? Spend some time jotting down some ideas in your writer's notebook about the "teacher as audience" and about "academic" audiences.

HOW WE ADAPT OUR LANGUAGE TO DIFFERENT AUDIENCES

All of us are constantly adapting our language to the people we're talking to, and the situations we're in when we talk to them. You probably use more formal language when talking to someone you don't know very well, especially if that person is in a position of authority. When you're with close friends, you shift linguistic gears and become more casual.

Think how strange it would be to use "pet" language, the language you use to speak to the dog or cat, when being interviewed by a prospective employer for a job at a fast-food restaurant: "Ya, Mr. Samuels, I'd love to work here, yes I would, yeah boy! Ruff ruff! That's a good fella, you hire me! Go get 'em! Smell those burgers! Ruff, ruff!" It would be just as bizarre to phone a friend and say, "Good evening, Janice, I'm calling regarding our upcoming plans to dine at Nick's Saloon and Deli—more specifically, the appropriate hour at which I might arrive at your domicile in my automobile to transport you to said establishment." Obviously, you'd use much more casual language than this; and yet, if Janice's father answered the phone, it wouldn't be so unreasonable to say, "Good evening, Mr. Johnson, this is Walter. May I speak to Janice, please?" At least, it would be more reasonable than saying, "Hey, this must be Janice's old man, right? How's it going, dude? Put Janice on the line, will ya?"

Usually, you make these kinds of adjustments in your language unconsciously; they're part of a complicated system of social roles we play and agreements we share about effective communication. If you use sophisticated language when giving directions to a child, she's likely to lose her way; if you tell dirty jokes at a formal cocktail party, you're likely to be left standing alone—even though you might tell such jokes in a less formal setting, perhaps even with some of the same people. Adapting to the audience means being sensitive not only to **whom** you're speaking but in what **context** or situation you speak to them.

YOUR TURN

Read the following exchange that occurred at a public copying machine. On the basis of their language, what might you say about these speakers and their "adaptations" to different audiences?

[A man is at the copy machine making copies; another man approaches the machine.]

Second Man: Excuse me, do you have a lot of copies to make?

First Man: Well, yes, actually, I'm copying this entire manuscript.

Second Man: I don't suppose I might sneak in for a copy of this letter, could I? I'd very much appreciate it; you see, my car is parked illegally outside, and I'm in a terrible rush to get this letter in the mail.

First Man: I'm sorry, if I let anyone and everyone make copies, I'd be here all day. I waited fifteen minutes myself to use this machine, and then it ran out of paper.

[Second man recognizes first man.]

Second Man: Hey, 'sat you, Charlie? Ha ha! Hardly recognized you under that beret. How ya doin'?

Charlie: Hey, Sam! [Laughs.] Oh, Polly gave this to me. Say, I've been meaning to give you a buzz. When are we gonna do that racketball thing we talked about, anyway?

Sam: Ah, it's the knee again. You know, same old problem. Listen, I gotta run; I'm parked on the bus stop out there, and the cops'll have my hide. Mind if I . . . ?

Charlie: Oh, sure, Sam, here, lemme move my papers out of the way. You need any change? I got a whole bucket of dimes here.

NOT Adapting to Your Audience: Why and When

Just as it's natural to adapt to different audiences in different situations, so are there reasons for **not** adapting to those audiences. Sometimes we do this on purpose and sometimes we just make mistakes.

Not Adapting to Your Audience on Purpose.   Usually, when we intentionally avoid adapting to audience, we do it to achieve special effects: to be funny or sarcastic, to alienate someone, or to show that we're a member of a certain group. Imagine a state trooper has pulled you over to remind you about your broken taillight. Saying to him, "Well, well, well, if it ain't Mr. Cop. What'cha got on me, huh?" would probably have a quite different effect from saying "Good evening, officer; what seems to be the problem?" You might vary your language in this way to imply something, to make a statement about the relationship you want to establish with your audience. The first response might say something like "I'm ready to argue with you for pulling me over because I've done nothing wrong, and I know all about you cops, always hassling people without good cause." The second response might say something like, "I'm ready to cooperate because you've got authority and as a good citizen I'll respect you." Neither response is "correct'' or ''incorrect''; they're just used for different purposes, to achieve different effects.

Intentionally varying your language can also say things about your feelings toward a **known** audience. Say you break up with someone you've been dating; you might find yourself using more formal, stilted language with that person, even though the two of you have become quite intimate. And if your new emotions aren't as fixed as you'd like them to seem, you might find yourself shifting back into a less formal style, as in this phone conversation:

> *Tyrone:*   Hello, Loretta, this is Tyrone. I'm calling about setting up a time when I might come by to pick up the belongings I left at your apartment when we were together. I know this may seem like an imposition, but since they do belong to me, I'd like to repossess them.
>
> *Loretta:*   Well, I'm rather busy today, Tyrone; I have a luncheon date with Robert. Perhaps I could leave your possessions with Mrs. Brown in the next apartment. She rarely goes out at this time of day, and I'm sure she'll be happy to hold your things for a few hours, at least.
>
> *Tyrone:*   That will be fine. And please be sure to include my Grover Washington tape.
>
> *Loretta:*   Ty! You gave that tape to me!
>
> *Tyrone:*   Oh, Lotty, I gave you everything I had! All I really want back is you. C'mon now, can't we talk? Gimme a chance!

We also routinely shift our language across different styles to indicate mood changes when we're with people we know well. Parents will often ''signal'' their anger to a child by using stiff, direct language, language that's quite different from the more personal and informal style they normally use:

> William Stuart Farnsworth, you march yourself right up to this room and clean up these toys!

And baby-talk is a popular way to admonish mature people:

> Aw, poor little Mikey, did it stub its little toe on the hammer it left in the middle of the floor? Here, let Suzy rub it better. There, now, don't cry. Maybe now little Mikey will think twice before he leaves his tools lying around for people to hurt themselves on!

Deliberately changing our language for different audiences can also be strategic. It's well known that Abraham Lincoln varied his speaking style when he gave speeches in the South and the North around the time of the Civil War, as did Martin Luther King when he was speaking to gatherings of whites or blacks during times of racial tension. Such adaptations can also be deceiving . . . or face saving. If you're speaking to a friend on a ''business-only'' phone and your supervisor walks into the room, you're likely to change your language suddenly from a casual, chatty style to a ''business'' style, and your friend on the other end of the phone will either ''get the hint'' or be quite confused.

YOUR TURN

Think of a situation (real or hypothetical) when you might intentionally avoid "adapting" your speech to your audience. Explain the situation. Then compose a dialogue (like the previous ones) that illustrates the case. If you can't think of a situation, try composing a script for the "business" phone case we described above.

Not Adapting to Your Audience by Mistake.   Usually when we're speaking with others, we pick up many "clues" about them as an audience and the contexts we're speaking in that help us to communicate effectively. Sometimes, though, we **unintentionally** misread our audiences, perhaps because we're too quick to make judgments about them. These unintentional errors can make us feel quite uncomfortable.

Imagine a situation that one of us experienced not long ago: a very old man with a cane shuffles up to your front porch looking dazed from the heat of the midsummer day. His shoelaces are untied, his shirt has come untucked, and he's glancing about as if he's lost his way. He asks for a glass of water. From his appearance, you assume that he's probably a little senile. Your context also gives you some clues: a few blocks away, there's a small retirement home, and on nice days the more physically able of the senior citizens there take short walks around the community.

From these clues, you might do as the author did, and make your language simple, comforting, and kindly, like a nurse talking to a patient: "Now, you sit right there on the porch swing and I'll get you a nice glass of cold water." In reality, the old man wasn't from the retirement home at all; he'd been taking his daily three-mile walk and had become very thirsty about halfway through. He turned out to be intelligent and articulate, and carried on an interesting conversation about the most recent novel he'd been reading. Using childlike language for this audience turned out to be inappropriate and a little embarrassing.

Most often we make incorrect judgments about our audiences from their physical appearances and mannerisms. During a recent convention, for example, a friend of ours left the hotel to buy his wife a gift at a nearby mall. It was Saturday, and he was dressed in a suit because he'd given a speech earlier that morning. But it's unusual for people to wear business suits at the mall on a weekend, so in each store our friend wandered through he was assumed to be a salesperson and was besieged with questions from the unsuspecting shoppers. When they discovered they'd "misread" their audience, their language changed from an abrupt, almost officious style to a more personal, friendly one. They used one kind of "language" for salespersons, and another kind for smartly dressed fellow shoppers.

Whatever the cause, these mistakes are a natural part of our social lives. Usually, they happen quickly because we don't have the time to analyze our social situations carefully. When we do have such an opportunity, however, it's worth taking some time to think carefully about how to shape and adapt our language to our listeners.

YOUR TURN

Using a tape-recorder or writing in a notebook, discreetly record some conversations to note how people fit their speech styles to their audiences and situations. Try crowded supermarkets, library lobbies, dorm cafeterias, coffee shops, or places where various kinds of people gather and where short conversations are common. After collecting your data, informally jot down your ideas about audience and bring these to class to discuss. You may want to think about some of the following:

What can you guess about the people you've listened to?

On what basis do you make those guesses? How much comes from language alone? How much from other things you observed in the context?

If you observed different kinds of people speaking to each other, what can you say about their language in terms of audience? Do they seem to be "adapting" their speech, and if so, how? What sorts of audiences are they? How can you tell?

Were there any occasions when someone seemed to shift her language when she spoke to a different person (for example, if two friends are talking in a coffee shop and one of them asks the waitress a question)?

Alternatively, try watching two or three very different TV shows at different times—a soap opera on a weekday, a Sunday football game, the 6 P.M. news, a late-late-night horror movie, Saturday-morning cartoons, etc. But instead of doing other things during the commercials, pay special attention to them. Jot down some notes about select commercials that come on during each of the programs you watch; then analyze them for their adaptations to audience. To what sort of audiences do you suppose these commercials are appealing? How do you know? What differences can you see in the language used in the commercials? Are there any that don't seem to adapt to their audiences effectively? Are there any that seem geared toward **everyone** and **anyone** as a possible audience? How do you know? Is there such a thing as a "general audience"?

Audience and Context

Contexts—particular places where language is used—can tell you something about communities of people and the way they see the world. Think about the differences in the "audiences" who attend meetings of two different organizations,— say, "Mothers against Drunk Driving" and "Citizens in Favor of Firearms"—or whose cars have very different bumper stickers—"God, Guns, and Guts Made America—Let's Keep All Three" and "Save the Whales." Or consider what sorts of audiences might be seen at two different kinds of performances such as a Verdi opera and a female mud-wrestling match. The audiences who attend each event will differ considerably (though, of course, there may be a few people who would attend both events).

A professor we know told us about a time soon after he'd moved to Oklahoma to teach, when a local rancher invited him to attend an illegal cockfight in an abandoned barn. The professor was excited—not so much about seeing a cockfight as learning something about local Oklahoman culture. When the rancher came to get him in his pickup, the professor was wearing some nice slacks and a sport-coat. The rancher advised him to put on old jeans, a cowboy hat, worn boots, and a denim jacket, and, at all costs, to "talk normal"—that is, to adapt his usually intellectual speech style to the community of people who attend illegal cockfights. Our friend learned some fascinating things about the attitudes and lifestyles of the people at the cockfight, but he did so only because he seemed like one of them. To have attended in the clothes of a professor and to have used professorial **language** would have been to alienate himself from the others, raising their suspicions and putting them on the defensive.

Of course, adapting to an audience isn't necessary all the time. In many ways, we express ourselves—what we really are beneath the many masks we wear—through the language we use most often and most naturally. Yet thinking carefully about contexts where other people express **their** true selves can help you to communicate effectively and persuasively.

That sort of thinking can also help you not to judge your audiences too hastily. When it's possible, try to use your context to make educated guesses about your audience, but think carefully about your judgments to be sure they're not unduly biased. Stereotypes do have their uses, but often they deceive us into acting or speaking in misguided ways.

Becoming sensitive to our audience is not something we can achieve quickly and easily; audiences are people, and people live and work and play in social or cultural contexts with which we may be unfamiliar. On a very simple level, if you don't make your living by drag racing or designing nuclear weapons or raising thoroughbreds or teaching scuba diving, you may not share the kind of "languages" these communities of people use—at least, when they're on the job. Exposure to different contexts may take many years. And people who are culturally or professionally or geographically restricted may not ever "see the world" through any other eyes than their own. By being sensitive to the many different kinds of people around you, though, you can learn a lot about audiences and their needs, beliefs, and attitudes. In turn, this new awareness can help you to communicate more effectively as you learn to adapt to other, less familiar contexts.

YOUR TURN

Imagine that you're out driving in your car one evening; it's dusk, and the remaining light is forming deceiving shadows on the road. Suddenly, a cat darts out from under a bush and runs right in front of your car. There's no time to stop, and you hit the cat, killing it instantly.

Luckily, the cat has a collar and a pet license tag. There's no one around and no phone in sight, so you put the cat in your trunk, drive home, and call the license bureau to find out who owns it. The license bureau informs you that the owner is 11-year-old Michelle Stein, who lives near the site of the accident.

You decide to call the Steins to tell them what happened. In your writer's notebook, first jot down five **concerns** you'd have in giving them this information, then write out a mock dialogue of the phone conversation **as you'd hope it would sound.**

Now suppose you call the Steins and Michelle answers the phone. You ask to speak to her parents, but they're on vacation, and the babysitter is busy cleaning up the finger paint that Michelle's toddler sister has spilled in the kitchen. You think about calling back later, when you can talk to the sitter, but you decide to tell Michelle the bad news instead.

In your writer's notebook, jot down several more **problems** you'd face speaking to Michelle that you might not have faced with her parents. (You might also consider whether there would be any differences between the Steins and the **babysitter** as audiences.)

Now write out a second conversation, this time with Michelle. But instead of writing the conversation as you'd hope it would sound, build some "problems" into it, and then try to solve those problems by being sensitive to Michelle as an audience.

WRITING AND AUDIENCE

In speaking, you adapt your language to your audience unconsciously and more or less automatically. In writing, though, you need to pay special attention to your audiences and what effect your choices will have on them. Why should something that's often unconscious now become something that requires careful thought?

First of all, when you speak, your audience is right in front of you. You can tell if your language is too sophisticated because the listener will frown or ask for clarification. If you're being too simple, or trying too hard to explain everything, your listener will nod or become visibly agitated, as if saying "Ok, ok, get to the point." But in writing, your audience is often distant, almost fictional. Sometimes you may not even know who, precisely, will be reading what you've written—only that they may live in a certain area, dress or talk a certain way, or hold certain beliefs. And sometimes you don't even know that much.

Second, in speaking you "compose" your language on the spot, which means you can adapt instantly as you get certain information from the audience. Even when you're giving a speech from written notes, you can make it sound bold and emphatic, slow and methodical, or casual and chatty. Many great orators make these decisions very quickly, based on what they can see in their audience (frowns of disbelief, smiles of encouragement, applause, boos, various states of unconsciousness, etc.). In writing, though, you can't instantly adapt your language because your audience must read what you've written only after you've written it. Later, we'll suggest some ways to develop "audiences in the mind" to use **while** you're writing and revising; but these are still only approximations of real audiences, and fictional ones at that.

Third, in spoken language we learn about audience from the day we're born. As young children, we find out quickly that we're supposed to be more formal and polite around guests—we're told constantly to say "please" and "thank you," or to say "may I" instead of "can I." And starting in kindergarten, we learn that school language tends to be formal and structured, very different from the language we use in the sandbox or on the playing field. The amount we learn unconsciously about **speaking,** then, is staggering. In contrast, the amount of writing we've done in our lives is minute. And usually we've written for very limited audiences. As a result, we're not accustomed to adapting our language to meet the needs and interests of diverse **readers.**

Finally, most speaking situations give us something we might call a "second chance." In reference to the previous "Your Turn," imagine that when you call the Steins to tell them about their cat, you explain: "I was approaching the stoplight at the intersection of 4th Avenue and Main Street, and the cat ran right in front of my car; I didn't have time to stop." If Mr. Stein asks you why you couldn't stop if you were slowing down for the light, you have the chance to explain that the light was green. That is, because you're **talking** to the Steins, you have the chance to do something that's perfectly natural when we speak: to **refine your meaning** for your audience.

Not so in writing. Once you've submitted your writing, you don't have those "second chances" to refine your meaning, to say to your reader, "No, no, what I really mean is. . . ." In writing, then, you need to be especially sensitive to your audience, anticipating many possible responses as you draft and revise, and ruling out those reactions that seem most unlikely. And, as we've suggested, there's no better way than the revision conference or the feedback from a "trial run" to help you refine your meaning **before** you submit a piece of writing.

YOUR TURN

Cindy, a university senior, will soon graduate with a major in Radio and Television and is starting to put together her résumé in hope of getting a job in her field. Ideally, she'd like to be a programming assistant at a TV station. Two years ago, she worked at a local movie theater as a cashier and helper. In her job, she sold tickets at movie time, ushered on weekends, helped to clean the theater between shows, and several times studied the movie listings and ratings to help Mr. Howells, the owner, decide what movies to order.

Cindy decided to ask Mr. Howells to write her a letter of recommendation for her job portfolio. Here's Cindy's request:

> Dear Mr. Howells:
>
> Remember me? I'm Cindy, and I worked as a cashier at your movie theater some time ago. I was wondering if you could write a letter to me about my work; I'm graduating soon, and anything you could say about me would be greatly appreciated.
>
> Thanks, and good luck with your theater!
>
> Very truly yours,
> Cindy Nelson

When Cindy sends this letter, she has "one chance" to make her meaning clear. If Mr. Howells' letter isn't very useful, she's wasted both their time, unless, embarrassingly, she wants to ask Mr. Howells to rewrite his letter.

Assume she sends it as is, and Mr. Howells mails her back the following letter of recommendation:

> Dear Cindy Nelson,
>
> Yes, you were a good employee. You did a good job selling the tickets, and you worked at a time when this theater was really getting off the ground. I remember, too, that you really did a good job of shining the glass on the postercases in the theater lobby. Hope you find a good job in whatever field you enter.
>
> Best wishes,
> Samuel Howells

Jot down some problems of **audience** in Mr. Howells' letter that would make it unlikely to be included in Cindy's portfolio. Then, looking over his response, jot down some ideas about Cindy's attention to the needs of **her** audience (Mr. Howells). What could she have written to Mr. Howells to ensure a better letter of recommendation? Rewrite Cindy's letter, and then write a response from Mr. Howells that she might find more useful.

The What and the How of Writing: It's in the Audience

As we explained in the Overview to Part 3, audience is closely intertwined with purpose. Both are part of your writing situation and help you to make specific **textual** decisions as you draft and revise your writing. For now, we'd like to focus briefly on how audience and text are tied together—how audience influences the decisions you make as you write.

In thinking about the content of your writing, you'll need to ask yourself how your audience will react to **what** you're saying—to the specific information or arguments or ideas you're presenting. In thinking about your composing choices, you'll want to ask yourself how the audience will respond to **how** you're presenting your information, arguments, or ideas: the kinds of words you use, the length and style of your sentences, your degree of formality, your organization of ideas, etc.

Consider the following situation. You're working for a large cafeteria on your campus. The cafeteria is run by a private company, but since it's housed in the Student Union building, the college community often uses that space for studying or socializing. Around lunch time, the cafeteria becomes crowded; diners are often seen wandering around with their trays looking for a place to sit. Many of the tables are occupied by students and faculty who aren't eating. Because your company wants to sell as much food as possible, you decide to print up little cards for each table that say something about the problem.

Here, then, you must make decisions about what the card will say and how you'll render that in specific choices as you draft and revise. And these choices will depend a great deal on how you think about your audience.

Here's one possible version, which one of us found in the cafeteria of a large state university:

> *Note:* There will be NO studying in this cafeteria from 11:30–1:00. You MUST be eating to remain here during those hours!
> The Management

And here's another version, this one from a cafeteria at a different state university:

> You are welcome to use this food service for study and social activities during all open hours other than 11:00–1:15 when your fellow university community members need it for dining. Please be understanding and considerate of the need to share and enjoy our university dining facilities and use them appropriately during all times of the day.

Clearly, these two messages are trying to convey the same basic information—asking patrons of the cafeteria to refrain from studying during lunch time. But the two texts are also very different in style, tone, etc. Those differences say a lot about how each establishment wants to relate to its audience.

YOUR TURN

In your writer's notebook, speculate for a paragraph or two about just what might be some of the differences in the two cafeterias' attitudes toward their audiences. You might want to ask yourself how you reached your conclusions about those attitudes. What kind of message is being **stated** through the language? What kind of message is being **implied?** Is language always a reflection of underlying beliefs and attitudes? If not, what could be going on in the minds of the two writers of these signs? (Feel free to invent some other circumstances that might explain why each writer made the specific textual decisions you see in the two signs.)

Finding a Balance

Being aware of your audience in writing is not always an easy process. That's because even when you're sure you've analyzed your audience in detail, you'll inevitably be surprised by an unexpected response. Audiences are people, and people are constantly changing and reformulating their ideas.

What, then, can being aware of your audience help you to do? Perhaps most importantly, it can help you to find **balance** in your writing—balance between yourself as a writer and your audience as readers. Balance so that you neither compromise your own beliefs and feelings nor insist on them pig-headedly. Balance so your audience will say, "I may not agree with this writer, but she sure has a good point and is willing to see other sides of the issue." Balance so you can express yourself **and** cause change, show someone your role **and** be sensitive to theirs.

In this way, audience stands at one end of a continuum, with "self" at the other. By "self," we mean the sorts of personal goals you're trying to accomplish in your writing, and the way you portray yourself—the "voice" you use or the "persona" you convey. If you strive too hard to appeal to your audience, you'll lose your "self," like a slave agreeing with everything his master says. If you get too caught up in your self, on the other hand, you may end up losing your audience, like the person at the party who rambles on and on without thinking for a moment whether what she's saying is worth her listeners' time.

To think further about this concept of balance, consider the following example. Imagine that you've been renting an apartment and are just about to move out. Your landlord says that you've done some minor damage to the apartment and refuses to return your security deposit. You think you've taken excellent care of the apartment, and you decide to write a letter to the landlord asking him for your deposit again. If you become too caught up in your self, you'll forget about how your audience, the landlord, will react to your letter. If you become too sensitive to the landlord as a reader, you may forget that you have a point to make, a goal you intend to accomplish. Here are two versions of such letters:[1]

Version 1

Mr. Gregory, alias Jerk:
You have no right to withhold my security deposit, and I demand that you return it. From the moment I moved into your seedy, run-down apartment, I knew right away that you were an evil crook, bent on exploiting students. Now I'm sure of it. You disgust me, with your beat-up old truck and your leering helpers who are always snooping around the place and taking coffee breaks every ten minutes. As for your apartment, it stinks. I've been miserable here; it's noisy, dirty, and uncomfortable. And I'm sure there are all sorts of violations of the housing code here—loose wires, leaking gas lines, clogged sewers. You better send me my money back, or else. I'll sue you, you bastard!

Version 2

Dear Mr. Gregory,
I know this is a real imposition, especially now that the holidays are approaching. But I'd very much appreciate it if you could think about returning my security deposit. I know that's a lot to ask, and that you probably need the money to make repairs on my apartment. I guess that's part of being a property owner. I'm sure it must be hard to keep your apartments in good working order. And, of course, there's a lot of regular wear and tear every day in these apartments, just from normal use. I certainly can sympathize with you and your workers; and I really hope you have a great holiday. Thanks for your consideration.

Mr. Gregory is very likely to ignore the first writer's request because the letter is so antagonistic, and antagonism usually builds defensiveness and adds to hostility. The writer seems to be thinking only from his own point of view, expressing his feelings instead of relating to his reader. But the landlord is also likely to ignore the second writer's request because the letter is so weak and conciliatory. Unless he's a very pitying man, he may think that returning the security deposit doesn't mean very much to the writer anyway.

Finding balance is not easy because language isn't simple: a single word can change the feel of an entire letter and imply something that wasn't intended. And the way language is interpreted varies from reader to reader, making it difficult to be completely certain what effect it will have. But

---

[1] We are indebted to Lee Odell for giving us the idea for this example.

thinking carefully about your **textual** decisions in terms of your **audience** can help you get the effect you hope for. How do we know this is true? We want to give you one more example, this one from a real experience.

A family we know in Buffalo, New York, bought a new car from a major American automobile manufacturer. But after two winters on the salt-laden roads of upstate New York, the car began to show signs of rust; the wheel wells were starting to rot away, and places on the front fenders had become pocked with little holes. Worse still, the guarantees had all expired, and our friends hadn't paid for any extra rust protection when they'd bought the car. So they decided to write a letter to the company to tell them how unhappy they were with their car.

As the family composed a first draft of their letter, they were very much immersed in themselves as writers: they complained bitterly about their car, criticizing the company, saying they would tell everyone about their terrible experience, and swearing they would do all they could to drag down the company's name.

As they thought more about their readers, though, they began to realize that such a bitter letter wouldn't have much effect on changing the company: the reader (most likely someone in the public relations department) would probably be uneasy for a moment, but would assume the company had lost a buyer. It wouldn't be worth trying to keep the family as loyal customers, so the company would probably send out a standard "form letter" apology.

The family's revised letter was much more sensitive to the intended audience. They pointed out that they had always liked the quality of the company's cars in the past, and that it was a shame that their family tradition of owning that brand of automobile was now sure to end. And even though they conveyed a strong sense of disappointment, they also recognized their audience's point of view: how difficult it is to make a high-quality product with escalating costs for materials, competition from Japan, and labor disputes.

Finally, they sent the letter off with a feeling that they'd made their point without condemning their reader, and that perhaps their letter could bring about some constructive change in the company so that future car buyers wouldn't be so disappointed.

A week later, they got a reply in the mail. It pointed out that normally there would be nothing the company could actually do about such a problem. In their case, however, an exception would be made. The letter instructed the family to take their car (now over two years old) to a nearby dealer. Waiting for them there would be a brand new car—the latest year of the same model—which they would be given free of charge, together with a five-year guarantee against rust. And the letter was signed by the president of the company.

In this case, the family had found a good balance between their interests and the interests of their audience, and so their letter had good results.

From the audience's point of view, the letter suggested that it was still possible to salvage the family's trust, by giving them a new car. And, in fact, it did: the family is still buying that company's cars.

YOUR TURN

Imagine that you've been asked by a social service agency to write three short leaflets (a page or so each) on heroin addiction. A picture of an addict shooting up will be used as the cover of the leaflet. The first leaflet will be distributed to a group of fourth-graders at a local elementary school. The second will be sent to a group of elderly people at a nursing home. The third will be read by ex-heroin addicts who were part of a special program to help them quit. First, plan briefly for writing these three short leaflets, and then try drafting them.

After you've completed your drafts, jot down in your writer's notebook some ideas about what you see in your drafts and what sorts of problems you faced trying to write the leaflets. You might consider the following questions:

> Even though you were writing about the same topic or subject (heroin addiction), you probably wrote about it differently for your different readers. What are some of the differences in the **content** of your writing? Why didn't (or couldn't) you write exactly the same thing for each group?

> No purpose for your writing was given in the assignment. What differences did you discover about **why** you might write to these groups? What reasons did you find for focusing on heroin addiction?

> Look at the **language** you used in the three leaflets. Are there any differences in your style or tone, your choice of words, the length of your sentences? Why didn't you simply use the same language for each audience?

> Think about the image you were trying to portray of yourself to your readers. Did that self-image change at all as you changed audiences? Think up a metaphor for your relationship with each audience (e.g., "like a father to his son," "grabbing them by the lapels," "hitting them over the head," "soothing and stroking," etc.). Why do you suppose you developed that sort of relationship? What does it say about your sensitivity to your audience?

WORKING WITH YOUR AUDIENCE DURING THE WRITING PROCESS
Planning

Just as it can help to begin thinking specifically about your purpose for writing during your early planning stages, so brainstorming for possible audiences can provide you with a kind of compass for making appropriate choices as you develop and draft your material. If you know in advance that your audience will be the striking members of a local union of janitorial workers, you'll make different decisions about what you write and how you write it than if your audience will be personnel management officers at a high-tech electronics firm.

Not all your writing, of course, will be (or can be) directed to such specific groups. If you're writing a letter to an established special-interest group expressing your views on a controversial issue in their area of concern, you'll probably have no trouble predicting their position. But if you're writing a letter to the editor of a newspaper, all you can know for sure are some general demographic characteristics of its readers (readers of the *Washington Post* or the *New York Times,* for example, will have a different profile from readers of the *Talahoochie Swamp Gazette* or the *White Supremacy Newsletter*). Beyond very general characteristics, you can't know much at all about a large audience. At exactly the same moment, your *Los Angeles Times* editorial on the issue of marijuana legalization may be read by a 27-year-old radical Marxist feminist, a 68-year-old furniture store owner with a son in treatment for heroin addiction, a 43-year-old taxi driver who thinks we ought to drop a hydrogen bomb on Moscow, and a charming little old woman who owns a Victorian bed-and-breakfast inn and doesn't know the difference between marijuana and marigolds. (We're stereotyping here, of course, but you can get the point.)

As you plan your writing, then, bear in mind that the specificity with which you can imagine your audience depends on how narrowly you can actually define it. Occasionally it's a group of people with similar attitudes, educational levels, and experiences, and you may know what those similarities are. At other times it's a much broader audience among whom these characteristics vary considerably.

The way you think about your audience will also vary in terms of your purpose for writing. If you're reporting the results of a two-year study of rabies in inner-city sewer rats, you won't have to think much about your audience's "opinions" on sewer-rat rabies; instead, you'll be trying to show that your study was conducted well and that you're reporting the results objectively and thoroughly. If, on the other hand, you're using the results of your study to persuade the city council to pump a million dollars into exterminating sewer rats because you found two cases of rabies in 18 months, be prepared to consider many points of view.

In any writing you do, you'll find it useful to consider the following questions about your audience during the planning stage:

Knowledge.   How much does your audience know about your subject? If you're writing about something highly technical, does your audience share your understanding and use of terminology, or will you have to translate this into something more basic? Very often, this consideration drastically changes the content of your writing. Are you writing to other people who raise expensive fantail guppies and already know the telltale symptoms of most scale and fin diseases, or are they innocent tropical fish novices who aren't even aware that guppies don't hatch from eggs?

Beyond their specific knowledge of the topic you're discussing, you also need to consider your audience's broader knowledge—their general level of education. A highly intelligent investment banker who knows nothing about how to waterproof her basement walls might read your home-improvement newsletter on the subject with greater ease than a worker at a muffler repair shop who has a ninth-grade education. If you're writing for the investment banker, you might have to define some of your terms more fully, but your language could be more sophisticated than if you were writing for someone who can barely read.

If your audience is sufficiently large, this question of education can leave you in a quandary. Do you risk sounding condescending by explaining too much in too simple a way, or do you risk frustrating your readers by assuming more knowledge than they have? In such cases, when you're sure you've found out as much as you can about your potential audience, it's better to err on the side of completeness and simplicity. If you've ever listened to a speech about some topic you know pretty thoroughly, you probably didn't mind it when the speaker went over something you already knew; such reviews are painless and can often be refreshing. But your reaction is very different when the rest of the audience are experts and you can't understand a word the speaker is saying.

Attitudes.   Characterize your audience's attitudes toward your subject as best you can. Can you know in advance how your audience feels about your subject? If you're arguing an opinion of some sort, will they approach your article already in favor of your views or opposed to them?

If there is no way of predicting how your audience feels about your subject, now is a good time to try some focused brainstorming, considering all possible points of view. Try drawing an "audience cluster" or tree: place your subject or topic at the center of the cluster (or top of the tree) and then create nodes or branches by filling in possible reactions or opinions of several different audiences. (Go ahead and stereotype for a while, as we did above: how **would** a taxi driver who wants to bomb Moscow feel about your topic? How about a radical Marxist feminist? How about your laconic cousin, your "old '60s type" friend, or your very conservative boss?)

Another excellent way to think of your audience while planning is to wear other people's shoes. If you're writing about something controversial, especially something that begs for a solution, first make a list of every argument you can think of in support of your solution. Then, for each argument, put on the shoes of someone opposed to your solution. How would they counter each support statement in your list? Once you've walked through your entire list in their shoes, put your own back on again. You'll be much better prepared to argue against their possible counterarguments because you've considered them fully. Or, better still, you may realize the genuine force of their reasons and grow less one-sided and doctrinaire in your own beliefs.

Interest.   How interested is your audience in your subject? If there's a chance their eyes will start to glaze over with indifference once they begin reading, you've got a very different sort of audience problem. Maybe they're not already charged up about racial discrimination in South Africa. What if they don't have a vested interest in the new tax law? What if cam-shaft engineering is about as interesting to them as ice scrapers and anti-freeze are to a Bahamian? In that case, it's up to you to raise their blood pressure a bit, get them to laugh, jump up, nod their heads in agreement, or make it worthwhile to disagree. How can you foreground for **them** that which makes the subject significant for **you?**

Relationship.   Who does your audience think you are? In much writing, your audience will know something about you before they begin reading. If you've been working in a small business for five years, anyone who's been there for more than a few months will probably know something about you—your past work, your attitudes, your beliefs about company policy, times you made a big success and times when you stumbled. In addition, your audience may know something about your position relative to theirs. If you're a stock clerk and you're writing to the chairman of the board about your low salary, you'll make very different decisions about your style and tone than if you're a store owner and you're writing a memo reminding your employees to come to work on time.

In other writing, your audience won't know you from Jane or John Smith; you're just the author of the piece they happen to be reading. Sometimes who you are won't really matter to your reader. Many people, for instance, can't tell you the names of the newspaper writers whose articles they read ten minutes ago over breakfast.

Your "identification" with your audience will depend on what sort of writing you're doing and what you hope it will accomplish. If calling attention to yourself as the writer of a piece is important for some reason, you'll make different choices than if you're simply reporting the facts. But it's important to remember that being noticed as the writer is not intrinsically any better or worse than remaining anonymous.

As you work on your draft, ask yourself some questions about your relationship with your audience: How do they feel about you? What is your status relative to theirs? Have you written anything in the past they might have seen, or do they know something about your actions or beliefs? Here is a good time to try a particle/wave/field on your audience—describing them as they currently are, then thinking of them more dynamically, as something in a state of change, and finally in terms of the field of relationships they maintain with you, with each other, and with the culture at large.

YOUR TURN

The following opening paragraphs on black walnut trees were written by a student in a composition class one of us taught a few years ago. The writer worked for the National Forest Service, and as part of his job he did research on tree growth. The assignment was to write an essay for readers in the community (a rural midwestern town of about 50,000 residents) on something he knew well or had expertise in, and which the readers would be interested in learning about.

Black Walnut Growth Increased When Interplanted with Nitrogen-Fixing Shrubs and Trees

Because black walnut (*Juglans nigra* L.) trees are valuable for both wood and nuts, new ways are always being sought to accelerate their growth. Recently, it was found that walnuts grow more rapidly when interplanted with nitrogen-fixing plants. We conducted this study to determine which species of nitrogen-fixing plant has the greatest effect on walnut growth.

This first paragraph was the beginning of his rough draft. After a conference group with three other members of the class, he completely revised the essay. Here's his new title and opening paragraph:

Black Gold . . . with Leaves

Black walnut trees produce the most valuable lumber and veneer of all timber species grown in the central United States. In December of 1965 near Franklin, Indiana, the Amos Thompson Veneer Company bought a black walnut tree at auction for $12,600. The Atlantic Veneer Corporation out of Beaufort, North Carolina, purchased eighteen black walnut trees near Pioneer, Ohio, for $80,000. One of these trees was valued at $30,000. Walnut logs, veneer, and lumber are used not only in this country, but are exported to other countries such as Germany and Japan for the production of fine furniture and paneling.

In your writer's notebook, spend a few minutes speculating on the differences between these two openings. Does the first version seem confident and well-written? If so, why did the writer change it so drastically? What shifts in purpose do you detect? What shifts in sensitivity to audience? Is the writer trying to establish a different relationship with his audience? Characterize the relationships.

Drafting and Revising

You'll find that your drafting process will be smoother, with fewer annoying puzzles, if you have a fairly clear picture of your audience and its characteristics before you begin writing. Keep your audience in the back of your mind as you go along, and your decisions—about diction, sentence complexity, and so on—will be guided almost automatically. Use your natural adaptation to different audiences to help you.

Would that writing were so simple! Very often, you'll find that in the heat of the writing struggle, you've taken a narrow perspective on your topic. After all, you can't think of everything; you may be so caught up working with your ideas that your audience has faded into the background. This is why it's absolutely essential to think carefully about audience as you revise your writing.

The finest way we know to get information about audience during the revising process is to ask one or more readers to role-play your intended audience. Give them the following questions together with your draft (these can also serve to help you role-play your own different audiences as well):

How would [intended audience] respond to this draft? Are there are specific parts (words, sentences, paragraphs, or sections) to which they might object, or which might result in undesirable responses? "Become" the intended audience; read through their eyes.

Is there a good match between the intended audience's knowledge or expertise and the language of my draft? Am I assuming too much or too little knowledge on the part of my audience?

Is my draft **too** sensitive to audience (wavering uncertainly between the technician and the layman, the for and the against, the left and the right)? Do I seem to be trying to please everyone and anyone, or **is** there clearly a specific audience I'm addressing or invoking in this piece?

Regardless of your own specific response, how interested do you think my audience will be in what I've written? Why?

Does my audience present at least some sort of challenge to me? If they already know about the subject fully, and if they're not interested in hearing what they know, and if they already agree with what I'm saying, is there anything in the draft which is worth reading?

Finally, consider writing a "justification" of your finished text based on your audience. Stand back from your writing and begin a parallel text that explains the decisions you made, referring specifically to the characteristics of your audience: "I began this paper by describing not just the statistics on illegal aliens in Florida last year but also their impact on the Floridian economy because I figured that a liberal senator in a northeastern state might not be aware of how severe the problem really is down there." Or, "I figured that the subject of illegal aliens might not be all that interesting to readers of our northeastern college paper, so I began my editorial with an anecdote about a young Floridian fisherman I know who's out of work because the illegal aliens are being hired by big fishing fleets at fifty cents an hour." You'll find that if you have trouble justifying each part of your paper in terms of your audience, you may have missed the mark. Originally, for example, we had three more pages on audience following the sentence you're now reading, but we couldn't justify it. We thought hard about you as our reader, and we decided you've gotten the point by now. So we dropped it.

Enough said.

Chapter Nine

SHARING THE LOAD: WRITING AND REVISING COLLABORATIVELY

Writing is almost always portrayed as a lonely, solitary business, and there's a certain amount of truth in this. Whether the image is as romantic as that of a tormented young poet scratching out his verses in a seedy garret, or as mundane as a modern college student pecking out the draft of a lab report in a dorm room under fluorescent lights, we usually see writers locked in single combat with their prose. Even if the writer is working in a crowded library or coffee shop, she's detached from the rest of the inhabited world.

But that's not the whole story, for in another sense writing is a most social business as well. Writing **is** communication, the attempt to reach out to other people, to deliver some sort of message, to make yourself heard. The lonely consumptive poet is writing not only "to his own soul" but also in hopes of publication. As a student, you're not writing in a vacuum, but explaining something on paper to your instructor or classmates, or to some fictional "general audience," or perhaps to one or more real readers beyond the classroom. The struggling writer is almost always struggling with and for an audience—even in diary writing, where to some extent there is a judging, responding part of the self sitting on the writer's shoulder.

Why we so often choose to isolate ourselves as writers has both cultural and psychological causes, but it doesn't have to be that way. Writers can give each other an immense amount of help (and moral support) at almost every point in the writing process. They can even go further and write collaboratively, joining forces to create something grander and smarter than any of them could have produced on their own.

The advantages of sharing your work with other writers, in part or in full, are many. Most obvious, perhaps, is that you and your friends, colleagues, or fellow students can function as sample audiences for each other, reading works in progress and responding to them. You can also share whatever "tricks of the trade" you've learned. Seeing how others approach writing greatly enriches your own repertoire of writing strategies. Not least of all, sharing work with other writers breaks down the discouraging and threatening walls we put between each other. Instead of being the one poor wretch who has real trouble writing, surrounded by a planet full of facile literary geniuses, you realize that, though some people enjoy writing, practically nobody finds it easy. It's a discovery you can't make too often.

In this chapter, we'll consider what writers can actually do for each other. The first half of the chapter focuses on the help you can provide each other as sample audiences. We'll show you how to solicit and make use of feedback to improve your work in progress, and how to give the sort of feedback that will help other writers do the same.

The second part of the chapter focuses on collaborative writing, where two or more writers are responsible for producing one piece of work. We trace the entire process of writing from first conception to final editing, suggesting how you can most usefully work together on each of these.

HELPING EACH OTHER TO WRITE

In most of the writing you do, you'll probably be solely responsible for your text. In your personal and business letters, your memos on the job, and your writing for college, yours will usually be the only name on the paper. Other people, however, can often help you produce your best work. The easiest way to arrange such help is simply to corner someone whose judgment you respect, present your work to her, and ask for her response. A more elaborate procedure, but in the long run probably a more powerful one, is to take part in a writers' group: several people who meet to discuss each other's work. The most productive writers' groups are those that meet regularly, every week or so, over a period of time. But even useful one-shot groups can be organized, in a dorm or sorority house or restaurant or wherever it's convenient.

Advantages of Forming a Writers' Group

In the middle of all the work you're doing to produce a piece of writing, you may think that spending time looking at other people's drafts or getting some feedback on yours is simply a bother; why not just go off to a corner and keep working?

For one thing, being exposed to other writers in the midst of their struggles can be an eye-opener. Each person approaches writing tasks differently. Some are furious brainstormers. Others sketch a few ideas and trust that in drafting they'll produce the rest. Still others go through draft after draft, each at high speed, until they've produced something they like. Simply watching other writers in action and comparing notes provides a sort of natural laboratory for examining how different techniques work in different hands. Sometimes a problem that you'd found impossible to solve in your own work simply vanishes when you look at it through another's eyes.

Second, you'll find that just talking about your work can be helpful, regardless of what the others say in return. In describing your work, your hopes, and your problems, you can sometimes talk your way into strategies you hadn't before considered. And whenever you explain your ideas to somebody afresh, you come to better understand both your ideas and your presentation. Even before you start rushwriting, you can benefit simply by telling your group what you plan to write about and something of how you might proceed. The group's questions requests for further information, expressions of interest, and nutshelling of your words encourage you to reexamine your ideas again and again until you've developed precisely the crystals you need.

The main advantage of a writing group, finally, is to provide you with a sample audience for your work. Simply by being there, listening to you, or reading your work, the group makes the whole idea of an audience more real. Keeping your audience imaginatively before you as you draft takes work. Having real faces and voices and personalities who will be reading your material gives you someone to focus on, someone specific to talk to as you write. This automatically helps you develop in your writing that mysterious quality called "voice."

Having several people in the group, each with his or her own peculiar temperament, interests, intellect, and assorted eccentricities gives you a sense for the range of effects your writing can produce. Ursula, who's an artsy, romantic sort, may consistently find your work intense and exhilarating, whereas Gene, who's in management, may find it self-dramatizing and silly. If you ever need to write a résumé and cover letter for a job application, you'll know whom to listen to more carefully. In time, you may get to know so well how different group members will react that you can use them as characters in written "dialogues" (see pp. 24–27) while you're developing your material.

If you read your writing aloud to your group, another excellent source of information is your own reactions. Note carefully how you're feeling as you read through each passage. Where do you really get involved in your own story, and enjoy sharing it? What seems to go smoothly and well? At what points do your ears and neck start to grow warm? What feels halting or seems to miss the point? What do you feel like hurrying over? Any of this you can note and recall later will help guide your revision.

Mechanics of a Writers' Group

To set up a writers' group, you need from three to six people who are also writing, and who are willing to meet to discuss each other's work. At a designated time, you meet for long enough to spend at least ten or fifteen minutes on each person's piece (this will vary, of course, depending on the number of people in the group and the length or complexity of the writing being discussed).

Each writer gets one 15-minute block of time. When it's your turn, you present your work, and the other group members respond with their observations, criticism, questions, advice, and general reactions to it. In presenting your draft, you can either read the piece aloud or provide members with copies of it. You usually get the most thorough feedback by providing copies at least a day before the meeting. Have the others read over your piece carefully before they arrive, jotting down their comments on the draft itself.

As the presenting writer, your task is to direct the group's attention and take note of what they say. It's essential that everyone gets a fair share of the available time for consideration of his or her writing. The group might even select a timekeeper to guarantee this. Beyond this formality (and an agreement that the purpose of the meeting is to accomplish a task and not to conduct a social hour) the groups should try to remain informal and relaxed.

YOUR TURN

1. Explain to someone the thoughts you have for a paper you're planning to write (or for which you just have notes). Afterward, answer

these questions in your notebook. How did your ideas change as you presented them? What did you learn about how to present your work? What were your listener's reactions? How might this help you when you actually draft the paper?

2. Read aloud a draft of something you've written. You might even ask your listener not to give you any feedback, just to see what you discover from your own reactions. Again, describe what happened. How will this information help you in revising?

Presenting Your Work to a Writers' Group

Taking the Right Attitude.   To make any use at all of people's reactions to your work, you have to go in with the right attitude. It's called humility. And by humility, we don't mean self-abasement. Don't toss your paper to the group, throw your arm over your eyes, and moan: "There it is. I know it's trash. I wrote it at three o'clock this morning with the baby crying. Go ahead, tear it to pieces." The message this really gives, obviously, is: "Spare me. Don't help me. Don't take me seriously. Above all, don't tell me what you really think."

By humility we mean the cool, mature, matter-of-fact realization that what you've written can be better than it is—something that's true of every piece of writing on the planet. Everything could stand work. With help, you really can make "silk purses out of sows' ears"—but only if you accept that you haven't got a silk purse to start with. Once this fact settles in, you'll no longer ask (with pathetic hopefulness), "Does this need any work?" Instead, you'll coolly and matter-of-factly ask, "How does this strike you? Where might I go with it? What works? What needs work?"[1]

Learn to detach yourself from your work. Don't take criticism of your work as criticism of you. Your work is objective; you've turned it into a text, a piece of writing, a thing. It sits outside you with its own strengths and weaknesses. It's not that you're being diagnosed by a panel of psychiatrists; it's more like your car is being examined by mechanics. Let your fellow mechanics help you find out what's making the funny rattling noise, or where you might install the fuel injector; then, in turn, help them with their machines. In any case, even if your work turns out to have serious problems, whom would you rather have point these out: your group members . . . or your teacher, editor, or boss? The writing group acts as a safety net between you and the reader that ultimately matters.

---

[1]These five words, "What works? What needs work?" can be almost chanted as a mantra throughout the revision process. The guru who first taught us this mantra was Donald Murray in his excellent *Write to Learn,* New York: Holt, Rinehart and Winston, 1984.

Before the Meeting. Again, for the most thorough feedback, provide your group members with a copy of your work before the meeting and ask that they read it. You might take the opportunity to direct to some degree the feedback you receive. Though you may be suffering the fuzzy blindness we all develop to recently completed drafts, you probably have at least some idea of the questions and problems you have with it. That paragraph about the Great Soufflé Disaster—it just feels too long (though you're not sure). Or the description of how to prune the azaleas seems (perhaps?) too sketchy to be clear. Or the two paragraphs about Atilla the Hun on pages 3 and 7 seem as if they belong together, but again you're uncertain. You'd like a second opinion.

So ask for it. Before you make photocopies of your draft, scribble those questions in the margins and ask your readers to pay attention to them. Or write your questions and concerns on a separate sheet of paper and attach it to the draft. Give your readers some idea of how they can best help you. To make the time they spend on your work most productive, there's a number of things they might need to know:

What kind of a paper are you working on? A proposal for a research project? A short story? A term paper?

Who is your audience? What kind of background do they have? Why would they be reading your work?

What are your goals for the paper? What do you want it to do for or to your readers?

Where are you in developing it? Is this rushwriting? An early draft? Almost ready to turn in?

What sort of help do you want? Are you testing out ideas? Searching for new angles? Or are you wondering about tone or persona? Do you want your spelling and punctuation checked? Are you worried about organization? Would it help to have your readers try to nutshell or outline your paper after reading it?

What are your specific doubts about the paper? What are you secretly afraid people will think of it?

Feel free to supply any or all of this information to your readers. On the other hand, you might just ask them something like, "Read this and tell me how you react to it." If you're completely at sea with your draft, that may be all you can do.

At the Meeting. When it comes time to discuss your work, take the responsibility to get the feedback you need. Ten to fifteen minutes is not much. If you have questions about major issues—tone, say, or organization—you want to make sure these get talked about. If someone starts pointing out each of your misspelled words, you need to steer the conversation in another, more fruitful direction. Not that misspellings are unimportant, but they can be pointed out just fine by circles on the text itself; they hardly require discussion.

Something else to watch for is the conversation growing murkily congratulatory. Out of politeness (and perhaps laziness) the first time a group meets, all the comments tend toward uselessly global praise. You get dialogues like the following:

Writer: What'd you think about it?
Reader: I really liked it.
Writer: Well, what did you like about it?
Reader: Oh, I don't know. Just kinda the whole thing.
Writer: The whole thing?
Reader: Yeah. I really thought it was good. It really flows.
Writer: Was there anything specific you noticed?
Reader: (Long pause.) The title. The title was really catchy. And kinda all this stuff through here. In fact, the whole thing. It was really good. I really liked it.

And so on. It all feels very cozy and safe, and none of it does the writer a damned bit of good. The problem isn't that it's praise. Starting with praise is fine; but even praise is more helpful when it's specific, focused praise. If it's all good, you need to press the questions, What works best? Where is it strongest? A reader who only gives you vague back-patting hasn't really given you any guidance. He's shirking his role as safety net—and wasting everybody's time.

One way to avoid this is to start by asking each group member to nutshell your paper, to summarize it in a single pithy sentence. You might even ask them to write these down, to prevent them all from echoing the first speaker. In this way, you'll find out immediately if what you thought you said bears any significant relationship to what the readers thought they heard. Prepare to be surprised. Each of them may well have a different answer.

From here the conversation may become more open-ended and freewheeling. It's your job to keep the conversation going and to channel it in useful directions. You need to interview your readers, to probe, question, raise issues, press for answers. If they're on a roll, let them roll. But anytime the conversation threatens to flag, it's up to you to raise another issue.

Whatever you do, no matter how severely tempted you may be, **don't go on the defensive.** Don't protect your work, or explain away the problems your group members point out, or insist that they're missing the point. Don't criticize their criticism. Don't bite the dentist for finding a cavity. Your job is purely to gather data of a particular type: that is, how your words affect a sample of readers. If something is unclear to them, or confusing, or boring, or offensive, **then it is.** They're doing you a favor to tell you so. If you attack them, or keep denying the validity of their claims, or refuse to listen to or believe them, they'll quit giving you the feedback you need. It won't be their loss.

Accept everything during the meeting. Your job is simply to question, listen, and take notes. Even if you're sure you're right, note down their reactions and move on to something else. You don't have to decide anything then and there. Once you have their reactions, you can go home and brood over what to make of them.

There's no way to make this process entirely comfortable or pleasant. Even if you knew your work was flawed, you always entertain the secret hope that no one else will notice. But they do. And it always takes a few hours to recover from having it pointed out, even if ever so gently. Grin and bear it. On the other hand, your work may be much better received than you expect. Sheer weariness often makes you see your draft as worse that it is. Finding out that other people actually laughed at the Soufflé Disaster can make it much easier to face the prospect of reworking it. And in any case, hearing how other people react to your writing is always interesting. Always.

After the Meeting. When you've finished with the group meeting, you may have mixed feelings about your draft. You'll know there is still plenty of work left to do, but you may feel a mixture of encouragement and dismay, gratitude and indifference, possibility and boredom. Some of your worst fears may have been silly, and you'll feel good; at the same time, others may have been right on target. Now is the time to sort it all out, put aside any negative feelings and approach the task of revising your work with common sense and optimism. At the very least, you **know** where some of the problems are now—and that can be a big relief in itself.

Before sitting down to revise your paper, take a few minutes to review precisely what you want it to do, and for whom. Pay special attention to any differences between your actual final readership and your sample readers. How close a match are they? If you're writing an editorial for your college paper, your classmates might be a perfect sample. Everything they say might be relevant. If, on the other hand, you're writing a technical report to be read by practicing chemical engineers, you may have to evaluate your group's responses accordingly. This doesn't mean you should dismiss them. Merely by being adult readers of English they have something very important in common with your final audience. But they might well need to have objects and concepts explained that your final audience will readily understand.

Carefully consider all the comments you receive. With each comment, try to get "inside it," to see your paper through your readers' eyes; try to find in yourself some echo of the reaction reported by your reader. If you can see for yourself the problems your reader saw in your paper, you'll be much better able to do something about them.

Remember the strength there is in consensus. When two or more of your readers describe how a particular passage comes across, they're probably right. In the very act of drafting your paper, you may have been blind to some matters. Your readers come to your paper fresh; no long familiarity with your subject has dulled or muddled their brains. Much of the time, the problems they point out are the very problems you yourself would discover, if you could just stick your paper in a closet somewhere and avoid looking at it for six months.

On the other hand, never let your readers' comments intimidate or tyrannize you. You're the final judge, the final authority on what you want your paper to be and on how you want to get it there. Just because a couple of readers said you should cut the dogfight scene doesn't mean you absolutely have to follow their advice. You may feel strongly about that scene; if so, ask yourself why they thought it didn't belong (if you didn't get around to asking them during the meeting). Maybe you can salvage it somehow and get around the problem. If not, cut it out with scissors and put it into your writer's notebook for another paper. It's still yours, whether you use it or not.

YOUR TURN

Below, we've printed an actual transcript of a session of five students in a writers' group.[2] The excerpt shows the group working effectively to help one writer improve her draft.

The writer, Alice, presented a draft of a personal narrative. Her account describes an incident from childhood: the time she was cracked across the nose by a baseball bat and knocked unconscious. The real interest of the story lay in her vivid description of the feel, sounds, sights, even smells, of the accident itself ("I smelled something tinny—like friction of metal against metal, or the smell of an electrical fire, which burned my sinuses"). Nonetheless, in drafting the piece, she had some trouble getting started. She began her rough draft like this:

> Storytelling is a true art. A good storyteller can describe a moment so that his audience will actually experience the event being described. The storyteller will use descriptive words to trigger similar memories of his audience. Following is a true story of an event that happened to me when I was about nine years old.

The discussion went in part as follows:

Amy: Why do you start off by saying storytelling is a true . . . or a good story can just . . . why do you start out talking about stories?

Alice: Well, cause I didn't know . . . because this is real details, you know. This is . . . this story. . . .

Alan: It sounds like she's going to start talking about storytelling.

Alice: This story, see, this is the name of it, "Description," and good storytelling is an art. And good stories can describe.

---

[2]We've borrowed this example from Martin Nystrand and Deborah Brandt, "Response to Writing as a Context for Learning to Write," in *Responding to Writing: Theory, Practice and Research,* ed. Chris M. Anson (Urbana, IL: NCTE, forthcoming).

Amy: Well, if you named it "Description" . . . "Description" just kind of summarizes that, you know. You don't really need that because that's not part of your story. And you don't go back to it, you know. Maybe you should go back to it.

Alice: Maybe that's how I could end it. I don't know how I would open it if I didn't, you know. What's going to make someone interested in this? What's going to make someone pick it up and read it?

Kristen: I thought it was neat here about . . . (indicates a particular passage). You could start with that. [The passage Kristen refers to reads: "What my eyes beheld was remarkable! On a vivid black velvet background shone five perfect, bone white stars. Each was perfectly shaped and had five points. They all moved slowly in a circular, clockwise motion."]

Mike: Yea, that's a good idea. Something like that. That's what I was thinking when you . . . when I read that.

Alice: That's how I should start it?

Kristen: Anything can happen in a cartoon. You could get . . . what you felt like . . . who's the guy on "Bugs Bunny?"

Alan: OK. What do you think? Me and the Coyote have a lot in common. Back when I was in ninth grade. . . .

Mike: I used to sit and watch cartoons when I was younger. And one day I had a similar experience . . . to be compared to somebody.

Alice: It's funny because you'd think that, you know, that's just cartoons. And all of a sudden you're laying there and you're seeing these stars.

As a result of this session, Alice overhauled her draft, and rewrote the opening of her paper. Here's the new opening:

> Last Saturday as I watched "The Road Runner Show," I saw Wile E. Coyote get cracked on the top of the head with an anvil. This happened when his well-planned scheme to capture the elusive Road Runner backfired as usual. As I watched, stars appeared and began to dance around his head. This sight triggered a memory of something that happened to me when I was about nine years old.

Study the two versions of Alice's opening and the transcription of her group discussion. Then answer the following questions in your writer's notebook:

What are the main differences between the first and second versions of Alice's opening? Look for the writer's purpose, the appropriateness of the opening for the kind of writing she's doing, and the use of details.

How would you characterize the group discussion? Is it smooth or disconnected, certain or tentative, formal or informal? Describe the comments the group members made on Alice's paper. What is their focus? What problems do they point out? Does a consensus emerge from the discussion?

How does Alice react to the comments she gets? What does she want the group to help her with?

When the group "vetos" Alice's opening, how does Kristen respond? What's useful in what she says?

What changes in Alice's revision seem to stem from the group meeting? What decisions has she made?

Responding to Someone Else's Work

On Being a "Sample Reader."   The nervousness a writer feels having her work discussed is more than understandable. When you show your work to others and ask their opinion about it, you expect to be nervous; if you care about the quality of your work, you probably should be. What's curious is that in giving feedback we're often no less nervous than in getting it.

Perhaps you've been in this situation before and know what we're talking about. The paper's in your hand. The writer sits eagerly, anxiously before you. You've read the paper. You know all the words. You know what the paper says, more or less. But then, what do you say? What do you actually tell the writer? How do you begin to help? Who are you to judge writing anyway?

In running writers' groups, it's been our experience that readers apologize almost as often as writers do. Over and over again we hear some perfectly lucid, sensitive, intelligent observation prefaced with a phrase like "Maybe I'm not reading this right, but what I picked up was . . . ," or "I'm not an English teacher or anything, but I think you might . . . ," or some other similar disclaimer.

None of this is necessary. You don't need to be an expert in English (or anything else) to provide very useful responses to the work of another writer. Sometimes, in fact, your very lack of expertise can be a real benefit, something the writer can use to his advantage. If the paper is an instruction manual on small engine repair, and you don't know a crescent wrench from a croissant, you may still be able to provide the most valuable feedback of anyone in the group. You may represent an important part of the writer's audience—the rank amateur—that she hasn't reached yet. For her instruction manual to be as useful as possible, it may have to help people at precisely your level of mechanical expertise. The same advice goes for expertise in grammar or style or other language matters. Your task is not to play English teacher, but to read as yourself and let the writer know how her words affected you. **You**. In all your unspoiled, lovely ordinariness.

So when you read a writer's text and she asks you what you think, don't worry about giving her The Truth about it. There is, after all, no **single** truth about the text; there is only the whole range of reactions it's capable of provoking in its readers. You needn't lay down the law; you need only report what happened **to you** as you read the piece. Your opinion is not the last work on the subject. Ideally, it's only one response out of a decent sample's worth of individual responses. It's the writer's duty to gather an adequate sample of responses, not yours to respond "for everybody."

You also don't need to worry about how you think you "should" respond to the words. Some people don't cry over accounts of little boys losing their puppies, just as others are bored by old Marx Brothers movies. You may just happen to be such a monster. Or suppose a writer ends her rousing editorial with a rhetorical question like, "Who then can doubt the wisdom of this proposal?" Stop a moment. Ask yourself that very question. Maybe anybody can doubt the wisdom of it. Maybe only a few unusually wise or foolish people might. In any case, don't let the writer get away with such a statement automatically. You know from the question what the writer hopes she has convinced you to believe, but what **do** you believe? In other words, how successful has she been? She needs to know this, and you can tell her.

YOUR TURN

Though you're perfectly qualified to provide someone with useful feedback on her writing, you'll always bring to the task your own unique background, knowledge, experiences, interests, and prejudices. You might help both your reader and yourself to make the best use of that uniqueness by working out just what your particular characteristics are as a reader. Answer the following questions. If you're participating in a writers' group, share these with the other members.

What is your social background? How and where were you raised? With which groups and types of people in the larger population do you identify?

What areas do you have special knowledge in? What special skills or abilities do you have?

What kind of reading do you usually do? How much do you read? What kinds of things do you never read?

What can a writer do to get your attention, keep you reading, make you root for her? What things do writers do that turn you off or annoy you or make you stop reading?

What advice would you give to anyone writing specifically for you?

Preparing for the Meeting. The fact that no one expects you to be a language expert may help to relieve any apprehension you might feel if you haven't worked in writers' groups before. On the other hand, that doesn't mean you can just recline in an easy chair and skim the members' drafts like so many magazine ads. You still owe it to the writers to read their work as thoroughly, sensitively, and intelligently as you can, and to think carefully about how to provide them the most useful feedback.

This takes concentration and time. All too often as we read we simply let the words flow over us without leaving much impression. A day later we'd be hard-pressed to remember even the topic of what we'd read, much less its structure, reasoning, tone, presentation, and illustrative details, or how we reacted to it page by page. For this, you need to read much more actively, probing and questioning the work as you go, and formulating, at least to yourself, your impressions of it. It's this active, concentrated reading that you owe your writer.

Beyond time and attention, however, you also need some method, some strategy, for working most productively in the time you have. Below we've detailed a procedure that, followed with some care, will help you read and respond to the work of another in a helpful manner.

Decide how far along in the writing process the piece is and what kind of feedback the writer needs. If the writer is sharing her first sketchy rush-writes or dialogues, all she needs to know is which ideas strike you as interesting and worth developing, or what else her material makes you think of. Organization is a minor issue, grammar and spelling distracting irrelevancies. On the other hand, if her writing represents a late, highly polished draft—one she's almost ready to turn in—the grammar, spelling, and visual appearance may be what she's especially interested in. Unless she seriously intends a major overhaul, suggesting whole new directions for development may be only discouraging and pointless.

Read the work from start to finish without stopping or pausing to mark anything. Relax, get comfortable, and read the piece attentively straight through. Don't read with an eye toward making comments, but simply to understand and enjoy the work. The point of this first quick reading is to reproduce as nearly as possible the first impressions and understanding of the final audience. Most prose, from novels to complaint letters, will only be read once by any given person. What the reader carries away after one read-through pretty much determines how effectively the piece accomplishes the writer's goals. Your writer needs to know what the effect was.

On the paper itself or on a separate sheet note your immediate reactions to it. How does the work make you feel when you're done with it? What mood does it leave you in? What do you feel toward the writer? Sympathy? Anger? Indifference? Are you fundamentally **with** the writer or **against** her? What does the paper make you want to do? Write to your senator? Dance on the rooftops? Take a nap? What images or phrases stick in your mind with particular vividness? What do you find yourself confused about? What answer do you instinctively feel like making? What kind of a letter are you tempted to send the author?

See how accurately you can reconstruct the paper. Start by nutshelling it. In one sentence, give the gist of the paper, its single main point. (Is that what the writer meant to say, do you think? Or do you think the writer intended to write one paper but actually produced something else?) What are the main points the writer's making? How does she arrange her material? You might try sketching an outline of the paper or drawing a tree of its organizational structure (see pp. 145–159).

Go back through the paper a second time, noting your reactions to it section by section in more detail. You should record any especially strong reaction you have to any specific part of the paper. If something excites you or confuses you or annoys you, make note of it. But attend also to when things are going well, when you feel yourself smoothly and easily carried along by the writing, without jars and bumps or tedium. This is harder to notice; it doesn't stand out like the rougher parts. But every half-page or so, if the writing simply seems to be working for you or if you notice even mild bright spots—neat turns of phrase, sharp images, sensible ideas—make a note of them. It's as important for the writer to know what works as to know what needs work. Not only does this help the writer fine-tune her sense of how language works, it keeps her from cutting into live flesh during her revision. Some paragraphs need to be put in a sort of game preserve to keep the writer from attacking them.

Write your reactions as precisely and carefully as possible, and in response to exactly what provoked them. You'll discover when you try to follow this advice that it's surprisingly difficult. We're asking for two kinds of precision: in the **description of the effect** and in the **location of the cause.**

Let the writer know as exactly as possible how you responded to the different parts of his work. Where were you feeling interested, calm, confused, annoyed, excited, hysterical, unsatisfied, hungry? Where did you find your mind slipping off the page into thoughts unrelated to the writing? Were there parts you wanted to skim? Did you have to reread anything two or three times before proceeding? What parts do you hope to remember? Did you feel your mind jumping around at any point or wrestling with the text, wanting to argue and blow whistles?

Try to pinpoint as precisely as you can what caused your reactions. Here you're pointing away from your subjective reactions to the words on the page. Sometimes something as small as an unfortunately chosen word—like "chick" or "broad" for "woman"—stops you in your tracks. At other times, whole long sections just seem flat or bland or uninspired. You might find that you've "read" three pages, but remember nothing about them. Trace back; find the paragraph where you started slipping away from the paper into melancholy broodings over the decline of Marvel comics. Or can you spot the sentence that really woke you up and drew you into the story?

The trick to giving useful feedback is connecting specific textual causes to your specific reactions. In essence, you're telling the writer something like, "I hear a tinny, high-pitched, airy whistling sound, and it's coming from that little shiny gadget right under there."

Feel free to report even vague, mixed, or changing responses to the writing. Your responses don't have to be strongly and clearly marked to be useful. They don't even have to be consistent. If after your best efforts all you can say is, "This passage through here just doesn't sit right somehow," you've still told your writer something. Or your feelings might be mixed ("I half think it's funny, but I feel a little insulted by it"); or the passage might change on you between readings ("At first it seemed too clever somehow; but when I reread it, it seemed really perfect"). In any case, let the writer know. You may not be alone in your ambivalence.

There's rarely a good reason for withholding any honest response arrived at after a careful, open-minded reading. Again, you're not laying down the law; you're only providing data. The writer can always choose to ignore your comment; she can't do anything with silence.

Don't feel obliged to know how to fix a problem you report. You don't have to be a gourmet chef to decide what tastes good or bitter to you. You don't need to know cars to point out to your mechanic the metallic grinding noise or the mushy feel of the brakes. It's exactly the same thing here. You might have a splendid idea of how to develop and refine the paper; and if you do, you might suggest it. But if something's bothering you, you should let the writer know, even if you have no idea how to remedy the problem.

If you want to mark grammatical, punctuation, or spelling problems, do it either after everything else or before really beginning. The best time to note run-on sentences, misspelled words, and so forth is after you've noted all your other reactions. Some people, however, can hardly read a paper with such problems; if you're one of these, mark them all first, then read the paper as if they'd all been fixed. Trying to catch these things as you read will probably prevent your attending to either content or mechanics very effectively.

Reporting your reactions. If you put yourself in the writer's place, you'll probably be quite tactful and helpful. You want both to give the writer the benefit of your observations and to inspire him to dive back into the work. You obviously don't want to humiliate or discourage him, but you also don't want to sing him a lullaby. It's no kindness to leave a problem in the draft unmentioned, any more than it would be to avoid embarrassing a scuba diver by quietly ignoring that little crack in her air hose.

You want to be encouraging, frank, and matter-of-fact. Although you don't want to ignore problems in the draft, you can well afford to understate them. Point them out clearly but gently. The writer provides all the "volume" at his end. When you discuss a writer's text with her, you're inevitably speaking through an emotional megaphone. Anything you say in a whisper is heard in a shout. Anything you say in a shout merely deafens.

Finally, when you point out something that doesn't work in the paper, try to find a second case where the writer tried the same thing but succeeded: "This part where you describe Jim seems sort of flat, but when you describe Julie in the next page I get a really clear picture of her." It's obviously encouraging to find a model of good writing in your own draft. If you've thrown one bull's-eye, you can throw another. You've got the ability; now it's just a matter of consistency. It's that kind of comment that provides both the inspiration to revise as well as very precise guidance on where and how to do it.

YOUR TURN

In Appendix B, you'll find some rough drafts of papers written by college freshmen. Read each draft as if you planned to sit down with the authors and give them your responses. Follow the guidelines we've suggested both for **what** and **how** you'd give comments to each author.

After reading and assessing and writing down your reactions, compare notes with three or four other people. What reactions, positive or negative, did you have in common? How did the work affect each of you differently? How did you vary in the way you phrased your comments? Which seemed more or less clear or helpful? Which ones might sting unnecessarily?

COLLABORATIVE WRITING

Most of the writing you'll ever do will probably be purely "solo." You'll bear the full responsibility for turning out the work; your name alone will go on the title page. If readers have any questions, complaints, or congratulations to offer, you'll be the person they bring them to. Sometimes, however, especially in work settings, you won't carry this sort of solitary load. It may happen that two people, or three, or ten, or an entire committee work together to create a single document.

Laws, business contracts, proposals, major technical reports are all usually the work of groups of varying size. The Declaration of Independence was written by a committee of five, including Thomas Jefferson (who did the actual drafting) and Benjamin Franklin (who did most of the revisions). Something like the proposal to develop a new spacecraft would entail the labor of literally dozens of writers. Closer to home, this textbook would never have been written if it had been left solely to the initiative of either of us. With two of us working at it, however, writing the textbook seemed less overwhelming, more like something we could actually finish before growing too old to enjoy the fruits of our labors. (We just made it, thank you.)

Though writing collaboratively has a lot to be said for it, it has its own problems as well. Productive collaboration requires all the writing skills and strategies we've discussed throughout this book, plus the ability to get along with and work well with other people. (As with any kind of work, the more hands you have to help, the more feet you have to trip over.) In this chapter, we want to map some of the hills and canyons of collaborative writing, suggest the most productive attitudes to carry into it, and give some pointers on how to make the work more pleasant and efficient (the two go hand in hand).

Advantages and Problems in Collaborative Writing

The most obvious advantage to collaborative writing is simply the division of labor. Four of you writing together can handle a large, complex assignment more easily than any one of you could alone. If, for instance, you need to write a long feasibility report, you'll face doing one-fourth of it with much lower blood pressure than you would the entire thing. Enough said.

Beyond that, however, the very process of writing together tends to be richer, more fruitful, and simply more fun than solitary drudgery. With several of you mulling over the same problem, the range of ideas and solutions you turn up will be much wider than any one of you could develop alone. And when the writers discuss their work together, the light bulbs go on by the dozens. Bob and Carol and Ted and Alice don't simply add together their best separate thoughts; the ideas of one strike up a chain of associations in another, which in turn remind a third of something else again, and so on. The play back and forth among so many minds together produces new thoughts geometrically.

Writing collaboratively also gives you an automatic sample audience. Such a team, in fact, is an almost ideal writers' group: every member is well aware of everyone else's task, audience, and purpose, and because they're all on the same boat in the same race, they're motivated to help out in any way possible.

A final advantage to collaborative writing is that, as a rule, fewer things are done thoughtlessly. In writing anything, you need to answer a number of questions of the sort we've discussed throughout this book: audience, format, organization, purpose, tone, and persona. When writing by yourself, it's often easy to forget the importance of these. When a number of you are working on the same piece, each of these issues pretty much has to come up for discussion, forcing you to think through and decide what to do about each one carefully. Though this can make writing as a team somewhat clumsy and slow at first, the result is a more carefully planned and written document.

The clumsiness of collaborative writing, though, is always a problem. Dividing the work up may make each part smaller and easier, but the total complexity of the project increases. Learning how to coordinate your efforts with those of your coauthors will take some time and attention.

Writers working together, in fact, run into much the same problems as those experienced by members of an athletic team, a military company, or an industrial work force. In each case, several people are working together toward one goal. If the group succeeds, all the members reap the same reward; if it fails, all endure the same punishment. To be perfectly fair, everyone would have to do exactly the same amount of work—which is of course impossible. Even if everyone has the same motivation, not every member of a work force has the same talents and capacities or even the same opportunities in terms of time, scheduling, and equipment. The result is that you have two equal and opposite worries: Will I be left holding the bag? (or) Will I let my coworkers down?

Added to these problems are others specific to writing. Each member of your group may have a different way of approaching the project: Bob's been explaining every technical term in his section, but Susan hasn't because she doesn't want to condescend to the audience. Kate's style has been informal and witty, whereas Russ's part is clinical and dry. If you bring these questions up for full, open, and cordial discussion, you'll probably resolve them fairly quickly. Sometimes, however, the different approaches either don't get discussed or your group doesn't agree on their importance. The result is a house built on a collection of incompatible floorplans: Tudor door here, Greek columns there, Spanish arches down one side, angular glass-and-steel patterns down the other. Or the group might agree on the general organization and approach, but the prose styles of the different writers might still clash—in which case, you've got a building with a coherent design, but painted in several different colors.

Strategies for Collaborative Writing

To collaborate successfully, each person has to pledge wholehearted cooperation. You have to accept that your entire relationship to the work you're producing differs radically from your relationship to a text you write alone. It's not that the work is, say, only 25 percent yours, with the other 75 percent divided equally amongst Ellen, Jose, and Muhammed. The fact is, the text belongs 100 percent to **every one of you.** Each of you may only have drafted one-fourth of the work, but each one is completely responsible for every word of it. Everyone in the group stands or falls together. You're in a position both of great power and great vulnerability.

Among other things, this should lead you to develop your material in a much more open and public manner than usual. Whatever shyness you may feel about your writing—particularly in its early, rough stages—must be laid aside in collaborative writing. You should be sharing your work with your coauthors at every stage in its development. Your brainstorming is **their brainstorming.** Your trees are **their trees.** Your rough drafts are the drafts of **their document.**

This also means refusing to take part in any picky, legalistic business about doing "only your share." To collaborate on a document of any length certainly means less work than writing the entire thing by yourself; but since the collaboration itself makes the task more complex, no simple division will tell you how much work you'll end up doing. If you're one of four writers, assume you'll do 35–50 percent of the work, not 25 percent. If you're one of ten, prepare to do 15–20 percent, not 10 percent. In collaborative writing six people each doing one-fourth of the work will just about get the task done. This is Murphy's Correction Factor for division of labor.

The general process for writing something as a team is no different from writing it yourself. The same stages we laid out in Part 1—developing your material, selecting and arranging, drafting, evaluation, and revision—apply to collaborative work no less than to solo performances. The most effective approach to each task, however, does change. Of the two most striking changes, we've already mentioned one: the work at every stage of the project becomes "public domain." The other major shift lies in the greater importance of early planning. Unless everyone's agreed on the trail before the hike begins, the entire project could be headed for the swamp.

Planning and Development. In the early meetings of your writing team, you should analyze carefully the assignment you're sharing. You should get all the questions of audience, purpose, and context out on the table.

With a clear, shared understanding of its goals, the team can then start brainstorming for ideas. One person should be appointed as secretary, and the other team members should start pitching ideas out as fast and freely as possible. It's best if the secretary has either a blackboard or overhead projector to write on, so that all members of the group can see all the ideas that have been offered.

The one rule is: anything goes. Members should toss out any and all of the ideas that occur to them. They shouldn't withhold or censor any of their own ideas, and they shouldn't evaluate or criticize any ideas of the others. Bad ideas may prove quite valuable, in that they might lead to good ones. There's no way to know in advance, and there's plenty of time to find out later. For now, all the group should be looking for is sheer quantity of ideas—good, bad, wise, silly . . . whatever. Get them out in public where they can prompt new thoughts in your coworkers. Obviously, any of the techniques suggested in Chapter Two can work for this: simple brainstorming, clustering, particle/wave/field, and others. The richest collection of ideas probably comes from giving several techniques a good run, since different approaches naturally pull different kinds of ideas and information.

Once this first wild and woolly brainstorming has played itself out, you can settle down as a group to mull over and evaluate the ideas. In the process, more ideas will arise, blend with the original dough, and turn into something else. Many of the ideas will drop away, as obvious dead ones. Others—ones you hardly considered at first—will look better over time. All of this is as it should be. You shouldn't think of this as "negotiating," but rather as "thinking out loud." Try to stay deliberately tentative and experimental at this point.

Don't worry too much about the agenda for these early meetings. Let the topics suggest themselves. If one of you gets on a roll, let him roll—and take notes. Don't be in a hurry to make final decisions about anything. The more complex the writing problem, the longer this activity will take. Be pre-pared to leave several meetings still feeling up in the air. These meetings should, however, have a fairly strict time limit. One hour, maybe two, is about all of this you'll be able to stand. Unless you agree on these limits beforehand, and stick to them, you'll keep chugging away, with less and less energy, patience, and effectiveness, until you're ready to collapse in a kind of surly exhaustion.

Though you should be willing to postpone making any final decisions, it's useful to spend the last few minutes of any meeting trying to pinpoint and define what you actually accomplished. If no final decisions were reached, what changes at least occurred in the team's outlook? What options did you discard? Which have come into prominence? What prog-ress did you make overall? Usually you can document some sort of progress, and it's encouraging to see this before calling it a day.

Over time, the issues you're wrestling with become clearer. Almost with-out noticing quite where or how, corners are turned, decisions are made. An outline or tree or other plan of the work begins to evolve in some detail. And the more detail, the better. If the danger in the early sessions is dis-couragement, the feeling that you're not making any progress at all, later on the danger becomes just the opposite, the illusion that you've made plenty of progress, and you can now all just go home and write.

Be careful about this. The outline you develop for your work as a team should be as thorough, as detailed, and as well-defined as you can make it. Any questions that you haven't discussed and settled in advance you will almost certainly approach, each in a different way. As a result, instead of finding the inconsistencies in your outline, where they're easy to fix, you'll find them in your combined rough draft, where they'll create a good deal more trouble. Would you rather have to tear down and rebuild a house, or simply redraw the floor plan before you start construction?

The ideal, in fact, would be to develop an outline so comprehensive and detailed that any one of you could write up any part of it. Not until every single team member could write the introduction equally well, review of research, methodology, results, or the conclusion, can you safely assume that the actual draft will be free of gaps, inconsistencies, and repetition. Given how much fresh invention always takes place in drafting, reaching such an ideal may be impossible; but the closer you come to it as a team, the easier later revisions will be.

Drafting. Once you've worked out and agreed upon a suitably detailed plan, drafting the document becomes a largely individual affair. If there's anything in this world two people cannot do, it's draft the same document at the same time. Here each team member will simply have to take her share of the work home and thrash it out herself, using whatever means she finds most comfortable.

But even here, you still stand to benefit by further meetings. Sometimes one of you will completely bog down on a section; you'll feel stalled, blocked, bewildered. The piece no longer makes sense to you, and you can't see how on earth to move it one paragraph further. You should feel perfectly free to bring the work to one of your team members, and that person should accept the draft as being as much his or her responsibility as yours.

Often your coauthor, simply by being fresh to the material, sails right past the difficulty that completely snarled you. In reading the draft, ideas strike your partner that would never have occurred to you. He or she can sometimes bang out the necessary pages in a fraction of the time you would have needed. At the very least, your coauthor can act as a consultant and point out the best road for you to follow. This assumes, of course, that all of you are working diligently and well, and that no one suspects anyone else of "dumping" the work. In short, thou shouldst always be willing to do for thy coauthors whatever thou wouldst have them do for thee.

Revising. Revising a collaboratively drafted document takes more ingenuity and patience than individual revision, but in some ways it's easier as well. You're not so much examining a complete, unified draft to see where it might develop or where it needs work as you're assembling the separate parts of the draft to see how they fit together. It's rather like assembling a prefabricated building or stitching together different patches into a quilt, while testing and refining each part separately.

The various separately drafted pieces of your text need to work together to form a consistent whole in terms of content, organization, and style. The ideas and facts and theory of the various parts obviously have to support each other; at the very least, you have to "get your story straight." The conclusion has to respond to all the issues raised in the introduction, the recommendations have to match the research findings, and so forth.

Consistency of organization is almost guaranteed if you're all working from the same outline; though even here, the arrangement of materials within sections often has to be parallel as well. If three tests are mentioned in order A, B, C in the methodology section, the results from them should be reported in A, B, C order in the results section, and evaluated in A, B, C order again in the discussion section. Once a pattern is established, the reader will look for the recurrence of it thereafter, and may be derailed if it's suddenly altered. Such things as the size and placement of headings, subheadings, and other visual aids also need to be standardized between sections.

Finally, the document should usually reveal a consistent sense of audience and style. Again, you should have discussed and decided these before anyone even begins to draft. But even with the fullest, more careful agreement on these, you may still find striking differences in style from one section to another. Different writers simply sound different. It's in fact one of the enduring fascinations in this business just how vividly different personalities shine through the words on the page. In collaborative writing, however, such differences are usually mere distractions. An instruction manual for computer software that moves for six pages at a formal, detached level and then suddenly turns friendly and casual will look like the patchwork it is. Since most collaborative writing is, in fact, on just such business or technical issues, the reader's concern is almost entirely with the content of the piece and not with the writers as personalities.

The best way to homogenize the prose style in a document is for all of you to rewrite **each other's** drafts. Nobody, again, has any business standing by his part of the draft as his own private property. All of the text belongs to all of the writers. You should be willing to relinquish control of your text to your group members, and you should be willing to revise their parts of the work according to your own best judgment of what will be best for the work as a whole. Obviously, you want to discuss each portion of the draft with the original writer and the whole group before doing anything major. You always want to arrive at the fullest agreement possible on every aspect of the work. But once you reach a consensus, any one of you should be able and willing to rewrite any part of the text to bring its style into conformity with the rest. (Your group may also choose to appoint one person to do this overall stylistic revision. If so, that person should probably be relieved in advance of some portion of the original drafting.)

If you do have the assignment of rewriting someone else's section, you should be willing to do so as thoroughly as you would your own writing. After all, it is your writing. Can this make for a touchy situation? Yes, it can. You don't want to offend or alienate your coauthors. Yet you shouldn't cheerfully okay work you think can be improved. In assuming this responsibility, however, you should be willing to give more help to every writer on your team than you would even in the best functioning writers' group.

Though we've been dwelling on the possible conflicts and difficulties involved, collaborative writing teams usually enjoy their work more than comparable groups of loners. The energetic sharing of ideas in the early phases, having someone you can turn to when you get stuck, the elaborate game of working the pieces of the document into a unified whole, and sometimes just knowing there are other people deeply invested in your work—all of these provide a richer, more encouraging, more entertaining atmosphere for writing than we usually enjoy huddled over our typewriters in solitary labor.

Some Final Tips

Procrastination. Procrastination is bad enough when you write alone, but in collaborative work it can really bring the roof down on your head. Your team members will sometimes need the material you've developed to carry on their own work effectively. Since every part of the document is often so tied up with every other part, you can bog down work on several sections by not keeping up on your own. Either your coworkers will have to stop work and simply wait for you, or they'll have to guess at what you plan to do and write accordingly. In the latter case, piecing together the group's work with any precision will be a lot more trouble.

Maintaining Contact.   Between even the best of outlines and the actual drafting of a piece, many things change. Details get added or dropped, new insights force a change of approach, certain ideas suddenly look as if they fit in one section rather than another, and so on. All of these erode the unity of the work in progress and require fine-tuning on the part of all the writers. In developing your own section, you'll often have insights and ideas you know would help your coauthors in their sections. For these reasons and others, you need to meet as a team regularly and discuss the progress of your work.

Ideally, you should establish some system for this from the very beginning. You should agree upon a regular time and place to meet. How you use these meetings depends on where the work is in the process. As a rule, your meetings will be busier toward the beginning and the end—in the development of the plans and the revision of the draft—than in the middle drafting phases. Nonetheless, the time should be available throughout the project, and all the writers should attend. Not only does this keep small problems from becoming big ones, it helps boost morale just to talk about the common labor. It almost always happens that you leave such a meeting more ready to work than you were when you went into it.

Renegotiating the Division of Labor.   In dividing up the various tasks among the team members, you try, of course, to give everyone a fair share. But how long any writing task will take is often anybody's guess. What seemed like a massive undertaking sometimes turns out to be much easier than anyone expected. More often (Murphy's Law again), a seemingly small section will reveal complexities and problems no one could have predicted. The result is that some team members polish off their assigned tasks quickly, while others become more and more overwhelmed.

It's only fair to keep in mind that the early division of labor was purely tentative, not final. For some writers to have to grind away for page after page, while others, by virtue of a simple miscalculation, get off much more lightly is hardly fair. It is, however, a splendid way to bog down the entire project. One reason for meeting at regular intervals, then, is to assess how the work of each writer is going and to redistribute the tasks as you go along. The tasks that turn out to be larger than expected should be divided up and taken over by whoever is free to take them on. Redistributing the tasks prevents resentment and ill-feeling in the group and speeds the task along as well.

Chapter Ten

WRITING WITH WORD PROCESSORS

THE ADVANTAGES OF WORD PROCESSING

Whatever other problems we face living in the closing years of the 20th century, we have at least been saved (if we choose to be) from the one part of writing everyone hates—recopying or retyping a manuscript after it's been revised. A brief century since the introduction of the typewriter, the slickest, easiest, and most playful writing medium yet has appeared—the word processor.

The really splendid characteristic of word processors is the amount of sheer drudgery they eliminate. Writing one word on a page with a pen or pencil requires almost no effort. Writing hundreds or thousands of them requires a lot. Two hours of writing an essay exam and your hand can ache. It's also maddeningly slow. With a typewriter, drafting becomes less of a problem, but what if you want to change something after it's typed? If it's only a word or phrase, you can go over it with white-out or carefully line through it. If it's any more than that, or if you want to add something, you'll have to write between the lines or in the margins; and then your neat, professional-looking paper suddenly looks a little shabby. And any major revision means retyping the work from page one. At two to four pages an hour, retyping a long work can consume hours or days of the most mindless, tedious labor.

As long as you're simply stringing words, and sentences, and paragraphs one after another, typing on a word processor is not very different from working on a typewriter. As soon as you need to change anything, however, the word processor really shows its power. Somewhere on the keyboard, there will be keys you can push that will move you to wherever in your text you want to work. Once you've moved, you can add or cut material right at that point, even if it's in the very middle of a sentence. The machine then straightens up the paragraph, and will later print it in final form.

Word processors also allow you to perform a task—called a "block move"—useful for larger revisions. Suppose you finish your rough draft and then discover that only in your concluding paragraph have you stated precisely what you've been trying to say all along. You realize that the conclusion should really be the introduction. A block move allows you to pick up the entire conclusion and quickly place it at the beginning of your paper, where you can smooth it out into a good introduction. Then, in an instant, you can travel back to the end again to write up a new, more appropriate conclusion.

Words, sentences, paragraphs, even whole pages can be cut with a few keystrokes. New material can be inserted wherever necessary. Large blocks of prose can be reshuffled any number of ways to see how they work before deciding on the most effective arrangement. And no matter how much slashing and patching and juggling you do, the final draft always looks perfect—like some minor masterpiece you tossed off in an idle hour.

What's more, the word processor actually encourages more revision by blurring the distinction between your "rough" and your "final" drafts. A rough draft on paper can limit the amount of revising you do. When the margins are filled with changes or when you can hardly read all your inserts and arrows and deletions anymore, you often decide you must be about done. But once you have some material down on a word processor, you can reshape and refine it, add to it, delete parts of it, even write in directions to yourself for future changes or additions, which you can later remove at the touch of a few keys. Your writing becomes essentially one, single, steadily evolving draft, with no real breaks between what's "rough" and what's "final." It's all always "rough," in the sense that you can make changes in your text whenever you please. And it's all always "final" since you can print out a reasonably presentable copy at any moment.

All these characteristics of the word processor free you to draft in a more flexible, open-ended way. You can write the various parts of your paper in any order you wish. You can add material to the beginning of your paper, or expand it in the middle, as easily as you can continue it at the end. You can write your paper in blocks, working on whatever material you're most ready to draft, rather than feeling compelled to start with the title and grind on through to the conclusion. And if you're writing a research paper, you can even keep separate files of notes from your readings and then slip them into your paper whenever and wherever you want.

Furthermore, your prose always looks first rate regardless of the shambles it's in conceptually. That in itself is encouraging. When you're painfully aware of how little sense you're making, the visible evidence of the struggle is no help; it's only adding insult to injury. A neat looking page seems somehow easier to repair, more hopeful.

For many people, word processing also has some wonderful psychological effects. When you put something on paper, it acquires a kind of inertia, a weight, a resistance to change. Once it's there, try as you will to fight the feeling, somehow you're committed to it. On a word processor, this is much less the case. What you write appears as transient, shadowy patterns of light on an electronic screen. A moment's effort put it there; half a moment's can make it vanish. It's psychologically weightless. You don't feel the same commitment to it. You can experiment with it, play with it. If you can't decide quite how to phrase something, you can dash off four or five versions, and then toss out all but the best. It's this quickness to eliminate failures and bury the evidence that led one writer to refer to word processors as the most "forgiving" of writing media.

Computaphobia

The simplest and most common fear people have of word processors stems from a deep, ingrained insecurity about machines themselves. Many people, rightly or wrongly, think of themselves as "not mechanically inclined," and they assume that computers can only be tamed by electronic wizards. The very thought of dealing with a computer makes them shudder. If you're one of these people, you need to learn to think about word processors as simply glorified typewriters and put aside all thoughts about "computers" per se. You don't need to understand chip architecture to write at a word processor, any more than you need to understand the chemical processes behind fossil fuel oxidation to drive a car.

Such fears can also result from imagining that you'll push the wrong button and somehow send the machine into nuclear meltdown or, worse still, that the machine will suddenly go sparking and clattering out of control and nothing you can do will stop it. Be comforted: neither of these will happen. Short of pouring a soft drink down the cooling vent or dropping the monitor down an elevator shaft, little you can do will permanently damage the hardware.

Other people are haunted by the fear that what they write on the screen somehow isn't "real writing," or, more plausibly, that the computer will "process" their prose, turning their writing into something cold and mechanical. A nationally syndicated newspaper columnist argued this point a few years ago, claiming that writing with a pen provided a sensuous contact with language that would be lost at the computer terminal. People who write at word processors, he warned, should not be surprised if their prose comes out like "processed" cheese—bland, colorless, without texture or taste. But students writing at the machines more often discover just the opposite. Because you can write so much more quickly on a word processor, you often phrase your thoughts in more immediate, rich, conversational language than you might by struggling over it by hand. Many students thus produce prose with a warmer, more personal voice than they did before.

For all that, the "velveeta-prose" worry isn't entirely groundless. "Overprocessing" **is** a danger for some writers. The very ease of revision leads some writers to polish and refine their writing into a kind of dull, flat "correctness," with nothing of their original voice or personality left. The technological "feel" of word processing can also cause some writers to begin sounding like computers themselves, as if they thought their brains and fingers somehow ought to be part of the whole elaborate system of chips and programs and files. But the technology is not so much to blame here as its user. Such writers need to learn to appreciate the distinctive sound of their own human voice and remember that, without the lively, complex personality using it, the machine is simply an idle box of parts and wires.

Of all the possible worries you might bring to word processors, one is quite justified: the fear that the machine will "eat" your work. Here is the classic nightmare: after much time and study, you master the commands and tricks of the word processor itself. For several days, you work on a paper, carefully brainstorming and drafting until you have almost seven pages. Late Sunday night, you sit down at the machine to produce a final, polished draft for Monday's class. You work diligently for hours, refining pages of text on the glowing screen. Finally, you're done. Your shoulders hurt and your eyes are sore, but you're finished, and you know what you've written is good. You want to print out a copy of your work and go to bed. You push all the right buttons and—**nothing!** Anxiously, you push the keys again—and then other keys. Still nothing. In a panic, you at least try to record your work onto your disk. Suddenly, the machine starts writing messages about disks and cables and faulty units and bad sectors or covering the screen with strings of cryptic numbers, all the while beeping and whirring—and then it goes blank! All your immortal prose has, as William Zinsser describes it, "vanished into the electricity."[1]

This **will** happen. Some portion of the work you do at a word processor will indeed disappear into its silicon gizzard, never to return. A power failure during a storm can wipe out everything you've been doing for the past six hours. Or, worse still, a disk with a hundred pages of text on it can decide to go bad—and your hundred pages are instantly lost. In short, although word processing may seem wonderfully magical, not all its spells are blessings.

But even here, there are "counter-spells" you can do to protect yourself from the worst. First, keep saving your file as you work. This transfers what you've been doing (which the computer is holding in something like a "short-term memory") to your disk, from which you can get it back no matter what happens to the machine. Second, always keep on hand at least two disks. Before you leave your machine, **always** copy your file from your text disk onto your second, "back-up" disk. Never get caught with only one copy of any file. If you've dutifully made a back-up copy of everything, then when that inevitable "bad disk" message appears, or when you inadvertently leave Disk #1 to curl up on a hot radiator or discover it in the jaws of your hyperactive poodle, you'll feel immensely smug and self-satisfied, knowing your work is safe on your other disk.

USING WORD PROCESSORS

Word processors can be used in every phase of the writing process, though it's not a given that they should be. Unless handled with tact and restraint, even their virtues can interfere with your writing process by leading you into "shortcuts" that prove less effective in the long run. The best use of word processors doesn't come from abandoning pen and paper completely. Simply because word processors do some things wonderfully doesn't mean they do everything even adequately. A large part of using the machines well requires you to observe your own writing process carefully to decide just when you should be sitting before the glowing screen and when you should still have your fingers wrapped around a peacock blue felt-tipped pen.

Using Word Processors in Brainstorming

In any brainstorming where you're simply spilling out your thoughts, following the train of your logic, getting feelings and ideas down in any rough words at all, the word processor is a boon. It's an especially good tool for

---

[1]*Writing with a Word Processor* (New York: Harper and Row, 1983), p. 51ff.

generating material using the techniques we mentioned in Chapter One: timed rushwriting, lists, sketches and studies, dialogues—anything, in fact, requiring only words, not pictures. Techniques that rely on visual aids, such as treeing or clustering, are still done best by hand. (Computers can do graphics, of course, but they require too much time and care to be useful for brainstorming.)

Looping.   One technique covered earlier that lends itself especially well to the word processor is "looping" (pp. 29–31). The word processor allows you to rushwrite and loop much more swiftly than you can by hand and to produce a more coherent body of material when you're done.

1. As with regular looping, write on some topic for, say, 20 minutes— then stop and save your text. (In other words, make sure it gets recorded on your disk.)
2. Take your break.
3. Return to the machine and read through your rushwrite on screen. Wherever something in your notes sparks a new thought, or wherever you see an idea that could bear some development, move the cursor to the "seed" itself and start adding the new material right there.
4. Pass through your notes in this way any number of times, continuing to expand whatever interests you right in the middle of the text.
5. As with all prewriting, keep at this until you either run out of time or decide that you have more than enough material. When you're done, print off the notes you have.

When you press the "print" command, the machine will type one long, richly developed rushwrite instead of several little ones. Furthermore, you'll find your material already fairly well sorted. You may still need to rearrange the major ideas in your writing, but all your thinking on any one subtopic should be roughly in one place.

If you want to develop separate rushwrites, of course, that's also possible. In that case, every time you find an idea you wish to develop, you could simply retype it at the bottom of your notes and work on it there. Or you might insert a "page break"—that is, move automatically to a new page—and begin your next rushwrite at that point. Then, when you print out, you'll get separate pages, with your various ideas developed to some degree on each. This might actually help you in organization, by allowing you to spread your pages around physically over a table or floor. Which method works better is something you'll have to find out for yourself just by trying them and comparing.

More Tips for Computerized Brainstorming.   So far we've assumed that you'll be rushwriting and looping entirely at the computer, though this isn't necessary. Another option combines the speed and ease of the machine with more leisure to ponder: do your brainstorming on screen for a while, then print out what you have and take it with you. In the slow quiet of your own room or the library or your favorite coffee shop, go over your material with a text highlighter or pen, and mark those passages you'd like to develop. Then expand on these either right where you are or back at the computer.

Some writers find word processors better for early high-speed brainstorming than for the more meditative staring-into-space sessions necessary to develop their ideas fully. Others find that they don't so much sit down and invent ideas as they just let ideas occur to them at random over the course of the day. No scheduled, deliberate development of their material is as useful as simply having a notebook and pen always within reach, to snare each new thought as it flies by. A word processor obviously doesn't lend itself to this kind of use.

You've probably already noticed that all brainstorming, however powerful it is in bringing up rich and original ideas, also brings up a lot of chaff. Often in your brainstorming you'll discover one usable idea buried in two pages of verbal underbrush. And sometimes the underbrush makes the idea very hard to see or keep track of.

Your useful ideas will become more visible if you clean out the underbrush early on. When you return to your rushwriting after the first session, simply delete the stuff you don't need. This keeps your work more manageable. You're less likely to become overwhelmed by your own productivity.

YOUR TURN

On your next piece of writing, try some of the following techniques and describe how they work for you.

Looping within your first rushwrite by adding new material wherever it belongs.

Rushwriting, printing out your material, and then developing it away from the machine.

Rushwriting, then stripping out obviously useless material and building on what's left.

Also try other idea-generating techniques that could be adapted to the word processor: listing, dialogues, etc.

Note: This is an excellent activity for someone just learning the word processor. It calls for you to write, insert, and delete, and it doesn't really matter how the final product looks.

Organizing Your Paper

Let's suppose you've been generating ideas for some time now and you like what you've produced. You feel ready to start organizing your material and get on with drafting.Your next tasks are to sort through what you've produced, decide what you want to use, and arrange it for greatest clarity, economy, and effectiveness.

Once you've printed out your notes, it's usually helpful to mark the key words and phrases with a yellow highlighter or to circle them with a pen. This gives you the opportunity to spot your major ideas at a glance. The words and phrases you highlight also provide you with tags you can use in sketching your tree.

Doing an Outline on a Word Processor.   The computer makes drawing up an outline especially easy since you can insert lines anywhere you like. This, in fact, allows you the top-down flexibility usually only possible with organizational trees. When you write an outline by hand, you're almost forced to work out the fine details of each section before moving from one major section to the next. You end up with something like this:

Character of Celie in *The Color Purple*
- **I.** Brutal childhood.
  - **A.** Mother dies
  - **B.** Incest—Pa
    - **1.** guilt and confusion
      - **a.** I (am/have always been) a good girl
      - **b.** telling nobody but God
    - **2.** protecting Netty
- **II.** Life with Mister

[and so on]

Suppose at this point you want to add something about Celie's being taken from school against her wishes. Or suppose you think of some important details associated with her mother. There's no easy way to make these changes on a hand-written outline. You can either squeeze them in along the margin, rewrite the outline from scratch, or skip them entirely.

With a word processor, on the other hand, all this becomes simpler, more logical, and more convenient. You can start developing your outline by listing just the major conceptual headings:

- **I.** Celie's brutal childhood—losing freedom.
- **II.** Knuckling under to Mister—freedom lost.
- **III.** Second childhood with Shug—the start of freedom.
- **IV.** Reconciliation with Mister—the final freedom.

This gives you your overall framework, allowing you to keep sight of the big picture while you develop the subsections. Once you've gotten this far (and you might try a number of outlines at this level before settling on one), you can go through a second time, adding only the second level of detail. This might produce the following:

- **I.** Celie's brutal childhood.
  - **A.** Ma's death and Pa's brutality.
  - **B.** Hope through Netty.

252

II. Knuckling under to Mister.
   A. The household slave.
   B. Losing Netty—Netty's advice.
   C. The bedroom slave.
          [and so on through the whole outline]

On your next pass, you carry the outline down a level further:

I. Celie's brutal childhood.
   A. Ma's death and Pa's brutality.
      1. Tie-ins between sex, death, and pregnancy
      2. Good girl or not? Celie's confusion.
      3. Telling God about it.
   B. Hope through Netty.
      1. Netty tries to teach self-respect.
      2. The survival value of education.
II. Knuckling under to Mister.
            [and so on]

On each pass, you can carry the outline to a further level of detail. Since the machine will allow you to insert a line wherever you like, you can revise the outline, adding here and cutting there, and substituting this section with that one, over and over until you have the most elegant, economical, richly detailed scheme you can devise. Word processors make outlines so easy and useful, in fact, that for the first time you might be tempted to write one even **before** writing your paper!

Scaffold and Brickwork Approach. Well suited to the word processor, this is a technique for fleshing out your outline with more extended writing, either fairly polished prose or loose notes. To use the "scaffold and brickwork" approach:

1. Work up an outline from your prewriting.
2. At each heading, write a one-sentence nutshell of what that section should say.
3. Type this sentence outline onto the word processor, leaving some space between each heading. This gives you your "scaffold."
4. Now move from space to space, drafting in full what you want to say in each section. This is the "brickwork."
5. Finally, delete the outline itself (remove the "scaffolding") and write in whatever transitions are necessary between your paragraphs.

YOUR TURN

Following the procedures we've described, try building a structure for your paper on the word processor. Then answer the following questions:

What were the advantages of using the word processor to help you organize the parts of your paper? What were some of the disadvantages?

Analyze your writing and organizing process; how much did you rely on paper and how much on the computer?

What happened when you began to outline your paper? Did you create the entire outline first and then begin fleshing it out, or did you create parts of it and change it as you began thinking about the contents of each section?

Write three tips for yourself about prewriting on the computer that you've learned from your experiences.

Drafting at the Word Processor

If you can do it, do it. Earlier in this chapter we sang the praises of the computer as a writing medium at some length. It's all true. A swifter and more effortless way to sling words across a page has not been invented. Though most people find drafting at the keyboard stiff and strange at first, they generally get used to it and are glad they did. Sentences form and fade in the imagination with the shimmering brevity of soap bubbles. By typing their drafts on the word processor, many writers discover that they dramatically raise their odds of capturing that first, fresh, natural sentence before it dissolves. We're less interested here, however, in repeating our earlier hymns to the machine than in suggesting adjustments you might want to make in your approach to drafting if you write on the screen.

At any given time, a word processor screen shows you only about a third of a page of your text—just a paragraph or two at most. Research has shown that although word processing seems to help writers improve the richness of their detail, their organization tends to suffer. When you draft by hand or on a typewriter, you can, by glancing repeatedly over your manuscript, see all your work at once. This helps you keep the shape of the work as a whole more clearly in your head.

If you run off on a tangent when you're drafting on paper, your manuscript will probably tell you. The little anecdote you began at page five is still healthy and going strong on page eight. Surgery is called for. On the word processor screen, the length of your detour is not as apparent—it keeps scrolling away into a computer nether-world until you back up to it. If you're not careful, all your essays will reveal the same organizational pattern: "And another thing ... , And if I might add ... , And furthermore. . . ."

Imagine, if you will, that you're painting a portrait, but at any one time you can only see one 6″ x 6″ square of the canvas through a sort of movable window you slide around over it. Except for that one small area you're working on, the rest of the picture remains hidden. What do you do?

If nothing else, you can move the window around a *lot*. On a word processor this means "scrolling" up and down freely and often to see where you've come from, where you're going, and how you can get there. This helps you to maintain the flow of your thoughts and to keep a sense of the overall shape and proportions of your paper.

You can also make frequent print-outs of your draft as you go along. This is especially helpful if you're working on a long piece, one you'll need several sittings to complete. Don't leave at the end of any session, if you can help it, without printing out what you've got—either all of it, if it's short, or at least the pages you've added. Read through the material at least once before your next drafting stint, perhaps making revisions on the paper as you go. These can be typed in first thing when you sit down again, or you can let them accumulate until after you've barged your way through an entire draft. In any case, bring the "hard copy" with you, and keep it, along with your tree or outline, beside you as you write. This represents a sort of compromise between paper and on-screen drafting. To return to the painting analogy, it allows you to keep uncovered at least those parts of the canvas you've already worked on.

Bridging One Day's Work to the Next. At the end of each drafting session you might also, before turning off the machine, make notes about the next short stretch you're going to write. Often our trees and outlines give us the overall structure of our work, but leave the subunits to be organized and filled in when we reach them. When you reach each small chunk in turn, it usually requires some time to sort out what you want to say about it, and in what order. If, after you start drafting, you realize you don't have time to complete the section, you'd hate to lose the brain work you put into it.

Your tree might, for example, show a node labeled "Duke's theatrics." Your intention, when you reached it, was to discuss the massacred "Shakespearean" speech given by the Duke in *Huckleberry Finn.* Just as you settle in your mind what you want to say about it, however, you realize your time is up—you have a bus to catch or an irate fullback wants his turn at the terminal. Though you won't have time to write the section just then, you don't have to lose all the thinking you put into it.

Instead, follow these steps.

1. Move down a line, and type a few rapid notes outlining just that section, the skeleton of the paragraphs or pages you'd write if you had the time. Print out a copy.
2. When you return to the machine, delete the minioutline from your file. Then, working from your paper copy, draft the paragraphs you had in mind.
3. Print this out along with the rest of your work for the day.

Writers often find that getting started proves difficult **every** time they start to draft. Each time they sit down they have to reconstruct the points they wanted to make, and how they wanted to make them. Carrying over an outline of the thoughts of the previous day helps them over this hurdle

255

and gets them started. Once they do get going, the momentum of the work then carries them along.

Overpolishing. As we mentioned above, in discussing the "velveeta prose syndrome," one danger of on-screen drafting is overcontrol. If, for instance, there's one particular phrase in your last sentence you decide isn't quite right, you can back up and change it in no time. Writing with pen and ink, or even on a typewriter, you might leave the shakey phrase in place and get on with the draft. On the computer, you'll be much more tempted to make the switch. It won't clutter up your text, and after all, what's five seconds' work?

Multiply that five seconds by a few hundred, though, and then add on top of it all the time you've spent thinking and rethinking and rethinking again each change, and you've used a great deal of time indeed. Your praiseworthy quest for clarity will keep you tinkering so obsessively with your last paragraph, you'll never get on with the next. You'll think you're writing when all you're really doing is waffling.

There's no foolproof guideline we can offer for how much polishing is enough or too much. Some writers simply work that way: each paragraph has to shine like a Christmas tree bulb before they'll start the next. Others sail recklessly through the first draft, leaving all the windy sentences and clumsy word choices in their wake, planning to clean up the debris later. Either approach works. It's just that the computer itself nudges you toward the slower, more meticulous, more painstaking approach to a degree that can waste large amounts of time.

If when you're drafting you're not sure whether to change something or not, **don't.** Leave it alone for the present and get more of your material down. If the passage really does need changing, you'll see better what it needs after you've let it sit awhile. On the other hand, many little problems you notice while drafting become impossible to find again when you reread your text after a break—which means they weren't worth worrying about in the first place. The moment you find yourself brooding over which of two exact synonyms best fits your meaning, and switching obsessively from one to the other and back again, stop yourself. Either put in the one you suspect is wrong and get on with your draft—anything to break the spell— or ask yourself if perhaps you haven't written enough for one stretch anyhow. It's often a symptom of fatigue.

The (Impatient) Ghost in the Machine. Many writers, finally, describe the feeling that word processors are somehow always "waiting" for them to get something down on the screen, always subtly but actively pressuring them to get on with their work. Most computers have internal air circulation fans that hum softly, and on many the cursor blinks on and off as if the machine were tapping its foot. Writers respond to this differently. Some find the mild impatience of the machine a tonic; it keeps them focused on the task at hand and helps them work more steadily and efficiently than they would otherwise.

For others, however, the machine's "waiting" is intrusive and bother-some. Some writers need to stare at the clouds or at pictures on their desks or at the people milling about outside their window. Some need to let their minds leave their work entirely, in order to come back to it from a new angle with new insights and ideas. For these people, the humming and foot tapping of the word processor may interfere with their best work. Others do most of their work comfortably enough at the word processor but fall back on pen and paper for the trickier passages, such as introductions and conclusions. These are all purely temperamental differences. Try everything and use what works.

YOUR TURN

It's time to put all this to the test. On your next assignment draft at least two pages at the word processor, print it out, and take it home. Then, in your notebook, answer these questions.

What material did you bring to the session? Did you have a tree or outline or notes? How did you use those when you were writing?

Were you able to stay in control of the whole section as a unit, or couldn't you "see the forest for the trees"?

What changes did you notice in your writing—in such things as level of detail, voice, organization, mechanics, etc.?

Where do you plan to go from here with this material?

Revising with the Word Processor

Although many writers still avoid their computers for brainstorming and organization, and others never become comfortable drafting with anything but a dozen sharpened pencils and a legal yellow pad, practically everyone who uses a word processor feels blessed in knowing that with the new tech-nology he **never has to type anything over,** no matter how drastically he alters it.

Serious writers are obsessive revisers. For them, the electronic secretarial skills of the word processor can save untold hours. The computer is not, however, always the best place to decide what changes you need to make. For this, you will probably still want paper. As we've pointed out, the com-puter screen offers "limited visibility." In revision, you'll want to see and manipulate your entire draft at once. You can certainly do "touch-up" painting and varnishing at the screen. But real **re-vision**—genuine from-the-ground-up structural reworking of your material—is never best done there.

So, print your draft and take it with you. Spread it out on your desk or your floor and start pondering what can be made of it. Then go after it with whatever tools you like: ballpoint pens, highlighters, different color felt-tipped markers. Decide where you would cut and paste—then draw arrows and circles indicating which paragraphs go where. Scratch out the parts that are vague or dull or snarled. Write in fresh words and phrases and details. Write "See Over" on a page, and on the back, draft those paragraphs the passage is crying out for. Or number each paragraph, and tree and retree the whole until the organization seems solid and strong. Then put it aside and go do something else for a while.

And then come back and go through it all again! One of the humbler beauties of "hard copy" is that you can carry it around with you to work on, wherever and whenever you please. The second time through your draft, you'll often notice opportunities for improvement that escaped you the first time. Others will only reveal themselves on the third, eighth, or fifteenth readings. Blue-penciling your way through your draft several times, preferably at intervals, helps you discover much more than if you tried to do all your revising in one, grim marathon session. And it's obviously more convenient to go through four stapled pages several times over a week than to set up shop each time at the word processor.

After this first cycle of revision, the fun part begins: entering all the changes at the machine. There's nothing much to be said about this, except that it's one of the most gratifying experiences in a writer's week. Right before your eyes, your feeble, tattered, leaky rough draft grows strong and colorful and seaworthy. The rotting old tub becomes a racing yacht; and then, with that great pleasure that comes from a good creation, you watch the printer launch a neat, tidy manuscript of your work.

Hacking at the Gordian Knots.   If you discover in your draft a clumsy or tangled paragraph that you don't immediately know how to revise, you might try using the computer to break the paragraph into separate sentences, leaving a line or two of space between each one. Then start playing with them. Tighten or rephrase each sentence individually. Delete the ones that seem superfluous. Add others that might clarify your meanings. Rearrange them on screen with block moves (it'll only take a second). Then, when you feel you have exactly the sentences you want in the order you want them, remove the empty lines and fuse them again into a single paragraph. The extra space you put between the sentences helps you see more clearly where the problems lie. You aren't as overwhelmed with the tangled, knotted mass of it.

Retyping Anyway.   After all we've said about revising on word processors, our final suggestion may horrify you: once you've got your work drafted and revised on screen, you might consider opening a new file, and typing it over again from scratch. Many writers find that by simply retyping something, they become involved in their text much more intimately than if they're just entering changes in an old draft. In the process of retyping, every paragraph, every sentence, every word comes in for reconsideration. The writers thus make many improvements they'd never have thought of any other way.

Others, in retyping their drafts, develop entirely new insights into their material, open up whole new veins of ore, discover new problems or arguments or examples. This is not, of course, the most convenient time to make such discoveries; but if the goal is the richest, sharpest, most interesting paper you can write on your topic, even such late guests are welcome.

As a less sweeping alternative, you could open a fresh file to start from scratch on a smaller section of your draft—one that you know isn't working out so far. Once you're reasonably happy with it, you can then electronically insert it into the appropriate section of your main file and just delete the old version.

SPECIAL FUNCTIONS OF THE COMPUTER

File Management

One of the more useful features of word processors is their "file management" capabilities. The computer allows you to store different kinds of material in different files, to save different versions of the same text, and to move material back and forth between the files you've created. You should learn the procedure for each of these as early as you can. Occasions will arise when the ability to do these might save you a good deal of time and trouble. The following are ways these skills might come in handy.

Stealing Your Own Rushwriting. Sometimes, while you're rushwriting or writing sketches and dialogues, you produce a passage that can be drawn straight into your rough draft. If you've done your brainstorming at the computer and saved it in a separate file, you can copy directly from your prewriting file onto your rough draft without having to retype anything. You'll likewise sometimes draft a passage that doesn't fit where you wrote it, but which you believe will be useful later. This you can ship back to the brainstorming file or to a separate "scrap file" for future use.

Notes and Quotes. In carrying out research for a paper, you might enter into one long file your summaries and paraphrases of what you find, along with those passages you think you might want to quote. Once this is printed out, it's easy to refer to as you draft. Then, if you do find a quotation you want to use, you can have the computer copy it straight from your "notes and quotes" file into your paper. This not only saves time, it lowers the chances of misquoting your source by retyping it incorrectly.

Saving Multiple Versions of Your Draft. Many writers fear that in revising a draft they might cut out or change something they'll wish afterwards that they'd left alone. Some writers are hesitant to commit themselves to a major change in their work until they've seen it alongside their original and can compare the two. Word processors allow you to do just that. Instead of continually drafting and revising on the same file, you can at any time make another copy of the file under a new name, leave your original alone, and work on the copy.

Once you've finished your original account of, say, visiting your cousin Max's farm, you might save two copies of it: "Farm 1" and "Farm 2." You might then revise "Farm 2" into an account of your harrowing accident on the tractor and your dog Hamilton's startling heroism. Now copy that, producing a third file, called simply "Hamilton," and continue expanding on all you remember about that amazing canine. In the end, you've got three different papers, any of which you might develop further or turn in.

Different Versions for Different Audiences. Suppose you're writing letters of application to different businesses. Your qualifications, how to contact you, etc., remain largely the same regardless of the prospective employer. On the other hand, you may have different angles, know different people, understand different things about each company. Here again multiple copies of the same text might come in useful. Once you've produced on your disk eight separate files, each with the same letter, you can call up each file individually and tailor it to the particular audience you're addressing. For similar reasons, you should keep your résumé on a word processor; not only can you add items to the résumé later without having to retype it, but you can easily create special versions of it, depending on the kind of job for which you're applying or the nature of your audience.

Alphabetic Files. Any file organized alphabetically—bibliographies, address lists, and so on—are secretaries' (and writers') worst headaches. Whenever a new item must be entered, the entire file has to be retyped. The word processor instantly eliminates that chore. Furthermore, most programs will let you import items from your list to use in a text. If you've entered into one file all the addresses of the persons and organizations with whom you correspond, you can easily plug these into whatever letters you need to send. Or, if your bibliography consists of 50 entries and you're only citing 15 of them in your paper, you can either make a duplicate file of the bibliography and delete the unneeded 35 or simply transfer the 15 needed entries into your text file.

Spelling Checkers

Spelling checkers are programs that turn your computer into an electronic proofreader. The program scans your text, compares each word in it with its own electronic dictionary, and writes on the screen any that it cannot find. That's all it does. As a result, the program will flag many of your misspellings—but not all. For example, it has no way of knowing if you've used the wrong member of a pair or trio of homonyms. If you've written something like "they're is a ship," or "there ship sank," or "their in great danger," the spelling checker won't bat an eye. In scanning your text, it will duly note that "they're," "there," and "their" are all recorded as legitimate English words and let it go at that. Instead, the error will probably be noticed by the first person to read your text. Let us hope that person is ewe, you're mother, or yore friend.

On the other hand, it will mark as misspellings anything it doesn't recognize, no matter how correct. Its data base contains only common nouns, not proper ones; as in Scrabble, names are taboo. A name like "Mark Green" it can handle, since "mark" and "green" will both appear on its list as regular words. But "Flannery O'Connor" will register as an error, and "Alice Walker" will be half right.

The moral is: use them, but don't trust them—at least not entirely. They are not—nor in the foreseeable future will they be—100 percent accurate. They're excellent at catching typographical errors since these rarely resemble anything English. But in the end, you still need to proofread your own drafts with a dictionary in hand.

The people who find spelling checkers most helpful are those who fuss and worry over every sentence they write, who feel compelled to break off their trains of thought to look up words in the dictionary, and who would freeze up completely if they suspected that their drafts were shot through with such mistakes. Some of these people find they can draft more easily and fluently, knowing they can correct all their typos and spelling glitches in a matter of minutes at the end of the session. Having the spelling checker there as a safety net allows them to perform the necessary verbal acrobatics with confidence. If you're one of these people, spelling checkers might make your life a lot simpler.

Style Checkers

These programs work much like spelling checkers. They scan your text for certain problems in usage and style, which they then call to your attention. They're not magical, and they can't really read. In fact, they're stunningly simple-minded—even the best of them. All they can do is tally and compare very simple items. For example, they can count the words from one period to the next and tell you whether your sentences are running a little long, a little short, or all too much of one length, compared with average English usage. Or they'll count "-tion" endings to words and, if the percentage runs too high, inform you that your style is "too abstract." Or they'll count "to be" verbs (is, was, were, will be, would be, are, am), and if the frequency reaches a certain level, cordially suggest that you make more use of active verbs to liven up your prose. (Movie buffs may remember in *Amadeus* the Emperor's airy criticism of Mozart's opera as having "too many notes." Enough said.)

Use these with care if use them you must. Every "problem" they point out may be a perfectly effective rhetorical strategy in context. Hemingway wrote predominantly short sentences, and his stories are good and true and fine. Winston Churchill produced stirring histories in a prose style that rumbles and rolls grandly down long flights from period to period without ever becoming wearying or confused. Philosophical treatises, as it happens, tend to be written more abstractly than auto mechanics' shop manuals—and the latter tend, for very good reasons, to have sentences that are short, choppy, and of a fairly uniform length. You are always the final authority on your own work. Only you know what effect you're trying to achieve. And even if you could tell the computer, the illiterate sparking rat's nest would never understand.

No computer will give you feedback as useful as that from your coworkers, classmates, or instructors. No computer, after all, has the foggiest notion what you're saying—much less if it's interesting or funny or profound or even makes any sense. And they can't see anything like "the big picture" in terms of organization or overall effect. You're writing for people. It's how they react that's important.

YOUR TURN

The last couple of "Your Turns" have asked that you brainstorm and draft at a word processor and record in your notebook how it went. Now revise the draft you produced on the word processor and answer these questions.

> Where and how did you do most of your revising? How much did you do on paper? How much on screen?
>
> Did you find yourself making different kinds of changes from one medium to the other?
>
> What changes do you notice in your writing, after revising it on the word processor? Look particularly at organization, voice, and style.

If you have access to a spelling or style checker, experiment with it. Run it over your draft once. What sorts of things does it pick out? What did you learn from it? How or when might it be useful to you?

PARTING THOUGHTS

You may have noticed throughout this chapter a strange blend of lavish praise for the word processor combined with a deep distrust. Both, we think, are valid. As with all powerful new technologies, the development of the machine itself is one thing, the development of the best way to use it is another. In the few years since word processors first became available, their obvious strengths have drawn so many writers and educators to them that we have a reasonably clear idea now how to exploit their potentials while avoiding their hazards. There's hardly a beartrap associated with the machines that someone hasn't fallen into—and bravely reported. This chapter represents in part the painfully won experience of those early word processor users.

From all this accumulated wisdom and experience we can draw two morals.

1. *Use the machine to enrich your writing process, not to hobble it.* We'd encourage you to discover as much about the computer's potentials as possible. Try everything. But never assume that just because you **can** do something on the screen, you **should** do it there. For any given task, from the earliest brainstorming to the final editing, you'll discover a number of usable approaches—from silicon chips to crayons. Whatever works, wherever it works, go with it. There is no guarantee, after all, that the lastest technology is necessarily the best technology for any given job. A Boeing 747 surely represents a greater technological feat than a Raleigh 10-speed bicycle, but whoever rode one to the zoo?

2. *Nothing the machine can do will ever teach you how to write.* Word processors eliminate an immense amount of drudgery. They also put you in more flexible control of your text. But they aren't critics. The business of writing is stringing words together so as to spark off a particular set of thoughts and feelings in the mind of your reader. The only way to discover how effectively you're stringing your words together is to have a fellow mortal read them and tell you how she responds. Programmers write for computers. You're writing for humans. There is a difference.

Appendix A

DEEP CASES FOR WRITING

INTRODUCTION: USING CASES TO EXPLORE THE WRITING PROCESS

What's a "Case"?

Imagine that one day you're walking down the street and suddenly you spot a wallet lying in the gutter, partly hidden by some leaves. You pick it up. Inside are some credit cards, photos, a driver's license with a picture of the owner (say, a middle-aged man in a business suit), and slightly over $200 in cash. The street is empty; no one has seen you pick up the wallet. Your dilemma: do you keep the money and throw the wallet away? Do you keep the money and send the wallet anonymously back to the owner? Or do you return both the wallet and the money?

What you've just read is a kind of "case"—a scenario which, in one form or another, has been used for centuries to explore issues of morality and ethics. Something like this case may have happened to you, or perhaps to a friend; but the case is designed as a **possible** occurrence that is then used for discussion, problem-solving, or practice.

Cases have long been used in business, law, medicine, the social sciences, and other fields to help people learn and practice the methods and thinking processes common to the discipline. Usually, a case involves some sort of simulation of a real problem or set of conditions. It's most often hypothetical, though it can be based on a real situation that serves as a good example of what typically confronts someone working in the field.

Why Use Cases for Writing?

Several times in this book, we've relied on short cases to illustrate our points or give you something to respond to in the "Your Turn" sections. You might be wondering, then, why we've included longer, free-standing cases for writing in this appendix.

There are several reasons. First, as we've pointed out before, the writing class is a special kind of setting, different in many ways from other, nonacademic situations in which you might find yourself as a writer. And because your writing rarely goes beyond the classroom in which you do it, it doesn't give you the sort of "hands-on" experience that helps you to learn how to do it well in many different situations. Think how hard it would be to become a chemist if all you did was learn textbook material and listen to lectures, without ever having the chance to run the kinds of procedures and experiments, in a lab, in which chemists are usually engaged. Imagine the difficulty of becoming a good photographer or visual artist if all you did was look at famous paintings and award-winning photographs in a book, or watch someone else take pictures or make sculptures. Visualize yourself standing up in court as a lawyer for the first time without ever having gone through a mock trial or building a defense based on an imaginary legal situation. Or think of facing an opposing softball team in the opening game of a season without ever having divided your own team up to compete in practice games. In these and most other activities, it's hard to imagine doing much more than a feeble job unless you've had some experience that in some way parallels the real circumstance. And that's exactly why schools have laboratories, fieldwork, and other sorts of opportunities for practicing law, photography, softball, chemistry, and art.

We think the same should be true for writing. In fact, because writing is such a varied process, entering into every aspect of our lives, the need to experience it in a **real** way, with many different readers and purposes, is absolutely essential to becoming better at solving the problems it requires us, again and again, to face.

But we often forget this need. By the time most of us reach college, the majority of the writing we've done has been one kind (academic papers) in one place (school) for one audience (teachers) and for one purpose (being evaluated as a student). Even though all this academic experience taken together might show lots of variety, writing only for school assignments is a little like trying to study the behavior of a robin by observing its actions inside a bird cage. We might reach some interesting conclusions but we wouldn't really know all that much about the normal lives of robins.

Of course, it's often difficult to set up many reasons for writing **within** a school that mirror reasons for writing **beyond** it: how often, for example, do you get the chance in general college courses to write a real corporate memo, a pamphlet for a social service agency, a feasibility study, a script for a high school documentary, a grant proposal for a federally funded project, or consumer instructions for assembling a lawnmower shipped in a box? Unlike medicine or law or TV broadcasting, which lend themselves to practice in a studio or surgery or mock courtroom, writing is an extremely varied activity that changes from place to place, from newspaper office, to corporate headquarters, to advertising agency, to geologist's laboratory. And because there is so much attention to learning the **subject matter** of the many courses you take, there is often little opportunity to practice the kind of writing that professionals in that field use beyond school; instead, your term paper assignment in Introduction to Macroeconomics may look a lot like your term paper assignment in History of Western Music: library research papers whose only difference is their content.

Your own personal solution to this problem should be to do as much writing as you possibly can of different types, especially for real purposes with nonacademic readers. Find reasons to write beyond school. Send letters expressing your political views to your elected political representatives. Write letters to the editor of local newspapers and magazines about current issues. Don't call your long-distance friends; they'll appreciate a letter more—and you'll save money, too. Get involved in local publications if you can—volunteer to write book reviews, movie reviews, album reviews, or critiques of local restaurants; sometimes you'll be rewarded with a pass to the movie or a copy of the book or album, or even a free meal at the restaurant. Write stories, poems, personal interest pieces on people in the neighborhood. Write complaint letters, advertisements for services you offer, descriptions of places you've visited for guidebooks that welcome tourists' comments for future issues. Become involved in internship programs at businesses and public service agencies and ask to do some writing for them. And, above all, keep a journal or "learning log" or "daybook" where you can write about your thoughts, observations, experiences, and plans, particularly about the subject matter you're learning in various courses. Try whenever you can to write, and you'll be surprised at how quickly your writing will improve, and how many more possibilities you'll find for it. In this respect, writing is a lot like running: you need to do it often—unless, that is, you want to be gasping for air and writhing with cramps every time you've gone the first 200 yards.

That's easy for us to say. There you are, two analytical papers due in the next three weeks, two major term papers looming on the horizon, and a thousand other things to do in your life. The hour you'd spend writing to your friend could be better divided into a ten-minute phone call and 50 minutes of review for the next psychology test. The letter to the editor can wait: environmental issues don't hinge on your protest of oil exploration off the Oregon coast. And the new Italian restaurant in town isn't waiting desperately for your expert pronouncements on the quality of its *cannelloni alla Veneziana*. Your professors, on the other hand, won't wait. In short, we know that you've probably got as much writing as you can handle right now, even if it's mostly school-centered, directed to teachers in response to their assignments.

But that's a compelling reason, we think, to take **some** of your school writing and turn it into writing whose problems resemble those that people face when they write in a variety of contexts, both academic and nonacademic. That's where the case approach comes in.

DEEP CASES FOR WRITING

In this Appendix, we've included three assignments we call "deep cases." We use the term "deep" because the cases are quite complicated, with much background information that tries to give you a picture of real people and a real context for writing.

Each case is designed to raise important questions about the basic perspectives we've explored in this textbook: the writing **process, audience, purpose,** and **content.** Part 1, on the writing process, should have provided you with useful strategies for working with these and other questions as you draft and revise your responses to the case assignments.

You may also be working through a case as you read and respond to one of the main chapters. If you're using this approach, we recommend that you link Part 2, on academic writing, with the "Social Issues 101" case; and Part 3 with the "Veterinarian's Nightmare" case or the "Machines and Green Thumbs" case.

Getting the Most from a Case

We've designed each of the cases in this Appendix to resemble typical writing situations people face in school or on the job. In real situations, your knowledge of people and events and history is complicated and rich. We've tried to reflect just a little of that richness by including considerable additional background material for each case. Some of this material will seem especially important to you; some of it will seem irrelevant. In the past, we've found that people disagree about what material is important, and that often leads to some stimulating discussion. We've also found that many of the **textual** decisions writers make when drafting responses to a case—what words to choose, how to structure the writing, what sort of style or tone to use, and so on—are based almost entirely on the circumstances of the case, rather than some "general" rules of good writing. You'll soon find that as you discuss your case with others who've responded to it, you'll become immersed in the world of the case and its situation. Don't be afraid to let your focus on "writing" merge with your focus on ethical or situational problems in the case. That's what writing is all about.

To get the most from the cases, we suggest you keep in mind the following points:

1. *Read the cases carefully.* We realize that we're providing you with information and background that, in an actual situation, you'd already possess. Unfortunately, we have no way to get around this problem, and that means that you have to "learn" the background well. Don't be reluctant to go back over the details in the cases, even as you write and revise.

2. *Follow the assignments* in the case as they're presented; don't skip ahead. We've tried to present you with "problems" that we hope will prompt you to rethink the drafts you've already written, mainly to give you practice with revision. If you look too far ahead in the cases before you begin writing, you'll spoil the fun.

3. *Don't be afraid to be tentative.* At first, you may feel that puzzling over a simple letter is a sign of weakness—after all, most good writers crank out simple letters effortlessly, right? Not so. The cases present you with ethical dilemmas, with problems of content, voice, style, tone, point of view, and audience that you'll need to work through carefully. If you find yourself struggling, crossing out words, rethinking, wondering, even testing out versions on a sympathetic listener, you're not alone. These cases have been used in dozens of classrooms and seminars and workshops, by high school students and college freshmen and third-year engineering students and businesspeople and nonnative speakers of English—even by teachers of writing!—and although almost everyone has enjoyed them, no one has ever told us they were easy.

4. *Don't feel that you need special knowledge* or experience to respond to the case. In the "Veterinarian's Nightmare," for example, you play the role of someone with a Doctor of Veterinary Medicine degree. But your lack of knowledge and experience in veterinary medicine shouldn't pose a problem for you in the case. In fact, we used this case once in a class of students majoring in preveterinary medicine, and their responses were very much like everyone else's. You'll find

that most of your concerns will be rhetorical—what language to choose, how to present the information, what background to include or not to include, etc.

5. Sometimes, you may need to *suspend your disbelief* a little and accept the events of the case as they're described. You might find yourself, for example, saying "I never would have done such-and-such in the first place." If such-and-such is an event already built into the case, there won't be much point trying to change it. Instead, work on getting your way out of the dilemma through your writing, given the background of the case.

6. *Above all, have fun with the cases.* Use them for classroom dialogue, debate, and sharing. Enjoy the problems you need to solve. After all, these are the mock trials, the practice meets, the rehearsals. Take some risks. Try out different possibilities. Laugh a little.

Designing Your Own Cases

If you enjoy the "deep case" approach, you may want to design your own cases for writing. The most effective and enjoyable way to do this is to collaborate with other people in a small group. If there are several small groups each producing its own deep case, the cases can be rotated and each group can then respond to another group's case assignment.

You'll soon discover that, like any writing, designing a case poses its own special problems. Whether you're working alone or in a group, you might find the following suggestions useful in avoiding some common pitfalls in case design:

Begin by Defining a Situation.   Brainstorm for possible scenarios involving characters in some sort of conflict. There are several ways to invent a rhetorical situation. For example, you could think up an interesting setting: a church or synagogue, a school, a department store, a street, a restaurant, a rock concert, and so on. Or you could start by describing some characters: an elderly couple, a police officer, some elementary school students, a sculptor. Eventually, as you conjure up images of problems and controversies, or background information involving characters in scenes, you'll begin to get some ideas for developing your case.

Remember to Involve Writing in Some Way.   How can you develop your case so that it hinges on one or more important pieces of writing (e.g., newspaper accounts, letters, reports, editorials and essays, and so on)? Often the fact that you'll need to develop a writing task for your case will help you to narrow down the specific background information you'll develop. If your reader can solve the problems you pose in some other way than writing, then create a situation for your case in which writing is the only likely course to take. In the "Veterinarian's Nightmare," for example, we made it clear that the reader, Mrs. Thompson, has no phone at her isolated beach cottage. You're forced to write.

Be Realistic.   Your case will probably contain two kinds of information: the description of the case, which usually leads up to the writing task; and considerable background and supplementary information, perhaps with additional problems and events. For both kinds of information, try to be true to the way that the world actually works; if your case is outlandish or too far-fetched, it may be amusing but it probably won't mirror common writing situations people find themselves in . . . and that's one of the main purposes of the case.

One way to be realistic in your supplementary information is to include other sorts of written documents as part of the case: letters and memos, police reports, news accounts, even controversial essays. Don't be afraid to contact other people for models of such documents. In the "Veterinarian's Nightmare," for example, we talked to several veterinarians, obtained a blank medical chart, and did some research on medical problems that can afflict dogs. The richer and more realistic your case is, the more fun your readers will have with it. Want to include a police report? Go down to the station and talk to the police; see if they have some forms you could use or old samples to give you some ideas. Need realistic sounding names? Open up your phone book and randomly select a first name from one person and a last name from another. Need a good location? Get out your atlas. Pick an interesting town or state and make up some street names. If your situation involves a common business like a fast-food restaurant, go down to McDonald's or Burger King and talk to the manager or give him or her a draft of your case. If it's unrealistic, you'll soon know—and you'll get numerous good ideas. Think of building the cases, then, as an interesting and amusing research project involving interviews, observations, perhaps some library research, and a good deal of collaboration.

Build a Dilemma.   We've found that people most often enjoy cases when they include several sorts of problems to be solved—even ethical and emotional ones because these, especially, must be worked out through writing. Once you've invented the basic scenario, try to devise some further complications. (You might even introduce these further complications **after** your readers have already drafted a first response. This will encourage them to rethink what they've written.)

In a case designed by some of our students, for example, you (the writer) are supposed to be the head of a small neighborhood organization. Recently, some new neighbors have moved into a vacant house on a pretty cul-de-sac near your home. Soon after they move in, their back yard starts filling up with junk—old tires, a refrigerator, scrap metal, some rubble, pieces of plastic, tin cans, and a variety of other discarded and unpleasant bric-a-brac. It soon becomes clear why: the new neighbors are modern artists, and they collect the junk to use in their many rather avant-garde sculptures.

But they never answer their door, as you soon discover, and they have an unlisted phone number. During one of the neighborhood organization meetings, the other members suggest you write a letter to the new neighbors asking them to do something about the problem. The case builds from there, and several further pieces of writing are involved.

At first, the designers of this case thought up a simple scenario: someone moves into the neighborhood and turns their yard into the local eyesore. So far, however, this scenario is too straightforward: there isn't much at stake, no real moral or ethical problem, and so the writing task would be quite simple: just write a letter to the neighbors asking them to clean up their junk-filled yard.

As the students worked on this case, however, they decided to make the new neighbors modern artists, so that from the artists' point of view, the junk is valuable and important. You can begin to see how much more interesting and difficult the case has become, just from this simple addition to the scenario.

What this means is that you should try not to "slant" the case too much toward any single point of view or solution. The more "obvious" and logical the response, the less you'll challenge your readers to think about alternative perspectives in what they write.

Consider Embellishing a Real-Life Problem. If you pay attention to the news, you'll often learn about situations that, with a little imagination, can make excellent cases. Recently, for example, we read an account in the newspaper about a situation that happened at a local high school. One of our colleagues, whose son attends the school, also gave us some further details about what happened.

Apparently, the high school administration had allowed the student activities board to set up an evening dance concert featuring a local rock band. The band was hired under contract to play for three hours. The high school administration signed the contract since the student organization was thought not to be legally in charge of the finances. The students then went ahead with the publicity and decorations, and everything was set.

On the night of the concert, the band began by playing some songs from the albums of popular "heavy metal" bands. Although these albums had been distributed by leading record labels and were available at most record stores, they included some songs whose lyrics the high school administration thought "objectionable." During the middle of their first set, the band suddenly found itself powerless: the high school principal had literally "pulled the plug" on the concert. The band was promptly asked to pack up their equipment, and to an angry, disappointed crowd, the principal announced that the concert had been officially cancelled because of the band's questionable moral character.

Although this event prompted considerable controversy (especially because the high school refused to honor the contract they'd signed with the band and was then sued by the band members), the scenario could be considerably embellished and made more interesting with the addition of a few details. If you were designing this as a case, you might consider including the lyrics the administration had found objectionable. You might write the "contract" the band had signed. You might include a picture of the band in action or do a mock newspaper article showing the principal pulling the plug. You might also include various reactions to the event in writing (say, from a "letters to the editor" section of the local newspaper) by a variety of citizens, students, musicians, pro- and anticensorship groups, and school board members. In creating all these additional details, you'd want to be sensitive to the range of issues the case raises, being careful to avoid slanting the case too heavily in favor of one or another group or perspective. In short, you could turn this actual situation into a rich, complicated, and interesting case for writing.

Our suggestion, then, is whenever possible to be imaginative, realistic, and complete. You'll find that both designing **and** responding to the cases will be a rewarding experience.

Finally, we want to make you an offer—a chance for you to have your case considered for inclusion in future editions of this textbook or in a special supplementary collection of cases we're thinking of publishing separately as the Appendix to this text. If you've designed a really powerful and interesting deep case for writing, send it (or ask your teacher to send it) to us at 209 Lind Hall, University of Minnesota, Minneapolis, MN 55455. Include your name, address and phone, and the name (and school) of your teacher, if you've produced the case in a course. We'll write back to let you know what we think. And if we use it, of course, you'll get full credit. Who knows? In a couple of years, your case could be read in hundreds of classes around the country.

And **that's** real.

Case 1: The Veterinarian's Nightmare

BACKGROUND

You're one of two veterinarians running a practice in a fashionable suburb of Denver, Colorado. Your partner, Mary Johansson, received her DVM degree (Doctor of Veterinary Medicine) from Cornell University five years ago and practiced in Jamestown, New York, for four years before joining your clinic almost a year ago. She specialized, both at college and in her

Jamestown position, in "small animal" medicine and minor surgery (i.e., house pets).

You received your DVM from Kansas State University in Manhattan, Kansas, nine years ago, where you specialized in agricultural veterinary medicine. For the first five years after college, you worked for the Nebraska Department of Agriculture. In your position, you inspected livestock, saw to the health of animals that posed a threat to the state's agricultural well-being, and conducted research on psoroptic scabies, a highly contagious skin infection that affected the sheep in several areas of Rock, Holt, and Garfield counties, Nebraska, during one summer. The following year, you received one of the state's four awards for promising research in eradication control.

In August two years ago, you learned from one of your Kansas State friends that the Denver veterinarian she was working with, Dr. James Bissonnette, had decided to retire. Unwilling to buy the Bissonnette practice

OAKVILLE ANIMAL HOSPITAL

herself, your friend soon took a job at an animal research institute in Los Angeles, but pointed out that the Bissonnette clinic might make a good investment. After investigating, you agreed, and made Bissonnette an offer. A month later, you packed your belongings and headed for Colorado to take over the Bissonnette clinic located near downtown Denver.

At the time you bought the Bissonnette practice, it had about 100 clients. Most of them used Bissonnette's services for their pets' yearly innoculations and occasional deworming, antiflea and tick scrubs, heartworm control, and other more or less routine work. For the last two years of Bissonnette's ownership, though, the number of clients had steadily decreased: many families near the practice moved to Aurora, Lakewood, Westminster, and other Denver suburbs and switched to the veterinary clinics in those areas. The new class of residents living in the burgeoning apartments and condominiums near the downtown area were mainly young professionals whose busy lifestyles (or rental leases) prevented them from keeping pets. Although you were aware of the drop in clients, Bissonnette's practice was cheap, and you saw a good chance to build it back up to its former prosperity.

Soon after buying the practice, you noticed some cheap office and clinic space for rent on the edge of Oakville, an upper middle-class Denver suburb. This space consisted of a waiting room, a small office, a receptionist's booth, two small examination/surgery rooms, and a room with ten cages for post-operative recovery and overnight cases. Although the building was badly in need of some repairs, you reasoned that the location would provide a growth in clients over the years. You hired a receptionist/secretary and an assistant, Jim Tufts, who would care for and feed the sick animals, clean the cages, do scrubs and grooming, and assist in the general duties of the clinic.

In its first year, the practice grew from just over 80 to almost 125 clients. You began to take on more elaborate surgical cases, and in the fall of that year, you took a five-year business loan at relatively high interest rates and had an addition built to the clinic to house up to 40 animals at a time. When clients saw the new addition, they began asking you to board their pets while they were on vacation, and soon this was generating some good income. You changed the facility's name from the "Rocky Mountain Veterinary Clinic" to "Oakville Animal Hospital."

Finally, the work became so hectic that you decided to take on a partner. Dr. Johansson read your ad in the classified pages of *Veterinary Medicine* and sent in her résumé. She was by far the best qualified of the applicants but insisted on being a full partner should she be hired. Not willing to pass up the chance to have such a well-qualified vet in your practice, you agreed to her terms, and she became your partner.

Soon after Dr. Johansson had begun working with you, however, a new clinic, the "Estate Acres Animal Hospital," was built in Oakville about four miles from your own. The hospital is architecturally very attractive, with nice lawns and lots of tinted glass, and a large parking lot. It is situated in

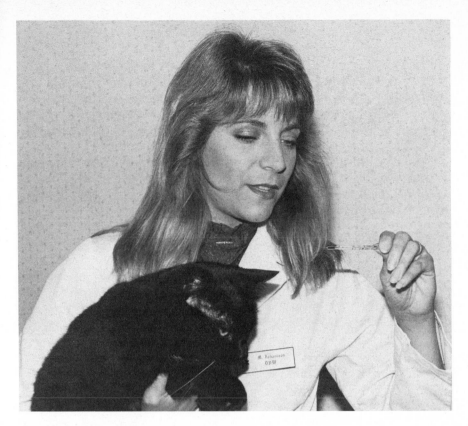

DR. MARY JOHANSSON

ESTATE ACRES ANIMAL HOSPITAL

277

an ideal location, close to two large malls and accessible from Route 85, a major thoroughfare connecting Denver with the southern suburbs. The facility boasts three full-time DVMs, two assistants, a receptionist, a full-time secretary, and a 24-hours-a-day, 7-days-a-week hotline in case of emergencies. Estate Acres has also been advertising a free "Pet-Van" service to transport animals to and from their homes.

Soon after this hospital opened, some of your steady clients asked you to send their pets' medical records to Estate Acres. You tried to beef up advertising and took out a larger *Yellow Pages* insert, but these had little effect. You're still losing a client or two each month.

The Present Situation

Martha (Mrs. William E.) Thompson is one of your wealthier clients who stayed with the practice from when it was run by Dr. Bissonnette. She owns an elderly Yorkshire Terrier, "Beckett." You've seen Beckett three times since taking over the Bissonnette practice, mostly for routine visits (see his

MRS. THOMPSON OUTSIDE HER DENVER HOME

medical chart below). Mrs. Thompson has been very pleased with your treatment of Beckett, and since the opening of Estate Acres, your only new clients have been half a dozen people she has referred to you. Several of these clients are also wealthy, and two of them own horses you now take

ANIMAL RECORD

OWNER'S NAME _Mr. and Mrs. William E. Thompson_ CASE NO. _019_
ADDRESS _363 Mountainview Terrace, Denver_ TEL. _617-2013_ REF. BY _(Bissonnette client)_
SPECIES _Canine_ BREED _Yorkshire Terrier_ NAME _"Beckett"_
SEX _M_ AGE _15+_ COLOR AND MARKINGS _Black and Tan_

EXAMINATION: NOSE _D - Runny_ EYES _Glassy + Liquidous_ SKIN _N_
BOWELS _N_ APPETITE _0_ COUGH _NONE_
PULSE _R_ RESP _R, SH_ TEMP. _N_

SYMPTOMS: _High Salivation, Mild Tremors, Panicked aura, dilated pupils_

DIAGNOSIS: _Philodendron Poisoning_
TREATMENT: _Liquid Diet for 48 hrs. - Antitussive drops - Remove all Plants from Vicinity of dog - Keep warm -_
REMARKS: _Dog was seen chewing on Philodendron leaves in early A.M. -_

CASE NO. 019

OWNER'S NAME Mr. and Mrs. William E. Thompson

SUBSEQUENT TREATMENT AND PROGRESS											
MO.	DAY	YR.	NOSE	EYES	SKIN	BOWELS	APPE-TITE	COUGH	PULSE	RESP.	TEMP.	TREATMENT AND REMARKS
9	4	84	N	N	N	N	O	N	R	IR	N	Possible onset of myasthenia gravis - swollen esophagus - mild paralysis after exercise - treated w/oral Inhibitors 1/wk -
9	14	84										Condition improved - Continue treatment
4	12	85	N	N	N	N	F	N	N	N	N	Annual Visit - Distemper Combination + check-up
1	8	86	N	N	M	N	F	N	N	N	N	Mild Sarcoptis mange - some secondary bacterial pyoderma - apply sulfur/lindane Treatment weekly for Sev. months
6	17	86	N	N	N	N	N	N	N	N	N	Condition improved - Continue applications -
10	30	86	N	N	N	N	N	N	N	N	N	Bacterial dip for fleas and ticks - full shampoo and grooming

ABBREVIATIONS: NOSE: D discharge, C clear. EYES: C clear, D discharge, GL glassy, U ulcer. APPETITE: F fair, G good, P poor, O none. SKIN: N normal, DA dandruff, EC eczema, M mange, RW ringworm, IM improved. BOWELS: B bad, C constipated, D diarrhea, DB diarrhea with blood, L loose, N normal, O no feces.

RESPIRATION: N normal, IR irregular, R rapid, SH shallow, S slow, W weak. PULSE: N normal, F fair, G good, IR irregular, IT intermittent, P poor, R rapid, S slow, W weak. COUGH: O none, DE deep, SH shallow, S slight, B bad.

BECKETT'S CHART

care of. In turn, Mrs. Thompson's friends are also beginning to recommend your clinic to their friends and neighbors, some with exotic birds and other animals for whose care they're willing to pay a good deal of money.

It's now February. Mrs. Thompson's husband passed away four months ago. She's decided to travel to her beach cottage in the Turks and Caicos Islands to recover from her loss and to get away from the cold for a while. She doesn't want to take Beckett, however, preferring instead to board him at your hospital. On the day she departs, her nephew brings Beckett in and gives you a note from Mrs. Thompson:

                                                    Sat., Feb. 7
Doctors:

I have asked my nephew, Charles Powers, to give you
this note along with Beckett. I had thought about
having him take care of Beckett, but he is leaving
tomorrow for London, so I am entrusting my little dog
to your excellent care instead.

As I told you on the phone Wednesday, I will be gone
for two weeks (I'm returning on Sunday, Feb. 22). If
anything should come up concerning Beckett, please
let me know immediately. I have no phone at the
cottage, but you can write to me at:

            "Villa Nueva"
            Box 312, North Caicos
            Grand Turk
            Turks and Caicos Islands
            British West Indies

Beckett likes to have one of these "Bonz" treats each
day, so I'm having Charles give you a box. Please take
good care of Beckett; he's all I have now that Bill is
gone.

                                        Mrs. Thompson

A few days after you begin boarding Beckett, he becomes ill. After investigating the problem, you and Dr. Johansson discover that he has a urinary blockage caused by cystic calculi (bladder stones). Dr. Johansson suggests immediate surgery, but you try instead to dissolve the stones with special injections.

Unfortunately, Mrs. Thompson can't be reached by phone, and the mail often takes up to a week to reach her cottage. You'd prefer to get in touch with her before operating on the dog, especially because she left instructions that you contact her should there be any problems with Beckett.

Finally, you decide you must operate or lose the dog. Since it's your turn to be on call for the weekend, you tell Dr. Johansson not to worry about coming in on Sunday, and you ask your assistant Jim to help with the surgery instead.

The operation turns out to be quite complicated, and you discover that the dog's bladder has begun to rupture in spite of the injections. Because the dog is over twelve years old, the operation weakens him considerably. You place him in a cage in the boarding area and keep him warm. Over the next few days his condition improves a little, but he's still seriously ill.

On the third morning after surgery, you arrive at the hospital to find that the temperature in the boarding kennels is 45 degrees; the thermostat has been turned down. All the animals have fared well except for Beckett, who has lapsed into a coma and is breathing faintly. You and Dr. Johansson cancel your day's appointments and take turns working on the dog for the better part of the day. By nightfall he's still alive but critically ill. Thursday his condition worsens a little, and in spite of your constant attention throughout the day, when you return on Friday morning, he's dead. Mrs. Thompson is supposed to return on Sunday, but in the meantime you've received a postcard in the Friday mail:

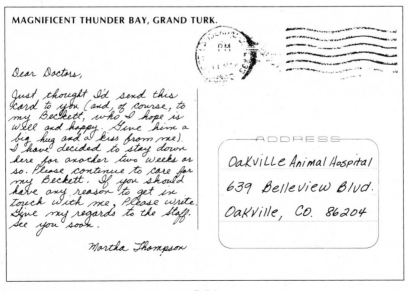

MAGNIFICENT THUNDER BAY, GRAND TURK.

Dear Doctors,

Just thought I'd send this card to you (and, of course, to my Beckett, who I hope is well and happy. Give him a big hug and a kiss from me). I have decided to stay down here for another two weeks or so. Please continue to care for my Beckett. If you should have any reason to get in touch with me, please write. Give my regards to the staff. See you soon.

Martha Thompson

ADDRESS

Oakville Animal Hospital
639 Belleview Blvd.
Oakville, CO. 86204

Because there's no way to reach Mrs. Thompson by phone, and because she's requested that you get in touch with her immediately in case there's a problem with Beckett, your task in this case is to write a letter explaining to her what's happened. The total bill for the cost of Beckett's boarding and surgery comes to $512.00. Additional background for the case will be provided as you draft and revise your writing.

YOUR TURN

1. Before planning your letter to Mrs. Thompson, spend some time analyzing your rhetorical situation:

   How important is Mrs. Thompson as an audience? Why?

   Although you know only a little about Mrs. Thompson, mainly from her notes, what sort of person does she seem to be? What effect could that have on the way you write to her?

   What concerns do you have about **what** to relate to Mrs. Thompson? Why are you concerned?

2. Begin planning your letter to Mrs. Thompson.

   Brainstorm a list of major points or create a tree of details to relate to Mrs. Thompson.

   Look for an organizing pattern in your brainstorming: what will you want to say first, second, third? Why?

   Who will you "be" as a writer? Will you use the plural pronoun "we," as in the entire clinic? or "I," as in you, personally, as surgeon?

   How much information do you feel ethically responsible for providing in your letter? Why?

   What sort of style do you want to use? Formal? Casual? Sermon-like? Eulogistic? Technical? Soft and mushy? Why?

3. Draft your letter. Keep track of your decisions as you write and speculate on them when you're done, in preparation for discussion.

JIM TUFTS AND HIS WIFE OUTSIDE JIM'S BROTHER'S HOME

Jim Tufts

Jim has been a faithful and diligent worker in your employ. For fifteen years, he'd worked in a steel plant in Pennsylvania, but was laid off two years ago because of plant cut-backs. Unable to find other work in Pennsylvania, Jim had' moved with his wife Jennifer and their little girl to Denver to live with his brother, who had some spare rooms in his finished basement.

Soon after moving your practice to Oakville, you advertised for a clinic aide, and Jim seemed the most eager of the applicants for the job.

Mrs. Thompson seemed especially to appreciate Jim, at least, based on the note she sent last year:

Dear Doctors:

What a wonderful job your assistant Jim did on my little Beckett's coat! Please tell him how much I appreciate seeing my wonderful Beck looking so good. It seems his skin problem has all cleared up, too.

I've been meaning to give you a picture of Beckett to pin up with all the others on your "pet potpourri board" in the waiting area, so I've included a photograph I took a few years ago when we entered Beckett in the Oakville Dog Show. Isn't his little bow just darling? Thank you again.

                                        Mrs. Thompson

BECKETT

© Michel Tritt/DOG FANCY

On Monday morning, three days after Beckett dies, your secretary finds a note and a time card mysteriously slipped under the front door of the clinic. It's from Jim Tufts, who's announced that he's quit his job.

```
Doctors:

    By now, you'll be wondering where I am. I just can't
face coming back, so I've quit. I'm sure now that I was
the cause of Beckett's death. I was cleaning the cages
last Wed. after you both left, and it was so hot that I
turned down the thermostat, and then forgot to turn it
back up. I figured you probably wouldn't fire me, but
I couldn't face working knowing that I'd probably
lost you your best customer. Just have Nancy send my
final check to my brother's address.
    I'm so sorry . . . I don't know what to say.

                                                    Jim
```

PAYROLL
TIME CARD

Print In Ink

Name __JAMES TUFTS__   Soc. Sec. No. __062-82-1137__

Date	A.M. In	A.M. Out	P.M. In	P.M. Out	Hours
1					
2					
3					
4					
5					
6					
7					
8					
9					
10					
11					
12					
13					
14					
15					
16	7:30	12:00	1:00	5:00	8½
17	9:00	12:00	7:00	10:00	6
18	—		1:00	9:00	4
19	7:30	12:00	—		4½
20	9:00	12:00	1:00	4:00	6
21					
22					
23					
24					
25					
26					
27					
28					
29					
30					
31					

Total Hours Worked __29__

Pay Period Ending __2/16 - 2/28__

PAYROLL — Disposition of Time Worked:

☐ Misc   ☑ Pay—Straight Time
☑ Biweekly   ☐ Pay—Overtime
                ☐ Time Off—Straight
                ☐ Time Off—Overtime

Reason for Overtime

_____

_____

_____

HOURLY RATE $ __6.50__

Type of Pay	Hours to be Paid	Amount
Straight Time	29	
Time and ½		
Shift Diff @ _____		
Other		

PAY THIS AMOUNT $ __188.50__

I hereby certify that the time recorded represents <u>actual hours</u> of employment for the period indicated.

James Tufts
Employee Signature

Authorized Signature

YOUR TURN

1. Assess your draft in terms of the new information you now have. Will this new information make a difference to what you include in your letter? Why or why not?
2. Make a decision about Jim's fate at your clinic. Then write a letter to Jim informing him of your decision (that is, if you think he should resign, confirm his resignation and make it official, providing reasons; if you think he should keep his job, don't accept his resignation and urge him instead to continue working with you).
3. Revise your draft to Mrs. Thompson if you feel the need to do so. Again, keep track of your decisions and be ready to discuss them.

Your Partnership with Mary Johansson

On the whole, your work with Mary has been good; you both get along well, though she is quite formal and professional, even when she's not working. She seems much more concerned with doing a good job as a veterinarian than with any of the "business" side of the partnership. However, when you first signed your partnership agreement, Mary insisted on writing into it some very particular "rules" that she said could never be broken as long as she was part of the clinic.

One of the items, for example, has to do with the payment of bills.

Article XXI

We further agree to enforce actively, regardless of circumstance, the partnership agreement policy on collection of payments. All clients will be required to make payment for services and materials on return of their pet. No bills will be sent or given. When special conditions exist, such as occasions when a client "gives up ownership" of an animal because of its illness or the high cost of treatment, a bill shall be sent to the client and payment must be made within ten days. If payment is not made, then legal collection procedures shall apply within ten days of the second notice of payment due.

Mary was also quite specific about "special circumstances," claiming that she'd known too many small clinics that had done poorly because every other client seemed to be a personal friend of the veterinarian, who "gave away" his or her services to be nice. She insisted on an item regarding these circumstances in the partnership agreement.

Article XXII

In the event of special circumstances, or of special relationships between a doctor and a client (excluding immediate family), we agree to enforce the payment of all services rendered, including the regular office, examination, consulting, or surgical fees, costs of all treatments and medicines, costs of all boarding, and costs of all other clinical procedures including house calls and other emergency visits. In addition, no client shall be entitled to any special treatment over and above standard treatment because of a special relationship or for the return of special treatment or consideration, or because of unusual extenuating circumstances such as the outcome of professional treatment, as long as this client is a regular client of this practice.

Costs for Treatment, Oakville Animal Hospital

Office Visit	$ 20.00
Shots	10.00
Distemper Combination	18.00
Stool Exam	15.00
Worm Diagnosis/Treatment	15.00
Antiinsect Dips & Baths	15.00*
Routine Shampoo & Brushdown	15.00*
Minor Treatments (pad cuts, etc.)	30.00
Minor Surgery	50.00**
Major Surgery (Spaying, etc.)	150.00 +
	**

*Ave. size dog. More or less depending on size.

**By weight. Estimate is for average-size dog in good
  health; actual charges will vary.

  Note: Costs for surgical procedures will vary
  depending on the severity of the procedure, the
  animal's condition, and the materials required for
  surgery (anesthetic, overnight boarding, etc.).

Boarding Costs at Littleton

Dogs	Day	Week	Add'l Days
Toy to Medium (45 lbs.)	$ 9	$56	$ 8
Large (45 lbs. and up)	11	70	10
Cats	6	35	5

Services: All animals are fed twice daily. Cages are
cleaned once a day. All dogs are walked twice a day
(unless sick) and are washed and groomed prior to
pickup for all terms over one week. For the boarding
of other pets such as tropical birds, please consult
the doctors.

YOUR TURN

1. Reassess your draft now that you have this new information. Is there anything you think you should change? Why? Does this new knowledge of the partnership agreement create any special problems in terms of the decisions you've made in your draft to Mrs. Thompson?
2. Decide how you'll handle the problem of billing Mrs. Thompson. Will you bill her in your letter? How? Will you reduce the amount of the bill or waive it altogether? Why? Will this compromise your partnership agreement?
3. Make any further revisions in the draft of your letter to Mrs. Thompson.

The Cremation Problem

As you're drafting your letter to Mrs. Thompson, you're reminded of the cremation laws in Colorado, and you retrieve the memo from your files, sent to you from Dr. Johansson soon after she joined the practice:

```
Doctor:

You might be interested to know that I received a
document from the State of Colorado reminding all
practicing vets of the Colorado Incineration Law for
dead animals. According to the law, we are required to
cremate all animals within 24 hours of death. I assume
you've always adhered to this law; it was the same in
New York, and we were careful not to violate it. For my
information, where have you sent animals for
cremation in the past?

                                        Mary
```

After digging through the files a bit more, you discover your reply to Mary.

Mary:

Thanks for your note. Only two or three animals have died in my care, and their owners took care of their burial. But in case we ever need to cremate an animal, let's use the Ridge Road Crematorium. Their fees are reasonable. Incidentally, we ought to charge that fee to the owners, plus delivery. Let's set it at $45.00. I do know one thing--the State means serious business about their reminder. Thanks for passing it on to me.

YOUR TURN

I. Again, reassess your draft in terms of this new information. How will you handle knowing about the incineration laws? Will you inform Mrs. Thompson about the fate of her dog's body? Are there any alternatives? If you decide to tell her, how will you do it? Where will you include this in your letter?

2. Make any appropriate revisions in your letter.

3. Think carefully about the ethical implications of your decisions— decisions you've rendered in your letter. If you've chosen to violate your partnership agreement, how does this violation differ from violating the Colorado State Law? What legal implications are embedded in the decisions you've made in your letter to Mrs. Thompson? What moral and ethical implications? What implications for your own survival and the survival of your business?

4. Again, keep track of your thinking for discussion.

5. Finish revising your letter entirely and turn it in—that is, assume it has been sent to Mrs. Thompson.

The Insurance Dilemma

You've finally polished your letter to Mrs. Thompson and sent it. However, you receive no reply after you assume Mrs. Thompson has gotten your letter. Instead, the following request comes to you from the Hartford Mutual Insurance Company:

HARTFORD MUTUAL INSURANCE COMPANY, INC.
179 W. 35th St.
Hartford, Connecticut 07942

Feb. 26

Oakville Animal Hospital
639 Belleview Blvd.
Oakville, CO 80204

Dear Doctors:

Recently, we received a call from Mrs. W. E. Thompson, one of your clients, notifying us of her dog "Beckett's" death at your facility. You may not be aware that for the past six years, Mrs. Thompson has had her dog's life insured with us against accidental injury and death.

The details of Mrs. Thompson's policy and claim are not important for the purposes of this letter. Specifically, however, we will need from you a short letter explaining (as nontechnically as possible) the events leading to Beckett's death, including your estimation of the cause of death. The primary need for this letter is quite obvious; but Mrs. Thompson has requested a copy, perhaps for her own clarification.

We appreciate your attention to this matter. Please address your reply to the attention of Myra Wilkinson, Claims Assessor.

Thank you.

Sincerely,

Robert E. Breck
Insurance Adjustor

REB:dd

YOUR TURN

Draft a response to the Hartford Mutual request. To do this, first generate a plan:

What will you tell Hartford Mutual about the incident? Will this differ from what you've told Mrs. Thompson? Why or why not?

What sort of audience is Hartford Mutual? Compare them with Mrs. Thompson as readers; what differences are there? Will these differences have any effect on your writing style, content, etc.? Why or why not?

What purposes do you have for writing to Hartford Mutual? Try to specify these—including any personal or psychological purposes you may have. Do your purposes differ from those you had for writing to Mrs. Thompson? If so, how do your different purposes affect your writing?

Consider the decisions you made in conveying information to Mrs. Thompson. Is there anything you want to withhold from either audience? Why or why not? What are the legal, ethical, and personal consequences of either withholding or revealing the details of the situation as you know them?

Looking back on your letter to Mrs. Thompson, are there any decisions you **would** have made differently had you anticipated the Hartford Mutual letter? What does this tell you about writing in general?

Draft your letter to Hartford Mutual. Then revise it carefully and be ready to submit it.

Mrs. Thompson, Curmudgeon

Assume that no matter how fine your letter to Mrs. Thompson, no matter how sensitive, or carefully revised and polished, Mrs. Thompson turns out not to be impressed at all by it. Instead, some time after you've sent your letter to Hartford Mutual, Mrs. Thompson sends you the angry attack on page 298.

Mrs. W. E. Thompson
363 Mountainview Terrace
Denver, CO 80212

March 8

Oakville Animal Hospital
639 Belleview Blvd.
Oakville, CO 80204

Dear Doctors:

I am writing to inform you that I had planned from the
start not to pay your bill for my poor little
Beckett's "treatment." I cannot but think that you
mistreated my little dog, and that it was sheer
negligence on your part that he caught a chill in the
recovery room and died as a result of an oversight on
the part of your staff (I am referring, or course, to
the thermostat fiasco, which your incompetent
assistant Jim has taken full responsibility for in
his letter to me dated Feb. 20, but which I am now
convinced is all your fault). When I boarded my dog at
your clinic, I assumed that he would receive the best
care you could provide. Obviously, I was mistaken.

I am seriously considering writing a letter to the
editor of the Denver Times, to warn unsuspecting
people of your clinic's unprofessional, money-
grubbing ways. You should be ashamed of yourselves.

In the event that you wish to pursue my bill, you may
contact my attorney, Mr. Cyrus E. Garnes of Spinner,
Peacock, Rawles, Garnes, and Wilson, Associates
(Denver), who will be more than happy, I assure you,
to take this matter as far as is needed for my
protection and personal satisfaction.

Please send my dog's file directly to Mr. Garnes for
his reference.

Sincerely,

Mrs. W. E. Thompson

YOUR TURN

1. Write a final, last-ditch attempt to appease Mrs. Thompson, if only to stop her from writing a letter to the *Denver Times*. As you plan for this letter, consider the following:

   What can you discern in the attitude, style, and tone of Mrs. Thompson's letter that will have an effect on your own response?

   Will your own attitude, style, and tone change as a result of Mrs. Thompson's letter? Why or why not?

   How are your purposes for writing different now?

2. Draft your letter.

3. As you review your letter for revision, what do you notice about its style and content? What are you telling Mrs. Thompson, and what purpose does each piece of information serve? What effect do you hope your contents will have on your reader? Why?

4. If you could have known **everything** about the outcome of the case beforehand, how might your decisions have changed?

5. How important is it to anticipate all possible consequences of your writing? What are the limits of thinking in such ways? When is it important or not important? Are there any lessons to be learned about anticipating the responses of readers in an academic setting, or doesn't it matter?

6. Keep track of your thinking in your writer's notebook and be ready to discuss these and other issues.

Case 2: Machines and Green Thumbs

BACKGROUND

During your final term in college, you decide to apply for a special internship program designed to give you experience working on the job while you gain academic credit (and make some money at the same time). Although the program is new, it has received enough funding to pay for the chosen student interns to travel to jobs that may be located many miles from campus.

You apply for the program and are notified that your application is accepted but that the kind of position you requested was not available. Instead, you have the chance to work as an intern in sales coordination at a small, recently incorporated company located in Providence, Rhode Island. Your job at Green Thumb, Inc., would be to assist the sales department in its routine work and also to help in the development of new strategies and materials relating to wholesale and retail marketing of the company's products. You decide that although it's not exactly what you'd hoped for, the experience will be valuable later on. And because Green Thumb is a relatively young company, your work there will give you a thorough look at how a business is run. You quickly accept the position.

Currently, Green Thumb, Inc., manufactures a single line of products: five engine-powered tillers and tractors for home garden use. The company plans to expand its products into other sorts of garden equipment and supplies; but it has proceeded very slowly from its family-based beginnings in the early 1970s, by putting all its energy into the few products it sells and by trying to build its reputation carefully and deliberately. Recently, Green Thumb moved its headquarters into the first floor of a new contemporary office building outside Providence.

GREEN THUMB'S NEW LOCATION

During your first week at Green Thumb, you spend most of your time getting to know the office personnel and learning about the routine work you'll be doing in your internship. So far, you feel pretty good about Green Thumb; the people are friendly in spite of their businesslike and efficient demeanor, and they've treated you with respect. In short, you're comfortable there—though it seems that the employees are expected to concentrate hard on their work. There is time for laughter and socializing . . . but never when it interferes with serious business.

One of your primary responsibilities, you learn, is to answer inquiries about the products Green Thumb sells. Unfortunately, Green Thumb has never produced any brochures or descriptive materials as a convenient way of responding to letters of inquiry about the company's products. There's been some controversy in the past about the possibility of such materials, with one side urging their development and the other side arguing the benefits of continuing to send individual, personal responses to each inquiry— at least until the company becomes too large to handle the volume of mail in that way. Those urging the development of brochures seem to be getting their way; recently, the president of the company, Ellen Fay, has suggested that someone try drafting a prototype of a descriptive brochure for consideration at a future meeting of the upper management.

In the meantime, you've been informed that it's your responsibility to answer each inquiry about the company's products in writing.

The Present Situation

It's your first official day of work. When the mail arrives, your immediate supervisor, Jan Harding, hands you a letter of inquiry from Mr. Cotton P. Haskins and asks that you respond to it as soon as possible.

Cotton P. Haskins
R.D. 1
Camden, ME 26101

Mar. 5

Green Thumb, Inc.
46 Bay View Rd.
Providence, RI 12180

Dear Sir or Madam:

I've heard a lot about the economy and quality of Green Thumb tillers and tractors, but I have had a hard time getting any information about them.

Could you please send me some information on your garden tillers, including costs, warranties, and wholesale or retail availability in my area. I have a 40 × 80-foot vegetable garden which I till yearly. The soil in this garden is light to moderate. I also wish to expand my garden by about 600 square feet this spring. The soil in the proposed area is heavy, with some roots.

Thank you very much.

Sincerely,

Cotton P. Haskins

YOUR TURN

Before reading any further, analyze Cotton Haskins' letter by jotting down some ideas in your writer's notebook in response to the following questions:

What's the purpose of Mr. Haskins' letter?

What does Mr. Haskins want to know? Why? What use will he make of the information you provide?

What are Mr. Haskins' specific needs as a reader?

What do you need to know to provide Mr. Haskins with what he wants? Make a list.

What can you infer about Mr. Haskins from the style, tone, and quality of his letter? Does his address tell you anything? Should it matter?

What else do you know about Mr. Haskins? How do you know it?

What problems might you face in responding to Mr. Haskins' letter? Why?

As you begin thinking about your response, you realize that you'll need quite a bit of information first. Now you understand why Jan Harding hadn't spent much time describing the Green Thumb tillers; she probably reasoned that you'd have to learn everything in the process of answering some of the inquiries, and that's why she kept on stressing that the office staff would be happy to retrieve any information you might need from the files.

To get you started, though, she gives you some files of basic information about the company's products. Although the filing system as a whole is extremely orderly, each file contains a variety of information and memos. You quickly learn that you'll have to take some notes on what's most relevant for the task at hand.

Jan has given you six files, from which you've taken some notes on relevant information. Review your notes from these files carefully, jotting down further ideas when you feel it's necessary.

NOTES FROM FILE 1: GREEN THUMB TILLERS

Green Thumb GT-01 "Moto-Till"

Moto-Till—Green Thumb's oldest product, dating from the beginning of the company in 1971.

Small, hand-held garden tiller driven by a 2-horsepower Briggs & Stratton 2-cycle engine. Single shaft; tills to the side (instead of to the front).

Moto-Till has a single forward speed. Controls are mounted on the handlebar.

Engine requires pull-starting (like a lawnmower). Has a single depth control that allows the user to vary the depth of tilling from 4" to 8" maximum by 2" increments.

The Moto-Till is designed to overturn earth, and this is its only capacity. Recommended for small garden work.

Moto-Till is the least expensive product—suggested retail price is $240.00.

Boxed, Moto-Till's dimensions are 38″ high x 25″ wide x 18″ deep. Weighs 48 lbs. 6 oz.

Comes in a single color, Vegetation Green. Manufactured of steel & aluminum with welded joints & seams; some rivets.

Requires generally light maintenance—periodic cleaning. Yearly or biyearly servicing recommended.

Green Thumb GT-04 "Pony"

5-horsepower Pony first introduced on market in 1980. More powerful than smaller "Moto-Till"—has advantage of rear tines (a rear set of spokes to dig the earth with) for reduced vibration. Has Briggs and Stratton engine.

Like Moto-Till, Pony is hand-operated. But wheels are powered by its engine, unlike Moto-Till, which relies on the turning action of the tines to pull it along.

Pony also features tractor-tread tires because it is often used on slightly heavier soil than the Moto-Till.

Unlike more powerful "Horse," Pony has only forward speeds, but it has both a fast and slow speed, whereas Moto-Till has only a single drive mechanism with one gear.

Pony features instant depth control. This is operated manually, with a lever on the handlebars.

Hand-pull starting is standard equipment on Pony. Can be purchased with optional electric starter for an additional $69.95. This version is listed as model GT-04B in the Green Thumb Line.

Pony has three functions in addition to soil tilling. It can chop, shred, and compost vegetation material (stalks, grass, weeds, soft roots, and thin branches).

Pony is approximately same height as Moto-Till, but is two-thirds as wide as the Horse. Suggested storage is in small shed or garage.

Pony has a list price of $575.00.

Constructed of steel and aluminum with welds and some rivets. Comes in two colors: Vegetation Green and Rust. Weighs 86 lbs.

Production discontinued briefly for 7 months in 1982 when a major design flaw was discovered in the drive mechanism. Design was altered and factory was remachined to produce updated model.

Green Thumb GT-06 "Horse"

Horse has Briggs & Stratton engine, 6 h.p. Introduced on the market in 1978 to compete with similar product manufactured by Troy-Built, Inc. List price is $760.00.

Like the Pony, the Horse has rear tines for reduced vibration. Also has power wheels with tractor-tread tires. Construction is similar—steel and aluminum, welds and rivets.

Two forward speeds, one reverse. Controls are mounted on the handlebars. Electric starting is standard feature.

Also has instant depth control, but it's automatic, not manual, as on the Pony.

Operated by hand. Also chops, shreds, and composts. Can handle slightly heavier material than the Pony.

Comes in two colors: Vegetation Green and Rust. Weighs 115 lbs. and measures slightly higher than Pony and ⅓ wider.

Comes with weatherproof vinyl cover.

Green Thumb GT-20 "Work Team"

Work Team is a much larger piece of equipment than the Pony, Horse, and Moto-Till, requiring seated operation instead of hand operation. Has a 12 h.p. Kohler engine.

More complex transmission (hydrostatic). Has hydraulic lift controls for lifting implements (mower, tiller, etc.).

Comes with a contoured seat made of durable leather-look vinyl.

Optional rotary mower attachment—for an extra $215.00 list. Mower attachment includes grass-catcher bag and frame.

Power steering is standard equipment. Tire chains and extra weights are optional (chains: $45.00; weights: $40.00) for heavy use.

Depth control for tilling is automatic but can be set to manual. Tills at variable depths from 2″ to 8″.

Has two forward and one reverse gear, with variable speed control (accelerator). Electric starting standard.

Comes in two colors: Vegetation Green and Tomato Red. List price is $1,600.

Weighs 315 lbs. and measures 30″ wide x 34″ long x 25″ high.

First introduced on the market in 1978 as part of a new line of heavier tractors.

Green Thumb GT-40 "DeTractor"

DeTractor is largest Green Thumb product, weighing 406 lbs. and measuring slightly larger than the Work Team. Comes standard with Lester 19 h.p. engine (2 cylinder). Retails at $2,115.00.

Transmission is hydrostatic, coupled to three-speed gearing (and one reverse). Has larger optional mower attachment (36″ compared with 24″ attachment for Work Team), which comes standard with grass catcher and frame.

Two colors: Vegetation Green and Tomato Red.

Has a three-point hitch for attaching other implements to the rear (carts, etc.). Also comes standard with headlights.

Seat is contoured (with back rest), leather-look vinyl. Comes with gauges for oil pressure and temperature.

Optional in-dash AM/FM radio (mono, with one speaker) is an extra $75.00.

Headlights are standard; single-beam. Also standard: power steering.

Special heavy-duty suspension system for rough terrain.

Standard composting and shredding functions. Reverse functions for tiller tines in case of binding from roots and heavy branches.

Automatic depth control. First introduced on market in 1981.

Also has optional snow-plow attachment ($215.00) operated by hydraulic lift controls. Chains and weights are same as for Work Team.

PHOTOCOPIES FROM FILE 2: GREEN THUMB GUARANTEES

Note: Copies of guarantees are inserted into packing boxes of all models; when delivery of equipment is requested, guarantees are given to the buyer at time of purchase.

Green Thumb Full One-Year Warranty (GT-20 & GT-40)

Green Thumb, Inc., warrants its Model GT-20 and GT-40 tractors to be free of manufacturing defects for a one-year period after the original date of consumer purchase. This warranty does not include damage to the product resulting from accident or misuse. If the product should become defective within the warranty period, Green Thumb will elect to repair or replace it free of charge, including free return transportation provided it is delivered prepaid to any authorized Green Thumb Service Facility. A list of authorized service facilities has been included with this product. Any questions regarding warranty service can be addressed to the company.

In addition, Green Thumb, Inc., warrants its Model GT-20 and GT-40 tractors to be free of defect to the drive train mechanism for a period of two years after the original date of consumer purchase. All other conditions apply.

Conditions. All Green Thumb repair service must be arranged through an official Green Thumb Authorized Service Facility. Any tampering with the products by the consumer or other party to effect repair will void this warranty.

All warranty claims must be accompanied by a full, dated receipt of purchase.

Green Thumb warranties are not transferable beyond original owner or purchaser.

Green Thumb warranties are not available for products used for commercial or rental purposes. Use of a product for these purposes will void this warranty.

Green Thumb Warranties do not cover transportation or other costs incurred from delivering products to authorized service facilities.

Green Thumb 90-Day Limited Warranty
(GT-01, GT-04 & GT-04B, GT-06)

This product is warranted against manufacturer's defects for a period of 90 days from the date of purchase from a Green Thumb distributor or authorized retail store. Within this period, we will repair the product without charge for parts and labor. Simply bring your Green Thumb sales slip as proof of purchase date to any Authorized Green Thumb Service Facility within the allotted time. Warranty does not cover transportation costs, nor does it cover a product which has been misused or accidentally damaged.

EXCEPT AS PROVIDED HEREIN, Green Thumb, Inc., makes no warranties, express or implied, including warranties of merchantability and fitness for a particular purpose.

This warranty gives you specific legal rights and you may also have other rights depending on your state of residence.

Notes from File 3: Distributors for Green Thumb Products

Distributors for State of Maine

Retail

Bob's Hardware, Augusta
True-Value South, Skowhegan
Kenson's Home and Garden Center, Rockport
Aurora Hardware, Farmington
East Coast Appliance Center, Bangor
Reliable Appliances, Portland
Lincolnville Hardware, Lincolnville
East Central, Inc., Brunswick
Waterville Small Farm Equipment, Waterville
Shields Bros. Hardware, Camden

Wholesale

Cory Farm Equipment, Bangor
Hanlon Small Farm Supply, Rockland
Waterville Supply Co., Waterville
Millinocket Equipment, Millinocket
Biddeford Till & Seed Co., Biddeford
Johnson's Farm Equipment, Bangor

NOTES AND SPECIMEN FROM FILE 4:
OPTIONAL SERVICE AGREEMENT

Notes:

Service agreements are purchased optionally from the dealer at time of purchasing product. It is the dealer's responsibility to inform the buyer of the existence of the service agreement and to enroll the buyer in the program at his or her request. All revenues from service agreements are sent to Green Thumb, Inc., by the dealer. Dealers are reimbursed by Green Thumb, Inc., for all servicing and parts covered under the terms of the contract, at a rate not to exceed $8.50 per hour for labor and Green Thumb's wholesale list cost for parts. All repairs unable to be made by the service facility will be made by Green Thumb, Inc., at no charge for delivery of equipment to and from Green Thumb Manufacturing, Providence, RI.

Specimen:

GREEN THUMB'S OPTIONAL SERVICE AGREEMENT

Congratulations! You're now the proud owner of a dependable Green Thumb tiller or tractor.

Green Thumb products are designed, manufactured, and tested to give you many years of effective, trouble-free service. However, any modern machine may require occasional servicing or repair. The Green Thumb Maintenance Agreement provides protection from unexpected repair bills beyond the terms of the warranty.

For $29.95 per year, Green Thumb will extend its full warranty protection **and** provide a free annual check-up through its authorized service centers. Should anything happen to your Green Thumb tiller or tractor (except for damage resulting from accident or misuse), simply take your equipment to an authorized Green Thumb Service Facility and it will be repaired free of charge.

In addition, you can pre-pay this fee for as many years as you wish, thereby making use of the low service agreement cost in the face of yearly inflation. Ask your dealer for the service agreement form. A list of authorized service facilities has been included with this product.

Note: Your service agreement must be made at the time you purchase your Green Thumb tiller or tractor. The service agreement extends the normal Green Thumb warranty by increments of one year from the expiration of the warranty. The service agreement applies only to the purchaser of the product; it is not transferable.

NOTES FROM FILE 5: AUTHORIZED
SERVICE FACILITIES

Facilities in State of Maine

Bob's Fix-It, Bangor
Portland Appliance Service Center, Portland
Garrison TV and Appliance Center, Bar Harbor
Shaver Appliance Service Corp., Lewiston
Route 1 Appliance Repair, Belfast
Shields Bros. Hardware, Camden
Al's Vacuum & Mower Service, Ellsworth
Raleigh Service, Kennebunk
Cory Farm Equipment, Bangor
Johnson's Farm Equipment, Bangor
Reliable Appliances, Portland
Lincolnville Hardware, Lincolnville

PHOTOCOPY FROM FILE 6

Camden, Penobscot Bay, and Surrounding Area

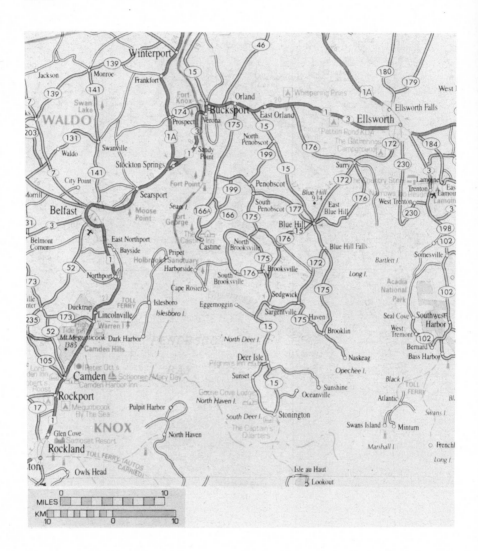

YOUR TURN

So far, then, you've gleaned as much information as you need from the files Jan gave you. Before reading further, **draft** an initial response to Mr. Haskins' letter.

To do this, brainstorm a **plan** for the letter first, based on the following questions:

1. What information from File 1 is relevant to the task? Why?
2. How much information in File 1 will you provide? What will you leave out? Why?
3. File 2 contains information Mr. Haskins has requested. What form will this information take in your letter? Why? How much will you include?
4. Files 3–5 also contain information relevant to your letter; but how relevant? How much will you include, and on what basis?
5. Based on your analysis of Mr. Haskins' letter and the information you have, try to specify your beyond-the-text purposes: what are you trying to do through the letter? Does it **all** relate to Mr. Haskins? What about Green Thumb? What personal purposes do you recognize?
6. Plan a structure for your letter. Will you follow the order of Mr. Haskins' requests? Will you begin with some sort of opening thanks or context-setting device? What material will come first, second, third? Why?
7. Draft your letter. As you do so, keep track of your within-text purposes; why are you making choices of structure, wording, style, and content? How do these choices relate to your beyond-text purposes?

THE WHOLESALE/RETAIL PROBLEM . . . AND SOME TEST DATA

After you draft your letter, you wonder whether it's appropriate to list both wholesale **and** retail stores in Mr. Haskins' area: should you list only retail stores? On what basis?

Jan is out of the office, so you decide to ask another member of the office staff whether it makes any difference. Chris, an executive secretary, remembers typing a memo on the matter of wholesale purchases of single items, and finds them in the files for you.

ITEM FROM FILES: INTERNAL MEMO ON WHOLESALE POLICIES

```
To:    Jon Sanders, Customer Relations
From:  Ellen Brown, Sales Distribution & Marketing
Re.:   Request for Wholesale Policies
Date:  Nov. 5, 1984

A policy was developed several years ago concerning
wholesale orders; we don't sell any equipment at
wholesale prices to individual customers. We ran into
a problem in Manhattan, Kansas, in 1979 when several
retail stores learned that we would ship orders of six
or more units at wholesale cost; members of local farm
groups were pooling their orders to buy the equipment
at under-retail cost, and our own wholesale
distributors were losing a portion of the market
because the retailers weren't selling as many units.
The wholesalers and retailers threatened to stop
carrying Green Thumb products.
   That doesn't, of course, preclude organizations
such as farm cooperatives from acting as wholesale
distributors of our products--just as retail stores
have the option of selling our products at whatever
price they wish below list. The Manhattan case was
difficult because the farmer "pool" could,
technically, have been considered an organized "co-
op" of some sort--if only to make a single purchase.
```

Digging through the back files to locate this memo, Chris also discovers two other memos on Green Thumb products, and decides you might be interested in seeing them:

ITEMS FROM FILES: INTERNAL MEMOS
ON TEST AND MARKET DATA

To: Jan Harding
From: Bob Skaggs, Quality Engineer
Re.:   Request for Test Report Data
Date: Mar. 7, 1983

Last year, we had an independent research and development firm do some tests on the most popular of the Green-Thumb models (GT-04 and GT-06). The tests were not intended for use in marketing or advertising for several reasons that Ellen Brown can tell you about. She also has the original report if you'd like to see it.

The results boil down to this: the Pony was able to handle almost all tilling jobs on broken ground (i.e., soil that has been previously cleared and tilled). However, when the Pony was subjected to a drag of 50 lbs. per square inch on the power train for 10 hours (imitating heavier soil conditions), it performed poorly, overheating and eventually breaking down. The Horse was capable of handling the extra load well, but after 75 consecutive hours it too began showing signs of failure, particularly in the throwout bearing of the gear mechanism. The extra load placed on the Horse would suggest that it's capable of handling most new ground except for very dense soil or soil with firmly set rocks or roots. For these jobs, it would appear that the tractor models are recommended.

To: Jan Harding
From: Ellen Brown
Re.:   Request for 1983 Research Data
Date: June 12, 1984

I'm having Janice send you copies of the most recent
market research data on Green Thumb tillers.

Briefly, the Pony took about 29 percent of the
medium-sized hand-tiller market in 1983--a good
chunk in the face of four major competitors. The Horse
fared badly, drawing only 5 percent of the larger
hand-tiller market. This was due in part to a higher
record of breakdown and repair between 1979 and 1981,
which seems to have resulted in some bad word-of-
mouth, at least based on survey data.

Overall, the Pony was preferred by 73 percent of
those who tried both models in recent research
demonstration surveys at eight locations in the
midwest. Most of those surveyed, however, were
looking for an economical tiller for use once or twice
a year on light or moderate soil in home vegetable
gardens.

YOUR TURN

1. Bearing in mind this new information, read through the draft of your letter. Is there anything you would now change in your letter? Why? Go ahead and make those changes if you wish.
2. One issue raised by what you've learned from the test data memos is whether your purpose is to "recommend" or "describe." Read through your revised draft. How much "recommending" have you done and how much pure, objective "describing?" For example, have you made a decision **for** Mr. Haskins about which machine he should consider buying? Review his letter; has he asked for recommendations? Are recommendations implicit in his request? Look at your descriptions of the equipment; is it possible to select details from the total inventory of information **without** "recommending," or making decisions based on Mr. Haskins' needs? Why or why not?

Jot down some ideas relating to these questions of purpose in your writer's notebook and bring them to class to discuss in light of your revisions.

PROBLEMS WITH MAINE RETAIL STORES

In reviewing the information from File 3 on wholesale and retail stores in the state of Maine that carry Green Thumb tractors and tillers, you notice that Shields Bros. Hardware, located in Mr. Haskins' town of Camden, is bracketed, with an illegible note scrawled below. Curious, you ask Chris what it means. Once again, Chris recalls typing up a series of memos about a problem with one of the Maine retail stores. In a few minutes, Chris locates the memos, along with one or two others that could be useful:

ITEMS FROM FILES: MEMOS ON RETAIL
STORES IN MAINE

```
To:    Jon Sanders, Customer Relations
From:  Ellen Brown, Sales Distribution & Marketing
Re.:   Lincolnville Hardware
Date:  August 12, 1985

Be advised that Lincolnville Hardware, in
Lincolnville, Maine, is no longer stocking the Pony
as of last Tuesday, when they sold their last unit.
The store number is 435.
```

To: Ellen Brown, Sales Distribution & Marketing
From: Jon Sanders, Customer Relations
Date: June 15, 1985
Re: Shields Bros. Hardware, Camden, ME

I thought this recent complaint letter would be
important to your department.

Mrs. R. E. Jacobs
160 Center St.
Rockport, ME 26112

June 10, 1985

Green Thumb, Inc.
46 Bay View Rd.
Providence, RI 12180

Dear Sirs:

I want to bring to your attention a problem I had
getting one of your products serviced. This spring, I
bought a Moto-Till from Kenson's Home and Garden in
Rockport. Two weeks later, the machine broke, and I
returned it to the store. They told me to take it to
Shields Bros. Hardware in Camden for servicing. Mr.
Shields refused to repair the machine, telling me to
return it directly to you.

You should receive the machine by UPS within a few
days. I would appreciate it if you would reimburse me
for the cost of mailing it to you. I expect it to be
repaired under my original warranty, and I suggest
you clear up your service and warranty policies with
Shields Bros. There is no excuse for putting your
customers through this kind of roundabout.

Sincerely,

Mrs. R. E.Jacobs

GREEN THUMB, INC.
46 Bay View Rd.
Providence, RI 12180

June 15, 1985

Mrs. R. E. Jacobs
160 Center St.
Rockport, ME 26112

Dear Mrs. Jacobs:

We have received your letter of June 10 describing the problems you encountered getting your Moto-Till serviced. Your guarantee slip has been located in our files. As soon as we receive your machine, it will be repaired free of charge and returned to you within ten working days at our expense. Unfortunately, under the terms of our warranty, we have no practical way to reimburse you for the shipping charges you paid to UPS.

We do apologize for any inconvenience this problem has caused you. Shields Bros. Hardward has been an authorized service facility for Green Thumb since 1976. We assure you we will investigate the problem thoroughly. In the meantime, the next closest authorized service facility is Route 1 Appliance Repair in Belfast.

Should you have any further problems, please do not hesitate to write to us or call our new toll-free number: 1-800-226-5932.

Sincerely yours,

Jon Sanders
Customer Relations

JS:pr

To: Jon Sanders, Customer Relations
From: Ellen Brown, Sales Distribution & Marketing
Date: June 16, 1985
Re.:   Shields Bros. Servicing

Thanks for passing on Mrs. Jacobs' letter to me. I
spoke to Sam Shields about our service agreement.
Apparently, he took over the store from his brother
Ed, who died last year, and had no knowledge of the
agreement we established with them in April of 1976
(on file). He found the agreement in their files and
has agreed to honor it for the time being, until he can
reassess his position.

I should point out, Jon, that Sam Shields is an
extremely abrasive, uncooperative man. He seemed
very reluctant to honor our service agreement, even
when I assured him that Green Thumb would reimburse
him for labor and parts at our fixed rate. He didn't
seem to understand the nature of the agreement, nor
was he eager to learn more about it.

I fear we haven't heard the end of this problem. I'm
bringing this to the attention of Washington Jones;
he may want to begin scouting for a new service center
in the Camden/Rockport area. Keep me informed of any
further developments.

To: Ellen Brown, Sales Distribution & Marketing
From: Jon Sanders, Customer Relations
Date: March 19, 1986
Re.:   Shields Bros. Servicing

We received another complaint about Shields Bros.
Hardware in Camden, Maine (see attached letter).
Apparently no one had taken any Green Thumb products
for servicing to Shields Bros. since the problem last
year (on file). This time, Sam Shields cleaned and
serviced a Green Thumb Pony under warranty and is now
trying to bill the customer for the work.
Should we remove Shields Bros. from the list of
service facilities and inform them that we have
voided our agreement with them?

Green Thumb:

    What kind of place are you people running, anyways?

    I took my tiller a pony to the service center.
Shields Brothers in Camden. I live out on Vinalhaven,
and thats not so close, and its all got to be done by
boat. Now I got a bill for something thats still under
the garantee. And Shields don't no nothing about it,
just keeps saying he'll send it to small claims
($118).

    Whats the deal. Do you pay me or what?

                        Joe Rider

To: Jon Sanders, Customer Relations
From: Ellen Brown, Sales Distribution & Marketing
Date: March 26, 1986
Re.:   Shields Bros. Servicing

I've managed to explain our servicing agreement
(again) to Sam Shields. Apparently, he's not happy
with the amount that we agreed to pay him for
servicing our equipment under warranty. I explained
the benefits to him as a retailer for following our
agreement, and this seems to have helped.

   In response to your question--keep Shields Bros. on
the list and let customers know it's an authorized
service facility. But in the meantime, keep in mind
the history here.

YOUR TURN

1. Analyze this new information from the files. Does it make a difference to the way you've responded to Mr. Haskins' letter? Why or why not?
2. Make any further revisions in your letter based on this new information. Then analyze your changes as reflections of your within-text purposes: are they necessary? Why? What role are you playing in making decisions about how to relate your knowledge of these files' contents to Mr. Haskins?
3. Assess your entire completed draft. What trouble spots did you have in writing it? Why? Develop a rationale for all your final within-text purposes, and write this out in your writer's notebook in preparation for discussion.

Case 3:
Social Issues 101

BACKGROUND

Imagine that you're a student in an introductory college course called Social Issues 101, a special topics course that focuses on "social ethics"—dilemmas in our society that cross the boundaries of religion, the law, medicine, education, culture, and other important institutions. Because the course ful-

The right to die ——
Decision : hospice
making ——
Whose?   hospi
Patient
Professio
Caretakers

Professor Wells in Social Issues 101

fills one of the distribution requirements for your major, it is quite popular and tends to close quickly during registration. However, you were lucky enough to get a place in the class of 40 students.

The teacher, Professor Lillian Wells, has chosen the topic of medical ethics for this first unit. She's placed on reserve at the library some magazines and readings focusing on the so-called right to die—the right to stop medical treatment for a patient who is still biologically alive but hopelessly ill. In class, the lectures and discussions have led to debate and argument on both sides of the issue—granting more freedom to allow patients to die versus enforcing the preservation of life in all circumstances, regardless of the patient's mental or physical state.

Although it's still quite early in the term, you've begun to get a sense of what Professor Wells is like as a teacher. The class discussions are interesting and provocative and provide a laugh from time to time, but Professor Wells demands that students come to class prepared. She's reminded your class that although Social Issues 101 is a popular course that fulfills one of the humanities requirements for most degrees, it's by no means a "blow-off" course. Her syllabus is quite rigorous, with several short papers, two exams, and considerable reading and informal writing. She seems fairly liberal, in the sense that she welcomes all views during discussion, but she doesn't appear to respect generalizations unsupported by specific examples, evidence, or careful argument. Often during discussion, she asks students to elaborate on their ideas and give concrete examples.

Recently, you also overheard a student who'd taken a course with Professor Wells talking about a time when he went to see her about missing several short assignments. Apparently, Professor Wells had said, "I didn't get where I am by treating education as if it's a big joke, and I expect the same attitude of my students."

Most of the students you've spoken to about Professor Wells, however, seem to respect her as a teacher, particularly for her fairness in grading, her insightful and carefully planned lectures, and her diplomatic and energetic way of leading class discussion. In short, she seems to be an excellent teacher—and certainly no pushover. Her class may be fun, but it won't be easy.

Professor Wells's handout describing one of the papers required for the course is on page 330.

Directions for Paper #1
Social Issues 101
Professor Wells

I have placed on reserve at the library a series of
articles on a question related to our focus this unit
on "social dilemmas." Read them carefully. The paper
for this unit is designed to give you practice in
reading, analyzing, and writing about one of the
burning questions of our time: What is the "right to
die" exactly? Who is, or should be, exercising it?
What are its moral and legal ramifications? How is it
different from euthanasia?
   Based on the readings, you will be writing a paper
of medium length on the problem of the "right to die,"
in response to one of the following topic questions:

   1. Present your own conclusions concerning when and
under what circumstances, if any, a patient's request
to terminate medical treatment should be honored.
Illustrate and defend your position by referring to
actual cases of patients in these situations.

   2. Discuss the case of Elizabeth Bouvia in light of
the various arguments presented in the readings.
Write your paper as recommendations to the hospital
in which she is in conflict. (Suppose the hospital
were run under the auspices of a Christian
organization.)

   3. How do you see the issues surrounding the
termination of medical treatment changing over the
next 20 years? Pay particular attention to economic
factors.

   You should include footnotes or endnotes for the
sources you use. This is a college paper; it requires
careful thought, and careful planning and writing. I
will not accept papers that are sloppily written and
without care for structure, grammar, and mechanics.
Revise, edit, and proofread carefully.

   Note: I will not accept late papers.

YOUR TURN

1. Spend some time analyzing Professor Wells's directions. First, what does she expect you to do in the paper? Based on your knowledge of her as a reader, will she be more favorably inclined toward papers that weigh both sides of the issue, papers that present one side as force-fully as possible, or papers with some combination? What is implied by her questions that accompanied the directions?

   Next, analyze the purpose of the assignment. Is it to prove that you've read the articles on reserve? Is it to see if you can determine a solution to the problem of the "right to die"? Is it to see how well you can read and write? What do you suppose she means by "analyze"? What are the differences in the purposes for each of the three possi-ble topics?

   Finally, develop some purposes of your own for the assignment, from the point of view of an enrollee in Social Issues 101. What can you gain from the assignment? How will this transfer to other areas of your interest? To what extent do your purposes relate to Professor Wells's? Although you can't know yet which topic you'll choose until you've studied the readings, is there one that appeals to you more than the others? Why? Is there one that seems "easier" than the oth-ers? Think carefully about what it means for a paper to be "easy." Now reassess your ideas about "ease" or "difficulty."

2. Before even looking at the following materials, do some thinking and writing about what you know already about the subject. Do at least one rushwrite on what you've already heard about the right-to-die issue, or even what you suspect logically the debate might entail.

   Do a list or cluster of the range of people this problem concerns. Make a note for each person concerning what you think his or her interest or position is likely to be. If you were planning to interview two people on the topic, which two from your list or cluster would make for the most interesting contrasting pair of interviews?

   Brainstorm a list of questions you could ask about the right to die. For you to develop a mature and comprehensive moral stance on the issue, what questions would you need to have answered? Think up as many as you can.

A FIRST PERSPECTIVE

When you arrive at the library to begin reading the articles on reserve, you discover that each magazine is in a separate folder and you can check out only one at a time. Several other students have already checked out some articles and are busy working on them in the reading area. The one you pick is a fairly lengthy article in the November 21, 1983, volume of *Maclean's* magazine—a magazine that, as it happens, you haven't heard of before.

As you head for the reading area, you realize you'll need to determine what kind of a magazine *Maclean's* is, as we discussed in Chapter Five. Who is its audience? What kind of coverage do you expect from it? You decide to examine the cover of your issue, along with the list of articles mentioned on the title page. Answer in your notebook the questions in the "Your Turn" section that follows.

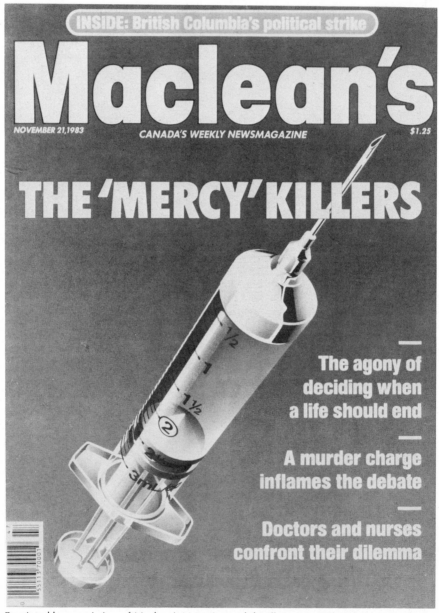

INSIDE: British Columbia's political strike

Maclean's

NOVEMBER 21,1983   *CANADA'S WEEKLY NEWSMAGAZINE* $1.25

THE 'MERCY' KILLERS

The agony of deciding when a life should end

A murder charge inflames the debate

Doctors and nurses confront their dilemma

Reprinted by permission of *Maclean's* Magazine and the illustrator, Rick Fisher.

Major Articles and Abstracts:

"The Eclipse of Arafat": U.S., Israeli and Syrian forces stood poised for new violence in the Middle East, but the real drama centered on the pressure on PLO leader Yasser Arafat. —**Page 32.**

"**Lutheran catholicism**": He inspired the Protestant Revolution, but 500 years after his birth Martin Luther's adherents are moving closer to Catholicism with the Pope's blessing. —**Page 49.**

"**British Columbia divided**": The province endured a second week of strikes as teachers joined civil servants in a dispute that threatened to paralyse British Columbia. —**Page 18.**

"**Fit queen for a crown**": Last week 23-year-old Cynthia Kereluk had already packed her bags to return to Edmonton when she learned that she had become the new Miss Canada.—**Page 40.**

Other departments mentioned on the table of contents:

Books	62
Business/Economy	42
Canada	18
Dateline	8
Films	54
Health	50
Law	58
People	40
Religion	49
Television	69
Theatre	56
Transportation	57
World	32

YOUR TURN

Does the cover look like that of an academic medical journal or a popular magazine? What do the cover art, the article title, and the subtitles down the side of the cover suggest about the magazine's approach to the issue? How would you describe the kind of language used in the title and subtitles?

What can you infer about the magazine's readership from the articles it carries and the lengths of them? To whom is it appealing? What U.S. magazines does *Maclean's* most nearly resemble?

After answering these questions, you proceed to read the main article and the sidebar article that accompanies it.

THE 'MERCY' KILLERS

By Val Ross

For 16 fitful hours after her birth, Candace Taschuck struggled for life in Edmonton's University Hospital, then died in her mother's arms on Oct. 8, 1982. Two weeks ago the Alberta attorney general's department charged a 36-year-old Israeli doctor, Nachum Gal, with capital murder in connection with her death. Baby Taschuk's parents, Robert and Sharon, of Two Hills, Alta., suspecting that she was brain-dead, had tearfully agreed to take their severely disabled infant off life-support systems at the urging of another doctor. The attorney general's department alleges that Gal, a visiting resident physician in Edmonton (page 29), had decided, without consulting the Taschuks, to ease and speed the baby's painful death with an injection of morphine 50 times the normal dosage. Reached at his mother's home in Jerusalem, an anguished Gal demanded, "Am I the only one charged?" So far, Gal *is* the first and only doctor to be charged with mercy killing in Canadian legal history. But, if he did it, he would by no means be the first to have done so. Euthanasia is classified as murder under the Canadian Criminal Code, but it is not an

A growing clamor has forced decisions about terminating the life of the severely ill out of the shadows

uncommon practice in Canadian hospitals, and there is a growing public clamor to control it.

The need for clarification of the law is urgent. The rapid advance of life-prolonging medical technology has blurred the traditional meanings of life and death and raised new questions about which lives retain their human value. Expensive hospital machinery can now extend life to those who previously would have been too sick to survive, placing an unwanted new burden of responsibility on the medical community. At the same time, death-with-dignity pressure groups urge doctors to "pull the plug" on the terminally ill and patients in a coma. And rights-for-the-handicapped advocates oppose any doctor who speeds the death of a patient incapable of making the choice for himself. The

growing clamor has forced the day-by-day decisions about whether or not to terminate the life of the severely ill out of the shadows. In the past year doctors, judges, politicians and the families of patients near death have become embroiled in an uneasy debate over who should decide who lives and who dies.

The problem is growing. Eike Kluge, a professor of ethics at the University of Victoria, estimates that each year doctors and medical staff deliberately assist as many as 800 infants and comatose and terminally ill Canadians to die. The Canadian Association for the Mentally Retarded estimates that the number is closer to 1,000. Until now, mercy killers who practised euthanasia actively (for example, with drug overdoses) or passively (by withholding lifesaving medical treatment) did so privately, after consultation with relatives. But today citizens have flung the doors open, goaded by the fear that without more control over medical decision-making they could someday become a doctor's abandoned experiment or an "artifact human" kept alive by medical technology. The public's clamor for more comprehensible and accountable decision-making is long overdue according to George Grant, philosopher and professor of political science at Dalhousie University in Halifax. Said Grant: "A society that fails to see the seriousness of these issues has given up the core of the Western tradition. I cannot think of a more important subject in the Western world." North Americans are confronting that subject with accelerating frequency.

● In March, a B.C. court ruled that the parents of Stephen Dawson had the right to deny their retarded seven-year-old son a potentially life-saving medical operation. Four days later the B.C. Supreme Court reversed that decision.

● In July, Canada's first court ruling effectively giving an individual the right to choose his or her own death emerged from a British Columbia Court of Appeal decision. The court ruled against force-feeding an imprisoned Doukhobor woman, Mary Astaforoff (Astaforoff was starving herself to death in a religious protest). Solicitor General Robert Kaplan ignored the court's decision and ordered Astaforoff force-fed and released from her prison last month.

● In October, Justice Minister Mark MacGuigan tabled in Parliament the Law Reform Commission of Canada's controversial report, *Euthanasia,*

Aiding Suicide and Cessation of Medical Treatment—and then hastily assured an anxious public that the government would not implement any of the recommendations immediately.

● Two weeks ago the U.S. justice department filed a lawsuit to determine whether a New York couple was improperly denying life-saving surgery to a handicapped newborn baby whom the press dubbed Baby Jane Doe.

Volatile notion: Underpinning the contradictory court rulings and inconclusive political response is the volatile notion of "triage," the concept that a human life can be selected for extinction if it lacks "quality of life." Triage used to mean the process by which battlefield doctors would give priority treatment to casualties who had a reasonable chance of recovery over those who would likely die. It has come to symbolize the cold-blooded ranking of human life into those who are fit to survive and those who are not. Still, when patients determine their own fate, the public's attitude toward euthanasia becomes increasingly tolerant: a 1979 Gallup poll reported that 68 per cent of those surveyed believed that doctors should not keep terminally ill patients alive when they formally ask to die. But the survey did not address the growing problem of patients who cannot decide for themselves—the very young, the retarded, and those in comas, like Karen Ann Quinlan, whom doctors have kept alive in New Jersey every since she fell into a drug-induced coma in 1975.

In those cases the power of life and death passes to other hands by default. Because courts have lacked precedents and because medical advice heavily influences the actions of the patient's family, the decision usually falls to the doctors. At one extreme of medical opinion are those who explicitly support triage. Last year Dr. Scott Wallace, a former B.C. Progressive Conservative leader, proposed a national referendum on permitting elderly patients to volunteer for death in order to free up hospital beds. In a controversial speech in Toronto in May, 1982, then President of the Canadian Medical Association Dr. Leon Richard asked who should have priority when health care resources were limited and suggested, "those who will return to the work force, those who hold key positions in business or industry...." Nor is the CMA's own ethics committee uneasy about the issue. Said Chairman Dr. Arthur Parsons of Halifax: "Who is going to get into the lifeboat? Is it

SOURCE: *Maclean's,* November 21, 1983, pp. 24–29. Reprinted by permission.

better to keep a severely retarded person alive or spend your tight resources on bypass surgery for a father of four?"

At the other extreme of medical opinion are pro-life doctors and nurses and allies of the handicapped, who argue that almost all life can have value. Speaking of baby Taschuk, Dr. Hugh Lafave, executive vice-president of the Canadian Association for the Mentally Retarded, commented: "They keep offering as an explanation that Candace would have been retarded anyway. Well, is that a reason for killing someone? The only reason I can see is that some doctor wanted to play God."

Still controversial as triage is, it is already practised in Canadian hospitals. According to Nerina Robson, past president of the Manitoba Association for the Mentally Retarded, attending doctors denied one Winnipeg woman kidney dialysis last year, apparently because she had Down's syndrome (she later died). Joseph Cawthorpe, a senior program staffer with the National Institute on Mental Retardation, charged that neglect in some homes for the retarded in the Atlantic provinces allowed people to die by denying them basic medical treatment. One woman at the Cormier special-care home in Buctouche, N.B., died of lockjaw 2½ years ago. Said Cawthorpe: "You have to work pretty hard at it for your patient to die of lockjaw in the 1980s."

Denying people treatment because they are retarded contravenes the United Nations Declaration on the Rights of Mentally Retarded Persons, the code of the Canadian Psychiatric Association and the beliefs of many doctors. But it is a common practice. Whether or not the Canadian public believes it is ethical will be the subject of intense debate this winter when the CMA-funded Task Force on Allocation of Health Resources, chaired by consumer advocate Joan Watson, opens the first of its cross-Canada public hearings on Jan. 12 in Toronto.

Morality: The vast majority of physicians are somewhere in the middle of the debate. They are uncomfortable with their terrible responsibilities but unsure that they can avoid them. Dr. John Anderson, a pediatrician with Halifax's Izaak Walton Killam Hospital for Children, said with a sigh: "I have quite a bit of difficulty with the notion of 'passive euthanasia'; you make an active decision not to support life. I am concerned that such decisions could escalate into actions that could be immoral." But Anderson himself has taken those troubling actions. He admitted: "It makes me terribly uneasy. In one case, after I turned off the life-support system I had to listen for nine minutes for the toddler's heart to stop beating."

In the face of those awesome responsibilities, physicians are no more equipped to cope than anyone else. A survey reported in the March, 1983, edition of the CMA *Journal* that 68 per cent of doctors polled had not even read the CMA Code of Ethics; in fact, they sought their ethical advice from their colleagues, who had no more background than they. As a result, they sometimes made life-and-death decisions on very subjective bases. "The child of economically comfortable parents has greater chances of receiving treatment," reported Joseph Magnet, University of Ottawa associate professor of law, in a comprehensive 1980 study of Canadian medical practice concerning defective newborns. Equally troubling was Magnet's finding that not one doctor he surveyed could articulate the legal doctrine of informed consent, which gives patients the right to sufficient information to make decisions about their own treatment. In fact, several doctors told Magnet that the idea of informed consent was "nonsense."

But even as the medical community struggles unhappily with the new moral questions, the courts are taking an increasingly active role. The most dramatic example of the growing activism of the courts was the controversial battle last spring over Stephen Dawson (*Maclean's*, March 28). Stephen suffered severe brain damage shortly after his birth. In February, 1983, a shunt, which drained fluid from his brain, malfunctioned. A neurosurgeon, Patrick Murray, visited Stephen once. On the basis of that visit, Murray advised the child's parents that Stephen would die painlessly if they denied him an operation for a new shunt. Later court testimony revealed that Stephen's mother asked Murray to "put him to sleep." B.C. social workers opposed the parents' decision and placed the boy in Vancouver's Children's Hospital to await the outcome of a custody battle. On the basis of testimony from doctors like Murray, provincial court Judge Patricia Byrne awarded custody to the Dawsons—effectively denying Stephen the operation. The B.C. pro-euthanasia lobby hailed her decision as a victory for the concept of "dying with dignity."

Overturned: But the B.C. Supreme Court overturned the decision. Medical personnel from Stephen's hospital, the Sunny Hill Hospital for Children, contradicted Murray's testimony that Stephen was "semivegetative." They pointed out that he could follow simple orders, throw a switch to start a toy train and was the only child in his ward to be selected for music therapy. Mr. Justice Lloyd McKenzie ruled that "the court's presumption must be in favor of life," and Stephen received his slightly belated operation. Today, Dawson "is doing awfully well," according to Maureen Harrison, Sunny Hill's director of nursing. She added,

"He is back in school and music therapy, and his vision seems to be getting better."

Life and death: The second Dawson decision changed the course of life-and-death decision-making, at least in legal theory. Said Prof. Ellen Picard, health law expert at the University of Alberta law school: "It has done wonderful things for jurisprudence in this country, giving us criteria and standards." But there are those who criticize the direction in which the Dawson case pushed the medical and legal professions. Dermod Owen-Flood, a Victoria lawyer who acted as amicus curiae (adviser to the court) in the Astaforoff case, asserts that "courts are not suited for dealing with life-and-death questions with scientific overtones." And Dr. John Crichton, chairman of the Canadian Paediatric Society's ethics committee, regrets that the case may have involved the courts more deeply in the medical decision-making process. Said Crichton: "I'm absolutely clear that the courts are too cumbersome. Most shunts, for example, should be dealt with in a matter of hours." Lefave of the CAMR disagrees. Said Lafave: "Clearly, doctors and families can be in conflict over what to do. Courts can stay up all night, and have, to reach a decision if that is what is medically required of them. These are not only moral but also legal questions."

But, as citizens demand clearer and more accountable medical decision-making, they are discovering that, despite the growing number of court precedents, the lawmakers themselves are still grappling with the basic issues. Said lawyer Flood: "The situation is still very muddy." And no one fears the imprecision of the law more than the doctors who must make the decisions. Currently, few doctors write down DNR—"Do not resuscitate"—orders for fear of legal liability. Instead, doctors and nurses try to communicate by codes written on the charts of dying patients.

Uncertainties: The University of Alberta's Ellen Picard submits: "The medical profession wants clarification. They feed on their own uncertainties." Because of that, the CMA, in co-operation with the law reform commission, the Canadian Public Health Association, the Canadian Nurses Association, the Canadian Bar Association and the Canadian Hospital Association, drafted a set of recommendations this fall in an attempt to clarify issues such as cessation of treatment. The findings will be presented to each of the organizations for ratification this winter. Prof. Bernard Dickens of the University of Toronto's law faculty says that the law reform commission's recommendations, tabled in Parliament on Oct. 25, will also carry great weight even though they have not, and may never, attain force of law.

The conservative but controversial commission report reaffirmed many of the principles already enshrined in the CMA Code of Ethics: the principle of informed consent; a patient's right to refuse treatment; and a doctor's right to discontinue treatment if it is not in the "best interests" of the patient and is not likely to be of therapeutic value (which theoretically would absolve doctors of the duty of supporting the life of a patient who did not want to live and whose condition they could neither cure nor improve).

Murder: The commission treats the explosive topic of euthanasia with particular care. It recommends that euthanasia should remain classified as murder under the Criminal Code. The commission argues that juries are already lenient with those who kill for compassionate reasons. As well, it says, changing the present status of euthanasia opens the door to abuse, such as offering murderers the excuse that their victims wanted to die. An example of the confusion that could arise if the commission had proposed widening the latitude of a euthanasia plea arose this year in California. Two doctors, Robert Nejdl and Neil Barber, faced murder charges because they had cut off the life supports of a patient after convincing his family that he had suffered irreversible brain damage. The deputy district attorney of Los Angeles, Nikola Mikulicich, told *Maclean's* that the prosecution viewed the case as an attempt by the doctors to cover up their own negligence in causing the patient's condition. But last month, after months of legal debate, an appeal court dismissed the charges.

While lawmakers and professional organizations painfully grope toward clearer policies, hospitals are already turning to another source of help—patients' advocates and hospital ethics committees, which provide considered opinions on problematic cases. At present there are only two hospital ethics committees in Canada, the older of which is at Foothills Hospital in Calgary. The media have hailed the committee as a pioneer, but its chairman, Rev. John Swift, points out: "We have no power. We are an ethics consultation service."

Economics: As reforms point physicians in the direction of more responsible and accountable decision-making, the financial limitations of the health care system drag them back to the prospect of triage. Said CMA ethics committee Chairman Parsons: "If you keep severely retarded kids alive, what do you tell the dialysis patients when you cannot afford their treatment?" The CMA insists that underfunding is forcing doctors to make economic triage-type decisions with increasing frequency. CMA spokesman Douglas Geekie suggested that one solution is to permit hospitals to raise needed revenues by extra-billing their richer patients—a practice that Health Minister Monique Bégin assailed once again last week. But permitting the wealthy to jump the queue while the ailing poor get sicker is just another form of triage, argued Victor Marshall, professor of behavioral science at the University of Toronto.

As the debate over whose life is worth fighting for continues, so does the pace at which changing technology presents a host of frightening new challenges to traditional human ethics. Medical triage is not the worst of them. Almost a decade ago the Institute of Society, Ethics and the Life Sciences at Hastings-on-Hudson, N.Y., advanced the provocative suggestion that brain-dead patients might be kept physically alive for "harvesting" of blood plasma, bone marrow and organs for transplants. After posing the ghoulish possibility, the institute's president, Dr. Willard Gaylin, warned that his suggestion could come to pass unless people finally tried to define what they meant by "human" and "alive." Added Gaylin: "There are no easy answers to these complex and painful questions." And those who seek answers at all, like Dr. Nachum Gal, often find that they have simply opened a Pandora's box.

With Jackie Carlos in Toronto, Rita Christopher in New York and Diane Luckow in Vancouver.

The cost of compassion

Maurre Nachum Gal, the doctor at the centre of Canada's current euthanasia controversy, was born Maurice Katzman in France in 1947. It was not until he started a research program at Edmonton's University Hospital in July, 1982, that he gave himself his Israeli name. When he returned to Israel permanently last February, says Hiske Breman, his friend and the mother of his three-year-old son, Eitan, he told nobody that his new name had been linked to a mercy killing. But Breman says his silence was characteristic. Indeed, late last week when *Maclean's* interviewed the shaken Gal, he would only confirm in a subdued voice that he had still not heard from the Israeli or the Canadian government about the charges he faces.

Canadian authorities now face jurisdictional problems in their attempts to prosecute Gal for murder. The main one is that the force of Canada's 16-year-old extradition treaty is in doubt. In 1978 the Israeli Knesset passed an amendment to its extradition law stating that Israeli citizens charged with felonies by foreign governments must stand trial inside Israel. Admitted federal justice department lawyer Oksana Kaluzny: "We are concerned that their law may be in breach of our treaty. This case is a potential precedent-setter in extradition law too."

The legalities are complex, but the facts of the case are clear. Candace Taschuk was born "basically dead," according to testimony given by Dr. Marc André Beaudry, a senior pediatrician in Edmonton University Hospital's neonatal unit, at a July judicial inquiry into the case. After the infant was removed from life-support systems at her parents' request, floor nurse Barbara Howell testified that she asked Gal to help relieve her pain. Howell said that she was surprised to see Gal write an order for 15 mg of morphine—50 times the recommended dose. The nurse administered it, and the baby died.

Last week Breman said: "Nachum is frightened. It must have been on his mind. I know him." But his fears may be unfounded. Asked whether an Israeli court would try Gal on the Canadian murder charge, Prof. Yoram Dinstein, rector of Tel Aviv University and former chairman of the university's law faculty, noted: "I doubt very much that it will happen, since euthanasia is so controversial. The attorney general [of Israel] has a lot of leeway on whether to charge or not." Even if Gal never stands trial, Canadian rights for the handicapped activists have effectively sent a powerful signal to well-intentioned mercy killers.

—VAL ROSS, *with Roberta Elliott in Eilat.*

YOUR TURN

What were the main issues raised by the article, "The 'Mercy' Killers"? What seemed to be the attitude of the writer, Val Ross, toward the issues raised? Define what the following terms and phrases mean in this article: death with dignity, triage, euthanasia, informed consent, artifact human, passive euthanasia.

Describe in a "nutshell" the story concerning Doctor Maurre Nachum Gal.

What new questions did the two articles raise for you? Rushwrite some additions to the list of questions you made when you first started thinking about the right-to-die issue.

ANOTHER FOLDER: THE TOPIC EVOLVES

When you go back to the reserve area, you discover that several other magazines have been returned. You still have a couple of hours before dinner, so you decide to make the best use of your time and read one or two more.

The next folder you check out contains another overview of the problem as presented in *Time* magazine about six months before the *Maclean's* article. Again, note the sidebar story that accompanies it.

Debate on the Boundary of Life

Medical miracles and the patient's right to die

Siamese twins, joined at the waist, with a common pelvis, were born in Danville, Ill., on May 5, 1981. The pair had three legs. The parents and doctor allegedly ordered all feeding stopped. They were charged with attempted murder, though the charges were eventually dismissed.

Former Schoolteacher Peter Cinque, 41, had lost his sight and both his legs to diabetes. He wanted to stop dialysis and other life-sustaining treatment. The hospital refused. On Oct. 22, 1982, a New York judge upheld Cinque's right to stop treatment. By then in a coma, he was disconnected from a respirator that day and died, alone, before his family could get to his bedside.

An elderly dying patient seemed to have slipped from life when Dr. George Dunlop, then a surgical intern at Cincinnati General Hospital, stepped in and managed to revive him. The patient, unable to speak, motioned for a pencil and wrote, unforgettably to Dr. Dunlop, "Why did you do this?"

No person's death is like another's, but these cases are not rarities. Four out of five people now die in a hospital or nursing home (only half did 35 years ago), and "most don't die unexpectedly," says University of Wisconsin Pediatrician Norman Fost. "They die as a result of a very conscious decision by doctors, along with the patient's family, to withhold treatment." The question becomes not how to save a life but when to let it go. Aided by artificial and transplanted organs and a jungle gym of gadgetry, doctors can now stave off death for long periods. The blessings of science have brought the curse of choices that raise confounding ethical and legal uncertainties. Is life, however tenuous or painful, always preferable to death? At what point should doctors stop treating terminally ill or permanently unconscious patients? Which forms of treatment or care can properly be denied to a patient? May the cost in money and resources be considered? Moreover, who has the right to make these decisions? "We are facing a moral vacuum," says Dr. Alexander Leaf of Harvard Medical School. "There are enormous disparities in views on whether you withhold certain therapies or do everything possible to keep a person 'alive.'"

Among major faiths, there is general agreement that it is morally permissible to allow a person to die if therapy would not lead to recovery. Views diverge, however, when this principle is applied to specific situations. The Roman Catholic Church has the most explicit position. The Vatican's 1980 declaration on euthanasia clearly permits an end to treatment that would only "secure a precarious and burdensome prolongation of life" when

death is imminent. Says Rabbi Seymour Siegel of New York's Jewish Theological Seminary: "It is the individual's duty to live as long as he can, but if a person is destined to die soon, there is no obligation to prevent that death from happening."

Last month the President's Commission for the Study of Ethical Problems in Medicine and Biomedical and Behavioral Research offered its recommendations on these questions in a 255-page report, "Deciding to Forgo Life-Sustaining Treatment." The study, the seventh published by the prestigious panel of doctors, lawyers, theologians and others since it started work three years ago, concludes that a competent patient, one who is able to understand treatment choices and their consequences, has the all-but-absolute right to decide his own fate. Declares Dr. Joanne Lynn, a geriatrician and principal author of the report: "An adult person of sound mind has authority over his own body." When a person is incompetent, says the report, a surrogate, usually a family member, should be named to make treatment decisions. The commission urges courts and legislatures for the most part to stay away. "The resolution of these issues," says Dr. Lynn, "should be left to people on the scene—the patients, their families and healthcare professionals."

The only force of the report's findings will

come in their contribution to the debate that already swirls around almost every aspect of this subject. The one issue involved on which there is a semblance of agreement is the definition of death. Traditionally, a person had been considered medically and legally dead when his heart and lungs stopped. Today, however, machines can prolong these visible signs of life even after the brain has ceased to function. The standards for determining "brain death," set forth by a 1968 Harvard Medical School report on irreversible coma, are now widely accepted among medical professionals. Thirty-one states and the District of Columbia have brain-death statutes.

Current laws also provide that a rational patient can make his own healthcare decisions in most cases. "A competent adult has the right to refuse medical treatment even if the ultimate result is death," writes Milwaukee Attorney Robyn Shapiro in the *Harvard Journal on Legislation*. "This right is grounded in the doctrine of informed consent and in the constitutional right to privacy." But as the case of Peter Cinque demonstrates, medical institutions do not always automatically honor a patient's wishes, often for fear of a malpractice suit by surviving relatives or a belief that the patient does not know best. Doctors who treat patients against their will, however, may be liable for battery or other charges.

It is a far more complicated matter when the patient is mentally ill, retarded, senile, brain damaged or comatose. Technically, he has the same rights as a competent patient. In practice, someone else must try to replicate the decision the patient would make were he able to speak for himself. This notion of "substituted judgment" was established judicially for an incompetent patient by the New Jersey Supreme Court in the 1976 landmark case of Karen Ann Quinlan, who had lapsed into an irreversible coma the year before. Pressed by her parents, the court ruled that her respirator could be removed if the Quinlans, her doctors and a hospital review committee agreed.

The New Jersey justices may consider yet another potential landmark case. In November 1982 Thomas Whittemore requested the removal of a nasal feeding tube from his aunt, Claire Conroy, then 83, who was in a New Jersey hospital unable to speak or move and suffering from advanced heart disease. Her doctor refused to do it. "He said to me, 'Mr. Whittemore, you can't play God.' And I said, "What are you doing? God's will is that this woman is ready to go. You're the one holding her back.'" Whittemore sought and received court permission to stop the feeding. "There is a point," wrote Superior Court Judge Reginald Stanton, "at which a patient, or someone acting for him if he is incompetent, has the right to refuse

treatment. That point is reached when intellectual functioning is permanently reduced to a very primitive level or when pain has become unbearable and unrelievable." Conroy died in February, though her tube was never removed because an appeal was to have been heard in May.

The Conroy case raises the issue not only of when someone should die but how. Is denying food and water to a patient, of any age, the logical extension of ending life-sustaining treatment? Yes, says University of Texas Law Professor John Robertson, author of the new American Civil Liberties Union handbook *The Rights of the Critically Ill.* "If you can legally and ethically take a respirator from a patient, the decision has already been made to let the patient die. Why, then, is it not justifiable to remove food?"

To many, though, there is a difference, if only one of sensibility. When Karen Ann Quinlan was taken off the respirator, her family fully expected her to die. She did not. Fed through a nasogastric tube, Quinlan, who turned 29 last week, continues to exist in a vegetative state in a nursing home. "She can hear me when I talk to her, and she can hear music. But no connection takes place inside," says Quinlan's mother Julia, who usually visits her daily. Though her daughter's recovery is impossible, she says, "We decided that removing the feeding tube was simply some-

thing we did not want to do."

The decision not to feed, or treat, an infant is an even more poignant one, and it is often made quietly for some of the 362,000 seriously ill infants born each year in the U.S. One recent case was far from quiet, however, and the result may change some pediatric practices. At his birth last April in Bloomington, Ind., "Infant Doe" had Down's syndrome, a defect associated with mental retardation, and a deformed esophagus that prevented him from eating and drinking normally. The parents, acting for their child, decided against repairing the esophagus. The effect would have been to starve the child to death, but the hospital sought a judicial order to allow the operation. The parents won in the lower courts, and the Indiana Supreme Court refused to intervene. While state officials raced to Washington to petition the U.S. Supreme Court, the week-old infant died.

When accounts of the case appeared in the press, the public reacted with horror. Pro-life groups lobbied President Reagan personally to prevent similar deaths. The result: new federal regulations seeking to prevent hospitals from denying food or care to handicapped infants. Effective last month, hospitals receiving federal funds must prominently post a notice announcing the federal policy and listing a confidential toll-free "hot line" to encourage reports of violations. The President's Commission denounces the rule, claiming it "adds further uncertainty to an already complex situation." Others contend that at best, it is inconsistent policymaking. "The Administration cannot cut programs for the handicapped," says Dr. Anne Fletcher, nursery director at Children's Hospital in Washington, "and at the same time want these babies saved." A lawsuit has been filed to block the rules. But already the first hot-line calls have come in, leading to an investigation of at least one false alarm involving ten children in a Tennessee hospital.

The President's Commission believes that Down's syndrome babies like Infant Doe are entitled to every medical effort because they can live, though it may be a limited life. Moreover, courts in the past have overruled some parents, such as Jehovah's Witnesses opposed to blood transfusions for their sick children. The Infant Doe case is thus something of an aberration. But it does add to the concern of those like Connecticut Pediatrician and Pro-Life Activist Paul Bruch, who is afraid that "the right to die could become the obligation to die, that somewhere along the line someone will decide that retarded people in a certain condition should all die."

Critics fear that the new federal regulations go so far that they would require the maintenance of all handicapped newborns, no matter how monstrous

or minimal their lives may be. "Withholding fluids or nourishment at any time is an immoral act," says U.S. Surgeon General C. Everett Koop flatly. The new rules may thus make doctors more hesitant to take what many had considered the more humane course.

Because of a recent case in California, doctors have yet another reason to fear the consequences of their actions. The case developed after Clarence Herbert, 55, a race-track security guard, suddenly slipped into a coma following a seemingly successful 1981 operation at Kaiser Permanente Medical Center in Los Angeles. With the family's consent, his doctors removed his respirator. "They said he was clinically dead and would never return," insists his wife Patsy. When Herbert kept breathing, the doctors cut off intravenous food and water, again with the family's agreement. Finally, eleven days after the operation, Herbert succumbed. After hearing a nurse's report, Los Angeles authorities sought to prosecute the physicians for murder. Last month a judge dismissed the charges, but an appeal is pending. The family now claims to have been misled about Herbert's condition and is suing for malpractice.

There is a growing body of such criminal and malpractice actions, but few medical professionals or lawyers welcome the second guessing of the legal system. Says President's Commission Chairman

Morris Abram, a New York attorney: "I cannot imagine anything worse than relying on a lawyer standing by the bedside leafing through papers to determine what treatment should be administered." He adds that legislation diminishing the privacy of the patient-physician relationship "would be mischievous and intrusive."

Some legislatures have sought to strengthen a patient's right to a say in the medical management of his death. Since 1976, 14 states and the District of Columbia have legalized the use of so-called living wills. Drawn up in case a person becomes incompetent, the document typically instructs doctors to stop "life-sustaining procedures" in the event of a "terminal condition." Some "right-to-die" laws attempt to make the directive binding on doctors, who may transfer medical responsibility for the patient if they disagree with his wishes.

The wills may also be of some legal help in states that have not authorized them, but their strength— the chance to speak explicitly about one's desires in the face of death—is also their weakness. For they may not cover the precise circumstances that occur. The President's Commission considers "durable powers of attorney" preferable. Forty-two states already have laws authorizing such documents. Both living wills and powers of attorney are easily revocable by a rational person, but the latter are more adaptable. They can empower anyone—relative, friend, adviser—to make any medical decision when the signee becomes incompetent.

Though little discussed because of its unseemliness, cost is also a factor in life-death decisions. The greedy relative who speeds a death to accelerate an inheritance is probably not a large problem outside of fiction, but the draining bills of prolonged hospitalization present real dilemmas. Should a daughter's carefully saved college-tuition money be spent to extend the life of a terminally ill parent? Even when the financial impact for an individual family is cushioned by Medicare or personal insurance, taxpayers and premium payers are affected.

There are times when the artificial prolongation of life is worthwhile, for example in the case of an accident victim whose organs may be used in a transplant. In addition, pioneering efforts such as those made for artificial-heart patient Barney Clark offer the promise of medical advances as well as the slim possibility of an improved life for the individual. The benefit to another's life was also paramount last week when a California woman who was declared legally dead nine weeks earlier after suffering massive brain damage gave birth to a child. Her vital functions had been maintained for a record period so that the fetus could achieve viability. Born after 31 weeks of pregnancy, her son is in good condition; the mother's life-support systems were removed following the birth.

Such unusual cases, and the many unique aspects of every case, are what makes an absolute rule so undesirable. Surgeon General Koop asserts that every physician knows the difference "between prolonging the act of dying and protecting the act of living." No doubt the dividing line between the two is a key determinant. And when in doubt, most authorities, including the President's Commission, would give the edge to sustaining life because of the high value society must and does place on it.

For Patrick McFadzen, 23, and his family, however, the presumption favoring life is exacting a terrible price. Nearly killed in a motorcycle accident three years ago, he has only a primitive brain function, but he feels pain and has suffered severe muscle spasms. "When his eyes were open," recalls his mother, "they were filled with terror." Last January he developed the ability to swallow and now can be fed orally. So no extraordinary efforts are being used to prolong his life at a nursing home in Two Rivers, Wis. He will survive indefinitely. "There are no clear answers," says his doctor, Steven Lawrence. "No judge in the land can adjudicate this type of human suffering." *—By Susan Tifft. Reported by David S. Jackson/Washington and Jack E. White/New York, with other U.S. bureaus*

A Family's Decision

Atlanta Journalist Roger Witherspoon and his wife Cynthia lost their first child, a daughter, in childbirth. A year and a half later, when Cynthia prematurely went into labor with their son Dax after only 22 weeks of pregnancy, the obstetrician warned them that the infant's lungs had almost certainly not developed enough for survival. Extraordinary measures could be tried if the parents wished to subject the baby to the process. Witherspoon's account of their decision:

I had seen the neonatal intensive-care units, big, immaculate rooms with stainless-steel-and-glass machines called Ohio beds, which cradled the premature infants. They were miniature people whose arms bristled with a series of tubes and needles going to a bank of computer screens and monitors. In a few cases, the infants thrive in that controlled, constricted environment, designed to give them the best chance to live. But most do not make it. They spend their brief existence in a sterile world, devoid of any real warmth or affection, a world filled with pain and discomfort. In my own view, the odds just were not worth it. I found it impossible to confront the vision of my child dying alone in a room full of machines—never having known what it is to be loved.

He was very still when born, and we thought he was dead. Then I thought I saw a hand move, slightly. But I had been up for more than 24 hours and thought it was just fatigue. Then he moved again. And the nurse gave him to me. He was strong enough, at that point, to hold one adult finger. He had my eyebrows, Cindy's long thin fingers, a head of hair, and a mouth that seemed a cross between us both.

The hospital was very accommodating. Cindy was wheeled into an adjoining empty recovery room, and her mother came in to join us. For a while, we were a larger family, taking turns holding the boy and letting him grasp and hold a finger. Memory says he smiled—though logic says that was probably not possible.

After ten minutes he could no longer muster the strength to hold on. His breathing became labored, and his heart was beating at a noticeably slower rate. The color of his skin, starting at his feet, began to lighten as it became starved for oxygen and blood. We watched death move upward in neat, horribly incremental stages. After 45 minutes, it embraced all of him, and it was over.

It took two weeks for the results of the autopsy to prove that Dax would not have survived the ordeal of the neonatal room had he been sent there. I was not aware that I had been worrying about it, but the news was a relief. In our case the decision was not life or death. The decision was between the sure odds of being a family, for however brief a time, and the odds of not being able to be a family at all. Though many of our peers disagreed, if fate forced a similar decision in the future, we would do it again. It was worth it.

YOUR TURN

What new kinds of information does this article add to the one in *Maclean's?* Find three new specialized terms or phrases and give definitions for them, based on how they're used here.

What was your reaction to "A Family's Decision"? How does it affect your thinking about the issue as a whole?

Again, what new questions do the articles raise? What else do they make you want to find out?

ONE CASE: MAKING THE PROBLEM REAL

The third folder you check out contains two separate articles focusing on the controversy surrounding the situation and behavior of one particular patient. The first, from *Newsweek*, gives a brief, presumably fairly objective history of the woman's case. The second is an opinion piece from the *National Review*, a magazine that appears to have a definite and deliberate political stance. On the magazine's title page and table of contents, you find the following information.

Article Titles and Abstracts:

"The Underhandedness of Affirmative Action": It's an insult to self-government. It amounts to a standing accusation against all white males. It contradicts its own avowed premises. Yet we continue to countenance it.

"Lebanon and Staying Power": The United States' experience in Lebanon affords a lesson in what power means.

"New York, New York": It's not such a long way from Tel Aviv. As Rainbow Jackson took Harlem by storm, Mondale and Hart were fighting it out over the question, "Where's the embassy?"

"How Does It Fare with Felipe?": Spain's new leader is not to be confused with his fellow socialist François Mitterand. So far, so good.

"The Revolt against Our Public Culture": America may not be a Christian nation, but where does it say we have to be heathen?

Regular departments carry names such as "From Washington Straight," "The Week," "The Right Books," and "On the Right."

A few pages further in you find a full-page advertisement for a book, entitled *Death at Chappaquiddick* with Senator Edward Kennedy's picture on the front. The headline, in half-inch tall bold-faced letters, reads: EVERY YEAR OR SO IT DOES YOU GOOD TO READ SOMETHING THAT WILL MAKE YOUR BLOOD BOIL. THIS WILL DO IT. The picture of the book is surrounded by clips from reviews, including such comments as these:

"Demolishes Teddy."

"The Tedrows succeed in demolishing Ted's flimsy accounts of the incident."

"A spate of books on the Chappaquiddick incident have recently appeared. By far the most devastating for the Senator is the book by the Tedrows."

At the bottom, there are a couple of short paragraphs, offering a money-back guarantee on the book; a little order blank to cut out and send in with ten dollars; and the final note: "P.S. Mary Jo Kopechne did not die from drowning."

YOUR TURN

Before even looking at the articles from either magazine, analyze what political stance seems to be suggested by the article titles, abstracts, and

343

other information on the table of contents of *The National Review*. What kind of book does *Death at Chappaquiddick* seem to be? If you were selling the book, where would you look for possible buyers? On the basis of these two pages from the magazine, how would you characterize the probable readership of *The National Review*?

You now settle down to read the two articles. You decide to nutshell each article as you read it so that you get to the core point each author is making.

The Most Painful Question

In conventional folklore, Elizabeth Bouvia might have been an inspirational figure. Paralyzed since birth by cerebral palsy, the tiny, 26-year-old quadriplegic grappled her way to a college degree, a pen-pal marriage and, briefly, a semblance of normal existence. But because she then decided her life was not worth living—and asked doctors to help her die— she has become an object of bitter legal wrangling and harsh public accusations. Lawyers for Riverside (Calif.) General Hospital, where Bouvia has been a patient since last September, have suggested she is a publicity-seeking nuisance. At a press conference, one provoked hospital official went so far as to call her "devilish and diabolical." Even spokesmen for the rights of the handicapped have denounced her for implying, as one of them put it, that "the disabled have nothing to live for."

In Bouvia's view, that is strictly a personal decision.

Having concluded, she says, that "the struggle is not worth it," and physically unable to take her own life, she asked doctors at Riverside to let her starve to death, administering only painkillers and hygienic care. Amid some disagreement of its own, the American Civil Liberties Union took up Bouvia's cause, arguing that under constitutional guarantees of self-determination, certain patients with failing kidneys, for example, have been allowed to refuse dialysis. When a California Superior Court judge ruled last month that Bouvia could not compel the hospital to let her starve, doctors began force-feeding her. But the ACLU has appealed for an order against the feeding, and Bouvia seems no less resolved to achieve her terminal goal. "I'm going to keep on fighting," she said with no apparent irony last week. "I'm not going to give up."

Will: To those who know her, the air of steely determination that Bouvia manages to exude from her frail, twisted body comes as no surprise. "Elizabeth has always had the ability to bounce back through her strong will," says Sheila Velez, a counselor for the California Department of Rehabilitation, who has worked closely with her since 1974. "It's the same thing now," adds Velez, "only the goals have changed."

Born in the west Texas town of Ft. Stockton in May 1957, Bouvia was diagnosed as a cerebral-palsy victim when she was six months old. Her parents divorced after moving to California, and at 10 she was placed in an orthopedic hospital, where she remained for seven years. Urged to enter a convalescent home, she turned instead to the rehabilitation agency. With Velez's help, she moved to a modern apartment complex in Riverside and enrolled as a social-work major at the city college, equipped with a tape recorder and a mechanical page turner. It was an exciting but trying time for Elizabeth, Velez recalls:

"She had to take control of her own social security, Medi-Cal [and] qualifying for federal grants and loans. But she maintained good grades through it all and pursued volunteer work, too."

The "happiest time" for Elizabeth was at graduate school in San Diego. She had begun corresponding with Richard Bouvia, a baldish, once-married factory worker from Iowa who was serving a prison term in northern California for attempted robbery. According to Richard, they fell in love "almost immediately" when she visited him, and a few months after his release on a work furlough in April 1982 they were married. But near the end of that year, things began to come apart. Elizabeth had trouble getting a work-experience placement in her graduate program. She dropped out, and as a result the state threatened to reclaim the free van that transported her to school. At the same time, she began suffering from a progressively acute arthritis.

Richard, meanwhile, was having trouble finding work and in vain sought a job back in Iowa. Elizabeth went with him, then moved to Oregon, where her father was living. Richard joined her there, but couldn't get a job and abruptly left again. "I just got fed up and walked out," he says. "It was my big mistake of the year. I think as far as she was con-cerned, it was the straw that broke the camel's back."

So it seemed. It was shortly after her separation from Richard last fall that Elizabeth signed herself into the psychiatric ward at Riverside General and began her quest for death. Picked up by the major media after a local reporter interviewed her, the story has brought her national attention. To date, around 1,500 pounds of mail have poured into her hospital room, along with 200 Bibles—some of them from people urging her to heed "the Lord's will."

Critics both inside and outside the hospital nevertheless see perversity in her stance. If she is so determined to end her life, they argue, why couldn't she have gone off somewhere and done it privately, instead of asking doctors to risk possible criminal charges of complicity in a suicide? To her lawyers' contention that she lacks sufficient control of her own limbs and body functions to kill herself, they reply that she must therefore accept the nutritional help it is the hospital's obligation to give her. "She's claiming the classic liberal right of self-determination, but tragically, she's not self-determined," says John Arras, who holds the post of philosopher-in-residence at New York's Montefiore Medical Center.

Hospice: Even so, some ethicists object to the im-position of force-feeding. Says Willard Gaylin, co-founder of the Hastings Center, which studies ethical issues in medicine: "The idea of a physician crawling on the chest of a patient to cram a tube down his throat is reprehensible." Gaylin agrees, however, that the idea of medicine as a caring profession should not be "contaminated." A hospice—usually a place for terminally ill patients—may be the place for Elizabeth, he feels. "Someway, somewhere, there should be help for her."

In the face of the controversy she has stirred, Bouvia maintains her characteristic stoicism. "I feel like I accomplished a lot when I was in college—but I've given it 26 years and what I've done with my life I've done," she said last week. "The quality of my life is over." She rejects any attempt at armchair analysis of her decision. And she turns down offers from sympathetic outsiders who offered to let her die in the privacy of their homes. By one not unreasonable conjecture, Bouvia, while not seeking publicity, may be asserting a deeply felt point: namely, a society that so reluctantly took responsibility for her life must now take some responsibility for her leaving it.

DAVID GELMAN with
DANIEL PEDERSEN
in Los Angeles

A RIGHT TO DIE?

ELIZABETH BOUVIA, a quadriplegic in Riverside, California, wants to starve herself to death. The hospital in which she spent seven months said, in effect, Not here. It obtained the backing of a local court for feeding Mrs. Bouvia by force. This decision—which has now forced Mrs. Bouvia to check herself out of the hospital—seems an abuse of the court's and of the hospital's power.

Not that I am in favor of suicide. But suicide is legal in all states of the U.S. that I am familiar with. For good reason: It is impossible to punish a successful suicide in this world, for he has left it. Wherefore the threat of punishment is unlikely to discourage would-be suicides. On the other hand, an unsuccessful suicide is not going to be cheered up by punishment and discouraged from trying again. Hence, there is no point in making suicide unlawful.

Morally, opinions differ: Some think suicide is licit, others do not. Most think, intuitively, that a suicidal person is deranged. Usually this intuition is correct. But not always. There can be rational reasons for suicide, although 90 per cent of people who commit suicide are permanently or temporarily deranged. Not infrequently they are despondent about a temporary situation and temporarily unable to grasp the temporariness of that situation. Thus, the present practice has much to be said for it: The cops usually take people who attempt suicide to a psychiatric hospital where they are observed to find out whether or not they are incompetent, in need of custodial or other care. If they are competent they are released. The two weeks of "observation," together with the failure of the suicide attempt, often are cathartic enough to prevent further attempts. Ideally more care is needed. Surely a person desperate enough, or deranged enough, to try suicide ought to be helped to overcome his problems if at all possible. Psychotherapy and social work could help. Yet hospitals seldom can give more than custodial care. Still, even the present, less than ideal, practice is better than nothing. It temporarily protects the suicidal person against an impulse that may be temporary, although, if he remains suicidal, not much help is provided.

Whereas 90 per cent of suicides are deranged, the remaining 10 per cent may realistically find their situation to be hopeless and rationally prefer death to life. Religious persons think it presumptuous to make decisions about their own death themselves. Religion requires us to leave this decision to God. But not everybody is religious. And the government in the U.S. is not meant to enforce religious doctrines. Rational suicide—such as the recent suicide of Arthur Koestler—is possible. It cannot be prevented by law, and I do not believe it should be, if it could be, although most of us intuitively, or doctrinally, oppose it.

However, aiding and abetting a suicide is regarded as a crime and can be effectively punished. There appear to be sound reasons for outlawing such aid. If we allow Smith to help Jones commit suicide, the help may be indistinguishable from persuasion and the persuasion indistinguishable from homicide. To be sure, there are cases in which such help is well intentioned and well motivated. But such cases are not easy to define in law. Thus a person who wishes to commit suicide must do so by his own efforts. If he is unwilling to rely on his own efforts it may well be a sign that he does not really want to commit suicide. Society certainly should not permit anyone to persuade, help, or push him.

SO FAR so good. But we must now consider the case of a person, Mrs. Bouvia, who wants to commit suicide, but is physically unable to do so by her own efforts. According to

SOURCE: *National Review,* May 4, 1984, pp. 45–46. © 1984 by National Review, Inc. 150 East 35 Street, New York, NY 10016. Reprinted with permission.

current law, even in such a case nobody is entitled to help her end her life by any positive act. But that is not the issue. She only wants to be left alone. She does not want to be helped. She only wants not to be forced, against her wishes, to take nourishment. Should she be forcibly prevented from starving herself to death? Should the hospital in which she was staying have been authorized to feed her parenterally against her will? Or through a tube in the nose? The hospital insisted that if it did not force-feed her it might be liable for abetting a suicide, and a California court authorized the hospital to force her to accept nourishment as long as she remained there. This interpretation of the law strikes me as perverse.

A few years ago a number of Irish terrorists starved themselves to death in British prisons to protest British policies. The British government certainly had the right to force-feed them, for they were convicts, not entitled to the liberties nonconvicts are entitled to. But the British government— wisely—allowed them to do as they wished, without fear of being accused of aiding suicide or of being held liable by the families of these men. The British government felt that even a convict should be allowed to refuse food if he so wished.* A hospital—or a prison—may be liable for failing to artificially feed patients who cannot eat by normal means, or are incompetent. But not a patient who will not eat. He has a perfect right to decline food, or medicine, or

an operation, if he so wishes and is competent to understand the consequences.

True, a hospital, unlike a prison, should not have to keep competent patients unwilling to accept its rules. But there are exceptions. For Mrs. Bouvia to be forced to sign herself out of the hospital was barbaric. In her condition Mrs. Bouvia needs painkillers and care not readily obtainable outside a hospital regardless of whether she wants to live or die. Nor could someone in her condition take care of herself outside a hospital. At this writing we do not know what plans Mrs. Bouvia has made, but barring special arrangements she would have to be visited by social workers and nurses, who, upon noting that she was starving herself, would regard it as their duty to take her to a hospital where she would be force-fed once more. Surely this would happen once she was in a coma, if not before.

WOULD IT have demoralized the hospital— patients and staff— to allow her to voluntarily end her days there? I cannot see why. Many people die in hospitals, involuntarily in most cases. The fact that Mrs. Bouvia would have been doing so voluntarily does not seem to me to be demoralizing—certainly not more so than keeping her alive by forcing nourishment on her, and having a guard at her bedside to prevent her from using the one arm she can (partially) control to remove the feeding tube.

The truth is quite sim-

ple. Mrs. Bouvia could, at least temporarily, be prevented from exercising an ability we all have—to starve ourselves to death— by the fact of her handicap. A competent person who is not physically incapable cannot be prevented from starving himself to death if he so wishes. Nor, as the case of the Irish prisoners illustrates, should such a person be forced to nourish himself. Mrs. Bouvia is mentally competent. But she is a quadriplegic. The California court has connived with the hospital to use her helplessness to impose a decision on her that could not have been imposed if she were not in the helpless condition that caused her to wish to starve herself to death. This is discrimination with a vengeance—discrimination generated entirely by Mrs. Bouvia's handicap.

The court and the hospital ought to be ashamed of themselves. Mrs. Bouvia ought to be permitted to receive what care she requires. She ought to be able to decline what she does not want. Surely her declination is neither frivolous nor incompetent. There are no indications of incompetence. She ought to be able—within the very small range fate has given her—to live and die as she wishes, even if many people may pray that she decide to live. But surely no one has a moral or legal right to force her to. □

*I am informed—I hope incorrectly—that some Irish priests encouraged the suicides. If so, these fanatics bear a heavy burden of responsibility for encouraging actions contrary to the tenets of the faith they and the suicides professed.

YOUR TURN

Summarize Van Den Haag's reasons for permitting Bouvia to die. Work out for yourself the similarities and differences between: 1) asking that medical treatment be terminated, 2) committing suicide, and 3) whatever it is you see Elizabeth Bouvia doing. Compare your own analysis with Van Den Haag's.

Suppose you were given the power of deciding Elizabeth Bouvia's case: what would you do? Is there anything else you'd want to know about the case before deciding? How would you defend your decision? Write out the answers to these questions in your notebook (for your own reference only).

COMPARING IDEAS: SOME COLLABORATION

When you return to the library the next day, you spot a couple of students from Social Issues 101 who are working together at a table in the "noise room," a soundproof study room that allows library patrons to talk without disturbing other readers. They invite you to join them. Each has checked out one folder, and they've worked out a system in which each person reads an article and then writes some notes about it. At the end of the session, everyone makes a photocopy of his or her notes and exchanges them for comparison.

You think this a useful idea, so they hand you one of the folders. It contains two articles about a speech made in 1984 by Richard Lamm, former governor of Colorado, on the right-to-die issue. The first article, in *Time* magazine, gives a brief account of Lamm's speech and its stormy aftermath. In the latter, from *The New Republic,* Lamm presents his own account of what he said, how it was taken, and what he really meant.

Question: Who Will Play God?

Colorado's Governor causes a furor on the issue of dying

The words seemed calculated to provoke an uproar. Elderly people who are terminally ill "have a duty to die," declared Colorado Governor Richard Lamm, 48, at a meeting of the Colorado Health Lawyers Association last week in Denver. "Like leaves which fall off a tree forming the humus in which other plants can grow, we've got a duty to die and get out of the way with all of our machines and artificial hearts, so that our kids can build a reasonable life."

An uproar is just what the Governor got. In Washington the American Life Lobby, an anti-abortion, anti-euthanasia group, quickly called for Lamm's resignation. Florida's Representative Claude Pepper, 83, Congress's leading advocate for the aged, accused the Governor of "downgrading the elderly." Lamm was confronted by angry older citizens in Denver. "I used to think the world of you, but I hate you for what you said," declared Lilian Bono, 76.

Lost in the ruckus was Lamm's original intent: to call attention to the alarming fact that "medical science is replacing God in deciding when we die,"

and to encourage discussion of the implications. "We can prolong our lives a few months or a year, but at what price?" Lamm asks. The Governor insists that he did not intend to endorse mercy killing: "In euthanasia, somebody else makes the decision. I am merely saying people have the right to die without medical science intervening." In addition, he notes, the "falling leaves" metaphor was an attempt to paraphrase an article in the *American Scholar* by University of Chicago Philosopher Leon Kass: "It was unfortunate that it suddenly became my quote."

However infelicitous his phrasing, Lamm was praised in some quarters for broaching one of the most sensitive issues of the day. Medical technology has become increasingly successful at keeping frail and withered leaves on the tree long after nature would have let them fall. Today, 80% of Americans die in hospitals or nursing homes, generally in the course of receiving some sort of medical treatment. Doctors no longer speak of death by "natural causes." Because physicians have the capacity to extend life, they often feel obliged to use it, observes Dr. Ber-

nard Towers, who helps direct a U.C.L.A. program for the study of medicine, law and human values. "Most people fear dying in the midst of electronic gadgetry," he says, "but it looks like there may come a time when we will not be allowed to die without an I.V. tube running."

The legal problems involved in allowing elderly patients to die have created a dilemma for physicians and hospitals, even when the wishes of patients or their families are clear. For instance, doctors at Good Samaritan Medical Center in Phoenix last week insisted that a court order be obtained before they would comply with an 83-year-old woman's wish to be disconnected from the respirator that was keeping her alive and in pain. Nearly three years earlier, the woman had drawn up a "living will," a document that requested hospitals not to prolong her life by extraordinary measures. Because Arizona does not recognize such a will (15 states and the District of Columbia do), doctors did not want to take legal responsibility for her death.

There is good reason for caution. In 1982 two physicians in California were charged with murder for complying with a family's request to remove feeding tubes from a hopelessly brain-damaged patient. The charge was dismissed upon appeal last fall. But, together with similar cases around the country, it has "sent a chill into the medical community," according to Washington Gerontologist Joanne Lynn, principal author of a 1983 Presidential Commission report on medical ethics.

Fear of legal reprisal has apparently led some hospitals to conceal decisions on life support so that no one can be held responsible for deciding to pull the plug. A New York grand-jury report last month charged administrators at a Queens hospital, widely recognized as La Guardia, with "shocking procedural abuses" in the care of elderly patients. According to New York State Prosecutor Edward Kuriansky, the hospital would put purple decals on the charts of patients who were not to be resuscitated should they start to fail. After death, the charts were destroyed so that there was no record of the fatal decision. La Guardia officials deny the charge, but there is no doubt that a number of American hospitals lack clear procedures for observing and recording the wishes of dying patients. Says Dr. S. David Pomrinse, recently retired president of the Greater New York Hospital Association: "In hospitals that have no rules, in the middle of the night you have a poor 21-year-old nurse trying to decide whether or not to call in the resuscitation team."

Because of the attention such cases have received in the past few years, many hospitals and states have begun to set guidelines so that life-and-death decisions are not made rashly in the heat of the night. By playing the gadfly, Governor Lamm may have promoted further discussion, and clarification, of a troubling ethical issue. ∎

When 'miracle cures' don't cure.

LONG TIME DYING

By Richard D. Lamm

LATE one March afternoon in a back room of St. Joseph's Hospital in Denver, I happened to remark, in the course of a talk to a small group of health lawyers and one reporter, that "we all have a duty to die." The next day, all hell broke loose.

The headline in *The Denver Post* announced: THE ELDERLY TERMINALLY ILL 'HAVE A DUTY TO DIE,' LAMM SAYS. The appalled health lawyers hastily called a press conference to try to correct the *Post*'s version, pointing out what I had actually said: that the terminally ill should be permitted to die with dignity instead of being hooked up

to life-support machines long after consciousness has faded and after there is no longer any hope of recovery. By that time, however, newspapers across the country were proclaiming that I wanted the elderly and dying to "get out of the way." For example, the New York *Daily News*, in its inimitable fashion, screamed: AGED ARE TOLD TO DROP DEAD.

Following the story, brutal as my statement appeared, I received close to three thousand letters. Despite the distortions, the vast majority of those who wrote to me agreed with the gist of what I had said. The response showed clearly that many people have come to believe that medical technology has run amok. "These machines are manacles, not miracles," wrote one woman. "There comes a time when aggressive treatment is not only counterproductive but

---

Richard D. Lamm is the governor of the State of Colorado.

SOURCE: *The New Republic,* August 24, 1984, pp. 20–23. Reprinted by permission of *The New Republic,* © 1984, The New Republic, Inc.

cruel." Another wrote of her mother, "who does not know me or other members of the family" and who is hooked indefinitely to a machine:

The family assets are expended at the rate of over $2,000 per month for part-time assistance in her care—money that she would have wished allocated to the grandchildren's education. . . . [S]o here I am, essentially with a corpse we cannot bury. . . . As you know, we are a medical family, and I am not decrying advancement in medical techniques or advocating euthanasia, but there comes a point that the perpetuation of a pulse and lung and kidney function exacts too great a price from family and society.

A third woman asked, "Who owns my body, Medicare, the hospital, the state, or me?"

It would seem that a new liberation movement is forming, a movement for liberation *from* our machines when they are used not to prolong living but to prolong dying. We have reached a point where doctors have the capability of keeping patients alive long after they have ceased to exist as thinking, feeling human beings. Do patients or their families have the right to refuse the "benefits" of these machines? This is partly a civil rights issue, partly a health care issue, and partly a very delicate and volatile issue of "substituted" judgment, where one person makes a life-and-death decision for another.

There is a relentless kind of technological imperative, particularly in the medical field: if we invent a machine, we have a duty to use it. In an article in *Nursing* magazine a nurse writes that we "can't shut our eyes" to the fact that resuscitation machinery is very expensive, and that "if the equipment is not used, there is no return on the investment." When faced with a decision to treat or not to treat a very sick patient, a doctor will usually order the available medical technology, no matter how ill the patient, no matter how much the expense drains resources from other patients. After all, in virtually every case, the patient or the patient's family isn't paying the bill. Instead, a third party insurer, or more often Medicare, stands ready to hand the doctor a blank check, leaving it to the doctor and the hospital to fill in the numbers. If a doctor doesn't order technological intervention in the last stages of the patient's illness, he is faced with the possibility of a medical malpractice suit, bad publicity, and a possible stain on his career. And there is no denying the fact that both he and his hospital stand to

gain financially from the intervention, even if it does nothing but draw out the process of dying for the patient. The final result is too often treatment that is scarcely distinguishable from torture.

There are a number of human forces at work here. Medicine is an "activist" profession and doctors are trained to see death as a failure. The families of the terminally ill often feel a moral ambivalence in the face of death. Patients themselves sometimes fear death more than the technology. But the overwhelming response to the furor I inadvertently touched off was captured in one elderly man's letter to me, "I do not fear death. I fear the indignity of deterioration, dependence, and hopeless pain."

THE EMOTIONAL toll on families and doctors faced with the choice between life-sustaining technology and death is only one part of the problem. Another part is the staggering financial cost. Last year health care nationwide cost $355 billion—$45 million an hour, 24 hours a day, every day of the year. Governor Thomas Kean of New Jersey describes health care as the "Pac Man of his budget," eating up his ability to solve other social problems. The time is not far off when there will be a direct conflicts between the health of the individual and the health of the society. We cannot afford all the medical miracles that the profession stands ready to give, and choices will have to be made about the distribution of limited medical resources. Technological immortality is running into fiscal reality.

A large proportion of our health care bill already goes for the care of patients who have no chance of recovery. We spend 28 percent of Medicare funds on the 6 percent of Medicare patients who die each year. In other words, we spend four times as much on these patients who die as we do on other Medicare patients.

One doctor, writing in *The New England Journal of Medicine*, sums up the dilemma:

Because of our great and proper humanitarian desire to preserve life, we have difficulty desisting in our medical efforts, even when the probability of the patient's recovery approaches zero, and even when the costs in a futile attempt to save one life may consume resources that might save many. The costs of trying to preserve the life of one cirrhotic patient with bleeding esophageal varices might be used to treat and prevent alcoholism in many persons. The cost of one heart transplant could support smoking-cessation programs, plasma-lipid-lowering diets, hypertension treatment, and physical-exercise programs for many. The cost of treating one premature newborn with respiratory-arrest syndrome could be used to provide nourishment for many expectant mothers, thus combating a major cause of prematurity.

Many of these high-tech procedures and machines (ventilators, nuclear magnetic resonance scanners, and renal dialysis machines for the terminally ill, among others) are so expensive that they interfere with our ability to pay for other medical procedures. The cost of high technology is one of the main factors cited by health care analysts for the decline in funds for prenatal care and health care for the elderly.

These machines present policymakers with much more difficult decisions than they had to face in the past. There was little moral ambivalence, for example, over the passage of comprehensive health care for mothers and infants in 1963. It is a different thing altogether, in a time of limited resources, to confront a choice between spending $100,000 for medical treatments in the last year of life and providing almost four thousand schoolchildren with lifetime immunizations from polio. The Colorado legislature, like many legislatures, has been reacting to federal budget cuts by cutting social programs, restricting A.F.D.C. patients to "emergency health procedures," and tightening eligibility standards for federal assistance of all kinds. Hospitals, state legislatures, and even the National Institutes of Health should be asking: how many Barney Clarks can this country afford?

T HE EASIEST issue both politically and morally is the "right-to-die" issue, and it is here that the new liberation movement is being felt. California passed the first right-to-die law in 1976, and nineteen other states and the District of Columbia have passed similar or identical laws. Such legislation gives doctors and hospitals immunity from civil or criminal prosecution if they have acted according to a "living will." The heart of a living will is simple: "If I should have an injury, disease, or illness regarded by my physician as incurable and terminal, and if my physician determines that the application of life-sustaining procedures would serve only to prolong artificially the dying process, I direct that such procedures be withdrawn and that I be permitted to die."

But if there is no living will, a host of questions arise. What is the duty of the medical profession? Whose judgment can be substituted for the patient's? When patients can no longer make their wishes known, who speaks for them? In cases when a family tells a doctor that no extraordinary measures should be taken to keep the patient alive, does the government or an interested observer have the right to intervene? Should nontreatment be a legally protected medical alternative? In many cases, medical technology is merely imposing life on a corpse: individuals who are brain dead are put on respirators and are continually resuscitated. In one a dying woman was resuscitated seventy times in a twenty-four-hour period, until she was finally allowed to die. It would seem that the best medical care does not necessarily make for the best treatment.

Should hope of recovery be a basis for determining the type of treatment a patient receives? And is recovery the restoration of full health, a return to a vegetative state without consciousness, or a state in between? As new medical technologies become available, we need to be assessing them in terms of the quality of life they offer. We need a better measure than merely the existence of a heartbeat. We must begin to distinguish between "biological life" and human life.

The courts have recognized three main criteria to guide medical professions in ambiguous situations. First, if a patient is brain dead the medical profession can declare him dead, even though his body functions. Second, physicians do not have to treat a "hopeless" patient. If no medical therapy can reverse a "hopeless" patient, treatment can be suspended. It is up to the medical profession to decide who is "hopeless." Third, in cases like that of Karen Ann Quinlan—in which physicians testified that they could not, under oath, foreclose the possibility of a "miracle"—treatment can be discontinued if there is "no reasonable possibility of a patient returning to a cognitive sapient state."

But these guidelines are minimal, and even the most fundamental question, "Is a person dead?," differs from state to state. Twelve states have not adopted the so-called uniform brain death law. In one New York case a 19-year-old man who had been shot in the head was comatose; he had no brain waves and no reflex responses, his pupils were dilated and fixed, and he was breathing only through a respirator. However, the district attorney warned the parents that if they discontinued the life-support system the state could lose the case against the assailant on the grounds that this was the actual cause of death.

In another widely publicized case, physicians in California ended life support for a comatose patient who was clearly never going to regain consciousness. Although the patient's wife and family had consented, an irresponsible district attorney charged the doctor with murder. The California Court of Appeals dismissed the charges, observing, "A murder prosecution is a poor way to design an ethical and moral code for doctors who are faced with decisions concerning the use of costly and extraordinary life-support equipment." The court considered the distinction between "ordinary" and "extraordinary" procedures, but instead adopted a rule that looked at "whether the proposed treatment is proportionate or disproportionate in terms of the benefits to be gained versus the burdens caused."

Whatever the ultimate standard, it is clear that most people recognize that at some point treatment becomes both counterproductive and cruel. Few would disagree with Pope John Paul II, who stated in 1980 that "When inevitable death is imminent in spite of the means used, it is permitted in conscience to refuse forms of treatment that would only secure a precarious and burdensome prolongation of life. . . ." The refusal of treatment "is not the equivalent of suicide; on the contrary it should be considered as an acceptance of the human condition."

The movement to reaffirm the dignity of human life and death in the face of possible technological immortality is growing slowly. People who do not want to be placed on life-support systems are exploring options, in addition to the living will, for determining the conditions for treatment or nontreatment of injury or illness. California and Colorado have passed bills allowing patients to appoint attorneys to represent them in medical areas. Patients who have a verbal understanding with their doctors that no extraordinary measures should be taken to prolong their dying could formalize that arrangement in a statement that would be placed in their medical records both in the doctor's office and at the hospital. These instructions would not be legally binding, but would carry a strong moral force.

But the best option currently available to the terminally ill is to arrange for hospice care. The philosophy of hospices is to ease the dying process by providing whatever pain medication or psychological support is needed. Hospices give terminally ill patients and their families choices about their care, including such extreme choices as refusing nutrition and fluids when death is imminent. Medicaid and Medicare should pay for hospice care as an alternative to hospital care for the dying because the cost is lower and the quality of care is higher. Some hospitals, like the Veterans' Administration Hospital in Denver, are beginning to allocate a few beds to hospice care for the dying. This allows the patient or his family to choose what kind of treatment he will receive in the last months of life.

However, these changes are occurring very slowly. In the meantime, countless human beings are hooked to the miracles of modern medicine, machines which too often offer them not recovery, but a living death. □

YOUR TURN

In jotting down some notes for your classmates, you decide to ask yourself some questions about the articles first, as a way to generate some ideas. Here are your questions:

How does the impression I got from the *Time* article compare with Lamm's account in *The New Republic?* What does the whole affair suggest to me about the way news is handled by different publications?

What does Lamm tell me about the financial aspects of the problem? How does he see the problem developing in the future? What does he offer as humane solutions to the problem?

Answer these questions briefly in your notebook. Define any new terms you see in the articles. Then exchange your notes with your real classmates and discuss the differences in your responses.

AN UNLOOKED-FOR, INTERESTING SOURCE

Over the weekend, you're roaming the stacks in the library to locate some sources for a paper you're writing in another course, when suddenly you spot a periodical called the *Journal of Christian Nursing*. Although you've never heard of this journal before, you think it might contain some interesting perspectives for your Social Issues 101 paper. You start flipping through some of the volumes and, lo and behold, you find a "case study" section in one issue containing five linked articles on the problem of euthanasia. Three of them look interesting enough to copy and take home with you.

Confronting the Right to Die

Caught between a Patient's Will and a Doctor's Order

Kay Sechriest

Mrs. Deem tried to die tonight. But we denied her the right.

Now, at home, I am writing with great fervor and conviction while my husband waits upstairs, half-angry, half-drowsing, not at all understanding my turmoil over a patient's near-death experience.

"No artificial means," her living will said. But the doctor had not written a do-not-resuscitate order. Nor had he said anything to the nurses about the living will kept in Mrs. Deem's chart.

The head nurse, like other older nurses in my hospital, believed the doctor's word is law. Nurses shouldn't challenge the doctors or introduce subjects they don't bring up. She didn't ask the doctor why he hadn't written a do-not-resuscitate order. As an LPN, I didn't challenge her decision.

At eighty-two, Mrs. Deem was tired and alone, ready to die; she told us so. That's why she signed the living will. Her last few days had been uncomfortable. After she fractured her hip, the physician on the orthopedic floor decided she needed to come to the cardiac unit for heart monitoring.

We pumped Mrs. Deem full of IV fluids laced with vitamins and made her wear an oxygen mask which she constantly tried to remove. She ate little by mouth and at times became confused.

She would hold out her hand as if asking us to take what she held. But when she released her fist, her hand was empty. The empty hand seemed to symbolize her present life—empty of meaning and dignity. With no family and no home but a nursing home, warm experiences and heartfelt love were far behind her now. Mrs. Deem's existence held only discomfort—even suffering.

Tonight, when we went into her room, we ignored her will. Her body still and breathless, her mouth open, her eyes closed, her color ashen, she appeared dead. As her heart slowed down to rest—perhaps to cease—we pounced on her, forced air into her lungs, called a code.

Quickly the code team came. Someone began chest compressions. Someone injected adrenalin. Someone else inserted an airway.

We gave Mrs. Deem breath, allowing her heart to pick up and go on. But did we give her life?

Now I'm home in my comfortable house in my warm robe, my coffee cup filled and close at hand, my precious family sleeping, quietly renewing themselves for another day. And I wonder about my patient.

It's not quite two hours from when it all started. Is she still alive? If so, is she lying there pink and warm, awake and alert, drinking a bedtime cup of tea, thinking of loved ones?

No. There are no loved ones left. But I care. If she could be better, aware and able to take some comfort out of just one hour, then I would wish her to live on. But if she lies there cold and gray, her heart fluttering, unresponsive, with her mind and soul suspended somewhere between life and death, then I wish her to die.

Is there not a time to die naturally, without interference, a place for us to go? When we have lived and strived and believed, is it not good to face the hour and go to the Lord?

Discussion Questions

1. What are the purpose and legal status of living wills?

2. Nurses are licensed to carry out physicians' orders but also feel ethically bound to honor patients' rights. Mrs. Deem had signed a living will, but her physician had chosen not to write a do-not-resuscitate order. Should the nurses have begun artificial ventilation when the patient stopped breathing? Why or why not?

3. The nurse asked, "Is there not a time to die naturally, without interference?" The writer of Ecclesiastes said, "For everything there is a season, and a time for every matter under heaven: a time to be born, and a time to die" (3:1-2). Once when he thought he might die soon, Paul mused, "For to me to live is Christ, and to die is gain" (Phil 1:21), and confessed, "My desire is to depart and be with Christ, for that is far better" (Phil 1:23). How should these texts inform our understanding of death, and more specifically, of a patient's right to decline life-sustaining medical treatments? What other Scripture passages apply?

A Theologian Responds: Assess, Don't Simplify

J. Robert Nelson

Mrs. Deem's tragic situation is typical of many which defy simple decisions free from moral and theological ambiguity. The case, described in utter simplicity, seems to indicate an equally simple response: Let her die.

It is hard to imagine that days, weeks or months of Mrs. Deem's existence could be "meaningful" or have any "quality," as the popular labels are used. The life she had was bringing her no satisfaction, only "discomfort," even "suffering."

Apparently no one wanted Mrs. Deem to continue living, except possibly the physician. The head nurse and Kay obediently followed what were apparently, but not explicitly, his orders: Monitor the patient's heart, provide IV fluids and nutrition, administer oxygen if she will accept it. Though no sedatives were mentioned, presumably she was in much pain due to her fractured hip.

When Mrs. Deem experienced a nearly (perhaps?) complete cardiac arrest, the nurses "pounced on her," "forced air into her lungs," and called the code team, which did its job successfully. Were these responses what the physician had instructed in such an event even though the patient had previously expressed her will for nontreatment?

Does a physician's failure to write "do not resuscitate" always mean "resuscitate"? In the Clinical Center of the National Institute of Health, the answer is yes. "Absence of an order not to attempt cardiac resuscitation shall be interpreted by the nursing staff as requiring such efforts should the patient have a cardiac arrest." (Medical Administration Policy No. 82-4, July 12, 1982.)

In any case, it seemed that no one would lament Mrs. Deem's death. She wanted it; so did the nurses; the code team had no personal interest.

If Mrs. Deem died and left an estate, it might revert to the nursing home after her bills were paid. Her death would free an unprofitable bed, medical personnel could attend to patients more likely to recover and society would be relieved of a burdensome member. Those who believed in God and the gospel of resurrection could serenely declare "She is with the Lord. Amen." Probably a nursing-home staff member would attend a burial conducted by an anonymous minister.

In its very simplicity, however, the case description omits certain needed data and also raises some difficult questions of law, medical practice, theology and social attitudes. For example, it is not reported whether this hospital, like many today, has an effective do-not-resuscitate policy.

Mrs. Deem is confined in Pennsylvania. This makes a difference. Those jurisdictions which have enacted "natural death acts" provide for directives signed by a competent person, usually fourteen days after the physician has certified that the patient's condition is "terminal" or "hopeless."

Even when the documents are duly signed, the courts are unlikely to support plaintiffs in malpractice suits against physicians who disregarded the instruments and continue treating patients. Physicians and nurses may be expected to show due respect for living wills, but they are not bound legally to do so. What state legislatures have done is to codify, but without enforcement power, patients' right to refuse treatment.

The living will was first advocated by The Euthanasia Society in America, which has since changed its name to the more innocuous Concern for the Dying. Various right-to-die organizations have promoted the wills, as have the American Public health Association and certain Christian hospital associations, both Protestant and Catholic. The case study does not tell us how, or with whose aid, or under what conditions Mrs. Deem signed her will.

Whether or not nurses must always obey physicians' orders is much debated today. This journal's readers must be highly sensitive to nurses' changing self-understanding and role, especially as they acquire greater skill and experience.

Some nurses have recently been charged and tried for deliberately exceeding physicians' orders in administering lethal doses of morphine. Would nurses in cases like Mrs. Deem's be legally culpable if they "just happened" to fail in their resuscitation efforts? Or if their failure was intentional?

Mrs. Deem's living will said "no artificial means." That summons up images of ventilators and other sophisticated machines. Since Mrs. Deem was not comatose, her situation does not coincide with that of the famous and late Karen Ann Quinlan. Even so, the permission to discontinue the respirator granted by the New Jersey Supreme Court (in re: Quinlan, 1976) has opened the way for comparable withdrawals of equipment needed for resuscitation.

But the categorical, literal rejection of "artificial" means of support or therapy may include every kind of treatment. Under certain conditions, "artificial" can apply not only to medicine, but also food and water, delivered either by nasogastric tube or by mouth (in re: Conroy, 1985).

Should Mrs. Deem have been starved and dehydrated to death? If she had been in New Jersey, and if she had continued to breathe after a respirator was withdrawn, as Karen Quinlan did, food and water could have been withheld, in accord with specified conditions.

In the Netherlands today they are not so delicate: Sedatives and curare can be given to hasten death, with legal impunity and immunity for all concerned.

I cannot share some people's abhorrence that any patient should be allowed to die naturally without interference, as a consequence of a degenerative disease. But neither can I feel the complacency, much less the satisfaction, of those disposed to expedite the dying process.

The presentation of this case suffers from sentimentality. Of course Mrs. Deem was not "pink and warm" or "drinking a cup of tea." Those conditions are not the alternative to death!

Moreover, the suggested biblical texts are of doubtful applicability. There are better ones. The oft-quoted brooding of the Preacher in Ecclesiastes that there is "a time to die" (3:2) is matched by his desperate, cynical assertion that humans die as animals do, that "a man hath no preeminence above a beast" (3:19 KJV). Such fatalism has no place in Christianity.

On the contrary, Paul's wish to end his earthly life so he could be eternally with Christ (Phil 1:23) is a maximal expression of assurance of and hope in resurrection. But it is not a death wish expressing his weariness of living. For the Christian, real living means to have been "crucified with Christ" so as to "live by faith in the Son of God" (Gal 2:20). Life is "in Christ" because Christ "is our life" (Col 3:4). Such are also Jesus' promises in John's Gospel, which is essentially the Gospel of life's affirmation.

It would be wonderful if a Christian physician, nurse or minister could turn to the Bible and find an unequivocal answer to the question about Mrs. Deem and the hundreds like her. But we are not granted this relief. What we do learn from the Bible is that all life is from God, that in matters of doubt there should be bias toward life, and that inevitable death is finally overcome by resurrection. For the rest, we must rely on empirical data and courageous judgment. ∎

The Nurse Responds: Living with Limitations

Kay Sechriest

Mrs. Deem lived, but only for one week. The days immediately after we resuscitated her were unpleasant ones; I believe she suffered. She was responsive for only a few moments at a time, and even then she was confused. She took no fluids or nourishment and moaned when touched or turned.

The physician discontinued her heart monitor, but I don't know that he ever wrote a do-not-resuscitate order.

I was off duty for a couple of days and learned of Mrs. Deem's death when I returned. No one on the floor seemed to know or care exactly how she died. I was disillusioned. *Why was I the only one who cared? She was given a few days of life—but of what quality?*

I believe Mrs. Deem evaluated her illness and inevitable death and was prepared to die rather than take the chance of living in an uncertain, uncomfortable state. That is why she signed her living will. But when her time came, we intervened.

Some patients have been brought back from seemingly hopeless situations to live full lives—often because medical personnel didn't give up. Yet I've seen many survive codes only to be connected to ventilators for the rest of their lives. Others, though breathing on their own, are brain damaged. I have wanted to scream to the physicians, "Let them die!" Yet only God can know what hidden purposes their lives may serve.

I can understand Mrs. Deem's physician's dilemma. He has vowed to do all he can to preserve life. But these days physicians consider not only their patients' wishes but also the possibility of malpractice suits from family members.

I often think of Mrs. Deem, pale and fragile, the first of many such cases for me, and I feel frustrated. I'm torn in one direction by the patients I care for, wanting to comfort them and respect their wishes and dignity. I'm torn in another direction knowing I must live with physicians' orders and the policies of my institution.

As a practical nurse giving daily hands-on care, I know some long-term patients well. But I also know I am only one member of a team with a definite line of command. I cannot make many decisions concerning my patients' care, due to lack of knowledge and experience. So for me, the answer is to give prayerful, individualized care while I continue my education. And I pray with each patient I care for, "Thy will be done." ∎

At the end of your next Social Issues 101 class, you approach Professor Wells and mention the articles you found. You tell her that you think they might be worth citing in your paper, but that you didn't want to do so until you spoke with her. She seems delighted that you had taken the initiative to find additional information on the topic, and encourages you to include them if they seem worthwhile. She also tells you to include any additional information you might find—but reminds you to use discretion in choosing appropriate sources, especially with respect to the three paper topics she has given the class.

YOUR TURN

Who is the apparent audience for the *Journal of Christian Nursing?* What are the shared assumptions of the nurse and theologian—and presumably of the magazine's subscribers?

Nutshell the essay by the theologian. Where exactly does he come down on the issue? What would be a fair paraphrase of his position?

Professor Wells tosses the ball back into your court and lets you decide whether your source is worth including in your paper. If you decide to use this source, what kind of use might you make of it? Or can you imagine a different writing assignment for which this source would be ideal? What might that be?

BEYOND THE LIBRARY: A SOURCE FROM THE COMMUNITY

A number of the articles so far have mentioned "Living Wills." You know from the articles, especially Lamm's, roughly what these are, but you decide that you'd like to see a real one to help you understand the issue more fully. A few phone calls later, you've gotten in touch with the Ethics Review

Board for the Med Dale Hospital near your college. The Board, you discover, keeps a standard Living Will on file. They send you a copy of the will. Examine it carefully.

GUIDELINES FOR TREATMENT

Living Will

Background and Definitions

The following guidelines are provided to aid those who may be called upon to make important decisions in the event of my serious illness or injury. I have drawn up these guidelines after serious reflection, inspired by a concern for the welfare of my family in the event I am rendered unable to care for them. These guidelines are not drawn up hastily or light-mindedly, but after long consideration and with a full respect for the gravity of the issues involved. I sincerely hope and trust that whatever medical professionals may be called upon to act in any of the situations outlined below will take my requests in this document seriously, and comply with my requests as far as possible.

These guidelines are based on two premises: (1) Life cannot be adequately defined in purely biological terms. In the absence of consciousness and any future hope thereof, a body with operating heart and lungs is rather an "animate corpse" than a live human being in any meaningful sense. (2) Life, human life, is communication, the ability to recognize others and be recognized by them, to communicate intelligibly and understand communications by them.

When communication with others becomes impossible for whatever reason—brain death, dementia, coma, etc.—whatever is of worth and dignity in my earthly life will be over. I have no further interest in being kept biologically alive thereafter, and would sooner be released before my purely physical maintenance becomes a destructive burden on the resources I have gathered for the good of my spouse and children.

Guidelines, by Mental State

I. *If I am conscious and mentally competent,* I expect to be told candidly and objectively all details of my illness and/or the full extent of my injuries, to have my prognosis explained to me, and to participate fully in important decisions concerning diagnostic and therapeutic measures to be taken.

II. *If I am conscious or semiconscious but of uncertain mental competence,* the person best able to assess my mental competence would be my spouse, ————, assuming he/she survives me and is not

358

impaired by illness or injury. Otherwise, the one most able to assess my mental competence would be ———.

III. *If I am comatose but recovery and restoration to or near my prior level of functioning appear possible, or if prognosis is not well established,* I expect that all available measures will be employed as indicated in an attempt to bring about such recovery and restoration.

IV. *There are other conditions, however, in which I would **not** want medical treatment (as defined below, section V).* These include the following:

    A. If I have been declared "brain dead" in accordance with standard criteria for brain death.

    B. If my primary physician and two neurologists agree that I have been in a "persistent vegetative state" for 72 hours.

    C. If I become comatose during the course of an obviously fatal disease, e.g., metastatic cancer or a demyelinating neurological disorder.

    D. If I am comatose as the result of severe injuries, such as extensive burns, multiple fractures or internal injuries, and my primary physician and two appropriate consultants agree that recovery and restoration will not occur.

    E. If I have been demented as a result of Alzheimer's disease or comparable process and am then hospitalized because of a complicating condition or injury, e.g., an infection or fracture.

    F. If, for whatever reason, my mental state precludes the possibility of future meaningful communication with other persons, and my physical condition requires more than routine food, drink, and basic bodily care.

V. *If any of the conditions in section IV obtain, I would **not** want:*

    A. To have resuscitation performed;

    B. To be placed on a respirator;

    C. To be kept on a heart/lung machine;

    D. To be placed on renal dialysis;

    E. To have any surgical procedure;

    F. To be fed by a nasogastric or gastronomy tube;

    G. To have a cardiac pacemaker;

    H. To have a plasma exchange;

    I. To have antiobiotics or other medications except for whatever pain relievers my primary physician may believe appropriate;

    J. To have intravenous fluids in excess of 500 ml/day;

    K. To have any other invasive procedures not specifically mentioned herein.

VI. I further stipulate that any of the measures that may have been instituted at such time as the prognosis seemed uncertain, or when recovery and restoration appeared possible, should be terminated when the prognosis changes to fall into any of the categories defined in section IV.

VII. Upon my death, I authorize whatever organs I have that may be of use to another to be removed for that purpose.

VIII. I neither request nor prohibit an autopsy, leaving that decision to my surviving next of kin.

IV. In other documents, I express my wishes for final disposal of my remains and an appropriate memorial service.

X. I have given copies of this document to my spouse, pastor, physician, lawyer, and two responsible friends. This document is to be considered in effect until such time as I deliberately rewrite its stipulations or repudiate it in writing.

YOUR TURN

What new insights into the right-to-die controversy does the Living Will give you? Where does it match your expectations? What about it surprises you?

If you could now interview a member of the board, what questions concerning their use of the wills, or any of their other policies relating to terminally ill patients, would you want to ask?

KEEPING YOUR EYES OPEN

Just a few days before your paper for Social Issues 101 is due, you're roaming around the bookstore during its "used-book blitz," a special sale when huge tubs of books are wheeled in for people to rummage through. You spot a collection of essays entitled *Ethical Issues in Modern Medicine*. Most of the articles seem only marginally related to the topic in Social Issues 101, but one, "The Function of Medicine," seems to hold some promise. You figure that at $1.25, you can't miss, so you buy the book and head home to see what you can glean from the article.

When you really get down to it, however, you find that the article is longer than you originally thought, and it's rather more abstract and sophisticated than the other sources you've read. Nevertheless, you decide to tackle it; the authors of the collection seem to be prominent people, judging by their affiliations, and perhaps including this source will give your paper a special edge.

The Function of Medicine

Eric J. Cassell

A thirty-eight-year-old man who had a mild upper respiratory infection suddenly developed severe headache, stiff neck, and a high fever. He went to a local hospital emergency room for help. Based on the progress of the illness and the age of the patient, the physician believed that the most likely diagnosis was pneumococcal meningitis, which was confirmed by examination. This kind of bacterial meningitis is almost uniformly fatal if not treated, but curable by simple antibiotic treatment. If treatment is delayed, although cure will result, permanent neurological damage is likely. The doctor told the patient that urgent treatment was needed to save his life and forestall brain damage. The patient refused consent for treatment saying that he wanted to be allowed to die.

TREATMENT REFUSAL AND ALLOWING TO DIE

Does such a patient have a right to be allowed to die? On the face of it the answer must be yes, because the patient cannot be legally treated without his consent. But I believe that it would be a rare hospital where such a patient would not be treated

From "The Function of Medicine" by Eric J. Cassell, M.D., *Hastings Center Report* (December 1977). Reprinted by permission of The Hastings Center and the author.

This article was prepared with the assistance of Nancy McKenzie. This work was supported in part by grants from the Henry Blum Research Fund and the Robert Wood Johnson Foundation.

against his will. The physicians would ask for a psychiatric consultation to declare the patient incompetent and then start therapy. Since penicillin works equally well against the bacteria whether the patient wants to die or not, he would recover.

Why do I expect (and sincerely hope) that such a patient would be treated despite his declared wish to be allowed to die? When a patient enters the hospital (or doctor's office) for help, he enters into a relationship with the treating physicians—and by extension with the hospital itself. While the nature of that relationship is still obscure, we know that when the physician enters the relationship he acquires a responsibility for the patient that *cannot* be morally relieved merely by the patient's refusal to consent for treatment. But more simply, the physician could not stand aside and allow the patient to die from a disease otherwise easily treated without feeling that he, the doctor, was responsible for the death.

The patient also has obligations. In giving himself into the responsibility of another, he is obligated not to injure the other morally or legally by making it impossible for the physician to act on the responsibility. In coming into the emergency room for help (he could have stayed home), he caused the physician and the hospital to become responsible for him without beforehand limiting the nature and degree of their responsibility. Although not meaningful in this case, such antecedent limits might allow the physician to refuse to enter the relationship.

In the situation I have described, by refusing treatment, the patient appears to be

SOURCE: *Hastings Center Report*, December 1977, pp. 16–19. Reprinted in John Arras and Robert Hunt, eds., *Ethical Issues in Medicine* (Palo Alto, CA: Mayfield, 1983), pp. 238–242. Reproduced by permission. © The Hastings Center.

committing suicide. If he jumped out a high window, he would accomplish his goal alone; here he is enlisting the aid of others. On the other hand, if he is not committing suicide, his motives are not clear. Therefore, if he resists treatment, the doctors might reasonably believe that the patient does not know what he is doing. The element of time appears to play a part. But time for what? A different but similar situation may make clear the function of time and what is lacking in this case of the man with meningitis.

A Jehovah's Witness, injured in an accident, comes to the hospital bleeding profusely. Blood transfusions are necessary to save the patient's life. The Jehovah's Witness refuses transfusions. While there will probably be much agonizing over the decision, or even recourse to the courts, the patient's right to refuse treatment (even though death will follow) may be, indeed has been, acknowledged. The situations are similar. The condition is curable, but without treatment death results. What is very different is that the patient's motive is well known and has been expressed and defended by an established institution, his church, over time. Further, the patient's decision is consistent with a set of beliefs that are well known, whatever we may think about them.

In addition to highlighting the element of time, the case makes another important point. The Jehovah's Witness did not ask to be allowed to die, he asked to be permitted to refuse treatment. That the decision may result in his death is not relevant. It is not death that is chosen. It is treatment (and its effects—religious in this instance) that is being refused. Most, if not all, instances chosen to highlight the discussion of the right to die, in medical cases, are really instances of the right to refuse the *consequences* of treatment of which death may be only one, and the least important at that.

For the first group of patients, those whose disease is curable but who will die without treatment, I conclude from my experience of how medicine is practiced in the United States that the patient's right to be allowed to die will not be honored. At least one reason the request will not be granted is that insufficient time is present to assess the patient's motives if they are not otherwise clear.

TREATMENT REFUSAL IN CHRONIC CASES

I believe the issues will be clarified by considering the second class of patients, those whose disease is not curable but for whom continued treatment will provide functional life over a long period. This class of patients is daily enlarged by medical advances, as chronic diseases from cancer to emphysema are more successfully treated. Instead of the man with bacterial meningitis, consider the case of a patient with sickle cell anemia requiring repeated transfusions, or a patient with chronic renal failure who needs dialysis several times weekly. If such a patient were to refuse treatment, could the same course be followed as with the man in the emergency room? It seems unlikely. A patient who refused further artificial kidney dialysis could be declared incompetent on the basis of the fact that his refusal constituted suicide. But what would happen then? Would the doctors in that kidney unit tie him down on the dialysis couch week after week? If it was a patient with anemia who required continued transfusions, would the doctors force the transfusions on the patient? Again and again and again? That does not seem reasonable. But, why not?

These patients also presented themselves for treatment and entered into a relationship with a physician and hospital. That relationship involved the doctor's responsibility and the patient's obligation. However, there are several crucial differences. In this instance, when the patient refuses treatment and asks to be allowed to die, can we claim that he does not know what he is doing? Obviously not. Patients with chronic diseases requiring long-term therapy are usually very knowledgeable. They have had plenty of time to learn about the disease, its treatment, and the consequences of both. Such patients learn from books, from physicians and nurses, and perhaps most important, from other patients. The patient has also had time to test his beliefs against the arguments of others. Certainly by the time he refuses further therapy, the patient will have been exposed to considerable argument. Discussion, however, is two-sided. Just as the patient has had time to acquire knowledge and test his beliefs, his doctors have had time to know the patient. During the weeks, months, or years that they have been treating him, the staff has an opportunity to know whether the patient's refusal of treatment and desire to die is consonant with all the other things they know of him.

When the man with meningitis refuses treatment and asks to be allowed to die, it does not appear to me to be a truly autonomous act. However, when a dialysand refuses further dialysis, his action appears to me to be much more the exercise of his autonomy. As the emphasis has shifted in the critical and theoretical examination of medicine, from the doctor's obligations to the patient's rights, there has been increasing discussion of the importance of the patient's autonomy. Autonomy appears to be the basis for the demand for informed consent. Patients' autonomy is also, it seems to me, the basis of the move to demystify medicine and make the patient a partner in his or her care. But what is autonomy?

AUTONOMY AND ILLNESS

Gerald Dworkin argues that autonomy requires both *authenticity* and *independence* (*Hastings Center Report*, February 1976, pp. 23–28). Authenticity is the true selfness of a person, the degree to which a person's beliefs, ideas or actions are truly unique despite their source.

Independence is above all freedom of choice. Freedom of choice requires three things: first, knowledge about the area where choice is to be made. One cannot make a free choice if he does not know what the choices are. Knowledge alone is not sufficient. To have freedom of choice one must also be able to reason, to think clearly, otherwise the knowledge is of little use. Finally, one must have the ability to act on one's choice, otherwise freedom of choice is meaningless.

When philosophers and lawyers (and many others) talk about rights they often speak as though the body does not exist. When they discuss the rights of patients they act as if a sick person is simply a well person with an illness appended. Like putting on a knapsack, the illness is added but nothing else changes. That is simply a wrong view of the sick. The sick are different from the well to a degree dependent on the person, the disease, and the circumstances in which they are sick and/or are treated.

Consider what autonomy means to a sick person, or conversely what illness does to autonomy. Let me start with authenticity. Am I my authentic self as I writhe in pain? When I am foul-smelling lying in the mess of my illness? In the first days after a mastectomy, it seems reasonable when the patient questions her authenticity—after all, our body image is part of our authentic self. It is common to hear patients say that they do not want visitors "to see me like this." Is that my authentic father lying there, weak and powerless, hooked up to tubes and wires? It is clear that illness can impair authenticity.

AUTHENTICITY AND INDEPENDENCE

But if illness has an effect on authenticity, what does it do to independence? The sick do not have the same freedom of choice as the well. Knowledge for the sick person is incomplete and (for the very sick) never can be complete even if the patient is a physician. For even the best-understood disease there are large gaps in understanding. Causes may be obscure and outcomes vary in probability. But the sick person cannot deal in percentages when what is wanted is certainty. For the doctor, these gaps are of less importance and uncertainty is his constant companion. Besides, as my colleague Jeremiah Barondess has pointed out, it is vastly easier for a physician to know what to do than to know what is the matter.

Not only is knowledge lacking for the sick person but reason is also impaired. In the simplest terms, it is difficult to be clear-headed in pain or suffering. The very sick may have impairment in the ability to reason abstractly even when their mental function is seemingly intact. Illness so obviously interferes with the ability to act as to require almost no comment. It should be pointed out, however, that a patient does not have to be bedridden to be unable to act; the fear of action born of uncertainty may be just as disabling.

Illness interferes with autonomy to a degree dependent on the nature and severity of the illness, the person involved, and the setting. What helps restore wholeness? Autonomy is exercised in relation to others; it is encouraged or defeated by the action of others as well as by the actor. For this reason wholeness can be restored to the sick (in the terms of autonomy) in part by family and friends. However, there are limits to the capacity of family or friends in returning autonomy to the sick, particularly in acute illness. Even the most loving well may turn aside from the ugliness, foulness, pain, and suffering of sickness. Merely the smell of illness and its mess are difficult for most people to overcome. They may be unable to see the sick person completely apart from the illness. Visitors in intensive care areas commonly cannot decide where to look and often end up staring more at the monitors and the equipment than at the patient. That person on the bed is simply not the authentic loved one, friend, or relative. These things

are especially true during acute illness, although when sickness lasts longer the family may successfully overcome their distaste.

The family is also injured by the damaged authenticity of the beloved sick person. As the sick person is not whole, neither are they. Similarly, family and friends cannot usually restore independence to the sick person. They too do not have the knowledge of the illness and although they can supply the ability to reason, their thinking is also clouded by emotion—by fear, concern, and doubt. Finally, while the family and friends can (and usually do) provide some surrogate ability to act for the sick person, they, like he or she, cannot act against the most important thief of autonomy, the illness.

THE PHYSICIAN AS RESTORER OF AUTONOMY

The doctor-patient relationship can be the source from which both authenticity and independence can be returned to the patient. The degree of restoration will depend on both patient and doctor and is subject to the limits imposed by the disease. I am also well aware that by his actions or lack of them, the physician can further destroy rather than repair the patient's autonomy. But here I am not speaking of what harm can be done but what good can be done. In the same manner, when I speak of the use of a good and potent drug, I would not focus on its misuse even though it may often be misused, nor concentrate primarily on its side effects, but speak rather of how it can and should be employed.

The mess of illness does not repel the physician and through training he is protected from defensiveness at the pain of others. For these reasons, he can see a parent where there is a father or a craftsman, attorney, or mother, aside from the sickness surrounding them. If he has known the patient for a long time, he knows the past or can construct it from conversation. He can talk of the future if he chooses. He helps restore authenticity by teaching the sick person how to reassert himself above his disability, by teaching how to be whole when the body is not whole.

The physician can also help return independence to the patient. He has knowledge of the disease and circumstances that the patient and family lack and he can search out the knowledge of the person necessary to make his medical knowledge meaningful to the patient. He can supply the ability to reason and help bridge the gaps in the patient's ability to reason. Finally, he can provide surrogate ability to act, against the illness if nowhere else. In so doing, the patient can be shown how to act in his own behalf and by that means reach a measure of control over his circumstances.

THE FUNCTION OF MEDICINE

The central question raised by the issue of the patient's right to be allowed to die or right to refuse the consequences of treatment: is the function of medicine to preserve biological life or to preserve the person as he defines himself?

I believe that the function of medicine is to preserve autonomy and that preservation of life is subservient to the primary goal. However, this issue is confused by several factors. First, it is obvious that the best way to preserve autonomy is to cure the patient of the disease that impairs autonomy and return him to his normal life. Second, the threats to life and well-being, and therefore autonomy, have been organized into a system of knowledge and a mode of thought called medical science which concentrate on disease and enlarging the system of thought, often forgetting the origins of the system in the human condition. That body of medical science and its derivative technology have acquired an existence now independent of their original function—understanding the sicknesses which rob persons of their independence and authenticity.

The issue is further confused because the underlying focus of medicine has increasingly become the preservation of the body and biological life. But until the last two generations it did not matter what the philosophy was, the tools of medical practice were so poor that medical care (although perhaps not surgery) had to function through the agency of the patient. The major tool of medicine was the doctor-patient relationship itself. Where that is the case, preserving the relationship and keeping it functioning requires the active participation of the patient. Where the patient's function is necessary, so is some measure of his autonomy represented. And it does not matter here whether the patient's autonomy was expressed primarily by the patient or primarily by the physician, so long as the actions and outcome were authentic to the patient, or at least perceived by the patient as authentic to himself. But, in an era of technological effectiveness, life at all costs seems to be a slogan and becomes a reality in the face of which autonomy is easily destroyed. The last thirty or forty years of medical history should not be allowed to eclipse the goals of the previous two thousand years.

Let us return to the cases. The patient with pneumococcal meningitis is treated against his will (correctly, I think) because the physicians have not had time to know whether his desire to avoid treatment is authentic while they do know it to be suicidal. Further, the only consequences of treatment that can be perceived are a return to health. It appears reasonable to me that *where doubt exists* doctors should always err on the side of preserving life. While there may not always be hope where there is life, there are usually more options. Indeed, in this instance, after he is well again the patient can, if he wishes, commit suicide.

The patient with end-stage renal disease presents a different problem. We allow him to refuse treatment and thus die because in his knowledge of the disease and its treatment and in our knowledge of him acquired during his treatment, we know his actions to be authentic. Further, allowing him to act on his desire preserves his independence. Here it is clear that the patient is not choosing death but rather avoiding the consequences of treatment. The issue is sharpened in the case of the terminally ill. If biological life is medicine's goal, then the patient should be kept alive as long as possible. If the preservation of autonomy is the goal of medicine, then one must do everything possible to maintain the integrity of the person in the face of death.

To medicine, as to mankind, death should not matter, life matters.

YOUR TURN

First, ask yourself, as always, who the probable readers of such a book of essays would be. As you read the article, nutshell each of its subtitled sections in turn. Note also its main terms; get them down into your notebook with a definition (in your own words) of each. Then answer the following questions:

How does Cassell present his case? How does he go about setting up his argument and making his points? How is his approach different from J. Robert Nelson's or Richard Lamm's?

Apply Cassell's logic to one of the people you've read about. What would Cassell's decision be in the Elizabeth Bouvia case? Write a dialogue of sorts between Cassell, J. Robert Nelson, and Governor Lamm on Bouvia's case and the other people you've been reading about.

Write a one-page summary of Cassell's article, quoting or paraphrasing wherever useful or appropriate.

CREATING AN EFFECTIVE PAPER

If you've finished the "Your Turn" exercises we've been suggesting, you should now have several pages of material in your notebook on the right-to-die issue generally and on these articles in particular. Given the exact nature of your assignment, there are a number of directions you could go with the material—both on the page and, more importantly, in your own head.

Return to the three topics in Professor Wells's assignment. Reanalyze the topics. Are you thinking about them any differently now that you've considered the issue carefully? Which one seems most interesting to write about? Why?

After brainstorming some possibilities for each question, choose one to write on. Then do the following for the topic you chose:

Tell which articles would be most useful to you. What especially in each article would you probably need to present in your paper, either by summarizing, paraphrasing, or quoting?

Develop a tree (see pp. 145–159) you might use in writing the paper.

Write an opening paragraph for the paper, presenting the thesis you'd be arguing and suggesting why the topic is important.

OTHER PROJECTS

Treat each question as if it were on the final exam for Social Issues 101, and write an essay-style answer for it. Take no more than 30 minutes for each question and don't refer to your notes.

Cook up five more questions on your own, of a sort that might work for a middle-length (5–8 page) paper. Then analyze each question in terms of how well you think it would work, what problems you might run into with it, etc.

Pick one of your new questions, and draw at least three possible trees that might help you organize a paper on it. Again, find what articles, or parts of articles, you'd want to use, and state what use you would make of each. Now, using the suggestions in Chapter Six, actually draft, get feedback on, and revise a paper based on the questions you chose from among those you cooked up.

Using the material in your research paper, write a letter to the editor presenting your views on the issue you've chosen. What changes in language, format, etc., do you need to make to reach this new and different audience? How do your purposes for the writing change?

Convert your letter to the editor to a letter to your local state senator or representative (assume Living Will legislation is currently being debated in the state legislature). Again, how do your purposes and tactics change?

Appendix B

SAMPLE STUDENT PAPERS

The following papers were written by three college freshmen at a mid-western state university. We offer them not as models for imitation but as the work of ordinary fellow students struggling, as we all are, with the business of getting thoughts, observations, and feelings down on paper.

The papers can be read (and discussed) in the light of much of what we've suggested in the body of this book. Most relevant, perhaps, are the chapters on revision (Chapter Three) and peer feedback (Chapter Nine). The sections on the use of timelines (Chapter Two) and on treeing and incorporating outside sources (Chapter Six) should also provide useful leads in your reading and thinking.

Imagine that the papers were written by students in your own class and that you will be meeting with them in a small writers' group to share feedback on each other's work. What would you tell each writer about your responses to his or her paper? What marginal notes would you make? What are the main issues you would stress in discussing each draft? How would you revise each draft if you'd written it yourself?

We've included here four papers. The first, "Memories," re-creates an experience of the author. The second and third, "Bear Problems" and "Bearly a Problem," discuss a local dilemma, drawing heavily from interviews. The two represent the rough and presentation drafts of the same paper. The fourth paper, "Termination of Treatment," analyzes an important social issue on the basis of the printed sources in Appendix A: the "Social Issues 101" case. In printing these papers, we've corrected some obvious typos as well as a few minor slips in spelling and punctuation. We've done this so that you can focus your attention on the broader issues, such as richness of content, organization, sense of audience, and so on. We've also left the footnote numbers in the "Termination of Treatment" paper to show when and where the author chose to document her sources. We're not reproducing her footnotes themselves, however.

Memories

By Michelle Costea

The memories are foggy, yet the impact still strong. I remember seeing Erika, her brother, and their parents through the window of the train. In a few minutes it would start moving and that would be the last in a long time that I would get to see her. Little did I know.

She had been my best friend; we had grown up together for a period of over four years. We were like sisters; lived in the same building, attended the same class in school, took part in the same circle of friends, and enjoyed the same activities. We had a true friendship, yet now that my family and I were leaving for the United States, it would be a long time before I would get to see her again. I was missing her already.

I don't quite remember having done this, but I was told that right before the train had departed I had run out to her and handed Erika my long-cherished ruby ring. This ring had had many memories and was a special piece of jewelry to me. I guess it must have been a pretty sentimental thing for me to do. She was in fact a very dear friend to me.

As I would daydream once in a while and think way back to the many good and bad times we had had together, it seemed as if these memories had blended into the world of unreality, as though they never had existed. Yes, I would think, distance and time can do such things. What a pity.

Yet I knew that one day I would go back to Romania and see Erika again. It didn't seem to be too much in the near future, but it was in my plans. I would visualize our reunion. After not seeing one another for over ten years, it would have been a spectacular event. I could see the expressions on our faces as we would catch that first glimpse of one another. I would feel the surprise, the astonishment, and the joy of seeing her again. Yet it was all in my mind, creating that which had not yet taken place, anticipating that which at the time I thought was only a matter of time. I knew nothing would get in my way. Little did I know.

A couple of years ago, one evening, my mother came up to me and my brother and announced to us that she had something very important to say. What could it have been? She didn't have too pleasant a tone of voice. Her words stuttered. What might have happened? We were both getting nervous. Our eyes would meet every few seconds in question of what could be going on.

I could feel my heart beginning to pound at an unthinkable rate. It felt as if it was going to jump right out of me. The puzzled expression on her face made me and, I could tell, my brother as well extremely curious. The time seemed to be standing still.

Then she finally began. Her words at first made no sense. I could not understand what she was getting at, but with each new beginning I started understanding more and more what the general idea of her announcement was. It sounded as though it must have been something she wasn't too comfortable informing us of. It seemed to be a touchy subject. That scared me. I didn't know what to expect of it.

The first thing I remember her mentioning was the big earthquake that had taken place a few years before in Bucharest, Romania. She began by describing the portions of the city that had gotten damaged by it. It was all very interesting, but what did it have to do with anything? My brother and I again would exchange glances. We thought it was all pretty weird.

She pretty much beat around the bush until she herself realized it was about time she put her guard down and simply say what she had to say. So now Erika and her brother were brought up. I could see my mother's face change to a pale color and her eyes begin to wander downwards. Her tone of voice to us became a warning that something very unpleasant was going to follow. It is unimaginable how puzzled my brother and I must have been by now. Then she said it. She took a deep breath and bluntly informed us of the horrifying news. My heart stopped in disbelief and horror. What about my plans for the future? And what about my memories of the past? Now they remained just that--memories. And the plans, just plans, never to be lived up to. How sad. She had perished in the quake.

Bear Problems

By Scott Brady

[Rough Draft]

The black bear population of northeastern Pine County in hunting zone 1 is rising and bringing with it numerous accounts of bear sightings and incidents, said DNR official Elmer Swensen. Because of these events, many people are afraid that bears may damage their homes and livestock. According to the game warden the increase is directly caused by the changes in hunting regulations in 1979, which were made to protect the black bear. A person may no longer shoot a bear on his deer permit; he must have a special bear permit. Only 3,550 of these were given out last year and only 300-400 bears were taken, said Mr. Swensen.

Because of this increase, the bears, which feed mainly on insects, nuts, and berries, are forced to invade one another's territory in order to find a sufficient food supply, Mr. Swensen stated. When this isn't enough, they will leave the woods in search of a better food source, Mr. Swensen said. This food source can be a dump, a garbage can, or as in several cases this summer, a person's home. Bears are normally afraid of humans, but will not be intimidated by them if they (the bears) are hungry. According to the game warden (Mr. Swensen), this summer is significantly worse than in previous years because the berries have grown very slowly because of the unseasonably cool temperatures this spring. Once the bears' berries are ripe many bears will return to the woods, he said.

The bears which don't return to the woods are causing some trouble in the small farming community of Bruno. Three examples of these problems were at the homes of Cliff Olson, Martin Lindsey, and Lyle Stray. According to Tom Olson, Cliff's son, two cows on their farm had their heads clawed and ears torn by a bear this summer. Now the whole herd sits in front of the house, scared to go out to pasture.

Martin Lindsey said that while he was away one afternoon this spring, a bear tore through the screen door of his home and ransacked the kitchen, leaving food and dishes scattered about. When he and his wife

372

returned, they saw bear tracks near the house. The bear had left by then but their dog was still hiding under the porch.

Another incident at the Lyle Stray home also involved a bear in the kitchen. According to a local newspaper, Lyle's wife, Sandra, woke up one morning and found a bear at the table eating butter. She called her neighbor Willie Stray, who came over with a rifle. Lyle and the neighbors tried to coax the bear out of the house, but he found a sack of sugar and again sat down to eat. That's when Lyle shot him. The bullet passed through the bear and into the cupboard behind him, ruining several pots and pans. The bear was dragged outside the home and the game warden, Elmer Swensen, was called.

Mr. Swenson said that one way to possibly prevent a bear from coming near a person's home is to rinse out cans and packages with food odors before throwing them in the garbage. Leaving food sit out or dirty dishes in the sink will also attract bears, he said.

According the Elmer Swensen, one solution for lessening the bear population would be to reinstate the former hunting regulations. This would mean that a hunter could shoot a bear and a deer on one deer permit. This would be statewide and would benefit zone 1, but might seriously harm the bear population in other zones.

Another more favorable solution, according to Mr. Swensen, would be to increase the number of bear permits issued in zone 1. This would ensure that bears in other zones of this state would not be harmed. He also suggested lengthening the bear hunting season to increase the chances of a hunter filling out his permit.

Bearly a Problem

By Scott Brady

[Presentation Draft]

Imagine the surprise of Duluth resident Martin Lindsey one recent spring afternoon when, after having been out shopping with his wife, Tiffany, he returned to find a large hole torn right through the screen door leading into the kitchen. Martin and Tiffany left the groceries in the car and cautiously crept in to inspect the damage. The gash in the screen was five feet across and a wooden slat was broken. Inside the cabin, the kitchen table was lying on its side, food and dishes were scattered about, and a large pot of soup that had been simmering on the stove was spread about the floor--what there was left of it. Vandals?

Well, not exactly. When Martin and Tiffany stepped back outside, they noticed two more telltale signs. Their young dog Mick lay huddled and shivering under the porch steps. And the broad, round tracks of a large bear trailed off through the soft ground and into the nearby woods.

A similar incident at the Lyle Stray home also involved a bear in the kitchen. According to a local newspaper, Lyle's wife, Sandra, woke up one morning to find a bear at the table eating butter. She called her neighbor Willie Stray, who came over with a rifle. Lyle and the neighbors tried to coax the bear out of the house, but the bear found a sack of sugar and again sat down to eat. That's when Lyle shot him. The bullet passed through the bear and into the cupboard behind him, ruining several pots and pans. The bear was dragged outside the home and the game warden, Elmer Swensen, was called.

Nor is it just vacationers and cabin dwellers who are having problems with the creatures. As if farmers didn't have enough troubles, they too are running foul of them. Cliff Olson owns a dairy farm in the small farming community of Bruno. According to Tom Olson, Cliff's son, two cows on their farm had their heads clawed and ears torn by a bear this summer. Now the whole herd sits in front of the house, afraid to go out to pasture.

Though here in the Twin Cities such stories are mostly amusing, to the people in the northern parts of the state, the bear problem this year has gotten serious. Because of the frequent sightings, and even breaking and entering, of the bears, many people are afraid that bears may damage their homes and livestock. Have the bears perhaps been protected too successfully?

Department of National Resources (DNR) official Elmer Swensen thinks maybe they have. According to the game warden, the increase in bear incidents is directly caused by the changes in hunting regulations in 1979, which were made for the protection of the bears. It used to be that you could shoot a bear on your deer permit, but that's no longer the case. Since the changed regulations, you now need a special bear permit to shoot the animals. Last year only 3,550 of these were issued and only 300-400 bears were taken.

Because of this extra protection of the bears, their numbers have risen. The bears, which feed mainly on insects, nuts and berries, are now forced to invade each other's territory for the food they need. And when the food in the woods runs out, they go in search of new sources. This can be a dump, a garbage can, or, like many similar cases this spring, Tiffany Lindsey's simmering pot of soup--the aroma of which almost certainly drew the bear into their house. (Any food odor--dirty dishes, food sitting out, empty but unwashed can and containers--all of these will attract the bears. When bear season comes, wash everything!)

Bears are normally afraid of humans, but lose their fear when they are hungry, Mr. Swensen explained. This summer the problems are worse than usual because the unseasonably cool temperatures have caused the berries in the woods to grow very slowly. Once the berries are ripe, most of the bears will happily return to the woods.

But what of next year and the year after that? According to Swensen, the bear population must be reduced. One solution would be to reinstate the former hunting regulations. This would allow hunters to shoot both a deer and a bear on one deer permit. But though this would benefit residents in hunting zone 1, it might seriously harm the bear population in other zones.

Another solution, which Swensen prefers, would be to increase the number of bear permits issued in zone 1. This would ensure that bears in other zones of Minnesota would not be harmed. He also suggests lengthening the season on bears to increase the chances that a hunter will bag his bruin.

Whatever the solution, it's bound to be controversial. As part of the natural wildlife of the state, many will claim, bears should be protected. If in fact their numbers are too high in zone 1, perhaps a better solution would be to capture and transport a number to other areas, as has been done with grizzly bears in Montana--and even with the Canada geese around the lakes in south Minneapolis. Though finding a bear in your recliner rocker might lead you to decide, "Enough is enough," it's the purpose of the Department of Natural Resources to find ways that all species--humans and bears--can live together.

Termination of Treatment

By Stephanie Schneider

"Today, 80% of Americans die in hospitals or nursing homes, generally in the course of receiving some sort of medical treatment."[1] Many of these patients are kept alive longer with no further living satisfaction, but merely to endure a great deal of pain. They simply experience an extension of their death process. It is unfortunate that today's great medical advances had to result with such impediments.

As a result of this technological progress and extended suffering, dramatic decisions are having to be made. In many cases it is almost essential not only for the well-being of the patient, emotionally and physically, but also the health of the family, to withdraw the treatment from the terminally ill patient. The question then arises, who has the authority or right to decide whether termination of treatment should be implemented, thus allowing the patient to die? Presently, with no distinct right or wrong guideline, decisions are being made inconsistently, by different people surrounding the patient. Yet with each decision there comes some sting of disapproval. Each individual situation is led by some initiator involved, who only wishes the best for the patient. These decision makers are often ridiculed by others involved and are sometimes even charged with murder.

When does the patient have a competent enough understanding of his condition to decide whether to die or not? Does the doctor have the right, legally or morally, to decide under the Hippocratic Oath? Can relatives objectively decide for the ill family member if he is unable to himself? And how does the law fit into such a moral issue? In order to realize the predicament of "deciding," each of these possible decision makers needs to be fully examined. A resume of each will be presented, pointing out reasons why and why they should not be considered authorities in the life-death decision. It will become quite evident that our society is far from determining the superior authority.

In order to understand the situation of the doctor we must analyze what the exact duty of the doctor toward his patient is. The moral duty differs from one doctor to another and there are as many variations as there are practicing physicians in the country. But for all the medical profession, it is linked to the Hippocratic Oath: "I will never give a deadly drug to anybody if he asks for it, nor will I make a suggestion to this effect."[2] To do otherwise would violate the innermost meaning of the medical vocation: heal where possible, care always, never harm.[3] This inner drive, which is characteristic of all doctors, can lead to much pain and prolonged agony on the part of the patient and his relatives. Unfortunate though it may be, some physicians refuse to stop treating a terminally ill patient as if they were curable, even to such extents as continuously reviving the body of a long-time brain-dead patient.[4]

Yet in some cases the life or death decision cannot possibly be made by anyone but the physician himself. Often terminally ill patients become so depressed, they cannot possibly make the decision at hand. (This will be discussed later in the paper.) Many times the machines and the different behavior of their loved one keep relatives from objectivity as well. "The mess of illness does not repel the physician and through training he is protected from defensiveness at the pain of others."[5] Through the illness, the doctor can still see the individual, and through the patient's requests and his own deductions, a reasonable decision can be derived upon.[6] So in many cases it seems that the doctor should have the authority to make the life-death decision.

A major issue in our country has always been the rights and freedoms of individuals. It is not surprising, therefore, that up for dispute is whether the individual patient, when terminally ill, has the right to judge whether termination of treatment should be carried out. Alice V. Mehling, executed director of the Society for the Right To Die says, "We want self-determination for the patient, whether that means continuing treatment or dying with dignity."[7] With this in mind one is bound to wonder if the patient is competent enough to make such a decison. Often

terminally ill patients are diagnosed as "too depressed" to make the
life or death determination, just as in the case of William F. Bartling.

Bartling lay dying of emphysema, complicated with a few other
diseases, when he asked to be relieved from his painful treatment and
allowed to die. As a result of being labeled "too depressed" to
completely comprehend his situation, he had to suffer for months, and
"while both sides squabbled in court, Bartling finally died, with the
ganglia of high-tech medicine still attached to his shriveled body."[8]
According to the idea of self-determination, Bartling was denied a
primal right. If a terminally ill patient is depressed and wants to die,
should he be forced to live? Is not forcing a patient to live through
longer suffering against the idea of "heal where possible . . . never
harm"?[9] If Bartling was judged incompetent to make his own decision of
death over life, what about living wills which are drawn up and signed
by quite competent adults?

Living wills are "documents declaring that the competent adults
signing do not wish their lives to be prolonged by medical means should
they face certain death from an illness or injury."[10] Even these
"insurance" statements don't guarantee anything for the patient.
Though through a survey it showed that doctors believe it right to
"withhold life support from suffering patients who are certain to die
and don't want their support, but that fears of legal action keep many
from doing it."[11] This fact almost pokes fun at the idea of individual
rights and self-determination when it comes to an almost certain and
painful death.

If the life or death decision is an individual one, who is responsible
to decide if the patient is unable to comply? Are the remaining family
members responsible when the patient is comatose or so delirious from
medications that a decision by the ill person is impossible? It is not
really possible for relatives to completely understand the position of
their loved ones, because they are so emotionally involved themselves.
What if they disagree among themselves? In more cases than not, when it
comes to relatives deciding the fate of their ill family member, the

court becomes involved. I don't believe, though our court system is quite respectable, that the law should have the power to decide on the fate of any ill person. Would it not be better to come as close to self-determination as possible through the patient's relatives?

Commonly when an argument between the physicians, relatives, or the patients themselves arises, the courts become involved. As far as laws go in the United States, fifteen states and the District of Columbia recognize the "living will."[12] This is included in the "right-to-death," natural death, or "death-with-dignity" laws.[13] These laws are so unstable, however, that for fear of lawsuits, doctors do not usually comply with them until specific court orders are given. Doctors have good reasons for their precautions. These "death-with-dignity" laws can also be stretched beyond the idea of terminating treatment. "In 1982 two physicians in California were charged with murder for complying with a family's request to remove feeding tubes from a hopelessly brain-damaged patient."[14] Though these charges were dropped upon appeal in the fall of 1985, one cannot help wonder how far one can go under such "death-with-dignity" laws. The tubes which were removed were feeding tubes and no terminal illness had been diagnosed. Is this truly what these laws were created for?

When courts themselves are forced to make the "terminating treatment" judgment, others are often called in for assistance. Often, at this point, relatives are asked for their preference, and if there is a "living will," it is taken into account, though it will not necessarily be extremely significant.[15] Moreover, specialists and doctors are asked to give their opinions. In one case the state supreme court turned to three hospital ethics committees to review a dying loner's case. The court followed their collected wisdom and ordered him off the respirator. "It is the first time ethics committees played a significant role in the court," says Dr. Ronald E. Crawford, a neurologist and ethics specialist. "This is going to happen increasingly in the future."[16] In this case it is glaringly apparent that there is no one decision maker. Perhaps all this indecision shows just how unprepared our society is to make life or death determinations for the terminally ill. At this point in time, I can't see any one way to handle the delicate situation of "mercy killing." It seems that any one group that gets assigned to decision making, whether it is the doctors, the patients, or the courts, a dragged out united determination including all parties is made. It is unfortunate, though this is the best process to date, that many terminally ill people suffer so long. Part of the problem is not fully understanding the emotional state of the terminally ill. "The very sick may have impairment in the ability to reason abstractly even when their mental functioning is seemingly intact."[17] What may help with future decisions is better understanding of the person dealing with the illness and restoring, as much as possible, the autonomy of the sufferer so that a resolution regarding life or death can be made collectively.[18]

The rapid technological growth our country has gone through has left little, if any, time to grow emotionally. Perhaps one day our emotions and understanding of the human mind will catch up to our technological leap. "In the meantime, while the law struggles along, patients, families, and doctors across the country make most life-and-death decisions privately--final judgments that the survivors must live with long after the courthouse doors swing closed."[19]

Index